Contemporary Reconfigurations
of American Literary Classics

Routledge Studies in Twentieth-Century Literature

1. **Testimony from the Nazi Camps**
   French Women's Voices
   Margaret-Anne Hutton

2. **Modern Confessional Writing**
   New Critical Essays
   Edited by Jo Gill

3. **Cold War Literature**
   Writing the Global Conflict
   Andrew Hammond

4. **Modernism and the Crisis of Sovereignty**
   Andrew John Miller

5. **Cartographic Strategies of Postmodernity**
   The Figure of the Map in Contemporary Theory and Fiction
   Peta Mitchell

6. **Food, Poetry, and the Aesthetics of Consumption**
   Eating the Avant-Garde
   Michel Delville

7. **Latin American Writers and the Rise of Hollywood Cinema**
   Jason Borge

8. **Gay Male Fiction Since Stonewall**
   Ideology, Conflict, and Aesthetics
   Les Brookes

9. **Anglophone Jewish Literature**
   Axel Stähler

10. **Before Auschwitz**
    Irène Némirovsky and the Cultural Landscape of Inter-war France
    Angela Kershaw

11. **Travel and Drugs in Twentieth-Century Literature**
    Lindsey Michael Banco

12. **Diary Poetics**
    Form and Style in Writers' Diaries, 1915-1962
    Anna Jackson

13. **Gender, Ireland and Cultural Change**
    Race, Sex and Nation
    Gerardine Meaney

14. **Jewishness and Masculinity from the Modern to the Postmodern**
    Neil R. Davison

15. **Travel and Modernist Literature**
    Sacred and Ethical Journeys
    Alexandra Peat

16. **Primo Levi's Narratives of Embodiment**
    Containing the Human
    Charlotte Ross

17. **Italo Calvino's Architecture of Lightness**
    The Utopian Imagination in an Age of Urban Crisis
    Letizia Modena

18 **Aesthetic Pleasure in Twentieth-Century Women's Food Writing**
The Innovative Appetites of M.F.K. Fisher, Alice B. Toklas, and Elizabeth David
Alice L. McLean

19 **Making Space in the Works of James Joyce**
Edited by Valérie Bénéjam and John Bishop

20 **Critical Approaches to American Working-Class Literature**
Edited by Michelle M. Tokarczyk

21 **Salman Rushdie and Visual Culture**
Celebrating Impurity, Disrupting Borders
Edited by Ana Cristina Mendes

22 **Global Cold War Literature**
Western, Eastern and Postcolonial Perspectives
Edited by Andrew Hammond

23 **Exploring Magic Realism in Salman Rushdie's Fiction**
Ursula Kluwick

24 **Wallace Stevens, New York, and Modernism**
Edited by Lisa Goldfarb and Bart Eeckhout

25 **Locating Gender in Modernism**
The Outsider Female
Geetha Ramanathan

26 **Autobiographies of Others**
Historical Subjects and Literary Fiction
Lucia Boldrini

27 **Literary Ghosts from the Victorians to Modernism**
The Haunting Interval
Luke Thurston

28 **Contemporary Reconfigurations of American Literary Classics**
The Origin and Evolution of American Stories
Betina Entzminger

Contemporary Reconfigurations of American Literary Classics
The Origin and Evolution of American Stories

Betina Entzminger

First published 2013
by Routledge
711 Third Avenue, New York, NY 10017

Simultaneously published in the UK
by Routledge
2 Park Square, Milton Park, Abingdon, Oxon OX14 4RN

First issued in paperback 2017

*Routledge is an imprint of the Taylor & Francis Group,
an informa business*

© 2013 Taylor & Francis

The right of Betina Entzminger to be identified as author of this work has been asserted by her in accordance with sections 77 and 78 of the Copyright, Designs and Patents Act 1988.

All rights reserved. No part of this book may be reprinted or reproduced or utilised in any form or by any electronic, mechanical, or other means, now known or hereafter invented, including photocopying and recording, or in any information storage or retrieval system, without permission in writing from the publishers.

Trademark Notice: Product or corporate names may be trademarks or registered trademarks, and are used only for identification and explanation without intent to infringe.

Library of Congress Cataloging-in-Publication Data
Entzminger, Betina, 1967-
 Contemporary reconfigurations of American literary classics : the origin and evolution of American stories / Betina Entzminger.
   p. cm. — (Routledge studies in twentieth-century literature ; 28)
 Includes bibliographical references and index.
 1. American literature—20th century—History and criticism—Theory, etc. 2. Canon (Literature) I. Title.
 PS221.E58 2012
 810.9'005—dc23
 2012013298

Typeset in Sabon
by IBT Global.

ISBN 13: 978-1-138-10932-2 (pbk)
ISBN 13: 978-0-415-53964-7 (hbk)

For Jason Moser

Contents

Acknowledgments   xi

Introduction: The Origin and Evolution of American Stories   1

1   Decoding the Cryptic Past: Richard Powers's and Louis Bayard's Reconfigurations of Poe's Short Stories   22

2   "A" Is for America: Revisions of *The Scarlet Letter*   43

3   A Draft of a Draft: Sena Jeter Naslund's Reconfiguration of *Moby-Dick*   66

4   Revising Alcott, Revising America: Reconfigurations of *Little Women*   83

5   The "Quintessentially American Book": Reconfigurations of *Adventures of Huckleberry Finn*   104

6   Life after Awakening: Anne Tyler's Revision of Kate Chopin's *The Awakening*   135

7   Plundered Narrative: Contemporary Rewritings of Faulkner's *Absalom, Absalom!*   150

Conclusion: The Future of Origins   170

Appendix A: Stealing Promethean Fire:
    An Interview with Novelist Louis Bayard   175
Appendix B: Interview with Sena Jeter Naslund   193
Notes   215
Bibliography   221
Index   237

Acknowledgments

I would like to thank Bloomsburg University's Research and Disciplinary Projects Grant and Bloomsburg University's College of Liberal Arts for financial support during the research of this book. In addition, I would like to thank the following research assistants for their valuable help: Brock Cahoon, Elena Brobyn-Navarro, Alexandra Martinez, and Erika Zaborny. Thanks are also due to colleagues who offered feedback during the drafting stages of this project, including David Cowart at the University of South Carolina and Cristina Mathews and David Randall at Bloomsburg University of Pennsylvania. I am also grateful to my family for their support as I worked on this book. Thank you Jason, Iris, and William. Louis Bayard and Sena Jeter Naslund graciously allowed me to interview them for this project, and Jon Clinch responded to my e-mails and discussed his work with me at his Oxford Public Library reading. I am grateful to them.

Portions of this book were previously published in slightly different forms: Part of chapter 5 first appeared in the *Southern Literary Journal* as "Come Back to the Raft Ag'in, Ed Gentry" in 2007 (from *The Southern Literary Journal*, Volume 40, Issue 1. Copyright © 2007 by the Department of English and Comparative Literature of the University of North Carolina at Chapel Hill. Published by the University of North Carolina Press. Used by permission of the publisher. www.uncpress.unc.edu); part of chapter 7 first appeared in *Studies in American Culture* as "Snow Job: Whitewashing History in William Faulkner's *Absalom, Absalom!* and David Bradley's *The Chaneysville Incident*" in 2005; "Stealing Promethean Fire: An Interview with Louis Bayard" first appeared in *Modern Language Studies* in 2012. All of these pieces are reprinted here with permission. Finally, thanks go to the Manuscript, Archive, and Rare Book Library at Emory University for granting me access to James Dickey's papers and for allowing me to include a photograph of a typescript page of *Deliverance* in this book.

Introduction
The Origin and Evolution of American Stories

Within the last thirty years or so, many well-received novels have overtly reconfigured aspects of American literary classics, offering readers new versions of familiar stories rather than startling originality. Unlike the postmodern parodies that characterized the 1960s and 1970s works of John Barth or Ishmael Reed, the more recent reconfigurations on which I focus offer respectful additions, almost homages, to the originals. A partial list includes Barbara Kingsolver's *The Poisonwood Bible* (1998), which reconfigures Louisa May Alcott's *Little Women*; Sena Jeter Naslund's *Ahab's Wife* (1999), which reconfigures Herman Melville's *Moby-Dick*; Louis Bayard's *The Pale Blue Eye* (2006), which reconfigures some of Edgar Allan Poe's stories; and Jon Clinch's *Finn* (2007), which reconfigures Mark Twain's *Adventures of Huckleberry Finn*. The number and popularity of these recent books suggest a curious trend for readers and writers, an impulse to retell and to reread books that have come to define American culture.

RECONFIGURATION AND POSTMODERNISM

To better understand this trend requires a more general understanding of postmodern literature. Literary borrowing, or intertextuality, is a frequently noted characteristic of postmodernism. Christian Moraru, for example, labels "intertextuality of representation" as the "unmistakable signature" of postmodernism (24). Moraru explores this intertextuality within literature as a reflection of a postmodern worldview: "In the name of an enlarged, cultural intertextuality, postmodern criticism propounds that a text—and a postmodern text more systematically than others—assimilates, re-presents a context because textual representations come about in collision with fictions, constructs, and representations of a more general kind, with the 'texts' of race, gender, sex, ethnicity, with the whole panoply of textuality writing our identities into a culture" (164). In other words, the intertextuality within literature reflects the more complex imbrication of individual identities, social categories, art, and society that sometimes goes unrecognized

Many critics acknowledge that a degree of intertextuality, the influence and inclusion of elements of an earlier work in a later one, occurs throughout literary history but has become more overt and intentional in postmodernism. Linda Hutcheon uses the term "historiographic metafiction" to describe these types of works: "fiction that is at once metafictional *and* historical in its echoes of the texts and contexts of the past" ("Historiographic Metafiction" 3). Postmodern writers who engage in historiographic metafiction rework historical moments, historical figures, and canonical literature into their contemporary fictional writing. They concern themselves with the process of narrative construction and how that process influences history and fiction. In addition, these writers concern themselves with the ways in which our constructed narratives then influence our reality.

Yet for Hutcheon, "Postmodernism signals its dependence by its *use* of the canon, but reveals its rebellion through its ironic *abuse* of it" (*A Poetics of Postmodernism* 130, emphasis in original). Hutcheon identifies parody or burlesque as driving forces in the historiographic metafictional texts she explores. Mark Currie further explains Hutcheon's term by pointing to the "illusion-breaking self-reflexivity" that characterizes such works (67). For example, near the beginning of *Flight to Canada*, a novel that displays all the characteristics of Hutcheon's "historiographic metafiction," Reed poses the question, "Who is to say what is fact and what is fiction?" (7) and follows with an account of Harriet Beecher Stowe's stealing the life story of Josiah Henson for her novel *Uncle Tom's Cabin*. In contrast, Raven Quickskill, Reed's main character, plans to write the story of Uncle Robin, an obsequious but crafty parody of Uncle Tom, in such a way that "to lay hands on the story would be lethal to the thief" (11). Reed's comic borrowing of characters, themes, and context from Stowe's work offers a clear and biting critique of the original, and his overt self-reflexivity destroys the illusion of reality in his storyworld. Similarly, in *Rewriting: Postmodern Narrative and Cultural Critique in the Age of Cloning*, Moraru looks at "counter narratives" by E. L. Doctorow, Robert Coover, and Paul Auster that rewrite earlier American texts in order to undercut them. As in historiographic metafictional novels, the themes and plots of the more recent reconfigurations that are the focus of this study often reveal a sophisticated examination of the process and implications of narrative constructions, but in contrast these authors refrain from self-reflexive peek-a-boo games that interfere with the reader's immersion in the narratives. They maintain the texts' illusion of reality, often referred to in theater as the "fourth wall." These authors also produce new versions that—rather than abuse or denigrate—respectfully add to or engage in a civil dialogue with their classic literary ancestors.

In his 1988 study *The Signifying Monkey: A Theory of African-American Literary Criticism*, critic Henry Louis Gates refers to "refiguration as an act of homage" among African American writers (xxvii), yet the texts discussed in this study suggest that such practice is widespread in contemporary

American literature. Clinch's *Finn*, for example, seems to honor its antecedent. This novel tells the life story of Pap Finn, a character created by Twain in *The Adventures of Huckleberry Finn*. In the appended author's note, Clinch writes, "Although I have approached [*Finn*'s] source material with the reverence that is its due, Finn himself has always insisted upon having the last word. Which is another way of saying that in order to learn the facts about Huckleberry Finn, you'll need to seek out an older and better novel than mine" (*Finn* 285). Clinch shapes his characters and plot with fidelity to Twain's work, shifting the focus to a character Twain shows only briefly and filling in the many gaps regarding this character's existence. By definition, then, these postmodern rewrites, or what I call "reconfigurations," respond to and give new trajectories to the classics they invoke. Yet these works are not parodies, because they do not "comically de-valorize" their "hypotext" (Herman, Jahn, and Ryan 419); nor are they pastiches, because they do not merely imitate the original. As Gates writes regarding the trope of Signifyin(g), "[T]he narrator's technique, his or her craft, is to be gauged by the creative (re)placement of these expected or anticipated formulaic phrases and formulaic events, rendered anew in unexpected ways" (61). Likewise, the reconfigurations on which this study focuses repeat with a difference, sometimes updating the tale to the present, as Anne Tyler does with Kate Chopin's *The Awakening* in *Ladder of Years* (1995), and sometimes maintaining the historical setting but telling the tale from the point of view of a peripheral character, as Clinch does in *Finn*.

These reconfigurations of American literary classics by contemporary American authors raise questions about the relationship of text to text, of author to author, of authors and texts to American culture, and of the reader to all the above. This study examines these novels in an attempt to answer some of these questions. Specifically, why do contemporary writers reconfigure earlier works? Why do they choose the daunting task of reinterpreting and retelling books that have come to define American culture? What does the popularity of this trend suggest about the function of literature in relation to readers, writers, and their culture? This study analyzes some contemporary American novels, written mostly in the 1990s and 2000s, with the earliest in 1970, and the American classics they reconfigure, written between 1830 and 1940. Readers could likely encounter these classics, written by Poe, Nathaniel Hawthorne, Melville, Alcott, Twain, Chopin, and William Faulkner, in a Great American Authors college course. Below, I sketch out three broad answers (aesthetic, market-driven, and cognitive) to the questions posed above, all of which can be simultaneously correct, but the last of which provides the focus for the remainder of this study. This last theory suggests that the trend of literary reconfiguration clarifies and makes explicit processes at work in literary history, cultural history, and human cognitive development.

I argue that by revising canonical American literature, contemporary American writers are (re)writing an American myth of origins, tapping into an existing cultural narrative and reshaping it to correspond to the contemporary writer's understanding of self and society. This impulse and the reception of these recent literary works validate contemporary cognitive psychological research about the function of narrative for the writer and the reader. Furthermore the contemporary novelists emphasize the cognitive function of narrative through embedded reading and writing functions (characters who read and interpret, characters who write) within their texts. The correlation between the novels' portrayal of narrative within their works and cognitive psychology is likely intentional on the part of the well-read contemporary authors, but the contemporary revisions also often underscore a similar function of narrative in the classic texts they revise, texts that obviously predate recent developments in cognitive psychology. In highlighting the construction and cognitive function of narrative in their own and in their antecedent texts, the contemporary writers suggest that such use of narrative is universal and essential to human beings. This emphasis on the construction and cognitive function of narrative also suggests that the individual narratives themselves, old or new, can make no legitimate claim to objective truth or reality, because the stories are always the product of a mind-shaping experience, and the desired myth of origins is, therefore, forever out of reach.

AESTHETIC REASONS FOR RECONFIGURATIONS

Writers have always been influenced by and borrowed from the works they admire, whether they be those of William Shakespeare, the bible, or folktales. One reason contemporary writers reconfigure classic texts is to acknowledge their debt to great writers and to assimilate some of those writers' creative power. Most writers were first lovers of literature. As writer Jonathan Lethem puts it in his essay "The Ecstasy of Influence: A Plagiarism," "Most artists are brought to their vocation when their own nascent gifts are awakened by the work of a master. That is to say, most artists are converted to art by art itself." The reading of a master, a "great book," engenders, for many, moments of epiphanic discovery—when one sees oneself and the world more clearly than before. In a letter to Thomas W. Higginson, poet Emily Dickinson describes this feeling: "If I feel physically as if the top of my head were taken off, I know *that* is poetry" (Higginson, emphasis in original). By memorializing an inspirational work in a new creation, a writer can pay tribute to it and attempt to replicate its effects.

Even without such a mind-blowing experience as Dickinson describes, the canonization of literary works implies a culture's judgment of their aesthetic worth. Most of the contemporary writers examined in this study were English majors or English graduate students, and many also taught English and creative writing. Repeated exposure to a work of literature in educational settings inevitably suggests an emulation-worthy status for that work. As Pallavi Rastogi says regarding epigraphs from canonical works, "In literary tradition, this method of using epigraphs establishes the connectivity of the literary method: the later writer places himself or herself in the tradition of the earlier writer, thus subtly seeking his or her own canonization" (278). Likewise, the contemporary writer of reconfigurations might be making a similar bid for recognition. Reconfigurations make literary influence explicit, and the explicitness suggests an attempt to profit aesthetically from literary devices that have worked so well in the past, to, in the words of novelist Bayard, "steal some of the original Promethean Fire" (298, this volume).

MARKET-DRIVEN REASONS FOR RECONFIGURATIONS

In addition to profiting aesthetically, though, contemporary authors stand to profit financially from their associations with classic texts. Bayard also acknowledges that reconfigurations are savvy marketing: Retelling a classic work allows readers to "know where they are, or at least they know where they're beginning, because they have some underpinning. Commercially speaking, it gives you a platform that a story about just any nineteenth-century character wouldn't necessarily have" (192, this volume). Many readers enjoy recognizing references to earlier literature in a new book. Doris Sommer suggests that discovering connections between individual texts entices the astute reader to "conquer" the text, "to get on top of it, to put one's finger on the mechanisms that produce pleasure and pain, and then to call it ours" (11). Matei Calinescu sees postmodern works as often "doubly coded" in this way, accessible without having read a prior, referenced work, but enriched by an understanding of the references. The double coding serves as a "strategy for attracting two audiences, a potentially large one and a small sophisticated one of 'secret sharers'" who get the references (446–447). Reconfigurations invite readers to solve an intellectual puzzle; they flatter readers who belong to the community of "secret sharers." Readers not only feel united with the author because they have read the same books (Keyser 92) but also feel a part of an imagined community of other readers (Guillory 42).

In *Transforming Memories in Contemporary Women's Writing*, Liedeke Plate argues that reconfigurations in the 1970s and 1980s, at least those written by women, were motivated by the desire to "counter a tradition of silence and alleged misrepresentation" in earlier literature (20). But in the 1990s, publishers began to recognize the commercial appeal of these reconfigurations and ushered more into the marketplace (21). Generally, publishers would rather produce a new book by a well-known author with an established audience than risk publishing a work by a new author, but a book by a new author that reshapes a familiar story by a canonical author reduces this risk. For a contemporary writer relatively unknown to consumers, connection to a canonical writer provides vicarious name recognition and association with a familiar category of literature. The reconfigured novels' sales and awards suggest that this strategy works: Among the contemporary novels discussed at length in these pages, one was named a best novel of the year by the *Washington Post*, the *Chicago Tribune*, and the *Christian Science Monitor* and was also named a notable book by the American Library Association (*Finn*); one won a PEN/Faulkner award and was a *New York Times* best book of the year (*The Chaneysville Incident*); five were *New York Times* bestsellers (*A Month of Sundays*, *Roger's Version*, *Deliverance*, *The Ladder of Years*, and *The Poisonwood Bible*); four were national bestsellers (*The Gold Bug Variations*, *The Pale Blue Eye*, *S.*, and *Ahab's Wife*); and one won a Pulitzer Prize (*March*).

COGNITIVE PSYCHOLOGY AND RECONFIGURATIONS

Most significantly, through reconfigurations, contemporary novelists convey their understanding, influenced by cognitive psychology and postmodern criticism, of the function of language and narrative within human minds and human societies—in this case, the American society. Recent cognitive psychology has found a strong link between narrative construction and human identity. According to Mark David Turner, "Narrative imagining—story—is the fundamental instrument of thought. Rational capacities depend upon it. It is our chief means of looking into the future, of predicting, of planning, and of explaining. It is a literary capacity indispensable to human cognition generally" (4–5). The human brain seems to be physically hardwired to use narrative to shape and to order experience in manageable ways. This capacity for narrative is an adaptation that has developed as part of human evolution. Anthony Paul Kerby claims that "self-narration is the defining act of the human subject, an act which is not only descriptive of the self, but fundamental to the emergence and reality of the subject" (4). In other words, self-narration not only separates us from less-evolved animals but also helps develop our higher-order thinking. For normal children, the practice of storytelling, through pretend play and recollection of events for those not present, emerges at around age three, shortly after the acquisition of language. Children who fail to develop this skill, or who develop it late, have other cognitive impairments.

Humans use narratives to understand themselves. In *How Our Lives Become Stories*, Paul John Eakin notes that narrative creates one's perception of oneself as an individual: Narrative is "deeply involved" in the "construction and maintenance of the extended self, that mode of self-experience that we are socialized to recognize as identity's core" (130). For many, psychological counseling consists of constructing a consistent life narrative to better understand one's past and to function better in the future. Many perceive the lack of a consistent narrative of the self as unhealthy and conducive of dysfunction. By ordering experience, then, narrative helps individuals improve emotional and mental security. For example, psychologists James W. Pennebaker and Janet D. Seagal conducted a study in which individuals wrote about "important personal experiences in an emotional way for as little as 15 minutes over the course of three days" (1243). They found that the practice positively influenced the individuals' mental and physical health (1243). Furthermore, the absence of narrative seems to correlate with the absence of recognizable identity. In *The Man Who Mistook His Wife for a Hat*, for example, Oliver Sacks discusses patients who, having suffered damage to the part of the brain that controls memory, lose all sense of self along with their recollection of the past.

Humans also use narrative to understand those around them and the events that fill their lives. According to Torban Grodal, narrative might "facilitate third-person empathic emotions" thorough its "capacity to refocus the story experience from a first-person to a third-person perspective" (153). The connection between narrative and the development of empathy is supported by the fact that Theory of Mind, cognitive psychology's name for an individual's ability to interpret what is going on inside another person's mind, develops in most children at about the same age as the ability to tell stories, at three or four. Those who have difficulty interpreting another's state of mind, such as people with autism, also have difficulty understanding fiction (Zunshine 195). In addition, we use narratives to sort out causal relations in past events, such as why an animal escaped the hunter's trap or why the applicant failed to get the job, and to prepare for future events, such as how to better trap prey or how to successfully land a job. Finally, we use narrative to commit events to memory in an organized way (Schank and Abelson 27) so we can draw on these memories later.

Literary narratives, ranging from the realistic to the fantastic, are a way of sharing versions of the internal narratives that we all construct, and, like internal narratives, they are not constructed by the simple transfer of the creator's sense data into language. People's brains do not simply mirror what their senses perceive, and postmodern narratives emphasize the disjunction between objective reality and human perception. According to Sacks, "Experience itself is not passive, a matter of 'impressions' or 'sense-data,' but active, and constructed by the organism from the start" (44). Hilary Putnam further articulates a model of "internal realism" to describe the relationship between the individual and objective reality: "[R]eality is accepted as existing 'out there,' but is only accessible to humans through human cognitive systems and, even then, only in the forms translated *by* those systems" (qtd. in Hart, "Epistemology" 321). The order and logic that humans impose on experience through narrative may not actually mirror external reality, but such illusion of order helps them function.

The way an individual orders sensory stimuli and experiences into consistent narratives is determined not only by the objective reality of those sensory inputs and by the distortions of his or her own perceptions but also by the influence of all the narratives he or she has constructed and heard in the past. The stories humans tell that constitute their identities are joint creations of their physical brain function and of the society in which they develop. In other words, narratives influence other narratives, whether internal or literary. Research psychologists Robyn Fivish and Elaine Reese, through the study of "memory talk" (when a young child and a parent discuss the events of a child's day), point out that this early self-narration is shaped by the child's interlocutors: "Parental styles of engagement can exert an enormous influence, transmitting both models of self and story" (Eakin, *How Our Lives Become Stories* 115). Parents ask questions, prompt addition of detail, and add in their own versions of events or parallel experiences, all of which shape the narrative of the child in one particular instance and shape the pattern of narrative construction that the child internalizes. Drawing on Fivish and Reese's research, Eakin concludes that "the child's sense of self emerge[s] in a crucible of family stories and cultural scripts" (117). Children and adults also receive large-scale models and sources of narrative coherence from political and religious ideologies, from scientific theory, from formal education, from literature (especially canonical literature), and so forth. These sources are then modified by the individual who has internalized them.

Often this influence and engagement occur without the subjects' conscious awareness. So, although individuals create narratives, narratives also create individuals. And, although individuals make up a society, societies also shape their individual members. Consistently, human beings compose and are composed by other people's stories, which they internalize, alter slightly, and perceive as part of themselves. In literary narratives, intertextuality concretely displays this process; a literary narrative composes and is composed by other literary narratives, which it internalizes, alters slightly, and presents as part of itself.

Cognitive psychologists developed the concepts of scripts and schemata to explain common storehouses of knowledge among members of a group. A script is a sequence of routine actions for certain routine activities, such as stopping at a red light, stored in the memory to be drawn upon when needed. Relating scripts to narrative, Herman notes:

> [C]omprehension of a text or a discourse—a story—requires access to a plurality of scripts. In the absence of stereotypes stored as scripts, readers could not draw textual inferences of the most basic sort—for example, that a masked character represented as running out of a bank probably just robbed it. . . . [S]tories stand in a certain relation to what I know, focusing attention on the unusual and the remarkable against a backdrop made up of highly structured patterns of belief and expectation. (90)

Schema are static models or prototypes of objects, experiences, or events also stored in the memory to be compared to new objects, experiences, and events in order to facilitate understanding. For example, a standard schema of a story is that it must have an engaging beginning that explains the characters and situation, a middle that develops those characters and situation and provides rising action, and an ending that resolves the conflict and provides closure for the reader. Often, this structure is represented by teachers on chalkboards by a convex curve depicting the story's beginning at the left, low side of the curve; the story's middle at the high, middle of the curve; and the story's ending at the low, right side of the curve. Readers who can easily visualize this curve have probably previously internalized this schema.

Within stories, whether formal literary ones, informal verbal ones, or internal mental ones, narrators rely on schemas for coherence. Schemas serve as norms for what is appropriate structure and content for a narrative, influencing, for example, the type and amount of detail in a story. These norms differ from actual experience, causing narrators to omit or to add information to enhance narrative impact, even if the narrative is only an internal one: As Schank and Abelson put it, "while our lives may not be coherent, our stories are" (27). The norms also vary by culture. Structure and information expected in one culture will not be exactly the same as that expected in another. Violating the schema too radically will cause narrative incoherence. Yet even though members of a culture share common schema, not all schema are shared. Individuals also form their own schema based on their unique experience, and even shared schema are colored by individual perception. Again, according to Schank and Abelson:

> Understanding, for a listener, means mapping the speaker's stories onto the listener's stories. . . . Different people understand the same story differently precisely because the stories they already know are different. Understanders attempt to construe new stories they hear as old stories they have heard before. They do this because it is actually quite difficult to absorb new information. . . . The real problem in understanding, then, is identifying which of all the stories you already know is the one that is being told to you yet again. (14)

As new schemas accumulate, old schemas adapt or evolve in light of new experiences.

COGNITIVE PSYCHOLOGY AND THE MYTH OF ORIGINS

As Kay Young and Jeffrey L. Saver put it, "Coming to narrative is a necessary feature of human development. And to the extent that culture is human development writ large, narrative becomes an inescapable constituent of culture" (73). Just as an individual's identity is made up of the individual's own and other's narratives, a culture's identity is shaped by canonical works of literature that are embraced and internalized by that culture. Building on the theories of Benedict Anderson and Walter Benjamin, Timothy Brennan notes the close connection between narrative literature and the development of national culture:

> Nations, then, are imaginary constructs that depend for their existence on an apparatus of cultural fictions in which imaginative literature plays a decisive role. And the rise of European nationalism coincides especially with one form of literature—the novel. . . . It was the *novel* that historically accompanied the rise of nations by objectifying the 'one, yet many' of national life, and by mimicking the structure of the nation, a clearly bordered jumble of languages and style. (49).

If, as Wilson says, individuals "are a composite of [their] stories," then our culture is a composite of our cultural narratives, and one's identity as part of that culture is marked by the degree to which one shares those narratives.

To understand how cultural narratives shape our national identity, think about the narratives in the form of history lessons that schoolchildren are taught about America. In elementary school, children learn that Christopher Columbus discovered America and that our country was founded on the principles of liberty and justice. These stories help children feel a sense of pride in their country and instill a sense of national identity. As adults, we learn that America was the land of an indigenous group with its own culture at the time of Columbus's arrival and that these people were decimated by Europeans. We also learn that our country was built just as much on slave labor and oppression as it was on the concepts of liberty and justice. Yet the earlier narratives are still a part of what we associate with our national identity. Anderson points out that an important aspect of narrative's role in constructing national identity is that it allows the uncomfortable parts of the nation's past to be rewritten into "a new form of narrative" that fits better with the nation's conception of itself ("Narrating" 659).

Classic literature contributes to our national identity in the same way as historical narrative. Such scholars as Harold Bloom, Anderson, and Jeffrey Olick have identified role of canonical literature in "memory-nation nexus" (Olick 2), arguing that the literary canon serves as "communal or societal memory" (Bloom, *The Western Canon* 18). Anderson connects this function of canon to the cognitive function of narrative more generally:

> All profound changes in consciousness, by their very nature, bring with them characteristic amnesias. Out of such oblivions, in specific historical circumstances, spring narratives. . . . [B]ecause it cannot be "remembered," [it] must be narrated. Against biology's demonstration that every single cell in a human body is replaced over seven years, the narratives of autobiography and biography flood print-capitalism's markets year by year. (*Imagined Communities* 204)

"As with modern persons, so with nations," Anderson continues. "Awareness of being imbedded in secular, serial time, with all its implications of continuity, yet of 'forgetting' the experience of this continuity . . . engenders the need for narrative of 'identity'" (205). Origins, the beginning of our individual and cultural narratives, are essential to understanding the identity that narrative helps create. As an example of the universality of such stories of origin, Anderson notes, "The conventional autobiography . . . almost invariably opens with unremembered information, and tropes of continuity. Thus, the author may tell us the date on which she was born, for which she must rely on circumstantial documentary evidence; and inform us about parents and grandparents, partly because . . . our idea of personhood, rooted in psychology and secular sociology, requires a framing in family genealogy and social history" ("Narrating" 659). Individually and collectively, humans try to explain their origins, believing that by understanding where they come from, they can better understand and explain themselves. Each culture has its own myths; the biblical story of Adam and Eve is a familiar Western myth of human origins. Columbus's discovering America and Huck and Jim's floating on the raft are familiar myths of American origin. For many, Huck and Jim, Ahab, and Hester are more real than any actual historical figure. The nature of their narratives allows the reader an intimacy with them that is not provided by historical documents. Together, the classic works form the beginnings of a collective narrative of American identity. They have become our cultural past and serve the function of an American myth of origins.

Sylvia Wynter explains that these tales of origin tap into cognitive patterns that have developed in the human brain and are important to our survival as a species. Animal instincts would normally induce greater competitiveness across family groups, but our evolved minds use narrative to override this competitiveness and to induce altruism and "conspecificity": "[W]e are co-identified only with those with whom our origin narratives and their systems of symbolic representations, or cultural programs, have socialized us to be symbolic conspecifics of, and therefore to display altruistic behaviors toward those who constitute the *nos* [us] on whose behalf we collectively act" (31). In other words, our origin narratives socialize us to identify with a larger group than just our blood relatives, producing altruistic behavior necessary for the formation of complex societies. By the same token, our origin narratives help us identify those who are not part of our society, so that we do not generally identify with "those whom our founding origin narratives have defined as the oppositionally meaningful markers of otherness to 'us'" (32). Wynter goes on to explain that these narratives and the worldviews they create can shift over time with the introduction of new thinkers and new ideas.

And it is not necessary for every member of the group to have read these classic texts to be influenced by them. Writer Lethem points out that certain texts, those that have been widely read and taught for some time, have "infiltrated the common mind" to "join the language of culture." Lethem refers to such books as "map-turned-to-landscape," suggesting that these nineteenth- and early-twentieth-century texts that were once merely representations of our culture have now become the culture itself. For example, without having read the novel, any average American, high school age or above, knows who Huckleberry Finn is and can give at least a sketchy overview of Twain's plot. The same could be said of Moby-Dick and Melville's novel. These characters and the basic events and themes of their novels are perceived as part of American history as much as of American arts. Because these books have "moved to a place beyond enclosure or control" (Lethem), many people know, via a lifetime of absorbed cultural references, the basic premises, characters, and plots of the classic tales even if they have never read them.

CONTEMPORARY AMERICAN AUTHORS AND MYTHS OF ORIGIN

Western myths of origin often involve an attempt to explain a troubling sense of loss or lack that we experience as humans. Jacques Derrida describes the human impulse to search for origins as "archive fever": "It is to have a compulsive, repetitive, and nostalgic desire for the archive, an irrepressible desire to return to the origin, a homesickness, a nostalgia for the return to the most archaic place of absolute commencement" (91). Because our ultimate origins, individually as humans and collectively as humanity, biologically and metaphysically, are both preconscious and prelinguistic, the objective reality of them is ultimately inaccessible. Charles Darwin metaphorically depicts this inaccessibility by comparing the record of human origins to a history text: "I look at the natural geological record, as a history of the world imperfectly kept, written in a changing dialect; of this history we possess the last volume alone, relating only to two or three countries. Of this volume, only here and there a short chapter has been preserved and of each page, only here and there a few lines" (qtd. in Beer 20). The connection of our forgotten origins with an absent or incomplete facility with language has also influenced poststructuralist thought. According to Jacques Lacan, "All signification is the result of a fortunate fall into a prison of signs" (qtd. in Bowie 67). Here, Lacan metaphorically connects the act of signification, using language, with the myth of Adam and Eve's ejection from Eden. Mark Currie further explains Lacan's connection of the loss of Eden with signification:

> Interpreting the sign then becomes a process of working backwards to the originary and mythical moment when the sign and the thing were unified, when the meaning of the sign was present. Writing is also a

> fall from presence since, like the sign, it is exterior to what it means, capable of signifying in the absence of the writer, demanding a kind of nostalgia for its origin, the moment when the mind that produced it was present, when it was full with signifying intention, or when it was speech. (82)

The fall into language separates us from a supposed earlier unity between signifier and signified, just as the fall from Eden separates us from a supposed prior unity with God. Just as the myths themselves attempt to account for our sense of loss or lack, the absence of these originary tales can create an even more frustrating and unsettling sense of loss and displacement, something with which postmodern thinkers are familiar. Contemporary American authors display an ambivalent attitude toward myths of origin. As Hutcheon and Currie point out, postmodern literature blurs the line between fiction and criticism, theory and practice, producing imaginary literature that engages some of the same questions and problems explored by contemporary critics (Hutcheon 90, *A Poetics of Postmodernsim*; Currie 53). This engagement with theory and philosophy produces in creative literature an awareness of postmodernist thought that has displaced many of our myths of origin, but at the same time it produces a wariness of the nihilism and disorder that can result from their absence. Postmodern theorists point out the illusory quest for one's beginnings, the yearning for the absence that was never present. Michel Foucault, for example, posits that the quester finds not "the image of primordial truth" but "'something altogether different' behind things: not a timeless and essential secret, but the secret that they have no essence or that their essence was fabricated in a piecemeal fashion from alien forms" (78). Like postmodern theorists, contemporary authors of reconfigurations emphasize the constructedness of origins, but they do so without abandoning all quests and without abandoning all myth, as long as myth is acknowledged as creative act rather than as objective reality. As Umberto Eco puts it, "The postmodern reply to the modern consists of recognizing that the past, since it cannot really be destroyed, because its destruction leads to silence, must be revisited: but with irony, not innocently" (qtd. in Hutcheon, *A Poetics of Postmodernism* 90). I would argue that the more recent contemporary works in this study approach the past neither innocently nor ironically. They simultaneously follow conservative and radical impulses in connection to the canonical works of literature they engage. By reconfiguring a classic work of literature, contemporary authors reenact the universal human quest for origins. But at the same time, these authors attempt to alter the trajectory of that cultural narrative and destabilize its claim to absolute Truth.

By revising the classic texts that compose our cultural narrative, contemporary writers mirror the way human individuals consistently revisit and refigure the past through language, via self-narration, in order to manage and to understand experience. Critic Guy Cook theorizes the relation of different types of literature to existing schemata: "[D]iscourse which is 'schema preserving,' leav[es] existing schemata as they were, and discourse which is 'schema reinforcing,' leav[es] existing schemata stronger than before.... The category of schema-refreshing discourse, whose primary function is to effect change in schemata, will include many of those discourses described as 'literary'" (192). Although Cook connects "schema refreshing discourse" with "literary" discourse, he makes a point to exclude canonical literature from this category:

> Literary discourses which were once schema-refreshing become schema-reinforcing.... This tendency of new form and content to become not only accepted but conventional, leads to a lack of fit between the literary canon and the category of "schema-refreshing discourse." This is hardly surprising, as the canon tends to be defined, not for a specific reader, but for—and by—a dominant social group speaking in institutions at a particular time in history. The concept of schema-refreshing discourse, on the other hand, must be related to as many variations as there are between epochs, individuals, and social groups.... Educational institutions, however, have a tendency to be a step behind. They canonize what was once (and exclude what is currently) schema-refreshing. (194)

If, as Cook suggests, canonical literature was once schema-refreshing but has become schema-reinforcing, one may view reconfigurations as attempts to reinvigorate, or to re-refresh, them. The contemporary reconfigurations of American literary classics attempt to rewrite cultural narratives in order to align them with an evolving society. What emerges are different stories, ones that reflect the contemporary writers' own perceptions and experiences (however those may be altered by the filter of fiction) but that maintain recognizable schematic elements in the form of intertextual references.

Contemporary authors ground their reconfigurations in the cultural narrative in a manner similar to that encouraged by T.S. Eliot in his 1922 essay, "Tradition and the Individual Talent." In response to modernists who valued novelty over tradition, Eliot writes:

> [T]he historical sense compels a man to write not merely with his own generation in his bones, but with a feeling that the whole of the literature of Europe from Homer and within it the whole of the literature of his own country has a simultaneous existence and composes a simultaneous order.... No poet, no artist of any art, has his complete meaning alone. His significance, his appreciation is the appreciation of his relation to the dead poets and artists. You cannot value him alone; you must set him, for contrast and comparison, among the dead.... The

necessity that he shall conform, that he shall cohere, is not one-sided; what happens when a new work of art is created is something that happens simultaneously to all the works of art which preceded it.

Contemporary authors of reconfigurations engage the canon differently than Eliot by revising one particular text in an extended form, but they share with Eliot a demonstration of the writer's cultural and literary knowledge, an invitation for the reader to compare old and new, and an adaptation of literary antecedents to a new time. Although one cannot draw an exact parallel between biological and cultural processes, this model of literary evolution resembles Darwin's model of human evolution, with gradual changes and adaptations over time and the most suitable characteristics being passed on to future generations. The similarity may not be accidental. Louis Cuddy and Claire Roche trace Eliot's influence by Darwinian theories through his mother's interests at home and through his Harvard education. They go on to argue, "Eliot juxtaposes his poetic forms and allusional strategies with the theories of evolution, anthropology, and eugenics—particularly Charles Darwin's principle of 'descent with modification'—to create his grand design for the unity and evolution of the human race and of existence as he had come to know it" (42). Likewise, the similarities among contemporary authors' practice of reconfiguration, biological evolution, and cognitive psychology may be attributed to the authors' own interests in these topics as well as to natural patterns in human physiology and culture.

Although they engage the tradition, contemporary authors do not view its influence as wholly positive, and it is through their radical responses to the canon, responses that exist alongside their conservative responses, that the contemporary authors show the influence of postmodern thought. As Ellen Spolsky writes, "[B]oth the deconstructionist debates of the last thirty years and the evolutionary argument collude in stripping us of our innocence. We are no longer able to continue as if words simply mean what they say, as if we did not know that words cannot be entirely reliably identified with the things they normally, habitually represent" (53). Ambivalence toward classic texts should not be surprising. French theorist Jean-Francois Lyotard defines postmodern as "incredulity toward metanarratives" (xxiv). Similarly, Foucault sees the canon as a nefarious disciplinary instrument of imperialist ideology. For him, the widespread dissemination and internalization of certain units of knowledge is a means by which those in power control language and thought. As he writes in "The Order of Discourse," "Doctrine . . . tends to be diffused, and it is by the holding in common of one and the same discursive ensemble that individuals . . . define their reciprocal allegiance. . . . Any system of education is a political way of maintaining or modifying the appropriation of discourse along with knowledges and powers which they carry." The reason some literary works become canonical, to be endorsed and disseminated by educational institutions and popular culture, is that they support a desirable image or ideal about a community, such as American society. In other words, they are powerful distributors of master narratives. In the case of a classic text like *Adventures of Huckleberry Finn*, these images or ideals might relate to the power of youthful innocence, the value of physical freedom and wide open spaces, and the importance of individualism and independent thought, all of which Americans generally associate with themselves. Eakin contends, "If narrative is indeed identity content then the regulation of narrative carries the possibility of the regulation of identity" (*Living Autobiographically* 33). Foucault seems to agree.

Resisting the canonical text's ability to regulate identity, contemporary authors of reconfigurations alter through their revisions the trajectory of the canonical narrative, showing that the process of regulation can be reversed; individuals can shape cultural narrative. In Kingsolver's *The Poisonwood Bible*, for example, the death of young Ruth May echoes the untimely death of Alcott's Beth March. But whereas Beth's death reminds readers of her self-sacrificing goodness and inspires her sisters' and her readers' guilt at not having been likewise, Ruth May's death inspires anger at the authoritarian father who sacrifices his child in the name of his mission. The readers are shown a different view of sacrifice and of authority, which will then influence their interpretation of Alcott's novel as well as Kingsolver's. The contemporary authors "refresh" the schema that we have internalized in connection with the classic text. Rather than disparaging or rejecting the canonical works, however, the contemporary reconfigurations invite readers to interrogate the classic texts' origins and to become conscious of their status as contributors to our identity. And according to Louis Mink, a familiar story is an ideal one with which to make this point: "The more familiar a story . . . the more one is likely to be aware of the arbitrariness of its construction, so that one's imagination can respond more alertly to connections (realized and unrealized) of structures to themes" (80). Through their metafictional plot elements, contemporary reconfigurations unsettle the notion of originary Truth in classic texts, yet the fact that the reconfigurations respectfully revisit these classics reasserts some of their cultural power.

Contemporary reconfigurations emphasize, just as recent cognitive psychology suggests, that what humans perceive as their experience is always already influenced by narratives they have internalized. Through metafictional plot elements, the authors highlight the power of internal and external narratives, the subjective nature of all language and all interpretation, and the problematic concepts of originality and objective reality. Tilottama Rajan posits that a "reading function" is inherent in all intertextual writing, because, through allusions and references to other literature, it makes the acts of reading, writing, and interpretation its implicit subject matter (67). For example, by titling his work *The Sotweed Factor* and retelling in fictional form Ebenezer Cooke's poem of the same name, Barth makes it clear that he has read and is responding to the earlier work. Gerard Genette calls this rhetorical gesture that identifies for the reader the "hypotext," or the earlier book, the "contract of transposition" (306). Barth's obvious rewriting calls attention to an exploration of the act and nature of composition. Barth's novel is metatextual, because it, at least in part, is a work of literature about the writing of literature.

The contemporary writers in this study make the implicit reading function of all intertextual literature explicit to underscore such metatextual concerns. Just like their readers, many of the characters in these contemporary novels read and interpret texts, such as historical documents or coded messages, and, like us, they believe they have come to understand these texts and their world, only to be proven wrong as the narrative unfolds. For example, in David Bradley's *The Chaneysville Incident*, John Washington reads and tries to decipher the meaning behind his deceased father's research notes in order to understand his own origins and his father's death. Still other characters in these contemporary novels, like their writers, create texts within the novels, such as letters and diaries. Readers use these documents to understand the characters and their world, only to discover later that the writing character is unreliable and their understanding is therefore flawed. For example, much of the text of Geraldine Brooks's *March* consists of journal entries written by Mr. March during his travels, interspersed with letters home to his wife. By comparing these two internal texts, the reader sees that Mr. March withholds much from his wife, and perhaps also from his readers. Through the reading characters and writing characters that the contemporary authors create, the authors highlight the fallibility and variability of interpretation and perception. By the contemporary novel's close, the reading characters come to realize their misapprehensions of the novel's embedded texts, and the reader comes to understand the writing characters' unreliability. From these characters, the reader infers the instability of meaning and interpretation generally, even in texts revered as literary classics. By calling our attention to the canonical work's continued influence on readers and then suggesting the instability of meaning in all texts, the contemporary authors encourage readers' more conscious selection of the narratives that define them.

Hutcheon writes, "Historiographic metafictions employ parody not only to restore history and memory in the face of the distortions of the 'history of forgetting' (Thiher 202), but also, at the same time, to put into question the authority of any act of writing by locating the discourses of both history and fiction within an ever-expanding intertextual network that mocks any notion of either single origin or simple causality" ("Historiographic Metafiction" 11–12). Conversely, because they are not parody in that they do not mock and ridicule their antecedents, the contemporary reconfigurations assert the potential authority of any act of writing. Melville does not own Moby-Dick and Captain Ahab. Naslund can say her piece about them and about all that they represent, adding what she believes that Melville neglects—in this case, the story of Ahab's wife. Because the reconfiguration does not degrade the classic text, it opens up the possibility for multiple interpretations without closure and without dismissal. Implicit in such a reconfiguration is the legitimate expectation that some other reader and writer will follow Naslund to tell the story again, this time perhaps giving the central role to Queequeg.

By reshaping *Moby-Dick*, or any other canonical work, without stripping its power, a writer reshapes a cultural narrative. By reshaping the canonical work to incorporate a contemporary voice, he or she acknowledges narrative as an ongoing process connected to identity and calls attention to the power of collective narrative to shape individuality and to form community. As Moraru notes, "Once we admit that truth has a memory, a cultural biography of becoming and adjustment within textual-material circumstances, we can no longer defend the hypothesis of monolithic and stable truth, of truth as a datum, meaning handed down to us as if authorized by an authority above history" (177). Calling readers' attention to the role of narrative in relation to identity, the reconfiguration empowers individuals to control their own identities by rewriting them.

METHODOLOGY

This study approaches its primary texts through close reading, informed by cognitive psychology, evolutionary literary criticism, and poststructuralism. On the surface, evolutionary literary criticism, which studies "the evolved human brain" (Spolsky 47) in the context of literature, may seem incompatible with poststructuralist notions of the constructedness and mutability of language, meaning, and identity. But many evolutionary literary theorists understand the mutability of language and meaning in terms of the brain's function. As Brian Boyd puts it, "If we are evolved creatures, our brains are not guarantors of truth, citadels of reason, or shadows of the mind of God but simply organs of survival, built to cope with the immediate environment and perhaps to develop some capacity to recall and anticipate." And evolutionary literary theorists do not suppose that the individual's brain interprets in a vacuum. According to Spolsky, "human bodies, minds, cultures, and theories" are "constructed (and variously so) by the interface of our genetic inheritance with the environment into which we are born, that is, by the constantly changing interaction of individual needs, hegemonic cultures, and an unstable class of culturally empowered arbiters" (55). Far from being mutually exclusive, poststructuralist literary theory and cognitive evolutionary literary theory can be mutually enhancing. I believe that this combined approach adds a useful complexity to the textual analyses.

CHAPTER CONTENTS

Each of the following chapters examines a particular American literary classic and one or more (by no means all) reconfigurations of it. In order to emphasize an evolution of the American cultural narrative, the chapters are arranged chronologically by the publication dates of the canonical texts being revised. Chapter 1, "Decoding the Cryptic Past: Richard Powers's and Louis Bayard's Reconfigurations of Poe's Short Stories," examines Powers's *The Gold Bug Variations*, a novel set alternately in the 1980s and in the 1950s that involves a quest for meaning, and Bayard's *The Pale Blue Eye*, a detective story set in the early nineteenth century. Both are contemporary reconfigurations of key stories by Poe, specifically his detective stories, such as "The Purloined Letter," "The Murders in the Rue Morgue," and their strange cousin, "The Gold-Bug," and his horror stories, such as "The Fall of the House of Usher" and "The Tell-Tale Heart." Both reconfigurations adapt the quest for answers or treasure prominent in Poe's stories to suggest that all human understanding, especially that contained in the always coded form of language, is suspect and illusive.

Chapter 2, "'A' Is for America: Revisions of *The Scarlet Letter*," analyzes John Updike's trilogy *A Month of Sundays*, *Roger's Version*, and *S.*, which retells Hawthorne's novel from the modern-day perspectives of its three main characters, Dimmesdale, Chillingworth, and Hester, respectively, as well as Bharati Mukherjee's *The Holder of the World*, set alternately in nineteenth-century America, England, and India and in 1990s America and India. Respecting *The Scarlet Letter* and its status as an American myth of origin, Updike critiques his contemporary American society through a comparison with the past, and Mukherjee extends the Americanness of Hawthorne's work into new geographic and cultural territory. Mukherjee's novel purports to tell the "real story" of the New England past, addressing without blame what she believes Hawthorne omits or minimizes, while at the same time undermining the notion that such a thing as a "real story" exists.

Chapter 3, "A Draft of a Draft: Sena Jeter Naslund's Reconfiguration of *Moby-Dick*," analyzes Naslund's novel *Ahab's Wife*, which, as the name suggests, tells the life story of Ahab's bride, whom Melville mentions only briefly in *Moby-Dick*. By rewriting *Moby-Dick*, Naslund reinforces this novel's position in the American canon, yet she also interpolates a new chapter into the American cultural narrative through her revisions. In retelling the tale from a female perspective, Naslund offers a feminist critique of American society and of the cultural narrative, adding voices to that narrative that she believes Melville omits. And although Melville was tortured by the inability to access origins or unmediated Truth, Naslund presents the resulting uncertainty as liberating.

Chapter 4, "Revising Alcott, Revising America: Reconfigurations of *Little Women*," examines three reconfigurations of Alcott's *Little Women*: Judith Rossner's *His Little Women*, a novel that recounts the lives of four sisters and their charismatic father in late 1980s California; Kingsolver's *The Poisonwood Bible*, which follows an American missionary family to Africa and back and follows the four daughters into adulthood in the second half of the twentieth century; and Brooks's *March*, which follows Papa March, the absent presence throughout most of Alcott's novel, on his tour of duty as a Civil War chaplain. By rewriting an American classic, the authors attempt to revise the narrative of American identity in a way that makes it more palatable to their understanding of themselves and the present. Each writer also, like the other contemporary writers in this study, incorporates reading and writing functions into her narrative to suggest that this act of reinterpretation and revision is an inevitable, unending, always provisional part of the human experience.

Chapter 5, "The 'Quintessentially American Book': Reconfigurations of *Adventures of Huckleberry Finn*," discusses four reconfigurations of Twain's novel. Perhaps because of the work's iconic status, many contemporary writers have offered their versions of the tale, and many critics have debated its merits. This chapter examines John Seelye's *The True Adventures of Huckleberry Finn*, which adheres to Twain's novel in almost every way except that it rewrites Twain's often critiqued ending; James Dickey's *Deliverance*, which relates the story of four men as they raft down a river in the 1970s; Nancy Rawles's *My Jim*, narrated by the wife that Jim leaves behind when he escapes with Huck; and Clinch's *Finn*, which offers the life story of Huck's drunken and abusive father, Pap Finn. These revisions allow the contemporary authors to pay tribute to the original book while overcoming what they perceive as shortcomings in the novel. The revisions also allow them to offer new literary interpretations of the American cultural elements Twain invokes. As with other contemporary writers who reconfigure American classics, these writers overtly call attention to the fallibility of language and the variability of interpretation within their texts. Their emphasis on misinterpretation, reinterpretation, or willful deception through language forms an analogue to the many varied interpretations of Twain's text and underscores that all knowledge is based on subjective perception and is always subject to reevaluation and reinterpretation.

Chapter 6, "Life after Awakening: Anne Tyler's Revision of Kate Chopin's *The Awakening*," reads Tyler's heroine as a matured version of Chopin's Edna Pontellier. Tyler's reconfiguration updates the first American feminist novel to the late twentieth century, but in doing so, it suggests that not very much has changed for women in nearly one hundred years. Tyler emphasizes the importance of narrative to self-definition, suggesting that more and better female models within the cultural narrative would help improve the status of women in American society.

Chapter 7, "Plundered Narrative: Contemporary Rewritings of Faulkner's *Absalom, Absalom!*," looks at reconfigurations of Faulkner's *Absalom, Absalom!* (1936). The most recent of the "classic" American texts featured in this study, this Faulkner novel, in particular, anticipates the contemporary texts' attention to revision, to the frustrating malleability of language and meaning, and to the relation of narrative to identity. Instead of reshaping and retelling earlier works of American literature, however, *Absalom, Absalom!* rewrites itself through the characters' preoccupations with cultural and personal history. The characters' preoccupations, then, are mirrored by the contemporary texts that revisit Faulkner's narrative in search of their own origins. Bradley reconfigures *Absalom!* in *The Chaneysville Incident*, a novel that oscillates among the 1980s narrative of John Washington, the mid-twentieth-century narrative of his father, and the late-nineteenth-century narrative of his great-grandfather. And Toni Morrison reconfigures Faulkner's work in *Beloved*, a novel set before and after the Civil War that explores the lasting trauma of slavery from the slaves' perspectives. Instead of using a (fictional) historical figure as a point of reference for their tales as Faulkner's characters do, Bradley and Morrison use a classic American literary work (*Absalom, Absalom!*) as a point of reference for their novels. Faulkner's characters and the contemporary novelists reshape their points of reference so the outcomes resonate more closely to the identities (cultural or personal) of their creators. These reshapings of experience (including the experience of narrative) through narrative help readers make sense of that experience. In this way, not only do the past texts influence the contemporary ones, but the contemporary ones also influence our interpretations of their antecedents.

This study's concluding chapter, "The Future of Origins," suggests other types of reconfigurations, such as film and television programs, that could be fruitfully analyzed to add to an understanding of narrative's function in human cognition and cultural evolution. Personal interviews, in which authors Bayard and Naslund discuss their works in relation to the literary classics that inspired them, appear in the appendix.

1 Decoding the Cryptic Past
Richard Powers's and Louis Bayard's Reconfigurations of Poe's Short Stories

One of the best-known and most popular American writers, Edgar Allan Poe is associated with the beginnings of the country's literature. Professor Alphonso Smith's words at a 1909 commemoration of the centenary of Poe's birth attest to this writer's association with American origins. Smith attributed to Poe "a patience and persistence worthy of Washington . . . a husbandry of details that suggest the thriftiness of Franklin . . . a native insight and inventiveness that proclaim him of the line of Edison" (qtd. in Peeples, "Poe's 'Constructiveness'" 178). Smith's words link Poe to the founders and inventors of the nation, assigning to him by association a similar originary role in the national literature. Poe's contributions to American letters were recognized by at least some of his contemporaries, who praised his work "in dozens of periodicals . . . [as]: 'unusually excellent'; 'some of the most popular tales of American origin'; 'one of the most extraordinary narratives ever penned'" (Silverman 154). Of Poe's collection *Tales of the Grotesque and Arabesque* (1839), a reviewer notes, "He has placed himself in the foremost rank of American writers" (155), and another reviewer describes Poe's "The Gold-Bug" as "the most remarkable American work of fiction published in the last fifteen years" (209). Poe himself self-consciously sought to shape the new country's literature, to "establish a native literary canon . . . giving America a literary order" in line with his own judgments and tastes (169). In fact, he identified his own period as the time in which American literature must begin in earnest: "[W]e are now strong in our own resources. We have, at length, arrived at that epoch when our literature may and must stand on its own merits, or fall through its own defects" (qtd. in Silverman 168).[1]

Poe's position in the American canon and the foundations of national literature is not unquestioned, however. In his own time, he often alienated fellow writers through his sometimes caustic reviews and alienated contemporary reviewers of his work through his sometimes bizarre and confusing tales. Louis Renza sees an uneasy fit between Poe and other early-nineteenth-century American writers: "Poe's kind of semiotic faithlessness has little place in a U.S. culture where one might think to invent or at minimum reconstruct a new identity from scratch. His vision, consequently, has little to do with ideas of American literary nationalism or exceptionalism" (34). Yet despite the fact that his vision did not jibe with that of his contemporaries, Poe's brand of literature, with its "semiotic faithlessness," and his view of the new nation fit quite well with many of today's postmodern writers. According to Renza, "[H]is works sketchily adumbrate a United States culture as itself at heart homeless and without identity, whatever the ideological fictions it tells itself from historical moment to moment to deny 'only this and nothing more': that everyone belongs here, because no one really belongs here" (35). The uncertainty, linguistic manipulation, pluralism, and rejection of metanarratives that Renza sees as characteristic of Poe's work and in contrast to that of his contemporaries presages some of the dominant concerns of postmodern literature. This pre-postmodern portrayal of language and identity coupled with Poe's attempts at canon formation explain why some postmodern American writers have turned to him when seeking American literary origins.

Two such postmodern writers are Richard Powers and Louis Bayard, whose novels, *The Gold Bug Variations* (Powers, 1991) and *The Pale Blue Eye* (Bayard, 2006), reconfigure some of Poe's short stories, updating them for a postmodern sensibility by strengthening the roles of women and African Americans and adding more overt socially conscious messages. Yet the contemporary novels also borrow and revise Poe's themes, such as a critique of America's economic system in the case of Powers, the death of a beautiful woman in the case of Bayard, and an obsession with deciphering codes in both works. In fact, all three writers explore the combination of power and language through codes as the dominant theme of their works. For Poe, Powers, and Bayard, the deciphering of codes and understanding of their messages attests to the role of narrative in human thought and relates to the human quest for origins. Unlike Poe, however, for Powers and Bayard, this meaning, this wholeness, this origin that the deciphered code promises remains forever elusive.

The primary literary antecedent for Powers's *The Gold Bug Variations* is Poe's "The Gold-Bug," a short story broadly about money, power, language, and the intersection of the three. First appearing in Philadelphia's *Dollar Newspaper* in June 1843, the story begins with an unnamed narrator visiting a friend, William Legrand, who is living in semi-exile on Sullivan's Island, South Carolina, after his family fortune has diminished. Living with Legrand is Jupiter, a manumitted black servant and caretaker who refuses to leave his former master. Near the story's beginning, Legrand excitedly tells the narrator of a fascinating gold-colored beetle that he had found on the island that day. Having earlier loaned the bug to another friend, Legrand proceeds to draw a picture of it on a scrap of paper that had been lying on the ground near the insect and with which Jupiter had first grasped the bug. While sitting by the fire and looking at the drawing, the narrator remarks on the beetle's resemblance to a skull. Irritated by the comparison, Legrand takes the paper, looks at it a few moments, and then locks it in a desk drawer. Sensing a change in his host's mood, the narrator leaves, only to be summoned about a month later by Jupiter, bearing a note from Legrand requesting another visit. Legrand, who appears to have gone mad, then takes the narrator and Jupiter on an expedition that eventually leads to uncovering buried treasure "of incalculable value" (Poe 335). In the second part of the story, published in the next week's issue of the *Dollar Newspaper*, Legrand explains to the narrator and the reader his knowledge of the treasure. The scrap of paper on which he had drawn the beetle was, he had discovered on closer examination, really a piece of parchment, which, upon being heated by the fire, revealed previously invisible coded writing, the skull being the only part of which the narrator had seen. Legrand deciphered this writing to reveal a treasure map left by the pirate Captain Kidd and then followed the map to the treasure.

In a letter to his friend Frederick W. Thomas, Poe says that he wrote this story, as he did his famous poem "The Raven," to make money: "'The Raven' has had a great 'run,' Thomas—but I wrote it for the express purpose of running—just as I did the 'Gold Bug,' you know. The bird beat the bug, though, all hollow" (*Letters* 287). Wealth was not only the author's aim in publishing the story but also at the core of its meaning. Jupiter's fear that his master's apparent madness results from his having been bitten by the bug hints at another type of "gold bug" that afflicts victims with the mad desire for wealth. As critic Terrence Whalen points out, the California Gold Rush did not begin until 1848, five years after Poe's story appeared in print, but a smaller gold rush took place in Georgia in 1828. Yet perhaps Poe's gold bug refers more generally to greed, although not necessarily directly linked to a gold rush. According to Whalen, the economic difficulties of the late 1830s and early 1840s fueled debates over the value of paper money versus gold and silver (197). Because of the nation's preoccupation with its currency, a tale about money was likely to gain public notice. The story metaphorically records Poe's own attempts to profit from his writing (turn his messages to gold) and, as Whalen points out, the economic concerns of his day: "[T]here are some basic correspondences between 'The Gold-Bug,' in which the central character converts a coded pirate map into pirate's treasure, and the general political context of Poe's day, in which partisan factions fought to establish the proper relation between a system of (paper) signs and the gold accumulated in various public and private treasuries" (201). Because of the unlikely sequence of events that leads to the treasure and because Poe emphasizes that the map itself is not written on paper but on parchment, Whalen sees the story as a parody of the government's attempts to promote trust in paper currency (219).

Others, however, have read this work as a critique of the capitalist system in which Poe lived and wrote, a critique concealed beneath the story's surface much as the treasure map is concealed until the correct methods are employed to read it. In the story's penultimate paragraph, the narrator asks Legrand about the skulls that they had found buried in the hole with the treasure, and the story ends with his reply: "It is clear that Kidd . . . must have had assistance in the labor. But this labor concluded, he may have thought it expedient to remove all participants in his secret. Perhaps a couple of blows with a mattock were sufficient, while his coadjutors were busy in the pit; perhaps it required a dozen—who shall tell?" (Poe 348). The corporeal remains lie in the pit, sacrificed to the treasure. Daniel Kempton suggests that the bones, "buried *within* the gold itself," hint at the cost, in concrete human terms and in spiritual terms for the author, of the mercenary drive (14, emphasis in original). The mercenary drive that drove Poe to compose a money-making tale, Kempton implies, also created in him a sense of having sold out and paradoxically became the subject of his social critique in that same tale.

Some of the same interpretations that readers see hidden beneath the surface of Poe's story are more overt in the work of contemporary writer Powers. In *The Gold Bug Variations*, Powers critiques more forcefully the problematic commingling of language, money, and power in our society. In the novel, Stuart Ressler, a 1950s molecular biologist, attempts to understand how life is formed by breaking DNA's hidden code, and Jan O'Deigh, a 1980s librarian, attempts to understand herself by researching the same subject. Their lives intersect when Jan begins a relationship with Todd Franklin, Ressler's early 1980s coworker. The once brilliant Ressler has faded into self-imposed anonymity as a graveyard-shift computer programmer. Ressler and Jan compare their searches to that of Poe's characters, even reading "The Gold-Bug" to make sense of their own quests. Powers's references to Poe indicate his indebtedness to this earlier writer's inspiration: "I have always tried to write my personal landmarks directly into my books in some way, if not in an acknowledgments page, then by some quotation or homage or identifiable theft that brands the book's indebtedness. So all those allusions or references: those are the people I'd like somehow to pay back" (Neilson 21). The fact that Powers pays homage to Poe in this tale about deciphering the genetic code and thereby understanding the origins of all life suggests that Powers sees Poe as an originator of sorts in his own right.

Like Poe, Powers writes about the destructive combination of knowledge and greed. Ressler knows that when one breaks a code to extend the bounds of human knowledge, one cannot control how the deciphered codes will be read in the future. Living in the early years of the cold war and remembering well the Manhattan project, Ressler, though close to understanding DNA replication, delays his research because he fears the uses to which his discoveries may be put. He believes that science has become a tool that perpetuates American capitalism, with catastrophic results: "A million species lost irretrievably by the time he dies, an acceleration of slaughter that can only be ignored by an effort of will. Not research's fault per se, but tied to the same destructive desire to grow, be *more*" (592, emphasis in original). As Powers states in his interview with Jim Neilson, "[T]he science that we do—and this is Ressler's point—remains as much a two-way proposition as any human story, and must stay accountable to both facts and values" (19). Like Poe, Powers suggests that greed can corrupt human quests and destroy human lives.

The novel's attack on commercialism becomes more obvious when, in the 1980s, a computer error causes a minor character to lose health insurance. When he suffers a stroke soon after, the insurance company at first chooses its bottom line over human life by refusing to reinstate him. Finally it is forced to do so by Jan, Ressler, and Todd's pseudo-terrorist tactics that combine literature, statistics, and computer programming to sabotage the company's computers and to defeat capitalist interests.

Also like "The Gold-Bug," *The Gold Bug Variations* is at once a capitalist success and a critique of capitalism. In interviews, Powers indicates that the serious author should follow the path taken by Ressler, eschewing fame and fortune in order to protect his or her values. Speaking about a later book, *Galatea 2.2* (1995), Powers speculates that the character Helen, a human-engineered artificially intelligent being, is killed by "the thing that pays the bills, that manufactures all the books, that arranges the shape of our lives . . . business" (Neilson 22). Speaking about literature in general, he states:

> I happen to believe that the deepest value of fiction is that . . . it is one arena where we can, at least temporarily, take apart and refuse to compete within the terms that the rest of existence insists on. Market value may come to drive out all other human values, except, perhaps . . . the completely barter-driven economy of the imagination. Fiction, when it remembers its innate priority over other human transactions, can deal not in price but in worth. (23)

These comments seem rather disingenuous, however, when considering that the paperback front cover of *The Gold Bug Variations* touts in all capital letters that the novel was a national bestseller.

Powers also adapts another aspect of Poe's "The Gold-Bug," a focus on codes and the nature of language. The desire to decipher codes, to strip away the barriers to meaning, suggests a quest for unity and wholeness characteristic of human uses of language more generally. I have suggested that contemporary American writers' reconfigurations of classic American writers are attempts to trace a way back to their literary beginnings, as individual literary beings and as products of our collective culture. Poe, however, was also a frequent borrower from the works of his predecessors. As he writes in one of his essays, "There is no greater mistake than the supposition that a true originality is a mere matter of impulse or inspiration. To originate is carefully, patiently, and understandingly to combine" ("Magazine Writing" 319).[2] Lilianne Weissberg convincingly argues that Poe reconfigures Daniel Defoe's *Robinson Crusoe* in "The Gold-Bug." In an 1836 review for the *Southern Literary Messenger,* Poe writes of the earlier work: "How fondly do we recur, in memory to those enchanted days of our boyhood when we first learned to grow serious over Robinson Crusoe!—when we first found the spirit of wild adventure enkindling within us; as by dim fire light, we labored out, line by line, the marvelous import of those pages, and hung breathless and trembling with eagerness over their absorbing—over their enchaining interest" (qtd. in Weissberg 149). Here, Poe describes an epiphanic moment of discovery with an earlier work of literature similar to that which many contemporary writers describe with the classic works they eventually reconfigure.

The impulse to reconfigure is in part inspired by the desire to recapture this wonder and excitement of the author's literary beginning. Beyond the author's individual literary beginnings, the layers of texts embedded in a new work through intertextuality resemble a trail of breadcrumbs pointing the way back to the culture's literary origins. The new narrative that incorporates the old forms a narrative of literary evolution, a narrative of narrative. Whereas Poe often leaves unacknowledged those earlier works from which he borrows, contemporary authors foreground their intertextuality, so the act of borrowing and the creation of the collective narrative itself becomes part of their works' focus. As Aleid Fokkema puts it, "Postmodernsim is not about the end of the story but, rather, about the story of story" (41).

The trail of breadcrumbs that points back to a narrative's origins for those who know how to follow, however, can also obscure those origins from a casual observer. Just as a reconfiguration imposes a layer of separation between the reader and the reconfigured narrative, so does the written word separate the reader from the meaning it signifies. John T. Irwin describes this as the "principle mystery of writing—that letters (written characters) on the surface of a sheet of paper somehow physically 'contain' or 'conceal' something metaphysical (thought)" (22). Human intellect makes symbolic thought and complex communication through language possible, but it also makes us aware of the gap between that language and objective reality. For example, language makes it possible for one villager to narrate a great battle for another, even though the auditor did not witness it, but the cognitive level that enables humans to use language also makes the auditor aware that the two experiences differ.

Poe, like many postmodern writers, recognized the obscuring potential of language, as the layers of text within "The Gold-Bug" reveal. Just as Poe's coded map marks the location of the treasure while delaying access to it, so too is language a marker for experience that actually distances us from it. As Irwin points out, this "mysterious concealment/containment" property of writing generally is "symbolized even more explicitly by Poe in another form of writing he was obsessed with, the encrypted message" (22). Michael Williams, for example, describes the layers of concealment that Legrand must work through in "The Gold-Bug" before his treasure is revealed: "[O]n the underside of the sketch of the bug is a text concealed by its invisibility; once the text is made visible, its words are concealed by its being in code; once the code has been broken and the words made manifest, their meaning is obscured by their use of pirate conventions and by their distance from their referents" (653). Poe also delays the reader's access to meaning in other ways within this story. The gold bug itself is an empty sign, as Legrand and the narrator point out. Although Legrand's and Jupiter's focus on the bug suggests that it is an essential part of discovering the treasure, any weighted object, such as a bullet, could have been used to drop a line from the skull nailed in the tree to the ground (Poe 348). Observing the excessive punning in the story, Richard Hull comments particularly on Jupiter's exclamation against "dat deuced bug" (326): "Thus 'dat deuced bug' is not only, from Jupiter's perspective an accursed bug—but a bug doubled in meaning, a bug punned. . . . To recognize that there are puns ought to be to recognize that there's more than one meaning to read. A deuced bug calls for a deuced reading" (7).[3] In this story in particular, the layers of concealment hyperbolize the always-present separation between language and experience.

Our awareness of this gap between language and its referents, which Shawn James Rosenheim describes as a "fundamental split . . . between corporeal presence and symbolic consciousness" (21), and our desire to bridge it create a sense of loss or of higher unity to be gained, what Jacques Lacan might call the real, what a religious person might call Eden or heaven,[4] and what Powers calls "a place where knowledge goes without saying" (491). This is the treasure buried behind Poe's map. The treasure to which the code leads the skilled interpreter is meaning itself, the place where signifier and signified are one. This feeling of wholeness and enlightenment provided by connection to art recalls Poe's words about reading Defoe's *Robinson Crusoe* and equates to what Powers calls a "Chapman's Homer" experience, referring to the John Keats poem that describes a moment of mind-opening discovery that accompanies a first encounter with a great work of literature (Nielson 21). One of Powers's characters experiences a similar epiphany. About his experience listening to Bach, Ressler says, "[F]rom my very first listening, this piece seemed to me less like music than a rescue message. Word from a place I had lived once, but could not find my way back to. . . . [I]t took the top of my head off" (189).

Like Powers and many other contemporary writers who reconfigure a classic work, Poe foregrounds the act of reading and interpretation in "The Gold-Bug" and in other stories,[5] calling attention to the way humans use narrative to make sense of their world. Humans create mental and written narratives to understand the chaos of experience, charting a trail of cause and effect, with an "X" marking the spot of the story's beginning and a star labeled "you are here" at the end. Reading and hearing others' narratives provides access to their interpretations of experience, to their mappings of events. As Powers puts it, "However much each of us might be locked in our own constructions, the view from somebody else's cell can help us revise our representations" (Nielson 16). Legrand searches for meaning in the text of the pirate map, discovering the sequence of events that it records. The story's second section traces not only the physical trail he follows but also the figurative trail of his thoughts, so that for the reader, too, the treasure of meaning is uncovered. Poe makes this treasure that Legrand seeks difficult to uncover but ultimately accessible, but for many postmodern writers, such concepts as Truth, meaning, and origins, although longed for, remain elusive.

Powers believes the human capacity for narrative facilitates survival, but he does not accept these narratives as accurate records of reality. In an interview with Neilson, Powers states that an important theme of his novels is the "bidirectional relation between narrative and cognition," adding that he uses the term "narrative" to "include the whole process of fabulation, inference, and situational tale-spinning that consciousness uses to situate itself and make a continuity out of the interruptive fragments of perception" (15). By "bidirectional relation," Powers indicates that cognition produces narrative and also that narrative produces cognition. Powers's understanding of the function of narrative is identical to that of many evolutionary literary theorists, who argue that storytelling is an evolutionary adaptation, the function of which is mental organization and social cohesion,[6] or as Powers puts it, "navigating runaway culture" (Burns 174). Holding an MA in literature as well as a BA in physics, Powers is very much aware of poststructuralist, social-constructivist theory that contends all knowledge and identity are constructed within societies and there is no basis outside a given social setting for evaluating that knowledge or for making generalizations about human identity. Many poststructuralists see evolutionary theory as reactionary belief in biological determinism, a heretical acceptance of meta-narrative. However, Powers and other scholars do not view these two theories as mutually exclusive. According to Brian Boyd:

> Just where is the problem in the supposedly devastating insight that meaning or knowledge has to be referred or deferred to other terms or experiences, themselves part of an endless chain of referral or deferral? How could things be otherwise? . . . In a biological view, our understanding of the world always depends on earlier and less-developed forms of understanding, on simpler modes of knowledge. . . .
> Evolution has no foresight and no aims, least of all an aim like truth. It simply registers what suffices.

Powers sums up this blending of biological and social constructivist theories as follows: "We may live our lives as a tale told, but the tale we tell takes its shape from the life we are limited to" (Nielson 16).[7] Here, the "life we are limited to" is our biological makeup and evolutionary adaptations to the environment, and the "tale told" is the meaning human individuals and societies construct to understand their existence.

The subjectivity of human perception destabilizes and individualizes the realities we construct through narrative, and the inexactness of the language with which we record and access those realities adds another layer of distortion. Through *The Gold Bug Variations*, Powers foregrounds a suspicion of language's ability to reliably convey meaning. Whereas Poe in "The Gold-Bug" writes, "[I]t may well be doubted whether human ingenuity can construct an enigma of the kind which human ingenuity may not, by proper application, resolve" (342–343),[8] Powers revises this statement: "Ressler knew how incalculably unlikely it was that a molecular duplication trick could hit upon a structure complex enough to probe its own improbability" (235). As the author says in his interview with Nielson, "[T]he book is about linguistic mutation and wordplay, and I tried to imitate my vision of the genetic code as a punning, runaway fecundity in the book's prose" (20). For example, Powers begins the book with a sequence of letters and symbols that resembles the one Legrand deciphers in "The Gold-Bug." Legrand painstakingly explains the meaning of this code and his method for breaking it, but Powers never refers to his code again, leaving it a mystery.[9]

This uncertainty in language troubles not only the readers but also the characters themselves: "Every part of speech is already a *figure* of speech.... Every assertion is already a comparison" (Powers 490, emphasis in original), laments librarian Jan. Later, she articulates the frustration caused by this distance: "[L]anguage makes it impossible to receive the exact message sent.... There's no jumping outside the medium to verify transmission" (516). Powers increases our awareness of the distance between message and medium by destroying, through self-referential formal devices, the realist illusion that many readers expect from traditional novels. Noting the structural parallels to Bach's *Goldberg Variations*, another artistic work frequently referenced in the novel, James Hurt remarks, "[T]he segmentation of the text, the numbering of the sections, and the subtitles all function ... to heighten our awareness of the text as text and of an 'arranger' presenting the text independently of the ostensible narrators" (35). Even the name *Ressler*, a homonym for *wrestler*, suggests the character's struggle for understanding that is a universal human struggle.

Powers's narrative technique further heightens the reader's suspicion of language, making the novel a quest for understanding for the reader as well as for the characters. Jan narrates one of the novel's time lines in the mid-1980s as she takes a year off work to research genetics, to ponder her failed relationship with Todd, to mourn Ressler's recent death from cancer, and to find herself. The other time line, intermingled with the first without transition, is a third-person limited-omniscient narrative of Ressler's life in the 1950s, as he struggles to decipher the genetic code as part of a university research team and as he begins and ends a passionate affair with a married colleague, Jeanette Koss. Due to similar styles and parallel themes and imagery, the reader suspects that Jan is also the author of the 1950s narrative. Only at the end of the novel do we learn that Todd actually wrote the past narrative during his self-imposed exile, ostensibly to finish his art-history dissertation but also to flee from guilt about cheating on Jan and to mourn the subsequent loss of Ressler. Instead of a completed dissertation, Todd returns with the narrative with which the reader has been engaged for more than six hundred pages. Upon retrospect, the overlaps and parallels between the two narratives, in which Jan and Ressler share experiences, such as the previously mentioned ones with Poe and Bach, and even the childhood memory of reading the encyclopedia cover to cover, heighten the reader's awareness that, despite the revelation that Todd has returned to commingle his narrative with Jan's, the real author of the text-that-is-only-a-text is Powers.

In a novel that reconfigures an earlier work of literature, Powers explicitly links his exploration of language to the biological reproduction and adaption of species. Through the parallel layers of near-duplication in the novel, Powers suggests a connection among these various processes. Each character of Powers's novel longs for understanding, "for the pattern of patterns, the structure that mirrored mind itself, gave it something to recognize in the landscape around it" (192). Eric Athenot sees the passionate but doomed love affairs, the aborted attempt at deciphering DNA, and the fused narratives that reveal the presence of the author as parodies of the never-ending human search for "access to prelapsarian completeness." The narratives that Jan and Todd compose serve as additional bids at this completeness. Todd's suggestion of commingling their two narratives to "make a baby" at the novel's end explicitly connects literary evolution and biological evolution, both of which simultaneously distance us from our origins and provide a trail leading back to those origins. Part of the collective narrative of a people is the literature of the people, a narrative that began long ago and will end far from now. As Powers puts it, "From the very beginning, my vision for fiction was predicated on the notion of interconnectivity and a view of 'long time,' in which every moment emerges out of a multivariate past and also retroactively changes those pasts" (Burn 169). By reconfiguring Poe, Powers ties his narrative to an ongoing narrative of what it means to exist in our world. Just as Powers appropriates Poe to make sense of twentieth-century questions, Jan and Todd appropriate Ressler's life to make sense of their own existence. In addition to deciphering meaning through DNA research and imposing meaning through their own narratives, two processes that overlap and intermingle, the characters use literature and music, Poe's "The Gold-Bug" and Bach's *Goldberg Variations* particularly, as a "triangulating sextant pointing back to the height of the ruined tower" (491). The artistic works of the past serve as part of the pattern, giving the characters, the reader, and Powers himself something to recognize in the landscape of the novel, something that points back to the treasure of Understanding.

In the last quotation above, Powers alludes, of course, to the biblical story of the Tower of Babel, in which human efforts to reach the heavens are thwarted when God curses them with different languages, making communication difficult. J.D. Thomas points out another biblical allusion in the novel's opening line: "Word came today" (11), which echoes the biblical story of creation: "In the beginning was the Word" (John 1:1) (19). Together, these two allusions again suggest the characters' desire for prelapsarian wholeness and unity, and the impossibility of that desire's fulfillment. However, through these references, Powers reminds the reader that his characters' quests are timeless ones that many experience. If the perfect union of communication and understanding are often figured in our imaginations as sacred spaces, Eden or the womb, then perhaps the earlier classic texts, also part of our collective imaginations, represent a marker on the route to recover such spaces.

At the same time, however, the references to Poe allow Powers to revise the earlier writer's vision of such quests and the possibility of fulfilling them, suggesting perhaps that no landscape lies behind the map. J. Hillis Miller contends, "The language of narrative is always displaced, borrowed. Therefore any single thread leads everywhere, like a labyrinth made of a single line or corridor crinkled to and fro" (24). The novel's vocabulary is on loan from other texts, the words of which have also been borrowed. Just as Powers reconfigures Poe, Poe in his turn reconfigures others. There are no master narratives, no urtexts, and the origins we seek are unattainable. Powers makes this point explicit when no ultimate treasure is uncovered in *The Gold Bug Variations*. Ressler abandons the attempt to break the genetic code, and Jan fails to understand the meaning of life and love. Further frustrating the reader's and characters' desires for answers, Powers echoes Poe's concluding line by also ending his novel with a question. After Jan and Todd have reunited, in response to Jan's objections that the relationship "would never last," we are left with Todd's oblique response: "Who said anything about lasting?" (638). Poe's final "Who shall tell?" (348), coming on the heels of Legrand's thorough explication of the map's meaning, refers to the fact that some secrets are unrecoverable and that some stories, particularly those of the murdered men in the treasure pit, are forever silenced (they can never "tell"). Powers augments this unsettling indeterminacy by refusing first to provide comforting solutions to the text's key mysteries and by then projecting the indeterminacy into the future. Echoing Poe's ending in Todd's final question, Powers emphasizes that, despite our need to understand ourselves through narrative, despite whatever clarity narrative may lend to that which has already transpired, the future is always unknowable. Narrative may record and help us understand our pasts, and it may help us predict the future, but the actual future is a treasure that narrative may never uncover.

In addition to the more overt and unsettling exploration of language's power to convey meaning, Powers adapts Poe to postmodern sensibilities in another important way: through his portrayal of female characters. Poe's "The Gold-Bug" is almost exclusively a male world. In fact, the only reference to a woman occurs when Legrand recounts learning the location of the treasure partly through the aid of one of "the most aged of the women" among the African Americans at the Bessop plantation (346). Although Legrand credits her for aiding his quest, the reader never sees her or hears her speak, and Poe devotes a total of three sentences to her. Critics have commented on Poe's objectifying and sometimes misogynistic portrayals of women in other works as well. In an analysis of Poe's detective story "The Murders in the Rue Morgue," in which two women are brutally murdered by what turns out to have been an escaped pet ape, Lawrence Frank observes, "In destroying the women's organs of speech, the Ourang-Outang [and Poe] blindly denies their status as human beings, confirming the darkest implications of male attitudes toward women" (182). Significantly, the women are dead and silenced before the story even begins. Irwin notes, "[T]he victims in the Dupin stories are all women and . . . their victimization has in each case a sexual dimension" (237). Poe seems to confirm Irwin's detection of a sexual dimension to his female characters' suffering in his famous comment from the "Philosophy of Composition." While explaining how he composed "The Raven," setting his process down as a model for other writers, he proclaims, "[T]he death, then, of a beautiful woman is, unquestionably, the most poetical topic in the world" (680). The beautiful woman must also be a dead woman to ensure her poetic worthiness, Poe suggests. Powers, by contrast, creates strong women who fill central roles in *The Gold Bug Variations*. With Jan and with a minor character, Jeanette Koss, Powers places women in roles traditionally gendered masculine, the amateur and the professional scientist, and he does so without desexualizing them. As first-person narrator, Jan controls the reader's point of view. She is an independent, intelligent, and articulate woman who, in contrast to many of Poe's female characters, survives.

Offering a darker reconfiguration of Poe's tales, Bayard's *The Pale Blue Eye* rewrites elements of several Poe short stories and includes the young Poe as a character. Bayard chose to reconfigure the work of a writer associated with America's literary beginnings, capturing that writer at his career's inception and setting the work in a seminal moment in American history, the early years of West Point and the nation's debate over the necessity of a national military academy. Bayard acknowledges Poe's connection to America's literary origins when speaking of the inspiration for this novel:

> When I was putting together the concept for this book, Poe was coming back to me in sort of an involuntary way, and I couldn't quite figure out why because I hadn't read him in something like twenty years, and I . . . gradually realized that he had been so absorbed into our cultural DNA that we no longer even recognize him, but he's part of our literature, and an essential part. Not just the fact that he created the mystery story, reinvigorated the gothic horror story, but he also laid the seed for science fiction with *Gordon Pym*, a wonderful book. The themes,

the obsessions and mono-mania of a lot of his characters figure very prominently in modern fiction, in Pynchon and Nabokov, people like that, Joyce Carol Oates, Stephen King. . . . I think he's one of the most important writers ever to come out of America. (179; this volume)

In *The Pale Blue Eye*, Bayard glances back to America's literary origins and pays homage to this literary forefather: "In terms of Poe, I think my debt to him is that he was the creator of the modern detective story, so it seemed to me a fitting homage to place him in one and have him fend for himself, as it were. . . . I think of my books as books that kind of read other books, and that's really where it comes from" (176; this volume). Here, Bayard calls attention to the reading function that Tilottama Rajan sees as implicit in all intertextual writing,[10] and he seems to connect his novel's interest in the nature of language and interpretation to a literary quest for origins that I shall examine below.

In addition to "The Gold-Bug," *The Pale Blue Eye* alludes to "The Tell-Tale Heart," "The Fall of the House of Usher," "The Murders in the Rue Morgue," "The Purloined Letter," the sketch "Landor's Cottage," and Poe's essay on the craft of writing, "The Philosophy of Composition."[11] The novel begins when retired detective Augustus Landor (the name combines those of Poe's famous detective Auguste Dupin and Mr. Landor from "Landor's Cottage") is summoned to the recently opened West Point Academy to investigate a mysterious death. The cadet victim, an apparent suicide, died by hanging, and, after the body had been discovered and moved to the hospital, his heart had been inexplicably cut from his chest during the night. After Landor agrees to take the case, he requests the help of a misfit cadet who has caught his eye, Poe. Poe, of course, actually attended West Point for one semester during 1830 and 1831 before being court-martialed for neglect of duty. The majority of the novel gives Landor's first-person narration of his attempts to solve the mystery, which turns out to have been a murder rather than a suicide and which appears to be linked to an occult ritual. In the course of the investigation, another similar murder occurs, but this time the victim's heart and testicles have been removed prior to hanging him. Punctuating Landor's narrative are Poe's first-person reports of his own undercover work on Landor's behalf, often followed by Landor's readerly responses to Poe's overwrought emotions and style.

Bayard, like Powers, responds to Poe's connection of poetry to the death of a beautiful woman, but he critiques Poe's portrayal of female characters more overtly than Powers. As Bayard says of Poe's female characters: "The women are ciphers; there's really no sort of plausible women, they're all just maidens or objects either of sex or horror" (180; this volume). Bayard has the young cadet Poe echo the author Poe's famous statement from "The Philosophy of Composition" to Lea Marquis, a young lady he admires: "I answered that quite the contrary, I considered Death—and in particular, the death of a beautiful woman—to be Poetry's grandest, most exalted theme" (191). The reader's response to this statement is immediately influenced by that of Poe's conversant: "For the first time since her arrival, she gave me the full gift of her attention—and then exploded into a paroxysm of laughter" (191). Lea's laughter ridicules the overly gothic declaration made by the more mature Poe of "The Philosophy of Composition" and adds to the reader's underestimation of the character that the narrator Landor encourages. We see an intelligent, vibrant, and beautiful woman's explicit challenge to the idea that true beauty resides in such a woman's demise.

Through her outright laughter, however, Lea appears more like a twenty-first-century woman than a nineteenth-century maiden, and the scene exemplifies the presentist bias that affects many contemporary reconfigurations of classic texts. The novel transforms the past, making it more accessible and palatable to contemporary readers and writers looking for the stability of origins, and it underscores the extent to which readers always transform texts by filtering what has been read through their own perceptions. Just as narratives provide a sense of unity and clarity to individual experiences, classic texts provide a sense of cultural cohesion and unity to a group's historical experiences. As with narratives of individual experience, the beginnings of collective cultural narratives reveal the influence of the narrator's and reader's perspectives at the moment when the story is told or read. According to Andreea Deciu Ritivoi, "[T]he story is continuously adjusted to accommodate and reconcile, if necessary, the self whose actions have already been committed with the self who makes plans for future action" (232). In other words, our present selves affect our understanding of our past selves, and we revise that which does not cohere in order to make a coherent narrative. Bayard's challenge to Poe's portrayal of women emerges even more clearly when, as a blood-soaked Lea dies at cadet Poe's feet, Landor hisses, "The death of a beautiful woman . . . [i]s it still a poet's noblest subject?" (374). Very soon, the ceiling collapses, and amid the falling debris they see Lea's mysteriously standing form, seemingly rising from the dead like Madeline Usher. The whole scene is more grotesque than beautiful, providing a graphic repudiation of Poe's pronouncement.

A presentist bias can also be detected in Bayard's portrayal of the African American character Caesar in *The Pale Blue Eye* in comparison to Poe's Jupiter in "The Gold-Bug." Critics have often commented on the racism apparent in the depiction of Jupiter. Kenneth Silverman, for example, quotes Poe's description of this characterization as a "perfect picture . . . no feature overshaded, or distorted" (206) and notes the appearance in other works of similarly denigrating portraits of African Americans that correspond to the author's racial attitudes: "Although in no way consumed with racial hatred, he considered blacks less than human—as did many other Americans in the 1840s—therefore 'utterly incompetent to feel the *moral* galling of [their] chain'" (207). Like "The Gold-Bug," Bayard's novel features only one African American character, in the role of servant. Although

Caesar's role may not seem very progressive, Bayard intends him as a counterpoint to Jupiter:

> In *The Pale Blue Eye* I made a point in having a black character Caesar who actually is intelligent, although it's interesting I used the phrase *intelligent*. I refer to him as an "intelligent Negro," and a black friend of mine just sort of winced when he saw it, because he thought it was a standard portrayal. Oh an "intelligent Negro," oh my gosh, he actually knows right from left! So I wasn't so conscious of that, but that language was absorbed from Poe, and James Fenimore Cooper, and authors of that era. They would have definitely commented on a Negro who was intelligent . . . and this is what I said to my friend. I couldn't pretend that Landor's attitude toward blacks would be the equivalent of somebody's today—that just wouldn't work. It would just be one of those anachronistic things that bugs me sometimes in some historical novels, when they bring their modern attitudes to bear in a way that doesn't seem plausible to me. (181, this volume)

Although Bayard says that he attempts to avoid overt presentism in his portrayal of Caesar, he still updates this African American character to more closely correspond to twenty-first-century racial attitudes. Merely a servant and a minor character, Caesar nevertheless gives Landor valuable information about the cadets at the academy, and he alerts the academy's commanders of Landor and Poe's location in the burning icehouse near the end of the novel, thus saving their lives. Revising Poe's portrayal of the African American servant character, Bayard also revises the master narrative of racism that is part of America's origins, making those origins more accessible to contemporary readers seeking a narrative of cultural experience.

Unlike the novel's portrayals of women and African Americans, the understated homoeroticism of *The Pale Blue Eye* is not a twenty-first-century updating of Poe's nineteenth-century attitudes. As Poe and Landor share information about the case, they grow closer until one evening, Poe awkwardly asks if he might linger in Landor's room after their business is concluded: "Our eyes met for a second, but it was a long second," says Landor, who also remembers looking "everywhere but at him" (234). Their relationship rises "to the next level of closeness: on the fumes of whiskey," and thereafter Poe steals to Landor's room almost nightly to drink and talk "for many hours in succession" (235), incurring the disapproval of the West Point administrators. Bayard points out that a similar bond of "great physical and personal intimacy" (186; this volume) exists between Dupin and the unnamed narrator of Poe's "The Murders in the Rue Morgue." The narrator of this story recounts that he "felt [his] soul enkindled within [him] by the wild fervor, and vivid freshness of [Dupin's] imagination" (243), and the pair arrange to live together in Paris, secluded from others and engaged in a routine that, had it "been known to the world," would have caused them to be "regarded as madmen" (243). The oddest part of the routine as described by the narrator is that the pair chooses to go out into the city at night and to remain shut in the house during the day. When at home, they read and converse, similar to a married couple. Perhaps the label of madness would arise not from their daily habits but from the domestic intimacy shared by two men. Homosexuality was associated with mental illness in the nineteenth century; in fact, the American Psychiatric Association included homosexuality in its *Diagnostic and Statistical Manual of Mental Disorders* until 1973. Poe's narrator, however, describes their union as "a treasure beyond price" (243), and Bayard describes it as being "as close as you can get in nineteenth-century literature to an advocacy of homosexuality" (186; this volume).

Given Bayard's revisionary approach to the female and African American characters, readers must wonder why he does not make more overt the homoeroticism suggested in Poe's story. The author, who lives with his long-time partner and their two children, was identified in his early career as a comic novelist and a gay novelist (Drabelle 6). His first two novels, *Fool's Errand* (1999) and *Endangered Species* (2001), are romantic comedies set in the gay community of Washington, D.C., and published by a small LGBT press, Alyson Books. Perhaps Bayard chooses not to accentuate the homoeroticism found latent in Poe's story for artistic reasons, such as character and plot development or historical accuracy, or perhaps he does so in order to appeal to a more mainstream audience than do his earlier books. The latter option suggests that, unfortunately, society's attitudes toward homosexuality have not evolved significantly since Poe's day.

Like Powers, Bayard also adapts from Poe an emphasis on the potential manipulation of language and the uncertainty of meaning. The detective story, a form that Poe is said to have pioneered with the 1841 publication of "The Murders in the Rue Morgue," lends itself well to the exploration of language and interpretation and their connection to human cognition. In his article "'The Murders in the Rue Morgue': Edgar Allan Poe's Evolutionary Reverie," Frank argues that the detective story, like the novel, developed "at a moment of social and intellectual crisis that it both recognized and defined" (169). Frank cites evidence of Poe's recognition of this social and intellectual crisis through the story's early scene in which Dupin displays his powers of observation and interpretation by tracing the narrator's train of thought, which begins when the narrator stumbles on some loose paving stones and includes reference to "stereotomy,"[12] Epicurus, and Dr. Nichols (Poe, MRM 245). Frank asserts, "[T]he loss of footing initiates the narrator's musings upon origins" (172), a subject that preoccupied many in Poe's day and culminated in the 1859 publication of Charles Darwin's *Origin of Species* (170). Epicurus and Dr. Nichols are associated with changing worldviews. According to the Epicurean system of cosmogony as explained by Lucretius, an "infinite number of worlds co-exist at the same time," and each world "comes into being by a mechanical process, grows for a time, and then begins to decline ... until it finally perishes altogether" (Solmsen 34); Dr. Nichols details in his 1837 book *Views of the Architecture of the Heavens* the nebular hypothesis of P.S. Laplace, which explains the origins of the universe without the aid of a divine creator (Frank 173).

Frank argues that after this early scene, the rest of the story "becomes an extension of the narrator's reverie" about the origins of the universe (173). For example, while deducing the solution to the murder, Dupin refers the narrator and reader to a passage from Georges Cuvier's *Animal Kingdom*. Frank quotes a passage from this work that is omitted in Poe's text but that offers a significant etymology of the name *ourang-outang*: "*Ourang* is a Malay word signifying *reasonable being*, which is applied to man, the ourang-outang, and the elephant. *Outang* means *wild*, or *of the woods*; hence Wild Man of the Woods" (qtd. in Frank 179). Frank posits that through the animal killer, a human ancestor of sorts, Poe evokes nineteenth-century anxieties about human origin and its implications for religious faith (180). To compensate for the "terror of a history secularized and devoid of design," the detective story offers the "creation of plot ... 'a sequence of cause and effect' ('The Gold-Bug' 581)—in the face of what may prove to be mere chance" (188). In detective stories, mysteries become solvable, providing comfort for those struggling with ontological uncertainty. Frank's insightful reading of Poe's first detective story and its social context highlights what many contemporary cognitive psychologists see as a primary function of narrative more generally: providing a mainstay against the chaos of chance. According to Jerome Bruner, narrative itself is a human adaptation, the purpose of which is to impose order on experience, making those experiences easier to understand and to share with others. Furthermore, the shape those narratives take is influenced by the conventions of one's culture as well as one's individual perceptions of experiences (15). So, the creation of plot is not a coping strategy unique to the detective story but is a coping strategy inherent in human thought. Building on this basic function of narrative, contemporary writers who reconfigure earlier texts create a cultural "sequence of cause and effect," a meta-narrative that links individual narratives across time, imposing a type of order on history and cultural identity. The postmodern writer, however, recognizes and underscores the constructed nature of such narratives, which, although an essential part of human cognition, do not correspond to any objective reality.

As discussed earlier, Poe himself emphasizes the separation of language and objective reality, but, unlike Powers and Poe, Bayard shows that the uncertainty of language can be manipulated for evil intentions. In *The Pale Blue Eye*, the reader comes to empathize with Landor, a world-weary and lonely, aging man, as he struggles to solve his last case. Bayard fosters our sympathies through Landor's periodic direct addresses to the reader ("You'll excuse me, Reader, if I paled at this last remark" [73]) and the seeming frankness of his narrative voice. Only after the (apparent) astonishing gothic resolution of the mystery does the reader learn, in chapter 41 of 43, that Landor is an unreliable narrator. The revelations of the previous chapter turn out to be only a subplot to the murders, the accused murderers turn out to be innocent (at least of murder), and the real killer turns out to be Landor himself. With his calm, rational voice that continues even into the chapters in which he reveals his guilt, Landor eventually comes to resemble the mad narrator of Poe's "The Tell-Tale Heart," who declares his sanity to the reader as he explains his careful murder of his elderly pale-blue-eyed housemate. Landor's unreliability extends to misrepresenting, or at least underestimating, the Poe character to the reader. Ultimately the character Poe, who, mainly through Landor's eyes, has come to seem at best a buffoon and at worst a murder suspect, discovers Landor's guilt.

Bayard further emphasizes the fallibility and unreliability of language by challenging Poe's own statements about writing within the novel. For example, Whalen argues that, as an amateur cryptographer, Poe hoped to capitalize on his skill by selling the value of cryptography to the public. In 1841, he published an article on "Secret Writing" for *Graham's Magazine*, in which he explained that secret messages might be used by governments in matters of diplomacy. Poe adds, "Good cryptographers are rare indeed; and thus their services, although seldom required, are necessarily well requited" (Whalen 202). He also boasts that he could solve any cryptogram sent in by readers and then proceeds to do so in subsequent issues. In another article on cryptography in *Graham's*, Poe quotes from a letter ostensibly written by a reader named W.B. Tyler, but which Whalen argues was probably written by Poe himself (209). The letter adds to Poe's earlier comments about the value of a coded diary:

> I have thus a record of thought, feelings, and occurrences . . . to which I may turn, and in my imagination, retrace former pleasures . . . secure in the conviction that the magic scroll has a tale for *my* eye alone. . . .
>
> What can be so delightful amid the trials of absent lovers, as secret intercourse between them of their hopes and fears,—safe from the prying eyes of some old aunt, or it may be, of a perverse and *cruel* guardian?—a *billet-doux* that will not betray its mission, even if intercepted. (Whalen 209, 211, emphasis in original)

The magazine articles glibly advertise to readers the merits of secret writing and Poe's own skill at its decoding, hoping to create a need for his services.[13]

The Pale Blue Eye includes several uses of code similar to the ones described by Poe in his essay, but, unlike Poe, Bayard emphasizes that secret writing and the knowledge to decode it may be used for treachery. The first message that Landor decodes is the last one revealed to the reader. In chapter 41, when we learn of Landor's guilt, we also learn of his reason for killing. His teenage daughter, whom the reader had previously been told had "run off," had actually been raped by three unknown men after a dance. The daughter refused to speak of the attack and later committed suicide.

After her death, Landor looks in his daughter's favorite volume of poetry and finds tucked away a chain she had taken from the neck of one of her attackers. The chain holds a cadet identification tag with the initials L.E.F. Landor quickly deciphers this code to learn the identity of the attacker: "It was easy work finding the owner. The names of West Point cadets were a matter of public record, and only one cadet had those initials: Leroy Everett Fry" (392). Landor stalks the young cadet until he knows enough about his habits to plot his revenge without being caught.

Examining Fry's body after being hired to solve the case, Landor pulls from his hand a torn and crumpled slip of paper with what appears to be a secret code: "NG/HEIR A/T BE L/ME S" (51). Landor confiscates the paper as a clue and later, with the help of Poe, deciphers it for the reader. In an exchange much like the one in which Legrand explains his decoding of the pirate map to the narrator in "The Gold-Bug," Landor and Poe piece together the meaning of the whole message based on the small remaining piece of it that Landor had found. They determine the note to have been an invitation for the young cadet to meet someone outside at night and, given the fact that he had gone out willingly, judge that he believed the note to be from someone he wanted to see. The late-night summons had led to his death, making this misleading message the novel's first indication of the fallibility of language and its potential for deception. This point is made stronger at the end, when we discover that the true author of the note was Landor himself, who wrote knowing that Fry would assume the letter was from a woman with whom he desired a tryst. Recalling one of the handy uses of cryptography presented by Poe in the voice of Tyler, this note proves to be a secret *billet-doux*, only this one is deadly rather than "delightful."

The purpose of codes is to add another layer to the separation that already exists between language and understanding, further distancing the uninitiated reader from the truth. The skilled decipherer creates the illusion that truth is just below the surface and that the unity between language and what it represents can be achieved with the right technique. By misleading the reader through Landor, revealing the truth only after we falsely believe the criminals have been caught, Bayard reasserts the indeterminacy of language and unsettles the reader's faith in representational systems. One representational system that has been critiqued is cryptographic writing and the value that Poe assigns to it. Yet Landor himself frequently calls our attention to the unreliability of language more generally. When interviewing a young cadet who had first discovered Fry's body, Landor notes, "Whenever he was moved to say what it was, it showed itself as *other*" (40, emphasis in original). Words fail to convey the meaning the young cadet wants them to. After reading cadet Poe's first report about his undercover work, Landor responds, "Well, that's Poe's version. Of course, you never can be sure about what someone tells you, can you?" (155). Here, Landor further undermines the reader's trust in Poe but, by extension, suggests that we should not trust language itself, even Landor's.

Bayard also includes a coded diary, similar to the one that Poe's Tyler touts in the "Secret Writing" essay. The deceased cadet had kept a journal in which he had "taken the usual precaution of crosshatching his entries—running vertical columns across horizontal ones—the better to foil the prying eye" (199), but Landor tells us that he has a "trained eye" for deciphering such messages. In this work and in his narrative about the case generally, Landor resembles Poe's analytical detective Dupin, who also reads and deciphers clues to solve his cases. Because small excerpts of Fry's diary are revealed to the reader and transcribed pages are turned over to the officer in command, the reader assumes that Landor mines the diary for clues that will lead to Fry's killer. In the end, we learn that the "treasure" Landor really seeks is the names of Fry's accomplices in the rape of his daughter. His discovery of the two other rapists' names leads to Landor's second killing, but before he can kill the third cadet, the young man flees the academy in terror.

In addition to calling readers' attention to the uneasy link between language and meaning, Bayard also unsettles the notion of originality. The novel suggests that Landor, whom the character Poe meets at age nineteen or twenty, is the inspiration for the character Dupin, whom the reader is to believe the character Poe will live to create. As cadet Poe forces Landor to admit his guilt, "He began to circle me—just as I had circled him in that hotel room and so many others in the old days—weaving loops round the guilty. Even his voice was beginning to sound like mine: the lilting rise and fall, the soft press of statements. An homage! I thought" (400). Just as Bayard creates an homage to Poe by reconfiguring him and his characters in *The Pale Blue Eye*, he also creates an impression that the real Poe's famous detective is an homage to a character created by Bayard. Furthermore, the association of Dupin with the duplicitous Landor raises questions about the reliability of Poe's character, whose discursive explanations of thought and method appear to hide nothing on first impression. In this way, Bayard changes the way we read Poe after having read this contemporary novel and disrupts the quest for a narrative of origins.

Similar to Powers, Bayard finally suggests that no ultimate wholeness exists in life or in language, and our attempts to fill the voids created by our human consciousness are futile. After Poe discovers his guilt, Landor lives alone, half fearing that Poe will reveal him and half fearing that he will not. One day he picks up a copy of Poe's recently published book of verse and reads the epigraph: "Tout le monde a raison":

Everybody is right.
Which is either the most wonderful or the most terrible thing I've ever heard, I can't decide. The more I chew on it, the more it gets away from me. But I can't help thinking of it as a private message from him. Whatever the hell it means. (410)

The words have no meaning for Landor, because, if they are true, then words have no meaning at all. If everybody is right, then nothing means anything. As does Powers, however, despite the instability of language and meaning, Bayard suggests that narrative is still a necessary strategy for coping with the perceived breaches between signifier and signified. Before the reader knows much of Landor's story, the character suggests his desire to tell it, to have it known: "But I do believe there's something about the human soul that wants to be known even in its ugliest corners. Why else does a man—myself included—bother putting words to paper?" (200). After Poe discovers the truth about Mattie's death and surmises Landor's involvement with the murders,[14] Landor shares his story with the reader and Poe. Already longing for death, even going so far as asking Poe to shoot him, Landor appears to live only to finish the narrative. The novel ends with a plea for a story in return: "Tell me now, daughter. In your own voice. . . . Tell me it will be all right" (413). That there is no response suggests the healing he seeks eludes him.

By reconfiguring the works of Poe, Powers and Bayard link their narratives to an ongoing American cultural narrative, while at the same time challenging the authority of that narrative. These two contemporary novels, set in different time periods, direct their attention to different ends of that American cultural narrative. Reconfigurations set in the contemporary writer's present seem to emphasize an examination of that present through the lens of the past, and reconfigurations set in the historical past seem to emphasize an examination of that past through the lens of the present, although both types of reconfigurations encourage a mental "oscillation" in which the reader holds "two texts simultaneously in mind" (Widdowson 504). Bayard's historical reconfiguration encourages us to look at America's past for the voices and subjects that were silenced and to interrogate those who did speak for their hidden messages. Powers's contemporary setting encourages us to see that the anxieties of the postmodern age, materialism and a perceived loss of ontological grounding, have plagued America since its early days, causing readers to ponder the potential consequences, if any, of current attempts at resolution. If language itself is unreliable, if the meaning that language seeks is ungraspable, and if originary texts themselves are not original, then the solace provided by a cultural narrative is in the process of creating that narrative again and again.

2 "A" Is for America
Revisions of *The Scarlet Letter*

"The opening scene of *The Scarlet Letter*," writes R.W.B. Lewis, "is the paradigm dramatic image in American literature. With that scene and that novel, New World fiction arrived at its fulfillment, and Hawthorne at his" (111). This work, for Lewis, is the crowning moment of Nathaniel Hawthorne's career and of American literature to that point. D.H. Lawrence shared this assessment, referring to *The Scarlet Letter* as "the most perfect American work of art" (qtd. in Tomc 491). The novel's ranking at the top of America's national literature stems not only from its intriguing plot, well-drawn characters, universal themes, and elegant style but also from its Americanness. Hawthorne's association with America's national literature is no accident. Hawthorne, Herman Melville, and *Democratic Review* and *Literary World* editor Evert Duyckinck were part of a group of nationalistic writers and editors known as "Young America" (Levine 231), whose agenda was to create and to support distinctive American literature. In fact, Duyckinck "wished to establish an American canon with Hawthorne at its head" (Castiglia 324). *The Scarlet Letter* eventually became the embodiment of this goal.

Evidence from the novel suggests that Hawthorne himself wanted to create an American book as well as a great book. In "The Custom-House," Hawthorne's introduction to *The Scarlet Letter*, he describes the Custom-House in connection with key national symbols:

> From the loftiest point of its roof . . . floats or droops, in breeze or calm, the banner of the republic; but with the thirteen stripes turned vertically, instead of horizontally, and thus indicating that a civil, and not a military post of Uncle Sam's government is here established. . . . Over the entrance hovers an enormous specimen of the American eagle, with outspread wings, a shield before her breast, and if I recollect aright, a bunch of intermingled thunderbolts and barbed arrows in each claw. . . . Nevertheless, vixenly as she looks, many people are seeking, at this very moment, to shelter themselves under the wing of the federal eagle; imagining, I presume, that her bosom has all the softness and snugness of an eiderdown pillow. But she has no great tenderness,

even in her best of moods, and, sooner or later,—oftener soon than late,—is apt to fling off her nestlings, with a scratch of her claw, a dab of her beak, or a rankling wound from her barbed arrows" (9).

Clearly, the passage above reveals an ambivalent attitude toward the United States, which is first personified as familiarly avuncular and then represented as cruel and "vixenly."[1] Likewise, the novel's main plot emphasizes the natural beauty and noble experiment of the New World as well as the cold oppressiveness of the early American Puritan society. Significantly, though, Hawthorne takes great pains to label the place where he found the scarlet letter itself and the notes that inspired his novel, a building that he later calls "Uncle Sam's brick edifice" (13), as American. This, he tells his readers, is an American tale. Within the main body of the narrative, after Chillingworth has died and left property in England to little Pearl, Hawthorne does not allow his narrative to follow Hester and her daughter to foreign soil. The narrative and the reader remain poised by Hester's cottage until Hester's "shadow-like" return (164). She lives her remaining years in New England and is finally buried next to Arthur Dimmesdale.

In 2005, critic Laurence Buell claimed that *The Scarlet Letter* "remains the single most taught long work of pre-modern American literature" (71). And this novel still has substantial influence on American letters: "Among major pre-modern U.S. fictions, *The Scarlet Letter* comes closest to rendering a myth of national origins. It has also become a masterplot for American writers" (71). Perceived as a myth of national origins, Buell suggests, the novel shows us where our nation and our national literature began. Much American literature since, he implies, imitates this early great work. Indeed, *The Scarlet Letter* has been the object of several contemporary American reconfigurations. The best known of these is John Updike's trilogy, *A Month of Sundays* (1975), *Roger's Version* (1986), and *S.* (1988). As Updike's novels have been discussed thoroughly elsewhere, this chapter only briefly examines them before analyzing in more detail a recent reconfiguration of *The Scarlet Letter* that has received less critical attention, Bharati Mukherjee's *The Holder of the World*. Like all writers of reconfigurations, Updike and Mukherjee respond to the classic text—in this case, *The Scarlet Letter*—that novel's place in the American canon, and the existence and function of a canon in the American culture. Through these foci, contemporary reconfigurations mirror and direct readers' attention to the way humans use narrative to understand themselves and their places in time and culture, they update a cultural narrative to more closely align with the contemporary author's sense of a national identity, and they underscore that, although such use of narrative is universal and essential, the individual narratives themselves can make no legitimate claim to objective truth or reality.

Hawthorne's association with the nationalistic goals of the Young America group suggests that *The Scarlet Letter* shapes an American myth of origins as much as it records one. Laura Doyle points out that he shapes this image of America by omitting references to political instability in the Massachusetts colony and in England and by omitting references to Indian wars, despite the fact that Salem would have been affected by all these conflicts during the period in which the novel is set. In addition, Hawthorne softens the punishment that an adulteress would receive at the hands of Puritan authorities; in actuality, the offender "would, at minimum, have been publicly stripped and whipped" (Doyle 254). Doyle sees these omissions as part of an agenda to mask the "foundational violence of colonization" (255) relevant in Hawthorne's own time to conflicts over "the Indian Removal Acts, the annexation of western territories and war with Mexico" (252). Gillian Brown, however, points out that, despite the inaccuracies, "generations of Americans have taken . . . the novel's representation of Puritan life in the colonies as an authoritative reference work on the New England Puritans" (125), illustrating the centrality of this text to the country's identity. As with all narratives of experience, such shaping of the historical identity may occur either consciously or unconsciously. As discussed in chapter 1, cognitive narratologists recognize that "[a]s we bring to life an event that happened in the past, we endow it with meaning that combines experience with expectation" (Ritivoi 232), shaping the past to better conform to our understanding of the present. Likewise, Hawthorne's perception of his American present influences his portrayal of an American past.

Hawthorne shapes this narrative of American experience in part from other narratives that had come before, adapting these earlier works to fit his own message and his own setting. Roberta Weldon notes that *The Scarlet Letter* contains references to "the most popular Christian texts of his day, including the Bible, Milton's *Paradise Lost*, Bunyan's *Pilgrim's Progress*, Renaissance devotional literature, and the ministerial biography" (14). Critics have also perceived the influence of more secular sources in Hawthorne's work. Nina Baym, for example, reads *The Scarlet Letter* as an "'anti-seduction' novel," revising the popular pattern of texts, such as Hannah Webster Foster's *The Coquette* (1797) and Susanna Rowson's *Charlotte Temple* (1794) (121). Richard Kopley sees the influence of more contemporary works in Hawthorne's novel, including Edgar Allan Poe's "The Tell-Tale Heart," Robert Lowell's poem "A Legend of Brittany" (1843), and Ebenezer Wheelwright's novel *The Salem Belle: A Tale of 1692* (1842) (18–19). David S. Reynolds argues, "Hawthorne sensationalized Puritanism by introducing fictional elements he knew were attractive to novel readers of the 1840s" (230). These elements, popular staples of mid-nineteenth-century fiction, include the sexual indiscretions of preachers and the redemptive good works of a fallen woman. Buell discusses the most overt borrowing in Hawthorne's tale. The final line of *The Scarlet Letter*, referring to the tombstone marking Hester and Arthur's grave and bearing heraldic symbols, reads: "On a field, sable, the letter A, gules" (Hawthorne 166). Here Hawthorne revises the final line of Andrew Marvell's poem "The

Unfortunate Lover," which reads: "In a Field *Sable* a Lover *Gules*" (Buell 75, emphasis in original). Through these allusions and references, Buell argues, Hawthorne "emphasize[s] something timeless, perennial" about his work: "Costumes differ, emotions remain the same. . . . *The Scarlet Letter*'s quiet affiliation with these texts helps establish *its* story not just as a Puritan tale but also as part and parcel of Euro diasporic collective memory stretching back to the Middle Ages" (76, emphasis in original). Buell sees Hawthorne aligning his work with an ongoing cultural narrative. Contemporary writers of reconfigurations do the same with an already-established American cultural narrative (established, in part, by Hawthorne). These contemporary writers, however, reveal a more overt indebtedness to a single source that serves to call the reader's attention to the constructedness of the original tale and its contemporary reconfiguration.

As with most of the contemporary writers examined in this study, Updike expresses admiration for the classic work that he reconfigures. James Plath quotes Updike's assertion that *The Scarlet Letter*, which the younger author first read at age thirty, was "the first American masterpiece" and that he was "struck by how 'right' everything is" in the classic novel ("Updike, Hawthorne" 122). Elsewhere, Updike states that his explicit goal in writing *A Month of Sundays*, *Roger's Version*, and *S.* was to revise this American myth: "*The Scarlet Letter* is not merely a piece of fiction, it is a myth by now, and it was an updating of the myth . . . that interested me" (qtd. in Plath, "Giving the Devil" 209).[2] All three of these novels are set in Updike's contemporary America and only loosely retell the plot of *The Scarlet Letter*. In each part of his trilogy, Updike imagines the twentieth-century equivalent of one of Hawthorne's three central characters and allows that character to narrate his or her own story.

Despite the different settings and plot trajectories between Updike's novels and *The Scarlet Letter*, each of Updike's three works contains overt references to Hawthorne's novel that alert readers to the connection. In *A Month of Sundays*, a sex-addicted Reverend Marshfield, whose wife's maiden name had been Chillingworth, spends a month in a sanatorium for wayward clergy after the discovery of his adulterous liaisons with members of his flock and the weakening of his religious faith. His custodian at this establishment, Ms. Prynne, instructs Marshfield to spend his days writing, and the novel consists of journal entries describing his thoughts and deeds, punctuated by undelivered sermons written during his "retreat." The novel's last entry, written gratefully to Ms. Prynne, with whom the narrator has just consummated his longing for sex, suggests, if not spiritual healing, then at least a renewed metaphysical awe.

Roger's Version offers the first-person tale of Roger Lambert, a professor of theology, whose younger wife, Esther, engages in an adulterous affair with her husband's graduate student, Dale Kohler. The names make clear that Updike's characters are analogs for Hawthorne's: Roger Lambert for Roger Chillingworth, Esther for Hester, and Dale for Dimmesdale. Jealous over his wife's affair, Lambert "works on Dale Kohler's psyche the way Roger Chillingworth worked on Arthur Dimmesdale's" (Wilson 246), surreptitiously torturing him with guilt and ravaging his religious faith. Updike suggests that the equivalent of Hawthorne's Pearl appears three times in the novel, "once as [Roger and Esther's son] Richie ('of great price'), secondly as Paula [Verna's daughter], thirdly—well why *does* Esther's weight at last swell to over a hundred pounds?" ("Special Message" 858). Updike's third hint above suggests that Esther is pregnant with Dale's child at the end of the novel, a point that he confirms in an interview with Donald J. Greiner (4). Among Updike's major characters, only Verna, Lambert's troubled niece, seems to have no equivalent in *The Scarlet Letter*.

In *S.*, one of the epigraphs from *The Scarlet Letter*, reminds readers of Hester Prynne's "dark and abundant hair" and "richness of complexion," physical traits shared by Updike's protagonist Sarah P. Worth. Derek Parker Royal points out that Updike includes a joke for the careful reader when he notes that Sarah's husband, a doctor, always has cold hands, making him Dr. "chilling" Worth. In addition, Sarah has an affair with the religious leader of a commune whose real name is "Art," reminding readers of Arthur Dimmesdale, and she has an adult daughter named "Pearl." Sarah frequently recommends the consumption of vitamin A, lives in an A-framed house while in the desert commune, and refers to her lesbian lover as "dearest A," reminding readers of Hester's scarlet letter. Because she does not fully trust Art, Sarah hides a mini tape recorder between her breasts to record conversations and sexual encounters, and James A. Schiff sees this as Updike's version of the sign proclaiming her adultery (27). In "Unsolicited Thoughts on *S.*," Updike writes, "American religion and its decay since Puritan New England would be a theme" in his trilogy of Scarlet Letter reconfigurations (859). In this way he also imitates Hawthorne by critiquing his society's present-day morals through a comparison with the morality of the past.

One of the major differences between Updike's fictional world and Hawthorne's is each world's attitude toward sex. Updike suggests that *The Scarlet Letter* appeals to him particularly because of the sexual content: "Hawthorne, indeed, of our classic writers, seems to be, recessive and shadowy as he was, the one instinctive heterosexual—which suggests how uncertain, how vitiated by Puritan unease and the love of freedom, the mating part of the American character is" ("Special Message" 858). Updike's novels bring this unmentionable subject out into the open. In contrast to the Puritan repression noted in *The Scarlet Letter*, where extramarital sex is a punishable crime and a guilt-inducing sin, Updike sets *Roger's Version* in a New England city, "like Cambridge where adultery is as common as aerobics and Freud has absolved us all" (qtd. in Greiner 3). Matei Calinescu points out that Hawthorne never mentions the word "adultery" and that Hester's sexual indiscretion has occurred more than nine months prior to the novel's beginning, but in *Roger's Version* the extramarital affair, "carefully evoked in the most minute detail, is at the center of the plot" (457). Although the settings differ, the same point could be made about the characters' promiscuity and violation of marriage vows in *A Month of Sundays* and *S*. Not only do they engage freely in adultery, but the characters openly admit it. In each of Updike's novels, an excessive desire to confess and to disclose sexual details replaces the shame and secretiveness, seen most significantly in Dimmesdale's long-delayed acknowledgment of his guilt, in *The Scarlet Letter*. As Sarah says, "Puritanism in my parents had dwindled to a sort of housekeeping whose most characteristic gesture was to take something to the attic because it was undistinguished or vaguely reminiscent of some relative we preferred to forget" (*S*. 263–264). Puritanism in the twentieth century has been tamed into "good breeding" or manners, and most critics seem to believe that Updike, although not above laughing at his characters' excesses and hypocrisies, sees some positive aspects in this change. For example, according to Schiff, Updike proposes, "[T]hrough acceptance of the body and its needs, the American self can rise from its bourgeois malaise, taste the exhilaration of freedom, and experience faith in the divine" (29).

Despite the revisions that Updike makes in order to align Hawthorne's America to a more contemporary view of culture, his grounding of the contemporary narratives in this classic work—one that he refers to as an American myth—suggests a desire to tap into an ongoing cultural narrative at its source. *The Scarlet Letter*'s associations with a beginning national literature and its emphasis on origins within the text make it a particularly appropriate subject for such reconfigurations. Critics have pointed out the novel's thematic obsession with origins, evidenced by the historical setting, the question of Pearl's paternity, and the "Custom-House" introduction that offers a fictionalized explanation for the story's source (see, for example, Kopley 17 and Grossman 14). Along these same lines, Calinescu asserts, "The success of Hawthorne's allegorical romance is at least partly due to the fact that it is the story of a letter . . . and *the letter*, symbolized by the first letter of the alphabet and thus charged with the meaning of all beginnings (including the American beginning), while also symbolizing writing/reading in general" (453, emphasis in original). As discussed in chapter 1, myths of origin reflect a desire to return to an imagined unity of perception and experience, to access our earliest states with consciousness intact. According to critic Gillian Beer, "In a world jostling with multiformality fissured by incomplete meaning, the dogged and dedicated search for the single solution, the recovered origin, becomes one pressing narrative response" (23). As Mukherjee's character Beigh says, "Together and separately we remember what happened to Hannah Easton Fitch Legge aka the Bibi from Salem, so that we may predict what will happen to us within our lifetime" (91). However, because our ultimate origins, individually as humans and collectively as humanity, are preconscious and prelinguistic,[3] they are ultimately inaccessible.

I quote here again Darwin's metaphorical depiction of this inaccessibility of human origins. "I look at the natural geological record, as a history of the world imperfectly kept, written in a changing dialect; of this history we possess the last volume alone, relating only to two or three countries. Of this volume, only here and there a short chapter has been preserved and of each page, only here and there a few lines" (qtd. in Beer 20). The record of humans' biological and cultural origins will never be fully recovered, just as the dawning of one's individual consciousness can never be fully remembered. The connection that Darwin draws between our forgotten origins and an absent or incomplete facility with language has also influenced poststructuralist thought. In *The Archaeology of Knowledge*, Michel Foucault says, "[T]he notions of development and evolution . . . make it possible to . . . discover, already at work in each beginning, a principle of coherence and the outline of a future unity, to master time through a perpetually reversible relation between an origin and a term that are never given, but are always at work" (22). This quest for origins, he continues, limits and shapes knowledge; it is futile because a single origin, in the sense that we imagine it, never existed at all. Jacques Lacan links the desire for origins to the development of myth and language: "All signification is the result of a fortunate fall into a prison of signs" (qtd. in Bowie 67). Here, Lacan metaphorically connects the act of signification, using language, with the myth of Adam and Eve's ejection from Eden, a place where understanding was complete, and signified and signifier were one. Contemporary reconfigurations of American literary classics participate in this narrative attempt to recover our origins while also calling attention to the human desire for unity and its impossibility. The classic texts serve as cultural myths of origin, which the contemporary authors attempt to access across the gulf of time, but in accessing them they alter them, just as all readers do.

Updike's trilogy, particularly the first two novels, shares *The Scarlet Letter*'s thematic emphasis on origins. In *A Month of Sundays*, Marshfield compares his role as author to that of a puppet master—"This is fun! First you whittle the puppets, then you move them around" (17)—who creates and manipulates his characters as he once assumed God controls humankind. According to John T. Matthews, "Marshfield at first celebrates the onanism of 'sullying' sexual and lexical clean sheets; writing begins for him as a kind of masturbation. . . . [H]e warms ironically to playing the creator" (352). Matthews links Marshfield's godlike status as author with the generative act of sex, which is his subject matter. By referring to his efforts as masturbation, though, because he writes in apparent isolation and approaches his subject without seriousness, he suggests that Marshfield produces no worthwhile issue. Later, however, "[a]s Marshfield exercises his creative freedom, his writing becomes a reflection and embodiment of himself" (352). Marshfield manages to create, or to conceive, himself in writing, much in the same way that all humans rely on narrative to remember experience, to understand cause and effect, and to construct a sense of their own identities.[4] George W. Hunt also sees in this novel a reference to the Bible and to *The Scarlet Letter* as originating sources. Marshfield tells us that the "motel" in which he is exiled "has the shape of an O, or more exactly, an omega" (8), and Hunt elaborates on the significance of this shape, linking it to

> 1) *Religion*. . . . Christ is described as the "Alpha and Omega." . . . 2) *Sex*. The association of the letter "o" with a woman's pudendum is common throughout literature. . . . 3) *Art*. Not only does the letter "omega," being the limit or the end of the alphabet, suggest the perverse limitations of all letter-writing that Marshfield experiences; but Omega, being at the opposite end of A, reminds us of this novel's upending of *The Scarlet Letter*, the kind of joke in which Updike delights. (187–188)

In Hunt's interpretation, three types of origin—divine, biological, and artistic—unite in Updike's reference to the Omega. *Roger's Version* also invokes the theme of origins, primarily through Dale, who searches for scientific proof of the existence of a divine creator and believes that an examination of DNA strands will yield this evidence. Here again, Updike unites a quest for understanding of biological and spiritual origins.

Like other contemporary writers, Updike undermines our faith in the written word in order to suggest the futility of this quest for origins through narrative. In emphasizing narrative unreliability, Updike again reconfigures an aspect of Hawthorne's text. Although Hawthorne sets up "The Custom-House" section of *The Scarlet Letter* to "offer proofs of the authenticity of [his] narrative" (8), he also points out that he has "allowed [him]self as much license as if the facts had been entirely of [his] own invention" (27). Lest we forget the interpretive role of the author and narrator, he thrusts this role upon the reader near the novel's end. When telling us of Dimmesdale's ascent to the scaffold and his marking of guilt, the narrator never describes exactly what those markings are or how Dimmesdale came by them, offering instead a few competing interpretations and saying, "The reader may choose among these theories" (163). On the surface, Hawthorne uses this device to suggest that there is some truth that he has not been able to recover, yet he also reminds us that tales are constructed by storytellers and story listeners. Even the meaning of Hester's scarlet letter changes in the eyes of those who behold it, becoming not a "stigma which attracted the world's scorn and bitterness" but "something to be sorrowed over, and looked upon with awe, yet with reverence, too" (165). Just as townspeople change their interpretation of the letter itself, so, too, does the reader alter the meaning of the novel that shares its name.

Unlike Hawthorne, Updike focuses not just on the variability of interpretation but also on language's power to deceive. Each of the first-person narrators in these three Updike novels is unreliable in ways that the reader comes to detect. Elisabeth Jay points out that Marshfield's sermons in *A Month of Sundays* "become an extension of [his] seduction tools," which he directs this time to "the warder-come-hostess of the sanatorium, the silent Ms. Prynne" (346). The reader, too, feels at once the lure of Marshfield's seductive charm and the threat of his deceptions. Roger Lambert is similarly misleading in *Roger's Version*. Dale and Esther's conversations and sexual encounters are rendered in such detail that the reader tends to accept these accounts as accurate until we remember that Roger, our narrator, has not witnessed any of them and has not conversed about them with either participant. They are products of his jealous imagination. In *S.*, Sarah often contradicts herself, making it difficult to trust her as a narrator. For example, in one letter to her husband, she claims to have relinquished materialism and scorns his concern with appearances, yet in the same letter, she offers lawn-care advice and urges him to send her half of the rental proceeds from their "Cape place" (68–69). These untrustworthy narrators emphasize that any text can mislead, warning the reader of "the seriousness of our interpretive responsibility" (Jay 350).

Whereas Hawthorne writes "The Custom-House" to assert the overall veracity of the narrative that follows, Updike's reconfigurations remind readers of their constructedness as works of fiction. For example, Matthews convincingly argues that readers are meant to recognize Ms. Prynne as a fictional narrative construction of Marshfield:

> Ms. Prynne is not a person but a creature of the manuscript, as her title might punningly suggest. The act of intercourse that takes place is really the climax of an act of discourse; Ms. Prynne's body, praised with scant detail, remains the emanation of writing and reading. From her first appearance in Marshfield's manuscript (as the presumed author of an erased comment) to her final reception of him into her "alarmingly liquid volume of the passage to your womb," she is described as much as a book as a body. (380)

With such wordplay as "Ms." and "volume," Matthews suggests, Updike alerts the reader of Ms. Prynne's wholly textual nature, and the sexual act that Marshfield describes at the novel's close is actually the union of the author and the reader through the body of the book. Similarly, Royal believes that Updike alerts the reader to the constructed nature of *S.* through bracketed comments in the transcribed tape recordings—"[*Responsive mumble.*]" (115), "[*Distant shout.*]" (119)—and by disrupting the hitherto consistent chronological order with the novel's last three letters. These strategies, Royal believes, indicate the presence of some unknown and unacknowledged editor who compiles Sarah's documents. To Royal's list of strategies, I would add the glossary that Updike includes at the end of the novel. Of the glossary, Updike writes, "[L]ike any footnote, it forms part of the text, and should be read through ... and its final entry, rather than the dying fall of Esther's last letter ... [is] the book's true conclusion" ("Unsolicited Thoughts" 859). As with the strategies Royal identifies, the glossary suggests the presence of a metatextual agent constructing the work. In addition, though, the glossary's final entry suggests the indeterminacy of meaning and the variability of interpretation:

> yuganaddha: A state of unity obtained by transcending the two polarities of *samsara* [existence] and *nivritti* [withdrawal or quiescence of the senses or mind] and perceiving the identity of the phenomenal world and the absolute (*S.* 299)

Of this term, Updike writes in "Unsolicited Thoughts on *S.*," "[T]he Sanscrit gurus meant either that there is no supernatural, or else ... everything is supernatural. What is, is absolute. The net of religious and philosophical terminology leaves reality exactly where it was before. Or does it?" (859). Updike points to the term's importance, but with the final question, he underscores its ambiguity and even the author's uncertainty about its meaning. By highlighting the unreliability and constructedness of his texts, Updike suggests the unreliability and constructedness of all texts, even Hawthorne's American myth of origin that serves as his inspiration.

Mukherjee describes herself as "an American writer in the American mainstream, trying to extend it" ("Four-Hundred-Year-Old Woman" 24), and readers can see this effort to extend the American mainstream through her reconfiguration of *The Scarlet Letter*. Like Updike's novels, *The Holder of the World* seems to respect Hawthorne's work as part of the American mainstream with which Mukherjee identifies, and her reconfiguration extends the work to better reflect her presence. The parallels between *The Scarlet Letter* and *The Holder of the World* become obvious only near the latter novel's end. Told from the point of view of a late-twentieth-century "assets hunter," Beigh Masters, *The Holder* recounts the search through historical documents and artifacts for a mysterious Puritan woman, Hannah Easton Fitch Legge, who, in the late seventeenth century, traveled to the Coromandel Coast with her husband, a factor in the British East India Company; was rescued during riots by a Hindu king; became that king's mistress (giving her the title "Salem Bibi"); was held captive by the rival Muslim emperor; and was believed to have been in possession of the Emperor's Tear, the world's most-perfect diamond. In the process of her search, Beigh's focus shifts from the diamond to Hannah herself, with whom she identifies. Beigh's final discoveries are aided by her boyfriend's research in virtual-reality technology, which allows her to "virtually" travel back to late-seventeenth-century India to witness Hannah's escape from Mughal Emperor Aurangzeb.

Upon finishing the novel, the parallels become more obvious to the reader. Beigh's historical research echoes that of Hawthorne's Surveyor Pue, who "devoted some of his many leisure hours to researches as a local antiquarian" (25), and who wrote "several foolscap sheets, containing many particulars respecting the life and conversation of one Hester Prynne" (27). Of course, Hawthorne's "The Custom-House" cites these notes and the scarlet letter twisted around them as the inspiration for the novel that follows.[5] Beigh's early fascination with Hannah begins while reading the trade magazine *Auctions and Acquisitions* (some critics have interpreted the journal, known as *A & A* for short, as an allusion to the scarlet letter),[6] where "the name Pearl [Hannah's daughter] . . . leaped off the page" (*The Holder* 69). Beigh, like the Hawthorne persona in "The Custom-House" and like Pue, becomes fascinated with the female subject of this research. Both novels are told from the perspective of the present-time narrator looking back on the past, although Mukherjee shifts from past to present and back again throughout the novel, while Hawthorne confines the present mainly to "The Custom-House" section. Mukherjee sets the early chapters of *The Holder of the World* in Colonial Salem, and she also recycles several of Hawthorne's character names, such as Hester, Prynne, and Pearl. Like Hester Prynne, Hannah creates exotic and luxurious embroideries, and both women use this skill as an outlet for repressed creativity and passion. Near the novel's end, however, Mukherjee offers a very obvious version of what Gerard Genette would call a "contract of transposition,[7]" settling beyond a doubt the connection between *The Holder of the World* and *The Scarlet Letter*: "We have the shipping and housing records, we have the letters and journals and the *Memoirs*, and of course we have *The Scarlet Letter*. Who can blame Nathanial Hawthorne for shying away from the real story of the brave Salem mother and her illegitimate daughter?" (284). As Christian Moraru notes, "*The Holder* ends with—or rather *at*—its source [the setting of *The Scarlet Letter* and the setting in which *The Holder* opened], by re-marking its textual origin. . . . And here we are, come full circle; here is Hawthorne's letter sanctioning this transhistorical and transcultural analogy" (164–165). Mukherjee's novel, of course, purports to tell the "real story," addressing what she believes Hawthorne omits or minimizes, while at the same time undermining the notion that such a thing as a "real story" exists.

Through her extensions of *The Scarlet Letter*, Mukherjee highlights Indian culture, feminism, and the need for religious tolerance. David Herman points out that most readers establish "a more or less direct or oblique relationship" between narratives they read and themselves, a process he calls "contextual anchoring" (8). Born in Calcutta, India, Mukherjee moved to the United States in 1961 and became an American citizen in 1988. As a reader of *The Scarlet Letter*, Mukherjee establishes a relationship that allows her to see herself in Hawthorne's narrative. In her study *Transforming Memory in Contemporary Women's Writing*, Liedeke Plate furthers Herman's point about the connection between readers and texts by suggesting that some readers make a record of themselves in a text by rewriting it: "Rewritings tell stories of reading.... They speak of how their writers 'received', understood, and interpreted what they read. Inviting a double, comparative reading, they also stage a particular scene of reading, one in which readers are encouraged to look again at the rewritten text, and to look at in the light of the new text" (41–42). Moraru articulates a similar point with specific reference to Mukherjee's novel: "*The Holder* [creates] a new relation between the canonical 'precursor' (Hawthorne) and 'imitator' (Mukherjee herself), through which the former Bengali, South Asian Canadian, Indian American, and—lately—American author reclaims the tradition of the American letters as hers and, for herself, a distinguished place in this tradition" (165–166). As a writer, Mukherjee composes this revised narrative that incorporates the self she imagines in the earlier tale, so her written work constitutes a variant reading of Hawthorne's novel.

Herman also points out that most readers imaginatively relocate themselves to the fictional "storyworld" while reading: "More than reconstructed timelines and inventories of existents, storyworlds are mentally and emotionally projected environments in which interpreters are called upon to live out complex blends of cognitive and imaginative response, encompassing sympathy, the drawing of causal inferences, identification, evaluation, suspense, and so on" (16–17). Mukherjee's reconfiguration, which locates its storyworld in the past and present, in India, England, and the United States, encourages this imaginative process, facilitating comprehension for people with similar backgrounds, but also opening up a new storyworld for European Americans, one made more accessible through its connection to a well-known narrative. In other words, *The Scarlet Letter* connections ease European American readers into the less-familiar storyworld of India. Respecting *The Scarlet Letter* and the tradition it inspired, however, Mukherjee intends to maintain the Americanness of the book. In an interview with Tina Chen and S.X. Goudie, Mukherjee says, "This is not a book about India, but about the making of America and American national mythology. That's why I used the two women characters, Hannah, the pre-America American, and Beigh, the post-de-Europeanized American, to dramatize the need to redefine what it means to be an 'American' in the 1990s."

It is no accident that Mukherjee choose the word "extend" to describe her objective regarding the American mainstream. As the word implies, seeds of the elements she emphasizes—internationalism, feminism, and religious tolerance—are present in Hawthorne's novel from the start, but Mukherjee emphasizes them to call attention to their place in American culture. Perhaps, like Buell, Mukherjee believes that readers have tended to ignore some important elements of Hawthorne's tale: "The cultural work that *The Scarlet Letter* has been made to perform is not quite the work it undertakes to perform. The book is arguably not an 'American' performance so much as one that critical and creative repossessions have by and large tended to Americanize in ways that play down its cosmopolitan and deracinated aspects" (80). Although I believe there is evidence of the novel's Americanness, as discussed above, I agree with Buell that Hawthorne also reveals the multicultural influence on early New England. For example, just before discovering the scarlet letter boxed away in an unused portion of the Custom-House, Hawthorne writes that he tries "to raise from these dry bones [old documents] an image of the old town's brighter aspect, when India was a new region, and only Salem knew the way thither" (25). The town's "aspect" was "brightest," in terms of its commercial and shipping interests, at a period just after Hester Prynne would have lived,[8] and the same attic that holds documents confirming this history also holds Hester's story. For many readers, however, this reference to India remains figuratively boxed away like the literal documents that bear witness to the trade.

Within the main narrative, however, Hawthorne briefly ushers forth Native Americans rather than Indians. According to Lucy Maddox, many nineteenth-century writers and reviewers saw the inclusion of Native Americans in literary works as a means of establishing a national American literature distinct from that of Europe (42). The limited appearance of Native Americans in *The Scarlet Letter*, however, may be attributed to Hawthorne's personal distaste for Indian stories. Anna Brickhouse quotes Hawthorne on the subject in "Sketches from Memory" (1854): "It has often been a matter of regret to me, that I was shut out from the most peculiar field of American fiction, by an inability to see any romance, or poetry, or grandeur, or beauty in the Indian character" (234). In *The Scarlet Letter*, a Native American brings Chillingworth to the village to receive his ransom just in time to witness Hester's humiliation on the scaffold: "An Indian, in his native garb, was standing there; but the red men were not so infrequent visitors of the English settlements, that one of them would have attracted any notice. . . . By the Indian's side, and evidently sustaining a companionship with him, stood a white man, clad in a strange disarray of civilized and savage costume" (44). The passage reveals the intermingling of Indian and English in the settlements as well as in Chillingworth. As Chillingworth says upon his meeting with Hester in the jail, "My old studies in alchemy . . . and my sojourn, for above a year past, among a people well versed in the kindly properties of simples, have made a better physician of me than many that claim the medical degree" (51). Although the Native American remains silent, Chillingworth testifies to his influence. His knowledge as a doctor, which not only enables him to do good but also aids his evil revenge against Dimmesdale, derives from European and Native American sources.

As Mukherjee reconfigures *The Scarlet Letter* in the early 1990s, Patrick J. Buchanan's "'Cultural Wars for the Soul of America' . . . were raging in their full fury, and non-white immigration had emerged as one of the major provocations" (Sen 46). Having recently become a U.S. citizen, Krishna Sen argues, Mukherjee no doubt felt personally threatened by these anti-immigration sentiments and chose a canonical work of American literature as the vehicle for her response. In her essay "Four-Hundred-Year-Old Woman," Mukehrjee says that she sets out to "redefine the nature of *American* and what makes an American by making the familiar exotic; the exotic familiar" (24–25). Mukherjee extends Hawthorne's connections between Puritan New England and Native Americans and between Puritan New England and India through her characters' merging of bloodlines, through her characters' geographic travel, and through the artistic blending of cultural styles, images, and works. In doing so, Mukherjee repeatedly conflates, compares, and blurs Native Americans with Indians, using the same word to refer to both. At one point, Beigh, playing dumb for a museum curator, distinguishes them by saying "Indian-Indian, not wah-wah Indian" (*The Holder* 14). Why does Mukherjee specifically emphasize these two groups, and why does she also blur them? First, she does so because the novel she reconfigures, *The Scarlet Letter*, also refers to these same two groups. More interestingly, however, the fact that the two groups share a name is a result of misunderstanding, as Columbus, supposing he had found a shortcut to India, first gave the misnomer "Indian" to Native Americans. Perhaps Mukherjee, in her novel that in many ways promotes cultural unity and understanding, is making an ironic jab at Columbus and his imperialistic impulse. In addition, Mukherjee's stated agenda is to redefine what it means to be American by making the familiar exotic; in doing so, she uses a group that is a familiar part of America's early history, Native Americans, and likens them to a group that most Americans think of as geographically and culturally distant. This comparison invites recognition of an important similarity between these two groups. The lands of Native Americans and Indians were both colonized by Europeans. America was no more a virgin wilderness waiting to be tamed than India was. With this reminder, Mukherjee challenges one common myth of American origins.

Physically blending Native American with New English, Mukherjee shows Rebecca Easton, Hannah's mother, abandoning her life in Puritan society and her child for the sake of her Native American lover. To have child and lover together is not possible in this society, because what Rebecca has done is "the ultimate unnatural crime of Puritan life" (30). Rebecca disappears physically from most of the novel's remainder, suggesting that this society cannot acknowledge such shameful connections. Likewise, Hannah represses the memory of her mother's departure, endorsing the fiction of her mother's death at the hands of Indians: "She wills the memory of this night away; she will orphan herself to that memory, deny its existence" (30). For the sake of self-preservation, Hannah alters the story of her origins to remove the taint of miscegenation, just as Hawthorne minimizes, and many readers ignore, the multicultural aspects in *The Scarlet Letter*, a novel some call our national "myth of origin."

As an adult, Hannah escapes her Puritan constraints physically and emotionally. For Hannah, India, where she travels with her husband, has "a vibrancy that sucked all breath out of her chest" (109). For a few years, however, she lives among the English and maintains most of her conventional attitudes and habits. Finding emotional connections with Indians, though, such as her servant Bhagmati and later her own Indian lover, Hindu King Jadav Singh, transforms her. As Mukherjee writes, "Many years later she called the trip, and her long residence in India, her 'translation'" (104). Far from feeling shame about her interracial union, Hannah celebrates the passion that she has never before allowed herself to experience. When Hannah later returns to Salem with Singh's daughter, Pearl, she does not shamefully hide in the wilderness as her mother did. Instead, she reclaims her mother for herself and her community, finding her "in a workhouse for the mad and indigent in Providence Plantations" (284). Hannah, Pearl, Rebecca, and Rebecca's five half–Native American children live together in a small house visited by "diverse men and women who came from curiosity and stayed for the wealth of [Hannah's] storytelling, the pungency of her opinions" (285). Mukherjee links this household, which "a more refined age in a more sophisticated city might have called a salon" (285), with the birth of America: One of the pungent opinions that Hannah and Pearl utter is, "We are Americans to freedom born" (285). Hannah's reclaiming of her mother suggests an acceptance of her whole self, and it is symbolic of the nation's acceptance of the multicultural components at its origins.

Mukherjee furthers this connection between New England and other cultures by juxtaposing and blending artistic expressions from diverse places and periods. The title of the novel, *The Holder of the World*, refers literally to a sculpture in Aurangzeb's royal chambers, but figuratively it stands for art itself, which retains culture for posterity and allows one to, in the words of Beigh, "with sufficient passion and intelligence . . . deconstruct the barriers of time and geography" (11). In fact, such a work of art first inspired the creation of this novel, when Mukherjee saw at a pre-auction viewing a seventeenth-century Indian miniature painting of a blonde Caucasian woman in Mughal court dress: "I thought, 'Who is this very confident-looking 17th-century woman, who sailed in some clumsy wooden boat across dangerous seas and then stayed there? She had transplanted herself in what must have been a traumatically different culture. How did she survive?" (Newman 69). This artwork records an early merging of American and Indian cultures; within the novel, it becomes one of the early clues that helps Beigh find Hannah when she discovers its likeness in a small Museum of Maritime Trade in an old New England fishing village (*The Holder* 18–19). The series of miniatures Beigh discovers "make [her], who grew up in an atomized decade, feel connected to still-to-be detected galaxies" (15), linking her with a world that is geographically and temporally distant.

Artwork unites across time and space, holding history and culture in its pages and frames, throughout the novel. One of the paintings Beigh finds in the museum depicts an Indian painter's imagining of young Hannah in New England: "She stands ankle-deep in a cove, a gold-haired, pale-bodied child-woman against a backdrop of New England evoked with wild, sensual color. . . . At the water's edge, a circle of Indians in bright feathered headdresses roast fish on an open fire. . . . Crouched behind her . . . black-robed women with haggard faces tug loose edible tufts of samphire and sea grasses." (15–16). Beigh's response to the painting is, "I was right—they were fascinated by us" (16), apparently just as "we" are fascinated by "them." For although Beigh glosses over the likeness, this Indian painting closely resembles an embroidery sampler created by twelve-year-old Hannah long before her travels began: "an ocean, palm trees, thatched cottages, and black-skinned men casting nets and colorfully garbed bare-breasted women mending them; native barks and, on the horizon, high-masted schooners. Colonial gentlemen in breeches and ruffled lace . . . pace along the shore" (44). Just as her Indian counterparts created an image of distant America, Hannah's imagination constructs a distant India.

Numerous other examples in the novel depict the merging of cultures through art and artwork's ability to hold the world for us to examine.[9] For example, while listening to Bhagmati recite the epic Indian story of Sita, the wife of King Rama captured and held captive by the "demon king Ravanna" (172), Hannah mentally draws comparisons with her own experience and with the contemporary New England narrative of Mary Rowlandson's captivity: "Rebecca chose to stay in her Lanka with her Ravanna. But Mary Rowlandson, the virtuous Puritan woman, had been dragged from Lancaster. Did Sita step out of her fenced garden because she heard . . . a knocking on her door, as though every bird, every flower, every sail at the horizon's edge were calling to her?" (173). Such comparisons of familiar stories to new ones is, as Roger Schank and Robert Abelson have pointed out, key to understanding (14). Not only do most humans attempt to understand unfamiliar stories in terms of ones they have heard before, but they also attempt to project familiar scripts and models onto the framework of new narratives. Cultural myths, such as that of Sita and biblical stories in Judeo-Christian societies, serve, according to Mark David Turner, an important cognitive function:

> Projection of one story onto another . . . is also, like story, a fundamental instrument of the mind. . . . The essence of parable is its intricate combining of two of our basic forms of knowledge—story and projection. This classic combination produces one of our keenest mental processes for constructing meaning. . . . The motivations for parable are as strong as the motivations for color vision or sentence structure or the ability to hit a distant object with a stone. (5)

Creating narrative helps humans order and understand their own experiences, and projection enables them to imaginatively place themselves in other's stories, to learn from them. Through art, Beigh finds common territory, "emphasizing cross-cultural continuities between East and West"

(Simon, "Hybridity in the Americas" 422). *Her* answer to the question she raises, which may differ from other's, stems from the imaginative union of these stories: "Where is Sita's version of her captivity in Lanka? . . . I may not have Sita's words, but I have the Salem Bibi's; I know from her own captivity narrative what Sita would have written" (*The Holder* 177). Of course, most of the Salem Bibi's narrative is constructed by Beigh herself. By building on the narratives of others, she betters understands those prior narratives as well as her own. She imaginatively creates her truth that brings the prior narratives together and answers the questions raised by them.

Another way that Mukherjee extends themes from *The Scarlet Letter* is by sending a strong feminist message through the parallels between her female characters and Hester Prynne. Although some critics note Hawthorne's conservative view of women's issues,[10] others agree that Hawthorne's Hester is anything but a weak woman, and her portrayal invites feminist interpretations. Baym, for example, argues that Hawthorne is "a feminist writer from *The Scarlet Letter* onward" (107), and Monika Elbert notes, "The book celebrates feminine intelligence, creativity, compassion, while it downplays, to Hawthorne's (and Hester's) credit, the popular and sentimental image of woman as dependent, or even worse, as victim of her romantic fantasies" (257). Less emphatically, Weldon asserts, "Hawthorne [is] difficult to categorize as a misogynistic or antifeminist writer" (4). Hester is clearly stronger than Dimmesdale, bearing the community's censure while protecting her lover and admonishing him to "Preach! Write! Act! Do anything save to lie down and die!" (Hawthorne 127). Unfortunately, the community denies the same opportunities to preach, to write, and to act to Hester, not only because of her scarlet letter but also because of her gender. A particularly clear message against women's oppression and in favor of women's empowerment comes near the novel's close, as Hester becomes a counselor and mentor:

> Women, more especially,—in the continually recurring trials of wounded, wasted, wronged, misplaced, or erring and sinful passion,— or with the dreary burden of a heart unyielded, because unvalued and unsought,—came to Hester's cottage, demanding why they were so wretched, and what remedy! Hester comforted and counseled them, as best she might. She assured them, too, of her firm belief, that, at some brighter period, when the world should have grown ripe for it, in Heaven's own time, a new truth would be revealed, in order to establish the whole relation between man and woman on a surer ground of mutual happiness. (165–166)

Here, more than any other place in the novel, Hawthorne reveals his sympathy for Hester and for women generally. The author, like his character, seems to look hopefully toward a time of gender equity.

Like Hawthorne, Mukherjee comments on the double standard for men and women regarding sexual activity. Beigh imagines Hannah's feelings after she witnesses her mother's departure with her Native American lover: "Has any child been so burdened? She has witnessed the Fall, not Adam's Fall, Rebecca's Fall. Her mother's Fall, infinitely more sinful than the Fall of a man. She is the witness not merely of the occasion of sin, but the birth of sin itself" (*The Holder* 30). Her mother's sin, the sexual sin of a woman, is "infinitely more sinful" than that of a man. Although neither Hawthorne nor the Puritan elders he creates seem content with the inequity, Hester's community punishes her for her sexual sin but not her male partner. Less-strict religious societies have traditionally overlooked male sexual activity outside marriage while holding women to more rigid standards.

In the quotation above, Mukherjee evokes the Puritan belief that Native Americans were minions of Satan, as well as the popular modern-day conception of early America as a Garden of Eden. This conception, a type of myth of origins, was perhaps first voiced by Columbus, who, on his third voyage to the "New World," near what is today Venezuela, believed he had found the actual Garden of Eden. According to Lewis, Hawthorne himself helped embed this notion of America as Eden into the collective consciousness: His Hester and Dimmesdale become the New World Adam and Eve after the Fall (111). When describing the infant Pearl, Hawthorne writes, "[T]he infant was worthy to have been brought forth in Eden; worthy to have been left there, to be the plaything of the angels, after the world's first parents were driven out" (61). Again, Mukherjee destabilizes an American myth of origin by showing that India is also Edenic, not yet fallen. Of a painting depicting a Caucasian man (probably Gabriel Legge) and an Indian woman against an Indian background, Beigh says, "It seems in every way a reversal of the familiar expulsion myths of Adam and Eve from Eden, Adam's fall, sinning all," and she titles the work "Entry into the Garden" (*The Holder* 207).

In this Edenic world, Hannah, like Hester, indulges in an adulterous love affair and becomes pregnant with her lover's child. Unlike Hester, she does not feel shame about her passion; on the contrary, at least in the eyes of Beigh, she is a "goddess-in-the-making" (163). In the narrative that Beigh pieces together, Hannah repeatedly shows her strength. She murders a Mughal general before he can murder Singh, she travels to the enemy's camp in a misguided attempt to orchestrate a peace settlement, and she finally returns to Puritan New England with an illegitimate daughter whom she proudly rears on the outskirts of town. As with Bayard's depiction of the female character Lea Marquis, discussed in chapter 1, the reader may detect a presentist bias in Mukherjee's characterization of Hannah. This proud, independent, even overtly feminist woman seems out of place in the seventeenth, or even the nineteenth, century. However, Hawthorne's description of Hester's thoughts reveals subtle parallels to those of the free-thinking Hannah. Just as Hawthorne says that Hester's scarlet letter is a passport that allows her to travel mentally and physically where others dare not, Rebecca, Hannah, and her daughter, Pearl, seem to live a particularly free existence in Salem: "The women had for so long indulged a liberty of eccentric dissent that their certification of certain extreme positions was considered advantageous to the maintenance of social order" (285). Far from being exile, Hannah's female household is Edenic. In the novel's present, Beigh herself and her boyfriend, Venn, have a relationship resembling the "surer ground of mutual happiness" (Hawthorne 166) that Hester prophesies. They live together without marriage, they are Indian and American, and they are professionals who value each other emotionally and intellectually. So, in her updated version of Hawthorne's tale, Mukherjee proves Hester's predictions right.

Perhaps the dominant theme of Hawthorne's *The Scarlet Letter* is the oppressiveness of Puritan religion. Near the main narrative's beginning, Hawthorne mockingly refers to the "Utopia of human virtue and happiness" that the new colony "originally project[ed]" (36), a project that is, of course, not realized. In describing the "severity of the Puritan character," Hawthorne notes that they are "a people amongst whom religion and law were almost identical, and in whose character both were so thoroughly interfused, that the mildest and the severest acts of public discipline were alike made venerable and awful. Meager, indeed, and cold, was the sympathy that a transgressor might look for, from such bystanders, at the scaffold" (37–38). Hawthorne's word choices here—*awful*, *meager*, and *cold*—emphasize the rigid quality of Puritan rule. Throughout the course of the novel, Hawthorne suggests that the characters' sins—the unlawful indulgence in passion, the cowardly and hypocritical failure to confess, the deceit, and the revenge—are not worse than, and indeed stem from, the Puritan society's harsh repression of the characters' humanity.

Mukherjee extends Hawthorne's appraisal of religious intolerance geographically and temporally. Like Hester Prynne, Hannah feels oppressed in her Puritan environment. Her adoptive parents fear her "wantonness of spirit," censoring her artistic embroideries and shutting her away from visitors lest she be tempted to sin or be labeled a witch. But the Puritans are not singled out for their denial of human passion and individuality. In this novel that draws from many cultures, one common aspect these cultures share is the oppressiveness of their dominant religions. The seventeenth-century Mughal Empire under Aurangzeb was characterized by religious suppression, much like Puritan New England. The historical figure appointed guardians of public morals, prevented the building of Hindu temples, and established a program to convert Hindus to Islam (BBC). Mukherjee's fictional Aurangzeb kills Hindu King Jadav Singh and his subjects, partly as a political maneuver and partly to cleanse the area of what he sees as Hindu idolatry: "The duty of the Emperor is to bring the infidel before the throne of judgment. There is no escaping the judgment of Allah" (*The Holder* 269). Aurangzeb believes that he fights a holy war and kills in the name of god, just as Hawthorne's Puritan elders believe their harshness against sinners is a holy duty.

Hinduism does not escape her censure, either. Mukherjee critiques an example of Hindu blind adherence to religion at the expense of human compassion. Hannah's servant Bhagmati, called Bindu as a child, tells of being raped by pirates at age ten and thrown into a river to drown: "A dishonored Hindu girl couldn't go back home. To have been abused was to have brought shame to the family for its failure to protect her" (223). But Bhagmati does not drown. She is pulled from the river by elephant washers and takes on a new life, surviving at odd jobs until she becomes a white man's servant and mistress and then, when he dies, Hannah's servant. Mukherjee writes that, although her family members are generally "decent and affectionate," they still disown her "in accordance with neighborly pressure and Hindu custom" (223). Lest we miss Mukherjee's irony when she notes that it is viewed as more cowardly to claim the dishonored family member than to disown her, she tells us, "Bindu, twice a victim, had run from her family, from her village, from all the familiar taboos and traditions" (224–225). Victimized not only by her rapists but also by those who should protect her, she rejects family and religion with a bitterness the reader shares. Mukherjee does not appear to critique the beliefs or believers of any particular religion; rather she critiques all those who, in the name of religion, value principles over people.

Mukherjee extends the parallel between Puritan New England and seventeenth-century India even further through the massacres that begin and end her novel. Framing the rest of the narrative, the two bloody battles have striking parallels. Near the beginning, Native Americans and colonists kill one another, Americans destroying Americans. Near the ending, Muslims and Hindus kill one another, Indians destroying Indians. The Nipmuc Indian braves who throw the head of a slain colonist for sport and the "rolling fire spreader" used to burn colonists' houses (37–38) resemble the Muslim general who uses an elephant to crush the heads of fallen Hindu soldiers (246) and the "burning balls of pitch" employed by the Muslim Army against the Hindu villagers (242). Both of these battles are linked to religious intolerance. Singh possesses an "unswerving hatred of all Sunni Muslims" (211), and for the Puritans the Indian massacre confirms that "they really *are* devils" (37, emphasis in original.). The battles as mirror images emphasize the ubiquity of religious intolerance and its inevitable disastrous consequences.

Mukherjee does suggest a positive view of spirituality, if not organized religion, through her portrayals of the relationships among her women characters. In an interview with Alison B. Carb, the author states, "I was born into a Hindu Bengali Brahmin family which means I have a different sense of self, of existence, and of morality. . . . I believe that our souls can be reborn in another body, so the perspective I have about a single character's life is different from that of an American writer who believes that he has only one life" (qtd. in Gonzalez 137). The idea of spiritual reincarnation is suggested with the connection twentieth-century Beigh feels for seventeenth-century Hannah. They are both white women with Indian lovers, but beyond that, without truly understanding why, she feels a kinship with this long-dead woman, and she intuits motives and emotions that she has no concrete way of knowing. Metaphorically, Mukherjee uses virtual reality to represent the concept of being born again in another time and place. When Beigh's boyfriend, Venn, takes her to his lab after having programmed in all her notes on Hannah, the Salem Bibi, Beigh enters a virtual seventeenth-century India, hoping to find the one answer that has eluded her, the location of the Emperor's Tear diamond. Beigh and the reader expect her to experience this new world through the eyes of Hannah, a woman we have come to think of as Beigh's counterpart. She awakens to seventeenth-century India, however, as Bhagmati: "[M]y hand is brown, with a tinkling gold bangle" (*The Holder* 281). This mental transformation suggests that on a spiritual level, humans are connected across time, geography, and race. Significantly, Beigh finds her answers only when she acknowledges this connection.

The virtual world created by Venn resembles the storyworlds that Herman describes: the "mentally and emotionally projected environments in which interpreters are called upon to live out complex blends of cognitive and imaginative response" (16). As with the concept of narrative storyworlds, however, the cognitive and imaginative response evoked depends upon the perceiver as much as on the environment, and this technology is one way that Mukherjee underscores the effect of perception on experience and interpretation. Having entered all of Beigh's research into the sophisticated, cutting-edge virtual-reality program he is helping create at MIT, Venn offers a trip to Hannah's time as a present to Beigh. Because of the word "reality" in its name, the reader may be tempted to mistake virtual reality for truth, for Hannah's actual fate. According to Randall Packer:

> Virtual reality is experiential and sensory—one does not simply observe the object, one is the object. One is not merely a detached observer—one enters into and becomes part of the landscape. The medium of virtual reality functions as an extension of the self, a reconfiguration of identity, intellect, dreams, and memories—ultimately blurring the boundary between self and exterior, between the real and the imaginary.

Although it blurs the boundary between the real and imagined, virtual reality is nevertheless constructed by a computer and by the participant's imagination. Mukherjee takes pains to remind us that the virtual experience is influenced by the participant: "The program will give you what you most care about; your mind is searching through the program though you don't realize it—it is interacting with my thousand-answer questionnaire—until it finds a place it wants to jump in" (*The Holder* 281). No two participants will experience it the same way. As Mukherjee states in an interview, "To me, creative imagination is the 'gatekeeper.' The technician downloads a statistics-rich experience; the artist, using the same program, wrests a vision. And each time you use that program, you learn or dislearn some element because 'you' are made up of a series of fluid identities. Similarly, each time you read *The Holder*, I hope you come up with new insights" (Chen and Goudie). The narrative experienced through virtual reality is to a large extent a creation of the participant's mind, just as literary narratives are created in part by readers, and just as all humans shape chaotic experience into manageable narratives.

Mukherjee further emphasizes the variability of perception and interpretation through the letters with which Puritans identify sinners, once again extending Hawthorne's strategy. Echoing Hawthorne, Mukherjee points out that, even in Hannah's time, branding with "the sinner's alphabet" no longer carries the stigma it once had in New England: "Adulterer, Blasphemer, Thief, Incest breeder—branded to his forehead or an Indian patch sewn to a woman's sleeve for miscegenation, no longer excited the intended pity or fear" (*The Holder* 41). Straying from the accepted views of the community, for Hannah's mother, Rebecca, the letters become an alphabet of revolt: "Rebecca was initiating her daughter into a whispered, subversive alphabet. 'A is for Act, my daughter!' . . . 'B is for Boldness,' Hannah pledged. 'C is for Character, D is for Dissent, E is for Ecstasy, F is for Forage. . . .'" (54). By linking multiple interpretations to the letters of the alphabet, Hawthorne and Mukherjee suggest in microcosm the multiple interpretations possible with any text composed of letters and words. The implication of this possibility for multiple interpretations is that, although art may be the holder of the world, no one text can be a universal repository of Truth.

Mukherjee also emphasizes the variability of perception and interpretation through epigraphs from John Keats's "Ode on a Grecian Urn" attached to each of the book's sections. Keats's poem offers a view of art contrasting the ones contained in Mukherjee's narrative. As Mukherjee says in an interview:

> The urn is still, the action is frozen, and one can only observe . . . action has been stuck in time and can't be redone. The people are always going to have their hand and feet in one particular posture, whereas with interactive technology, you're changing the narrative by inputting new information according to your new mood. . . . The individual experiencing the image, not simply the image itself—both are going to be transformed by the interaction. (Chen and Goudie)

Likewise, through reading and interpreting a narrative, the reader and the reading are transformed. "Ode on a Grecian Urn" depicts the urn as a vessel of meaning that is permanent, unchanging, but Mukherjee suggests that we must fill the vessel with ourselves to understand the meaning; we must ravish the "unravish'd bride" (Keats). By emphasizing the role of the interpreter in shaping and creating the narrative past, Mukherjee emphasizes that this interplay between artist and interpreter transforms art from the "foster-child of silence and slow time" (Keats) to the "holder of the world."

As with the other contemporary authors in this study, Mukherjee also calls attention to the frustrating mutability and uncertainty of language and its power to mislead. Hannah, being courted by the dashing Gabriel Legge, knows better than to believe his tall tales of adventure. Later, when listening to Bhagmati's stories, Hannah again discovers that "reciters . . . indulge themselves with closures that suit the mood of their times and their regions" (*The Holder* 176). The storytellers and their audience influence the tale told. Even Hannah herself is associated through her embroidering with an excessive outpouring of imagination. As Shao-Pin Luo points out, "The embroidery provides an outlet for Hannah's emotions and fights of imagination and, with a pun on embroidery as the 'embellishment of tales,' for the stories of her memories and fantasies" (92). Mukherjee hints that Hannah may not be completely reliable, and the author also reminds us that Hannah's story is filtered through a narrator's perception, a perception influenced by Beigh's own time, region, and personal needs and desires. More than once, Beigh prefaces parts of her narrative with such words as, "I need to believe" (*The Holder* 109). Time and again, the reader is reminded that Beigh is a researcher piecing together an incomplete history and filling in the gaps. The pieces that fill the gaps are composed of Beigh as much as they are of Hannah.

Contemporary authors, such as Updike and Mukherjee, recognize the frustrating need for connection with our distant past but also recognize the futility of trying to achieve it. Mukherjee comments on this frustrating impossibility in the last line of *The Holder of the World*: "time only to touch and briefly bring alive the first letter of an alphabet of hope and of horror stretching out, and back to the uttermost shores" (285). The first letter, of course, refers to the "A" of *The Scarlet Letter*, but our ability to access only one letter of an alphabet suggests the large gaps that remain forever unfilled. Updike and Mukherjee supplement the iconic status of *The Scarlet Letter* as American myth of origin with newer versions, but they remind us that these are simply versions, not reality. Likewise, their reconfigurations undermine *The Scarlet Letter*'s claim to authoritative Truth while still respecting that novel's value as a work of art.

3 A Draft of a Draft
Sena Jeter Naslund's Reconfiguration of *Moby-Dick*

Sena Jeter Naslund's 1999 novel *Ahab's Wife* explores in more than 650 pages approximately twenty years in the life of a character only briefly mentioned in Herman Melville's *Moby-Dick*. In Melville's novel, we learn from characters' remarks that Ahab has a wife much younger than himself back in Nantucket; that they married three voyages ago, the first voyage occurring the day after their wedding; that he sometimes misses her; and that together they have a young son. Melville never gives this character a name, but Naslund names her Una Spencer, after a character from Edmund Spenser's *Faerie Queen*. Although Ahab receives greater emphasis in Una's story than she does in his, their marriage is not the sole focus of her tale; in fact, as the novel's first line reveals, "Captain Ahab was neither [her] first husband nor [her] last" (1). Like many other contemporary writers, through her reconfiguration, Naslund pays homage to a great American classic but adds her story to it. By doing so, she adds her voice to the American cultural narrative, while simultaneously suggesting that this artificial product, narrative, reflects individual perceptions rather than reality.

Melville's *Moby-Dick*, like Nathaniel Hawthorne's *The Scarlet Letter*, is one of the classics that has come to define American literature. In *The Broken Estate: Essays on Literature and Belief*, James Wood claims, "Melville founded American vernacular prose equally with [Mark] Twain," and he "Americanizes Shakespeare" (38). Like Hawthorne and Poe, Melville called for a distinctive American literature to rival that of England, a national literature that he saw already blossoming in the works of some of his century's prominent writers, including Hawthorne. In 1850, as he composed *Moby-Dick*, Melville published in the *Literary World* "Hawthorne and His Mosses," his famous review of Hawthorne's *Mosses from an Old Manse*, in part to praise the work of the older writer whom he admired and who had recently become his friend, but also to advocate a national literature and to further the goals of the Young America movement. He devotes long passages of the review to American literature generally rather than to Hawthorne's work specifically. "Let America then prize and cherish her writers," he exhorts his readers; "yea, let her glorify them" ("Hawthorne" 525). Melville further calls for the celebration of our national writers above those of Europe:

And while she has good kith and kin of her own, to take to her bosom, let her not lavish her embraces upon the household of an alien.... But even were there no Hawthorne, no Emerson, no Whittier, no Irving, no Bryant, no Dana, no Cooper ... were there none of these, and others of like calibre among us, nevertheless, let America first praise mediocrity even, in her own children, before she praises ... the best excellence in the children of any other land. Let her own authors, I say, have the priority of appreciation. (525–526)

As the quote above illustrates, parts of Melville's book review read like a Young America manifesto. He goes so far as to connect American literary prestige to national power more generally: "While we are rapidly preparing for that political supremacy among the nations, which prophetically awaits us at the close of the present century; in a literary point of view, we are deplorably unprepared for it" (527). Supporting American writers, he suggests, strengthens the political power of the nation. Although this sentiment is at least partly self-serving for a writer struggling to support himself with his craft and longing for literary fame, it also conveys the jingoistic attitude that Melville genuinely shared with the other members of Young America.

Melville's fiction also reflects his interest in American prestige and development. John P. McWilliams, in *Hawthorne, Melville, and the American Character: A Looking-Glass Business*, sees this concern in *Moby-Dick*, a novel that begins and ends in an American setting but that otherwise takes place in the oceans of the world: "The persistency with which Melville applies images of the American prairies to the whale and the sea reflects the important cultural fact that the American of 1850 saw his nation taking possession of two frontiers simultaneously. Ishmael describes sailors as pioneers, the whale's forehead as 'the Prairie,' and rolling billows as grassy Western glades" (157). Not all of his contemporaries discerned the American flavor of *Moby-Dick*, and Melville's efforts at national literature become more obvious in a later work, *The Confidence Man* (1857), which Sheila Post asserts was written in response to *Putnam's Magazine*'s "lament that 'our first novel of [American] society has yet to be written'" (129). In this novel, Melville adopts an "American place, the Mississippi River, and the persona of what critics of the day referred to as 'an original American idea,' the confidence man" (129), causing *Putnam's* to praise this work "as a 'thoroughly American story'" (130). Regardless of his contemporaries' views of *Moby-Dick*, however, many critics today share James Barbour's opinion that it is "the great American novel of the nineteenth century" (25).

Although Melville attempted to create a national literature, his influences include American and European authors who link his work, like that of contemporary American writers of reconfigurations, to an ongoing literary tradition. The eight pages of extracts that precede *Moby-Dick* indicate that this novel reads and responds to a wide range of other texts. Some of the most important influences, which also inform the main body of the novel, are several books about whaling, such as American Owen

Chase's *Narrative of the Most Extraordinary and Distressing Shipwreck of the Whale-ship Essex* (1821). In this memoir that inspired Melville, Chase, the first mate of the Essex, recounts a shipwreck and its aftermath that resulted from being rammed by a sperm whale. Melville also draws information about whales and whaling from William Scoresby's *Journal of a Voyage to the Northern Whale Fishery* (1822) and Thomas Beale's *The Natural History of the Sperm Whale* (1839), among others (Parker 432–433). Other important influences that shape *Moby-Dick* include the King James Bible; the dramatic works of William Shakespeare, which Melville praises as the pinnacle of literary achievement in "Hawthorne and His Mosses"; and Thomas Carlyle's *Sartor Resartus* and *On Heroes, Hero-Worship, and the Heroic in History* (435). In addition, Robert Milder argues, "*Moby-Dick* owes much of its boundless ambition to the fertilization by Hawthorne, to whom the book is dedicated" (32), and, as mentioned above, whose *Mosses from an Old Manse* Melville read and reviewed while composing his novel.

All great writers such as Melville owe a debt to the literary tradition that precedes them, but postmodern writers of reconfigurations differ in that they direct the reader's attention to specific canonical texts to which their novels overtly respond. As a writer and an English professor with a PhD in creative writing, Naslund well knows *Moby-Dick*'s iconic status in American literature, and she comments in an interview that "the glory of [Melville's] writing" inspired her (204, this volume). Naslund recalls analyzing what makes *Moby-Dick* and Mark Twain's *Huckleberry Finn* "candidates for the great American novel" (195, this volume). Both, she notes, are "quests over water"; in both works, characters transcend "cultural barriers of prejudice"; and both are "accessible to a lot of different sorts of readers" (196, this volume). She resolved to follow this formula in her own novel, *Ahab's Wife*.

Because of her admiration for Melville's work, Naslund also resolved to be "scrupulously true" to it wherever her novel intersects with *Moby-Dick*, scouring it for references to Ahab's wife and incorporating Melville's limited information about this off-stage character into her book. She uses a passage in which Ahab gazes into Starbuck's eyes and sees there his wife and child as evidence of Ahab's tenderness toward his family, noting, "I wasn't interested in skewering Ahab for being a bad husband" (198, this volume). Yet she is also not interested in writing about a "sweet, resigned girl," which is exactly how Captain Peleg describes Ahab's wife in *Moby-Dick*. To justify her creation of a strong female character, she compares Melville's Peleg to Shakespeare's Polonius, "full of ideas that didn't hold water" (198, this volume). Of course, Melville himself establishes a precedent for comparing his characters to Shakespeare when he compares Ahab to King Lear, Pip to Lear's fool, and Starbuck to Hamlet. Reviewers of *Ahab's Wife* also note Naslund's respectful treatment of Melville. Greg Changnon of the *Atlanta Journal and Constitution* approves the "short Melvillian chapters, [the] double title and [the] 19th-century prose." The *Kirkus Reviews* asserts that Naslund's novel is "[a] genuine epic of America: an inspired homage to one of our greatest writers that brilliantly reinterprets and, in many ways rivals, his masterpiece" (*"Ahab's Wife"*). Yet with Melville's canonical status so well established, to what end does Naslund offer her homage?

A cynical or unappreciative reader might agree with *The Nation*'s Tom LeClair, who sneers, "[M]aybe *Ahab's Wife* is like the widow Una becomes. She inherits Ahab's property and capitalizes on his wealth" (46). LeClair suggests that Naslund, and perhaps other contemporary writers of reconfigurations, unfairly profits from Melville's reputation rather than earning a literary reputation of her own. But as the *Kirkus Reviews* quotation above notes, Naslund does more than merely imitate or borrow from *Moby-Dick*; she also reinterprets it. By offering a form of homage to Melville's novel, Naslund reinforces its canonical status, its place in the American cultural narrative. At the same time, however, she adds some of the tales that Melville left untold. In doing so, she alters future interpretations of *Moby-Dick* and revises the cultural narrative it helps compose.

As noted in this study's introduction, narrative is something humans "virtually have to do" (Schank and Abelson 27) in order to thrive. Naslund expresses this human need explicitly through Una, who says, "I had begun to see my own life as a story and myself as the author of it" (158). Many people remain unaware of authoring their self-narratives, yet cognitive psychologists believe they still process new experience and information through mental stories. As fundamental to human society as individual narratives are to human beings, a cultural narrative helps establish cultural identity, and that cultural identity in turn shapes the society's stories. In order to be coherent to others, we shape the stories we tell according to culturally established norms, leaving out what does not fit and emphasizing what our society values (Schank and Abelson 27). But as individuals with individual perceptions, we introduce small differences with each new story, and those differences may eventually become a part of the larger cultural narrative, gradually influencing the norms that define storytelling and our society. As Michel Foucault puts it, this story may become part of the culture's "truth":

> Each society has its regime of truth, its "general politics" of truth: that is, the types of discourse which it accepts and makes function as true; the mechanisms and instances which enable one to distinguish true and false statements, the means by which each is sanctioned; the techniques and procedures accorded value in the acquisition of truth; the status of those who are charged with saying what counts as true. (72–73)

Our cultural narrative, then, consists of stories we tell ourselves about ourselves over time. These stories are accepted as "truth" about ourselves by the collective society, and those who pen the stories are often considered canonical writers. T.S. Eliot commented on the value of connecting one's contemporary stories to the stories of one's culture's past, praising James Joyce's *Ulysses* for "'manipulating a continuous parallel between contemporaneity and antiquity' as a way 'of controlling, of ordering, of giving shape and significance to the immense panorama of futility and anarchy which is contemporary history'" (qtd. in Kroeber 166). In Eliot's statement, we see a collective cultural narrative functioning in the same way individuals' narratives of self function, ordering experience in order to make sense of it and to make it into history. A historical novel that reconfigures an American classic, such as *Ahab's Wife* or Louis Bayard's *The Pale Blue Eye* or the historical narrative strand of Bharati Mukherjee's *The Holder of the World*, interpolates a new chapter into the American cultural narrative.

What does Naslund add to Melville's story that she hopes will become a part of our collective narrative? As suggested above, one of the key stories Melville chooses not to tell is that of Ahab's wife. Gerard Genette labels this type of reconfiguration the "revaluation of a character," which "consists in investing him or her—by way of pragmatic or psychological transformation—with a more significant and/or more 'attractive' role in the value system of the hypertext [rewrite] than was the case in the hypotext [original text]" (343). More than simply giving the details of an individual woman's life, though, Naslund attempts to inscribe the historical role of strong women indelibly onto the story of American identity. According to Liedeke Plate, "Naslund's novel engages tradition as canonized to open it up to subjects forgotten or repressed, bringing them within the purview of canonization as cultural remembering" (144). Those forgotten or repressed subjects are often women. In fact, as Jeannette King notes in an essay on *Ahab's Wife*, Leslie Fiedler's 1959 study of American literature, *Love and Death in the American Novel*, identifies the boys' adventure story as the primary concern of America's defining literature, including *Moby-Dick*, *The Adventures of Huckleberry Finn*, and other works (182–183). The omission of women's stories is not characteristic of all American literature of the nineteenth century, however. During and shortly after their lifetimes, the works of Harriet Beecher Stowe, Louisa May Alcott, Kate Chopin, E.D.E.N. Southworth, and Augusta Jane Evans, female authors of fiction about women's lives, were better known and, by many, more respected than Melville's. The process of canonization helped partially erase, at least for a time, these women's works from the cultural memory. The fact that some of them were reintroduced into the canon in the late twentieth century emphasizes how cultural memory can evolve through the influence of new voices, such as Naslund's.

In interviews, Naslund has often commented on the inspiration for this novel and its feminist spin on *Moby-Dick*. During a series of long car trips with her preteen daughter in the early 1990s, they listened to books on tape, including *Moby-Dick*. Taken with the beautiful language and the larger-than-life characterization, her daughter memorized and recited some of

Captain Ahab's speeches. Naslund recalls her pride that her daughter "has a good ear and can tell what good literature is," but also her disappointment that the book lacks an important female character, "one with whom she could identify and memorize her speeches" (195, this volume). She also makes note of the lack of strong female role models in American literature generally, citing the few prominent women characters, such as Hester Prynne of *The Scarlet Letter* and Edna Pontellier of *The Awakening*, as unsatisfactory options (203, this volume). Eventually, Naslund developed her plan for *Ahab's Wife*: "I wanted to write a novel about a woman quester and have it end in triumph, not defeat" (201, this volume).

Recent cognitive psychology can help explain why strong female role models in literature may help young women become stronger women in society. According to David Herman, we process new information by means of scripts, or internal narratives: "Stored in the memory, previous experiences form structured repertoires of expectations about current and emergent experiences" (89). Without relevant previous experiences, new information will be more difficult to understand and process, and new situations more difficult to negotiate. Reading stories about strong female characters adds to our repertoire of expectations, making it more likely that young women can envision themselves in strong roles and that strong women will be more acceptable in society. As an adult, Naslund's character Una reflects back on the role of childhood reading in shaping her experience as a woman: "And the women in Shakespeare who impersonated men! I had done that, too. Perhaps I had stepped so easily into the idea from having read him" (417). From Shakespeare, Una learns feminine strength but also the necessity of disguise. In *Ahab's Wife*, she will transition into acceptance of female strength in women's clothing, an unapologetic model for future readers.

Chronologically, Una's story begins when she is twelve, approximately the same age as Naslund's daughter during those long car trips, a transitional age from girlhood to womanhood. From the start, courage and adventure govern her life. When she refuses to bow to her father's religious fanaticism, her mother sends her to live with her more liberal aunt and uncle, who are lighthouse keepers. When she is sixteen, two young men visit the lighthouse island, and, wanting to view their approaching boat, Una climbs to the top of the lighthouse: "I imagined the tower itself was proud of me and enjoyed the passion of my rising knees and feet" (66). Una's ascent is figured as mastery over this giant phallic symbol, and when she reaches the top, she battles an angry sea eagle for command of this perch, earning the admiration of the two young men. This scene also reminds readers of the fairy-tale damsel locked in the castle tower, awaiting the rescue of approaching knights. Una, however, figuratively slays her own dragon by fighting off the sea eagle and descends from the tower under her own power. Soon after, impatient with waiting for life to come to her, she disguises herself as a boy and ships with a whaling vessel. Although Una's adventures may seem improbable, Lisa Norling, in her study *Captain Ahab*

Had a Wife: New England Women and the Whalefishery, 1720–1870, confirms that nineteenth-century women sometimes sailed with their husbands and, less often, disguised themselves as men to join whaling voyages. On board, Una plays the roles of cabin boy, lookout, and tutor, earning the respect of her captain and the crew through hard work, intelligence, and skill. Yet she also explains how she handles some uniquely feminine challenges, such as managing her menstrual periods. These are not the concerns of Ishmael and Queequeg or Huck and Jim, but Naslund shows readers that a girl can make her own quest over water.

As a result of her seafaring adventures, Una endures the tragedies of shipwreck, cannibalism, the death of one close friend, and the madness of another. Afterward, she returns to a more traditionally feminine way of life in response to the violence she witnessed, and she seems equally capable in both environments. As a girl, Una had learned to sew from her mother and her aunt, and even then she had imagined the adventures of her female relatives: "When one stitches, the mind travels, not the way men do, with ax and oxen through the wilderness, but surely our traveling counted too, as motion" (70). When Una first sights a whale, she compares its motion, "sewing the water with her body" (149), to that of a needle through cloth, and upon her return to land, Una plans to make her living by sewing. In an interview, Naslund says, "[T]he needle is the female response to the harpoon, it's about creating something while the harpoon is an instrument of destruction" (Sullivan 2). Naslund celebrates the adventure and creativity of the traditionally feminine life, offering it as a positive alternative to the brutality of whaling.

And Una's life as a woman is adventurous. Her second marriage, to Ahab, occurs halfway through the novel, and the two are drawn together because of their similar natures. The morning after their first night together, however, Ahab embarks on another whaling voyage, and Una soon learns that she is pregnant. She finds intellectual and emotional companionship during her husband's long absence from, among others, historical women, such as Maria Mitchell, the first person to discover a new comet by telescope, and Margaret Fuller, the nineteenth-century feminist writer. Although the frequent intersection of Una's life with those of famous nineteenth-century figures may sometimes seem contrived, Naslund uses these historical figures to bear witness to the existence of real, strong women during the nineteenth century. As King points out, "When . . . Fuller says to Una, 'You are the American woman' (591), she is asserting that women, too, are part of the American tradition so firmly identified as male in nineteenth-century fiction" (185). Such women as Una are not only the product of imagination. King also points out an important contrast between Una's story and that of many nineteenth-century fictional heroines: The novel does not end in her marriage, because marriage is not her primary aim. With her first premonition that her husband may not return, Una's independence comforts her: "No, I do not unmarry Ahab. But I marry myself. I take my fate as within"

(Naslund 561). After learning of Ahab's death, she grieves and then recovers to live happily without him. Marriage in the novel can be joyful, but it is not the only path to a woman's fulfillment.

Another feminist statement made by Naslund gazes back further in literary history to one of Melville's own primary influences, the King James Bible. Melville names several important characters after biblical figures, and the fates of these biblical figures foreshadow the fates of characters in *Moby-Dick*. For example, the biblical Elijah, a prophet, accurately foretells the demise of King Ahab. In *Moby-Dick*, sailors believe old Elijah to be a madman, but his prophecy also proves accurate when he tells Ishmael and Queequeg, "Shan't see ye again very soon, I guess; unless it's before the Grand Jury [Last Judgment]" (Melville 91). The biblical Ishmael, Abraham's outcast son, parallels the isolation of Melville's Ishmael, particularly at the beginning and end of the novel. Most importantly, the biblical Ahab is an idolatrous king, destroyed by God for his wickedness. Similarly, Melville's Ahab would "strike the sun if it insulted [him]" (140), and he challenges heavenly authority, embodied as the white whale, leading to his ultimate destruction. Although Melville never names his Ahab's wife, the biblical Ahab marries Queen Jezebel, a figure who, for many today, has come to embody female immorality and evil. According to biblical scholar Janet Howe Gaines, "she has been denounced as a murderer, prostitute, and enemy of God" (qtd. in Satchell). Yet Gaines and other feminist scholars see Jezebel as a scapegoat to "misogynistic biblical writers" (qtd. in Satchell). Michael Satchell believes that the scriptural evidence does not substantiate Jezebel's wicked reputation, and he sees her as a "blood-stained yet strong-willed, politically astute and courageous woman" living in a time of few rights and minimal status for women. Although Naslund does not go so far as to name her character Jezebel, her creation of *Ahab's Wife* works to redeem strong women from automatic association with evil. In addition, by reminding us that the biblical Ahab had a wife who strongly influenced his reign, Naslund underscores this character's relative weakness and inconsequentiality in *Moby-Dick*.

In addition to creating a feminist counterpart to supplement *Moby-Dick*'s voice in the American cultural narrative, Naslund intensifies some of Melville's themes, particularly those of sexuality and race. Fiedler and other[1] scholars have noted the homoeroticism in *Moby-Dick*, particularly in the description of Ishmael and Queequeg's "marriage" and in chapter 94, "A Squeeze of the Hand." Leland S. Person, for example, argues that "[f]rom *Typee* forward, Melville experimented with alternative forms of gender and sexuality identity. . . . Employing a remarkable array of semantic and narrational tricks, he disguises sexuality and sexual transgressions in ways that co-opt his readers, most of whom, I think he is betting, will get his jokes and thereby reveal themselves to be in secret sympathy" (245). As Person here suggests, the subject of sexuality, like the whale that the *Pequod* hunts, remains mostly beneath the surface in *Moby-Dick*. Naslund acknowledges, "Melville in *Moby-Dick* is an advocate of cultural and religious tolerance" (Haynsworth 65), adding that, as a late twentieth-century writer, she can be more "frank about homosexuality than Melville could" (206, this volume). *Ahab's Wife* includes two male couples who defy society's expectations through their homosexuality, and Naslund recognizes the complications of such defiance. For one of these couples, the affair ends tragically in madness and death, and for the other, the relationship offers the hope of happiness. In *Moby-Dick*, Ishmael and Queequeg's union begins on land and then quickly retreats to the freer existence at sea. Naslund reverses this pattern by placing the earlier, failed union at sea and the promising union within the community on land.

Naslund also offers more overt statements about nineteenth-century racial politics than Melville does in *Moby-Dick*. Melville uses Ishmael to proclaim the justness of racial equality, for example, jeering at those who suppose that "a white man were anything more dignified than a whitewashed negro" (62). Readers of Melville's time were also sensitive to the messages of racial equality in the text, some even reading it as an allegory about the U.S. dilemma over slavery. For example, critic John Stauffer cites an 1856 essay published in *Frederick Douglass' Paper* by James McCune Smith that "likens the *Pequod* to the ship of state in American politics" (224). McCune Smith sees the *Pequod*'s destruction as a warning to "American leaders" who continue to oppress African Americans (225). Naslund, however, believes that Melville, writing in the mid–nineteenth century when slavery was the chief political concern of the country, misses an opportunity to address this issue clearly (204, this volume).

Ahab's Wife directly engages the subject through the character of Susan, a runaway slave who hides from bounty hunters in Una's cabin. She also speaks directly to Melville here, echoing Ishmael and Queequeg's bedroom scene at the Spouter Inn when she places Susan in bed with Una: "I wanted to say upfront, Melville, I hear you, and I'm coming along right behind you" (204, this volume). Instead of a loving masculine embrace, the two hide from the hunters, share body heat, and perform an activity "that is quintessentially female" (204, this volume), delivering Una's baby. Before Una's baby is born, Susan's entrance into the scene is also a symbolic birth. Having hidden between the bed's two mattresses while Una was up, Susan emerges as Una's labor intensifies: "From between the two mattresses, under my back, I felt her body moving. And though I saw nothing, I imaged with my inward eye her fingers grope the edge, her head and neck thrust through, and then in a smooth lunge . . . she slid out onto the floor" (Naslund 8). Naslund's text has given birth to the slave that she believes Melville excludes. Susan later flees north across the frozen river in a scene borrowed from the nineteenth-century's most influential abolitionist author, Stowe, but she and Una maintain a long-term bond through letters. By incorporating this iconic scene of Eliza's escape from *Uncle Tom's Cabin*, published just one year after *Moby-Dick*, Naslund illustrates what Melville might have done.

Naslund also adapts Melville's theme of spiritual quest. Through this quest, literally embodied as Ahab's hunt for the white whale, Melville evokes the thematic quest for origins that we also see in the works of Edgar Allan Poe, Hawthorne, and the contemporary writers who reconfigured them. Ahab struggles to understand and to confront the agency behind the white whale, to know what force, if any, it represents: "If man will strike, strike through the mask! How can the prisoner reach outside except by thrusting through the wall? To me the white whale is that wall, shoved near to me. Sometimes I think there's naught beyond. . . . That inscrutable thing is chiefly what I hate" (Melville 140). The uncertainty of who or what controls human fate affronts Ahab's sense of justice, and he vainly seeks certitude. John Bryant points out that Melville frequently has Ahab use genealogical metaphors to express his ontological questions ("Moby Dick as Revolution" 78): "Where is the foundling's father hidden? Our souls are like those orphans whose unwedded mothers die in bearing them: the secret of our paternity lies in their grave, and we must there to learn it" (Melville 373). These metaphors make clear that Ahab links the mysterious agency that drives the white whale to human origins.

As do Poe's detective stories, *Moby-Dick*'s concern with human origins reflects a general mid-nineteenth-century anxiety. Geological and astronomical discoveries of this time period challenged long-held beliefs in divine creation and in the Great Chain of Being, which ranked all creatures in order of their likeness to God (Harvey 72; Eric Wilson, "Melville, Darwin" 133). Eric Wilson sees references to current scientific theories and the unease they produced when Melville mentions Louis Agassiz, a Swiss-born professor of zoology at Harvard, and Frederic Cuvier, a French zoologist, both pre-Darwinians. Melville also includes in his extracts a quotation from Charles Darwin's *The Voyage of the Beagle* (1839), which he refers to as *Darwin's Voyage of a Naturalist* (Eric Wilson "Melville, Darwin" 140). Unlike many of his contemporaries, however, "[Melville's] interest, ultimately, was less in the Christian theological ramifications of deep time than in the rawer metaphysical proposition of unrecoverable primordialness" (Harvey 74). The white whale's mysteries, then, represent this "unrecoverable primordialness" in the novel. Along these same lines, Wilson, arguing for the influence of Darwin's *The Voyage of the Beagle* on *Moby-Dick*, asserts that Ishmael "is drawn to the sea as his progenitor, perhaps the common source of life from which he descended, possibly the spring of everything" ("Melville, Darwin" 141), and he ultimately survives, because, unlike Ahab, he is able to adapt, in good Darwinian fashion, to a new way of seeing the world: "[T]he evolving earth is ever unfinished, a vibrant rough draft. Ishmael concludes his classificatory efforts by deciding that true systems are ever uncompleted, that the world, like his book, is Darwinian—a work in progress, always open-ended" (145–146).

Like Ahab, Una experiences spiritual uncertainty, but she is more accepting of it. After attending a Universalist church, she feels a kind of peace.... To believe it was not necessary. Merely to know that some people had invented a more liberal view of Christianity loosed the bonds of the old dogma and its dependence on damnation. I had thought there to be only one Christian Way, straight, narrow, exclusive. And here was a road that went off at right angles, that could bend and double back, that was open to whatever sheep might wander onto it. (Naslund 338)

Although she does not reject religion or spirituality entirely, she rejects the necessity of adhering to one specific set of beliefs and rituals. Una finds the greatest harmony with Unitarians, because their religious skepticism matches her own. In contrast with Ahab's anger at controlling force he cannot see or understand, Una feels liberated by a lack of certainty. As Naslund puts it, "[Ahab] wants to strike through the mask to get at whatever is essentially genuine, authentic experience. My Una's questing has more to do with engaging the imagination. There is not that demand that there be something that you can get to when you strike through the mask. One can create a sense of oneness with nature" (202, this volume). Rather than being a source of frustration or a target for defiance, the unknown, for Una, is a source of inspiration.

Melville and Naslund link spiritual ambiguity to the indeterminacies of language. Melville scholarship and the text of *Moby-Dick* offer evidence of Melville's dual preoccupation with understanding language and understanding God. In a letter to a friend in 1849, Melville writes of Shakespeare's works, "Ah, he's full of sermons-on-the-mount, and gentle, aye, almost as Jesus.... I fancy that this moment Shakespeare in heaven ranks with Gabriel, Raphael, and Michael. And if another Messiah ever comes twill be in Shakespeare's person" (Wood 32). In this letter, the reader detects awe and envy. The great writer is first elevated to the level of angels and then to the level of God himself. Wood argues that language was for Melville what the white whale is for Ahab:

> *Moby-Dick* is the great dream of mastery over language.... Melville saw—and *Moby-Dick* is the enactment of this vision—that language helps to explain God and to conceal God in equal measure, and that these two functions annul each other. Thus language does not help us explain or describe God. Quite the contrary, it registers simply our inability to describe God; it holds our torment. Yet language is all there is, and thus Melville follows it as Ahab follows the whale, to the very end. (39)

As Wood states, *Moby-Dick* reveals the similarity between Ahab's struggle and Melville's. Ahab's desire to strike through the mask metaphorically describes a desire to unpack metaphor, to strip away vehicle from tenor, or to at least firmly fasten them together for one unchanging meaning, similar to the way Tashtego hammers a sky-hawk to the mast of the sinking *Pequod* at the end of *Moby-Dick*.

Naslund also unites literary themes with spiritual ones in *Ahab's Wife*. She echoes Melville in comparing great writers to gods: "Shakespeare, and all the other gods—Milton, Bunyan, Homer" (236). Later, in a sermon, Una's Unitarian minister speaks of God the Creator as an artist and of metaphor as "a mirror, a magic glass by which we see what we would otherwise not see" (342), suggesting at once that art is a channel through which we may understand God and that the earthly world is the metaphoric vehicle that helps us perceive the tenor that is God. Naslund explicitly connects the quest for spiritual meaning to the quest for literary meaning by borrowing Melville's metaphor: "[Words] are but a mask. Not the mask that conceals, not a mask that I would have you strike through as mere appearance, or worse, deceitful appearance. Words need not be that kind of mask, but a mask such as the ancient Greek actors wore, a mask that expresses rather than conceals the inner drama" (148). Here, she seems to talk back to Ahab, telling him not to rail against the uncertainty but to embrace it. At the same time, however, she herself pins Melville's meaning down by making explicit the connection between literary interpretation and religious understanding that remains implicit throughout *Moby-Dick*. Naslund's use of this metaphor strikes through the mask of Melville's, ironically disambiguating it when her character seems to welcome ambiguity.

In "Language and Meaning: An American Tradition," Philip Gura argued thirty years ago that Melville's understanding of language was influenced by the theories of a nineteenth-century Congregationalist minister, Horace Bushnell. In his 1849 "Preliminary Dissertation on the Nature of Language, as Related to Thought and Spirit," Bushnell suggests that language is in constant flux, an imprecise tool for expressing God's reality, but the best tool available to humankind. Because of the distance between human thought and God's truth, the only way to convey meaning is through indirection, which is ultimately unsatisfactory (Gura 14). As Gura points out, Bushnell's theories resemble those of twentieth-century literary theorist Jacques Derrida, in which every act of decoding is ultimately another encoding. Meaning or Truth is always deferred, always just out of reach. Perhaps the best example of this theory's influence on *Moby-Dick* is in chapter 42, "The Whiteness of the Whale." Gura suggests, "The whale . . . cannot be understood in one way or the other, but only as a symbol of the final inapproachability of any objective fact" (18). Near the end of the chapter, however, Melville suggests a more frightening, and more postmodern, interpretation. Rather than representing the inapproachability of any objective reality, perhaps the color white represents the absence of any objective reality: "[B]y its indefiniteness it shadows forth the heartless voids and immensities of the universe, and thus stabs us from behind with the thought of annihilation" (165). More terrifying than an evil force that controls our fates is the idea that nothing but chance and chaos control our fates. Neither heaven nor hell awaits us, only extinction. Under this interpretation, Melville pushes the theories of Bushnell to a darker place. Rather than explaining that God cannot be directly expressed or understood in human language, he suggests the possibility that God does not exist at all.

Gura also discusses the theories of another nineteenth-century philosopher, A.B. Johnson, arguing for his influence on Henry David Thoreau. According to Johnson, language is an unreliable system of signs that only leads humans away from God's reality: "'[T]he moment . . . information is clothed in language, either articulately or in thought,' man begins to wander 'from the substance of the universe to the shadow,—from the realities of creation to the artificial and conventional forms by which men communicate with each other'" (Gura 4). Again, Gura points out the similarities between Johnson's theories and those of twentieth-century theorists, such as Ferdinand de Saussure, who posited that human language (the signifier) has no essential connection to what it represents (the signified). Meaning is arbitrarily agreed upon by human convention, and each sign has meaning only within the system of other arbitrarily agreed-upon signs. Although Gura does not develop this connection, we can also see Johnson's influence on Melville, especially in Ahab's frustrated attempts to "strike through the mask" to understand the reality behind it. If we need not rely on signifiers, perhaps we can see the essence of that which we wish to signify. Metaphor, symbols, language itself is an obscuring shroud that interferes with our ability to perceive the essence of things. Throughout *Moby-Dick*, Ishmael's word choices reflect this inability of language to represent meaning, as he frequently invents words—such as "uninvitedly"—or refers to that which he attempts to describe as "nameless" (Smith, "The World and the Thing" 261–262), and Queequeg's tattoos offer further evidence of the inadequacy of signifiers. Although they are ancient holy markings, these tattoos have lost all meaning, because no living person knows how to read them. They are signifiers without a signified. To circumvent language, Johnson argues for perceiving the world through one's senses, but Melville suggests that the white whale himself, an element of nature, is but a signifier. Ahab's ultimate failure to strike through the mask and to confront that which it signifies suggests that signifieds—again, if they exist—remain forever out of human reach.

The resemblances of *Moby-Dick*'s meditations on the nature of language and reality to those of twentieth-century literary theorists suggest that Melville was a thinker ahead of his time and perhaps explains why this novel did not receive acclaim during the nineteenth century. The novel also exhibits characteristics more often connected with postmodern writing through self-referentiality and metatextuality. Like the contemporary writers in this study, Melville suggests the unreliability of language and the subjectivity of interpretation and then calls the reader's attention to the book as a composition in language, an object of interpretation. For example, in chapter 89, "Fast-Fish and Loose-Fish," Ishmael's explanation of whaling etiquette merges into a critique of property laws and labor exploitation. In the final sentences of the chapter, though, Melville extends his analogy even further: "And what are you, reader, but a Loose-Fish and a Fast-Fish, too?" (310). A reader is a fast-fish in that the words have been penned in the reader's absence. We can do nothing to change them; we are stuck. At the same time, a reader is a loose-fish in that the interpretations are the reader's own; we are free to take the author's words in directions of our own choosing, escaping the author's control. Metatextuality also appears in chapter 32, "Cetology," which categorizes various types of whales using the same terms with which printers classify the sizes of books: Folio, Octavo, and Duodecimo. Here, the author emphasizes that this novel about whaling is also a novel about writing. The chapter ends with Melville's most overt self-reference: "This whole book is but a draught—nay, but the draught of a draught" (125). By labeling his book a draft, he implicates his own words in his critique of language, inviting our skepticism. Further, he invites revision, suggesting that the version of reality he has constructed is incomplete and ongoing.

Proving herself to be a loose-fish and a fast-fish, Naslund accepts Melville's invitation by reconfiguring his novel in *Ahab's Wife*. And, like Melville, she repeatedly emphasizes the uncertainty of language and the variability of interpretation. As Ahab says to Una while she is still married to Kit Sparrow, her first husband, "Beware the treachery of words, Mrs. Sparrow. They mean one thing to one person and the opposite to another. . . . Words seem to be well-woven baskets ready to hold your meaning, but they betray you with rotted corners and splintered stays" (Naslund 297). Kit seems to echo Ahab's thoughts when, during a moment of paranoid delusion, he comments, "What do names matter? They're only code" (312). On the surface, Ahab is maddened by his quest for revenge against the white whale, and Kit is maddened by guilt and grief over his own actions and the death of his friend. Refusing to believe that others do not share his thoughts, Kit assumes they speak in devious code. Yet all words are merely code that humans use to name concepts, arbitrary signifiers loosely attached to the signified. Kit and Ahab struggle to make logical sense of the world that has caused their suffering rather than accept its ambiguities, and this futile struggle drives them mad.

Some, though, find the variability and instability of language and perception exhilarating. Early in the novel, Una recalls a childhood conversation about religion with her mother, who tells her, "Perhaps we each adopt or create our own truth" (22). If she is right, then objective truth does not exist. Individual origins may be unrecoverable, but each person must create his or her own stories, with linked beginnings, middles, and ends, to come to terms with his or her experience of the world. Unlike Una's fanatically religious father and unlike Captain Ahab, Una's mother is undisturbed by this uncertainty. And Una is her mother's daughter. Thinking about her past, she writes, "Perhaps the mind . . . is a glistening, pink cave. As a child that image was available to me, for my mother read aloud how Plato likened his mind to a cave. But his was dark instead of pink. With this writing I wish to enter that opalescence and inhabit the pearly chamber of memory" (19). Loosely borrowing from Plato's allegory of the cave, Una admits that the images available to her through memory may not be reality, but neither are they Plato's shadowy prison. The beautiful pink cave is a yonic symbol that feminizes creativity through imagination. Naslund makes a similar point in her most recent novel, *Adam and Eve* (2010): "[The novel] asks one to embrace the imagination, not as something false, a poor substitute for reality, but on the contrary, as the best we could do; we should glory in it" (209, this volume). *Ahab's Wife* explicitly links this subjectivity and variability of interpretation to literature as well. In a letter to Una, Susan, the runaway slave, writes of her continued efforts to learn reading and writing, using Ralph Waldo Emerson's "Nature," after Una has first taught her to write her name: "I've taken the sentences all apart so that they are just a string of words. I've learned them all. Now I can put them back together to make my own meanings instead of those of Mr. Emerson, the author" (Naslund 655). Although Susan uses the sentences to learn the basics of reading, the same image applies to more sophisticated reading/interpreting of literature. Naslund herself has carefully read *Moby-Dick*, has taken Melville's sentences apart, and has reassembled them to make meanings of her own. The author sums up her thoughts on language and meaning as follows: "What I get around to saying is (a) I love language, (b) I'm suspicious of words, and (c) nonetheless it [language] can go a long way. The [Greek] masks were very large so that audiences could see them in the back of the amphitheater. So they were masks that revealed, which is a paradoxical idea that tickles me" (210, this volume). Unlike Captain Ahab and his creator, Una shares her postmodern author's sense of play and freedom when faced with an uncertain system of meaning.

The structure of the narrative also conveys Una's greater comfort with unchartered and unstable mental terrain. Humans continuously form mental narratives of experiences in order to understand them, and usually these are structured linearly to emphasize cause and effect. According to Elinor Ochs and Lisa Capps, "[T]ellers seek the clarity and coherence that linearity offers. . . . Linear narratives channel events into a temporal flow, thereby making even 'terrible things' somewhat comprehensible" (44). Although we find out through other characters about events that happened before Ishmael begins his narration, the actual narrated events of *Moby-Dick* unfold linearly. *Ahab's Wife*, however, destabilizes that structure, beginning in the chronological middle, flashing back to the beginning, catching back up to the book's starting point, and continuing on to the end. Again, according to Ochs and Capps, "Nonlinear narration opens narration to multiple truths and perspectives and the realization that certain life experiences resist tidy, ready-at-hand interpretive frameworks" (45). Una as narrator says that she begins her narrative with the most difficult part, the death of her child and her mother, to have them over with. In doing so, she denies herself and her reader the softening effect of context and the explanatory solace of narrative cause and effect. These unexplained tragedies, once told, free her to tell the rest of her tale.

Like Melville, Naslund also embeds metatextual references that call attention to this work as a construction of language, rather than fostering an illusion that the narrative conveys objective reality. For example, as Melville does in *Moby-Dick*, she connects the journeys over land and sea within the novel to the literary journey the reader makes through reading the novel (147–148). Also, in a playful poke at Melville, she foils his famous opening line, "Call me Ishmael" (Melville 18), when her Nantucketers are unable to recall the *Pequod*'s sole survivor's name (578). This example confirms the warning of Naslund's Ahab that the corners and stays of words may rot and splinter, thus mislaying the words' intended meanings. More explicitly, the novel repeatedly emphasizes that Una is an author creating an autobiographical work, but one that is fictionalized. Una proclaims near the end of her tale that "adherence to fact is slavery" (610), which raises doubts about the life-story she has just disclosed. In an interview, Naslund also refers to the "tyranny of fact" that "makes an aesthetic shape difficult or even impossible" and argues that "memory and the imagination are very close together" (210, this volume). Several witnesses of the same event may recall the event quite differently, and a writer of autobiography may remember the past differently than others with whom that past was shared. As Kay Young and Jeffrey L. Saver point out, "Fidelity—stable recall and self-interpretation of the past is not a property of the human brain and mind. The varied subjectivity of literary autobiographic productions has its root in the inescapable subjectivity of the brain's narrative and memory system. This variability of memory, however, does not detract from the primacy of narrative recall in organizing human experience" (79). Narratives of past events are never wholly accurate, yet they are a necessary component for a whole sense of self in the present. Narratives of self are continuously revised, coloring past events with present knowledge. Postmodern reconfigurations foreground this process through their revisions of the cultural narratives embodied in the classic texts.

Cultural narratives are never wholly accurate yet are necessary components of our cultural identity. Contemporary reconfigurations offer revisions of past narratives that update them in light of present knowledge, forming a continuous coherent narrative that connects our present to our past. Just before the novel's epigraph, Una asks Ishmael if he minds that they write the same book: "Think of the Cathedral of Chartres," he replies. "Think of its two towers. They do not match at all. Built perhaps a century apart, or more; but without both spires, our Chartres would not be Chartres" (Naslund 663). Here, of course, Naslund intentionally echoes Melville's Ishmael, who links his book to the uncompleted Cathedral of Cologne: "For small erections may be finished by their first architect;

grand ones, true ones, ever leave the copestone to posterity" (Melville 125). Cultural narratives, like cultural landmarks, may evolve over time, always leaving completion "to posterity." Melville's *Moby-Dick* does not include the story of Ahab's wife, just as Chartres originally had only one spire. Now we have the added spire of Una's story, and our *Moby-Dick* is forever altered by it. When Una says that her work is also "but a draft of a draft" (Naslund 663), she extends Melville's earlier invitation to other stories and future writers. In fact, Naslund herself adds a small sequel in her next novel *Four Spirits* (2004), in which a descendant of Susan reveals this character's fate. The metatextual references in contemporary reconfigurations call upon us to see them as narrative, necessary tools but not Truth, subject to change and revision. Unlike Melville and Ahab, Naslund and her main character accept the indeterminacy of their tale, viewing it as liberation rather than torment.

Although *Ahab's Wife* does not engage in the ironic parody of *Moby-Dick* that is often associated with the term, in other respects the novel exemplifies what Linda Hutcheon labels historiographic metafiction, a work that "self-consciously explores the status and function of narrative as an ideological construct shaping history and forging identity rather than merely representing the past" (Nunning 216). To the American cultural narrative of which *Moby-Dick* is a key component, Naslund adds the wife's voice and amplifies the voice of the slave and the homosexual. Some skeptics might accuse her of rewriting history, but the revision calls attention to the way literary classics shape history and continue to shape our cultural identity in the present. As Naslund herself says in an interview with Janice Kennedy, contemporary reconfigurations "may be something of a millennium event. We want to look back at the past and see what we want to bring with us into the new era—and in what form we can bring it." The desire to connect to the past is a desire to understand our identity, and together the classic text and its revision link our contemporary identity to our cultural past. At the end of *Ahab's Wife*, Una the narrator says of herself and Ishmael, "Each day and forever, by the ticking of the mantel clock and by the dark wheeling of the cosmos, we have given time a home" (Naslund 666). Through Una, Naslund has given the time of *Moby-Dick* a home in the twenty-first century and has shaped American historical time to reflect the concerns of the present.

4 Revising Alcott, Revising America
Reconfigurations of *Little Women*

Louisa May Alcott's *Little Women*, first published in two volumes in 1868 and 1869, recounts the experiences of four middle-class girls (Meg, Jo, Beth, and Amy March) and their mother in New England during and after the Civil War. The novel was in many ways progressive for its time period, showing more independence for women than was conventional, and Alcott herself was a women's-rights activist. For me, and for many female readers of a certain age, Alcott's *Little Women* is the novel that first inspired our love of literature. My mother recommended it, and I checked it out of my elementary school library. Because it was much longer than any book I had previously read, I renewed it week after week, slowly digesting it under the patient and approving eyes of Mrs. Williams, the librarian. Many famous female writers have also remarked on the importance of *Little Women* to their girlhoods.[1] This chapter explores three female writers—Judith Rossner, Barbara Kingsolver, and Geraldine Brooks—who not only read and absorbed *Little Women* but also responded to it through novels that rewrite Alcott's work.

During the author's lifetime, reviewers praised *Little Women*, which sold well, but did not claim literary greatness for it (Englund 205). Written as a book for girls, this novel never received the critical respect afforded to works by Edgar Allan Poe, Nathaniel Hawthorne, and Herman Melville. *Little Women* has, however, remained popular since its publication and was celebrated by some of its early readers. Sheryl Englund notes that Ednah D. Cheney, the author of an 1889 biography of Alcott, "appeal[ed] to American readers' nationalist or regional pride in Alcott's depiction of New England domesticity . . . and conclude[ed] that Alcott deserves 'the lasting gratitude of her country' (289)" (210). In Cheney's words we see literary nationalism like that which fueled the writing and reception of Hawthorne, Melville, and, to a lesser extent, Poe. A great literature was, Cheney implies, a source of pride and a sign of a great nation. More recent readers also associate Alcott with American pride and ideals. Madelon Bedell, for example, in her preface to a 1980 biography of the Alcott family, writes, "I knew that Jo March was Louisa herself, a female Horatio Alger who rescued her family from poverty with the writing of the legend in *Little*

Women" (xii). Bedell compares Alcott and her character Jo to the author of iconic nineteenth-century "rags to riches" stories, such as *Ragged Dick* (1868), which, although not respected for their artistic merit, became the popular emblem of the American Dream. In the latter half of the twentieth century, feminist scholars began to examine *Little Women* and its impact on American culture, and the novel has gradually achieved some acceptance as an American literary classic, making its way into literature classrooms and literary studies.

In her examination of a 1994 film adaptation of *Little Women*, Englund points out one example of popular culture's association of Alcott with canonical American literature. The film merges details of Louisa May Alcott's life with those of her character Jo, a conflation fostered by the somewhat autobiographical nature of the characters. Like the March family, the Alcott family consisted of a mother, a father, and four daughters, the second of whom, like Jo, was a writer, and the third of whom, Elizabeth, died young from the effects of scarlet fever, as does Beth March. The conflation of author and character was further fostered by the early marketing strategies that encouraged the public to think of Jo as Alcott (Englund 200). Near the film's end, Jo, played by Winona Ryder, unwraps a copy of her newly published book, and the camera zooms in on its title page. The title, of course, is *Little Women*, written by Jo March rather than by Louisa May Alcott. In addition to substituting the character's name for the author's, the film's close-up also reveals a substitution for the original publisher. Alcott's novel was first published by the Roberts Brothers firm, but the title page we see in the film lists as publisher the prestigious James T. Fields, "one of mid-nineteenth-century Boston's most eminent literary figures" (199). Englund sees this substitution as "an implicit attempt to link Louisa May Alcott to Fields' list of elite canonical authors, which included such figures as Hawthorne, Emerson, and Thoreau," thereby "rais[ing] Alcott's cultural capital" (199–200). Whether intentional or not, the substitution suggests *Little Women*'s rising status in American literary history.

As are the stories of Poe and the novels of Hawthorne and Melville, this novel of Alcott's that inspired contemporary reconfigurations is also inspired by an earlier text. Although her primary influence, Puritan John Bunyan's *Pilgrim's Progress*, is a seventeenth-century British text, it nevertheless helps Alcott tap into the American ethos. Alcott draws her epigraph from Bunyan's work, and as the novel opens, the four March girls are each given a copy of it as a Christmas gift. Some of Alcott's chapter titles—such as "Playing Pilgrims," "Amy's Valley of Humiliation," and "Meg Goes to Vanity Fair"—indicate parallels between the two texts, as the girls embark on their own spiritual pilgrimage to overcome their flaws. As Anne Lundin points out, the pilgrimage motif was popular in nineteenth-century literature, and Alcott's portrayal of it influenced other writers of her time: "As the genesis of the American family story, as a secular parallel to the sacred pilgrimage, *Little Women* frames the field of value and action from which children's literature sprang in late-nineteenth-century America." Part of the reason Alcott's novel proved so influential to the American family story was that the holy pilgrimage motif taps into early conceptions of American identity. Calling for a renewed connection to American ideological origins in his book *Who Are We? The Challenges to America's National Identity*, American political scientist Samuel P. Huntington writes, "In the seventeenth and eighteenth centuries, Americans defined their mission in the New World in biblical terms. They were a 'chosen people,' on an 'errand in the wilderness,' creating 'the new Israel' or the 'new Jerusalem' in what was clearly the 'promised land'" (64). Huntington goes on to say, "[The] Puritan legacy became the American essence" (65). If Huntington is correct, his theories help explain why Bunyan's *Pilgrim's Progress*, with its own Puritan holy pilgrim, was so popular in nineteenth-century America[2] and why invoking this text in *Little Women* helps Alcott tap into that "American essence."

According to Nancy Armstrong in *Desire and Domestic Fiction*, eighteenth- and nineteenth-century novels, such as *Little Women*, "helped to formulate the ordered space we now recognize as the household, made that space totally functional, and used it as the context for representing normal behavior" (23–24). So, Alcott invokes an existing American identity and further helps shape that identity through her portrayal of her mostly female American family. The fictional *Little Women*, based on Alcott's childhood family life, helps shape American readers' understanding of what a normal home life containing normal women should look like. Americans associated this image of the ideal family, in turn, with the identity of the nation. As Gillian Avery notes, "For Americans, the household community was a microcosm of the ideal republic they saw themselves to have created; all its members were independent and working towards the same purpose, for the good of the whole" (44). We can see these values portrayed in *Little Women* as Marmee and her daughters each contribute their share to charitable work and to the support of the family. Although she bases her ideal March family on her own, however, Alcott omits many of the real struggles that would have made her fictional family seem less than ideal. In an essay about Bronson Alcott, written for the *New Yorker*, Brooks notes that in 1844, Abigail Alcott threatened to take her children and leave Bronson over his failed experiment with a utopian community called Fruitlands. Toward his daughter Louisa, Bronson was often critical and encouraged her when young to think of herself as a misfit (Trites 10). Far from the ideal patriarch, Bronson failed to earn enough to support his family, leaving Louisa and other relatives with that financial responsibility. According to Roberta Seelinger Trites, from 1848 to 1852, when Alcott was between the ages of sixteen and twenty, she "worked as a teacher, a governess, a tutor, and a servant" to help support her family (10), and she continued supporting her family after she began making a comfortable living by writing. The Marches were so influential in part because readers connected them with

Alcott's real family, but, as we can see, this fictional family creates a false and unrealistic ideal.

The desire to reconfigure *Little Women* as a contemporary novel may have been inspired in part by Rossner's, Kingsolver's, and Brooks's early love of this novel, a type of homage to a book that introduced them to the world of literature. Yet by rewriting this American classic, the authors also attempt to revise the narrative of American identity in a way that makes it more palatable to their understanding of themselves and the present. Liedeke Plate points out that such feminist revision of a classic text is a paradoxical act: "[W]omen's rewriting [is] a form of cultural recall that is directed at remembering differently, challenging the canon, yet re-inscribing it" (132). The revision keeps the canonical work alive but changes our reading of it. Such revision underscores the interpretive role of the writer and the reader in all narrative. To further emphasize this interpretive role, Rossner, Kingsolver, and Brooks, like the contemporary writers that this study has examined so far, incorporate reading and writing functions into their narratives to suggest that the act of reinterpretation and revision is an inevitable, unending, always provisional part of experience.

In her 1990 novel *His Little Women*, Rossner recounts the life of a California movie producer, Sam Pearlstein, and his four daughters, the products of three marriages, from the 1950s to the late 1980s. The four daughters provide the most obvious parallel to Alcott's novel. The eldest, none-too-subtly named Louisa Abrams, writes autobiographically inspired fiction, as did Alcott. Rossner's character Nell, the second daughter, whose name echoes the monosyllabic *Jo*, narrates the tale, although by profession she is an attorney who only dabbles in writing. Sonny, the third daughter, dies tragically young, as does Alcott's Beth, and Liane, the youngest daughter in Rossner's narrative, is also the most selfish and beautiful, like Alcott's golden-curled Amy March. Although acknowledging the canonical status of *Little Women* through her reconfiguration, Rossner also questions some of the earlier novel's most basic assumptions. Through the differences between Rossner's fictional family and Alcott's, we see Rossner's challenge to family and gender norms portrayed by Alcott. And by using plot details to underscore the uncertain and shifting divide between truth and fiction, Rossner suggests that the concept of the perfect nuclear family as a cornerstone of American society is itself a fiction, although even its fictional portrayals have sometimes had the power to shape reality.

In *His Little Women*, Rossner encourages readers' continued scrutiny of the line between truth and fiction to determine just where it lies. The author's maiden name, Perelman, closely resembles the name *Pearlstein* that she gives to the charming but fickle father figure in the novel, and Rossner's father was reportedly an alcoholic (Miller), like Pearlstein. Like Pearlstein, Rossner grew up in New York and married three times, and, of course, like her characters Louisa and Nell, Rossner is a writer. Louisa's autobiographical fiction, in fact, leads to a libel suit that drives the novel's plot. Not only does the novel obscure the line between fictional events and Rossner's biography, but it also blurs the distinction between the character's fiction and the character's "real" life. In her narration of the libel trial, Nell quotes "unaltered (though not uncut)" court transcripts (292) and offers "an outline of Campbell's [the plaintiff's] life as pieced together from information we obtained" during the trial (270), as if these are real historical events with nonfictional documenting evidence. What is truth and what is fiction, the reader begins to wonder? By asking how much lived experiences influence the fiction writer's creations, Rossner also raises the obverse question: How much does the storytelling impulse influence most peoples' understanding of their lived experiences? Nell articulates the question in this way: "My father said once that when Louisa discussed some familiar incident or argument he could recognize the words or deed, but they'd become part of a story that was foreign to him. I have had the same experience, and I am curious to know whether this trick of altering reality is unique to the storyteller or whether we are all of us constantly filling in between reality's dots to make a story no one else sees in quite the same way" (278). Like the other writers of reconfigurations in this study, Rossner implies that, to some extent, we all experience life as a story. People tell themselves stories to process the past and to connect the past to the present. Such narratives "provide a sense of meaning or order to the world or access to a supramundane world" (Boyd, "Evolutionary Theories" 162).

Writers broaden and lengthen this sense of meaning and order by connecting their contemporary stories to past stories in the form of classic literature. To forge these connections, though, necessitates revision. One aspect of *Little Women* that Rossner pointedly revises is the image of the wholesome and supportive nuclear family. Rossner could probably not have found within the United States a setting that differs more from the one Alcott chooses. Instead of austere, moral nineteenth-century New England, Rossner chooses twentieth-century California's movie culture, with its stereotypical excess and materialism. As Nell describes it, "[M]ovie people surrendered to the domination of sex much earlier than the population at large, its pleasures and intensities being even more welcome in a place where people need constantly to convince themselves that they're real" (122). As this quotation reveals, even in her setting, Rossner evokes the blurred boundary between truth and fiction. Furthermore, in contrast to the everpresent and ever-inspiring angel in the house, Marmee March, in *His Little Women* we have a series of ineffectual mothers who remain mostly behind closed doors in alcoholic stupors. In contrast to Mr. March, whose physical absence is balanced by his spiritual presence and who reassuringly returns before the novel's close, we have Pearlstein, who, though physically present for most of the novel, is spiritually disconnected from others and who creates in his daughters the disconcerting sense that he is always on the verge of leaving. In contrast to the ideal March marriage, the devoted and enduring foundation on which the children develop, almost every marriage in *His Little Women*, most notably Louisa's, Nell's, and Pearlstein's three, end in divorce. Rather than being physically and spiritually nurtured into strong, moral adulthood, Rossner's children are physically and spiritually abandoned by their parents. Louisa even abandons her five-year-old son, just as she had been abandoned at five by her own father.

One child in particular, Sonny, suffers tragic effects due to her emotional abandonment. Her nineteenth-century counterpart, Beth March, dies from the long-term complications of scarlet fever, contracted while caring for sick neighbors. As death approaches, she is more beloved by her family and more angelic. By contrast, Sonny, feeling emotionally isolated from her parents, finds a substitute in Estella, the family's Mexican maid, the only person who can comfort or discipline Sonny as she grows up. Later, as a teenager, Sonny also finds a compelling emotional resonance in a novel she discovers. The novel, titled *A Servant's Diary*, details an erotic "orgie a trois" among a wealthy married couple and their servant, Elena (149). Estella finds a well-thumbed copy of the book in Sonny's room, is "intrigued by the title and the author's Spanish name" (218), and reads the book. *A Servant's Diary*, it turns out, was written by Louisa under a pseudonym, and Estella, "being smarter than Sonny . . . was certain which couple and maid they were supposed to be about" (218–219). Denying any truth to the pornographic scenarios in the novel, Estella feels insulted and betrayed by the entire family. She leaves them to return to Mexico without even saying good-bye to Sonny. Trained throughout the novel to question the separation between fiction and reality, the reader wonders how much of the book is based on truth and how much, as Estella contends, is based on lies.

Distraught and drug-addled over this latest abandonment, Sonny finally commits suicide, "driving her car off a mountain road less than a mile from the village where Estella lived" (266). Sonny's isolation from family, the tawdriness of the circumstances, and her death by her own hand form a stark contrast to the death of Beth, who, "like a tired but trustful child, clung to the hands that had led her all her life, as Father and Mother guided her tenderly through the Valley of the Shadow, and gave her up to God" (Alcott 382). Through the Pearlstein family as counterpart to the Marches, Rossner suggests that the image of the idealized nuclear unit that helped shape society's conception of a normal family is today more of a fiction than a reality. Furthermore, the novel's unremitting interrogation of the boundary between fiction and reality and its association with Alcott's nineteenth-century classic suggests that such a family always was as much a product of fantasy as it was a product of reality.

Another aspect of *Little Women* that Rossner revises is the novel's portrayal of gender roles. Although this nineteenth-century novel places an unconventionally high value on female education and allows its female characters, especially Jo, more than the usual self-direction, Rossner's reconfiguration suggests that she believes the female gender roles in Alcott's novel are oppressive. The title of Rossner's book, of course, echoes the title of Alcott's, and Rossner uses a quotation from *Little Women* as epigraph that reveals the source of both titles: " . . . I know they will remember all I said to them, that they will be loving children to you, will do their duty faithfully, fight their bosom enemies bravely, and conquer them so beautifully that when I come back to them I may be fonder and prouder than ever of my little women." As Mr. March reveals in this letter home to his wife and daughters, despite his temporary absence, these little women are his, and their independence is restricted by memories of his words and their faithful duty to his authority. As Jo says, "I'll try and be what he loves to call me, a 'little woman,' and not be rough and wild, and do my duty here instead of wanting to be somewhere else" (14). According to Jane Goldstein, Mr. March's "views shape the daily choices of his family's pursuits at home through his letters and the common goals he has discussed previously with his wife. Marmee actively upholds the principles she shares with her absent husband" (54). In addition to reiterating Mr. March's patriarchal proprietorship in her title, Rossner shows that gender roles have not changed so much in one hundred years. Despite his neglect or outright abandonment, all four of Pearlstein's daughters are dependent on him financially and emotionally. Nell and Louisa repeatedly rely on him to get them jobs, and his younger daughters live in his house, partaking of all the luxuries available to a successful California movie producer. Nell and Louisa also shape their lives by childhood memories of his words and by efforts to secure his faithfulness and love, and Sonny and Liane destroy themselves, or nearly so, by acting out their anger at being raised by servants and money rather than emotionally present parents.

Rossner's revision of *Little Women* challenges Alcott's portrayal of female gender roles and of the nuclear family. By updating some plot elements and characters, Rossner does not suggest that nineteenth-century perceptions of gender and family are bad and twentieth-century perceptions are good, but rather that in all times, such perceptions are often based on illusions. By pointing out these illusions, she suggests the necessity of continued revision in the stories we tell ourselves and in the society those stories intend to reflect.

Kingsolver also uses literary revision as a vehicle to encourage cultural revision. Through the first-person narratives of a mother and four daughters taken to Zaire by their missionary husband and father, Kingsolver's 1998 novel *The Poisonwood Bible* reconfigures Alcott's novel. Even though she does not wholly accept the ideals portrayed in *Little Women*, her comments about the earlier book indicate her admiration for it. Before writing *The Poisonwood Bible*, Kingsolver writes in a 1995 essay, "I, personally, am Jo March, and if her author Louisa May Alcott had a whole new life to live for the sole pursuit of talking me out of it, she could not" (Alberghene and Clark xvii). Later, after the publication of *The Poisonwood Bible*, Kingsolver says about her novel, "Certainly I considered that other famous family of 'little women' as I was writing. . . . It was one of the most beloved books of my childhood" ("F.A.Q.").[3] Kristin Jacobson comments on some of the "compelling connections" between *Little Women* and *The Poisonwood Bible*:

> The Price family in *The Poisonwood Bible* loosely but distinctly parallels the March family in *Little Women*. Both stories have minister fathers and families comprised of four girls. The Price girls' character flaws especially coincide with the March daughters' failings that set *Little Women*'s narrative in motion. Rachel Price mirrors her precursor Meg March, who thinks too much of her looks and hates to work. Both Leah Price and Jo March are tomboys who long to be somewhere else, and Adah Price and Amy March are similarly selfish, "defective" girls—Amy endures ridicule due to her nose, and Adah's noticeable birth defect sets her apart physically and emotionally. Devoid of moral or physical defects, the family favorites Ruth May Price and Beth March die tragically young. (105)

Jacobson also points out the two novels' similar emphasis on the making of home and family, although the setting, the home, the family, and the authors' attitudes toward them differ greatly.

Reconfiguring *Little Women*, a novel that has become associated with the ideal American family and the ideal American woman, helps Kingsolver achieve her "primary goal," which "is not to represent Africa," despite the fact that most of the novel is set there, "but to revise America's representation of itself" (Koza 288). One of the items that the Price family carries in their American baggage to the Belgian Congo is a picture of the current American president, Dwight D. Eisenhower. Kingsolver uses this detail to emphasize that even though they are far from home, they are still American. Earlier in this study, I suggest that reconfigurations that maintain the historical time period of the classic work emphasize an examination of the past through the lens of the present, and reconfigurations set in the author's current time period emphasize an examination of the present through the lens of the past. Yet the first half of *The Poisonwood Bible* is set in an intermediate past, 1959 to 1960, as the Congo struggles for and wins its independence from Belgium, and readers are encouraged to examine this temporal setting from the perspectives of past and present. We view the Price family's intrusion into Africa in light of what we later learned about the U.S. involvement there and from the perspective of the less-paranoid, post–Cold War world, and we also see in their failing attempts at maintaining a home and family a distorted image of the nineteenth-century ideal influenced by Alcott's novel. As Kingsolver recounts through the voices of the Price women, after the Congo's independence in 1960, the U.S., fearing communist influence over the new government, supported the overthrow and murder of its first elected leader, Patrice Lumumba. Kimberly Koza asserts, "Kingsolver seeks not only to illuminate a dark corner of American history but also to encourage her American readers to see themselves in relation to that history" (288). The Price family's resonances with the March family help her do this as well as interrogate the model of the American family and American female identity. Although *Little Women* grants the American woman more autonomy in some areas than many other novels of the time period, it also celebrates American power structures that had held women voiceless for so long, such as Christianity, capitalism, white privilege, and patriarchy. Kingsolver's reconfiguration of *Little Women* emphasizes that these power structures are oppressive, interwoven forces embedded in American identity.

Unlike the Price women, Alcott's March women learn that self-sacrifice is a virtue. The novel's second chapter features the four daughters donating their Christmas breakfast to a needy family, and Beth, the most virtuous March girl, seems almost angelic in the death she peacefully faces after a long invalidism. At first, the Price girls also sacrifice much to obey their missionary father's every command, leaving home, friends, school, and modern conveniences behind to travel with him to his post in the Congo. Because the novel reveals their thoughts through first-person narrative, however, we know that they are often unhappy about such sacrifices. Their ultimate sacrifice comes when the youngest Price daughter, Ruth May, is killed by a deadly green mamba snake after the father has refused the villagers' and his church superiors' instructions to leave the Congo. Her death coincides with the murder of Lumumba, and she becomes a symbolic victim of the patriarchal white structure embodied by the missionary father, who believes he has a God-given mandate to remain despite blatant evidence to the contrary. Rather than praise her example, however, the other Price women rebel, just as Africans are rebelling against Belgian control. Kingsolver overtly links the rebellion of the African nation with the rebellion of the white women.

One of the ways that Kingsolver displays their rebellion and conveys her social critique is by highlighting language's multiplicities of meaning and the fallibility of communication. The inherent uncertainty of meaning that appears in other reconfigurations discussed in this study appears in *The Poisonwood Bible* as a problem with translation. Discussing a familiar Bible passage, Brother Fowles, a former missionary, states, "Was it a *camel* that could pass through the eye of a needle more easily than a rich man? Or a coarse piece of yarn? The Hebrew words are the same, but which one did they mean?" (248, emphasis in original). The answer, of course, is uncertain, and the one that has been accepted is the less obvious of the two choices. Words, Kingsolver suggests, often go astray of their intended meanings. While writing this novel, Kingsolver spent much time "perusing a huge old two-volume Kikongo-French dictionary, compiled early in the century (by a missionary, of course). Slowly I began to grasp the music and subtlety of this amazing African language, with its infinite capacity for being misunderstood and mistranslated" ("F.A.Q."). This language gap fuels the tensions between the missionary, Price, and his flock. In the words of daughter Leah, "Everything you're sure is right can be wrong in another place. Especially *here*" (505, emphasis in original). It takes the daughters nearly thirty years to gain such understanding of the variability of interpretation—that Truth for a white missionary from the U.S. is not necessarily the same as Truth for a black villager from the Congo—and it is something that apparently never crosses their father's mind. Adah notes that the language barrier often causes him to utter gibberish to his flock: "*Bangala* means something precious and dear. But the way he pronounces it, it means the poisonwood tree. Praise the Lord hallelujah, my friends! for Jesus will make you itch like nobody's business" (276). As Pamela H. Demory points out, "Price is completely unaware of his mistake, so while he believes he is a master of the language—the very Word of God—the text reveals him to be a fool, preaching what his daughter takes to calling behind his back 'the gospel of poisonwood.'" Not only are his sermons confusing and often irrelevant to the lives of his flock, but at times they are also dangerous, as when he insists on baptizing the village children in the same river in which a child, before his arrival, had been attacked and killed by a crocodile.

The villagers of Kilanga, where he preaches, appropriate and revise Price's sermons as a way to resist his control, emphasizing the connection between language and power and the ability to shift language in order to shift power. As the mother, Orleanna Price, puts it, "Africa swallowed the conqueror's music and sang a new song of her own" (*Poisonwood* 385). At one point, having heard from white men that "Jesus and elections" are both "good," the village chief interrupts Price's sermon to hold an "election on whether or not to accept Jesus Christ as the personal Savior of Kilanga" (333). Price's insistence that such an election is blasphemy appears to contradict what the villagers have already been told about Christianity and democracy, so, despite the minister's protests, they vote and reject Jesus. Adah eventually understands that in the Congolese language and worldview, the change of words means the change of reality: "It is a dangerous thing, I now understand, to make mistakes with *nommo* in the Congo. If you assign the wrong names to things, you could make a chicken speak like a man. Make a machete rise up and dance" (213). The lesson that readers learn is that words, individually or in a novel like *Little Women*, can shape identity, but people can also shape words into new meanings through appropriation and revision.

In *Little Women*, the straightforward linear narrative told from a third-person omniscient point of view gives readers the reassuring illusion of an orderly existence. If the book's young female readers, like the March pilgrims, stay on their paths and continue striving to overcome their flaws with the help of God, Marmee, and Father, then they, too, will eventually reach the Celestial City. Unlike Alcott, Kingsolver disrupts the reader's desire for stability by allowing each of the Price women to tell her own first-person tale of occupation and rebellion, tales that differ from, and even contradict, those of the others. Susan Strehle observes that, through the collection of brief first-person narratives, the Price women reject the religious word of the authoritarian father "to embrace words—plural, secular, nuanced, spoken, interpreted exchanged, and affirmed" (426). And Kingsolver herself notes the connection between this pluralism and political control: "This novel is asking, basically, 'What did we do to Africa, and how do we feel about it?' It's a huge question. I'd be insulting my readers to offer only one answer. There are a hundred different answers along a continuum" ("F.A.Q."). Repeatedly, Kingsolver shows that the meaning of an action depends on the interpretation of the observer, and the action of the novel reveals that the interpretations that are most often heard are those of the white men in power. Also connecting the control of language to power, Demory observes that the women in the family are "regularly silenced by [Nathan] Price. In giving them a voice, Kingsolver comments on the political, social, and family constraints that keep them from speaking." Turning the patriarchal tables, Kingsolver denies a narrative voice only to the head of the Price family.

The novel abounds with conflicting interpretations of actions. According to daughter Leah, for example, her father's holy mission is to "tell the stories of Jesus, and God's love. Bring [the Kilanga village] all to the Lord" (*Poisonwood* 286), and for most of her childhood in the Congo, she believes his failures are due to the faults of others. Her more ironic and skeptical twin sister Adah, however, develops the palindrome "Amen enema" to describe their father's forceful ministry. In another example, Leah tells us that her mother frequently sends her away from Price's side, because she resents Leah's imposition on his time and privacy. We learn in a later section by Orleanna that she sends Leah away so the worshipful daughter will not perceive her father's indifference to her (98). The novel's multiple voices—demonstrating the lack of authoritative Truth—make the reader suspect all narratives, even those master narratives of Christianity, capitalism, whiteness, and patriarchy.

The Poisonwood Bible reveals the oppressiveness of these master narratives for the natives and the pilgrims: Capitalism originally motivated whites to exploit the Congo, white superiority made them feel they had the right to do so, and Christianity helped them justify their actions to themselves. But the Price women, as the Kilanga villagers had already done, eventually rebel against Price's control, fleeing the village and the social constructs Price represents, to continue their journey on their own. Whereas *Little Women* ends with the surviving March women all comfortably married, Kingsolver's *The Poisonwood Bible* ends with the surviving Price women all happily independent. Alcott, however, did not plan to marry off all her characters. In a letter, she comments that Jo should have remained a "literary spinster," but "publishers are very perverse & won't let authors have their way so my little women must grow up and be married off in a very stupid style" (qtd. in Maibor 108). Due to societal pressures, Jo's author compels her to marry, in turn reinforcing a social structure that expects marriage and subservience of all women. Single or unconventionally married, each of Price's three remaining daughters eventually assails elements of the oppressive system and adjusts them to her own needs.

Rachel, the oldest Price daughter, appropriates and revises the capitalism that drives the marriage plot of *Little Women*. Despite the fact that the women can and do support themselves—Marmee, Meg, and Jo work outside the home during the father's absence—the driving force of Alcott's narrative supports the idea that women themselves are commodities of exchange in a capitalist society. Although Marmee does not want her daughters to marry solely for money, she acknowledges that money is necessary in a marriage and that the source of that money is male: "Money is a good and useful thing . . . and I hope my girls will never feel the need of it too bitterly, nor be tempted by too much. I should like to know that John was firmly established in some good business which gave him an income large enough to keep free from debt and make Meg comfortable" (188). At the novel's end, all the daughters marry men whose incomes will support them comfortably, and Amy, the most acquisitive daughter, is rewarded with the "best" marriage, to the wealthy Laurie Laurence, emphasizing that to be a success in a capitalist society, to accumulate material goods and wealth, a woman needs a wealthy husband.

Rather than relying on a man to provide for her, at *The Poisonwood Bible*'s end Rachel owns and manages the Equatorial Hotel in South Africa with a staff of female employees: "I have created my own domain. I call the shots. . . . I'm making a killing" (511–512). Her international visitors, however, sometimes mistake the nature of the establishment: "They look at me stretched by the pool with all the keys on a chain around my neck, and one look at my pretty young cooks and chambermaids on their afternoon break. . . . And guess what: they'll take me for a madam of a whorehouse!" (515). The implication is that women, particularly economically successful ones, need husbands to make them respectable, but Rachel assures them that her sexuality, like her money, is her own. As Jacobson points out, however, although she achieves financial and emotional independence, Rachel is still constrained by notions of white privilege (115): "The restaurant is for paying guests only, which is, needless to say, whites, since the Africans around here wouldn't earn enough in a month to buy one of my *prix-fixe* dinners. . . . So I built them that shelter, so they wouldn't be tempted to come in and hang about idly in the main bar" (461–462). She appears comfortable with the social and economic separation of the races as long as she belongs to the group on top.

The capitalist system depends to a large extent on exploiting others. Both in Kingsolver's 1950s and 1960s Congo and in Alcott's nineteenth-century U.S., the exploited Other was usually black. Although *Little Women* is set during the Civil War and the father serves with the Union Army, the novel barely mentions slavery or African Americans, highlighting the privileged status of the March family in that they do not have to think about race on a daily basis.[4] For the most part, whiteness is a given, and the only people who are visible in the Marches' world, the only people the readers could imagine finding in such a world, are white. This silence manifests the reality of white privilege in the time period. By setting *The Poisonwood Bible* in Africa where the whites are a minority, however, Kingsolver ensures that her characters must at least acknowledge their racial privileges. As a child, Kingsolver herself spent two years in the Congo with her family: "I came home with an acutely heightened sense of race, of ethnicity. I got to live in a place where people thought I was noticeable and probably hideous because of the color of my skin" (Kanner). Daughter Leah feels a similar conspicuousness, and she actively attempts to erase it along with her racial privilege. After a few years in the Congo, Leah falls in love with and marries an African, her father's former translator, Anatole. During Anatole's sentence as a political prisoner, Leah remains in Africa awaiting his return. Alone in her African community, she feels that her neighbors label her as a foreign exploiter, although their treatment of her is "deferential and reserved" (*Poisonwood* 472). She wishes "to leave [her] house one day unmarked by whiteness" (504), and she sometimes feels that her "skin glows like a bare bulb" (472). Unlike her sister Rachel, Leah wishes to live in Africa like an African, and she rejects the privileges that her white skin might afford her.

Another honored institution in *Little Women* that *The Poisonwood Bible* undermines is Christianity. In her essay "Can a Woman Be an Individual? The Limits of Puritan Tradition in the Early Republic," Linda K. Kerber notes that the Puritan church, so much a part of the early republic, so much the backdrop of *Little Women*, and so much associated with American identity, according to such literary critics as Sacvan Bercovitch and such political scientists as Huntington, preached repression and sacrifice. By the late eighteenth and nineteenth centuries, church membership was predominantly female, the men having rejected the restraints of the church (Kerber 171). Puritan Christianity, however, still corresponded with and helped reinforce the roles expected of women in nineteenth-century America. *Little Women* celebrates Christian virtue, but from a feminist standpoint the reader may see its oppressiveness. One of the most important lessons that the outspoken Jo learns is to control her tongue in the name of Christian goodness. Regarding her daughter's temper, Marmee advises Jo to "watch and pray" (Alcott 75), and she tells her, "My child, the troubles and temptations of your life are beginning and may be many, but you can overcome and outlive them all if you learn to feel the strength and tenderness of your Heavenly Father as you do of your earthly one" (76). Although Alcott intends the scene as a valuable moral lesson for her character and her reader, the feminist reader may see that Jo has been effectively silenced in the name of her heavenly and earthly father. As Maria Soledad Rodriguez argues, "[Marmee] becomes the spokesperson for the patriarchy, for the father who is present through her when she enforces his domestic ideal of little womanhood, taking special pains to help Jo suppress her personality as she had done with her own" (18). In addition to revealing Christianity's role in gender oppression, nineteenth-century women's literature also sometimes overtly links Christianity with an imperialist mission. For example, in *The American Woman's Home*, Catherine Beecher and Harriet Beecher Stowe look forward to a time when "these prosperous and Christian communities would go forth and shine as 'lights of the world' in all the now darkened nations" (Kaplan 589). The word choices of "light" and "dark" insinuate a racial domination, and the connection of prosperity and Christianity hint at capitalist exploitation in the name of Christ.

In *The Poisonwood Bible*, Kingsolver explicitly links religion with oppressive silence and economic exploitation. Strehle notes, "Kingsolver takes care to root Nathan's religion in American Puritanism" (417), emphasizing his connection to American origins and the book's association with *Little Women*. Price's daughter Leah, once his most loyal follower, begins to bridle against her father's authority after nearly a year in Africa, and she also begins to question his religion: "But where is the place for girls in that Kingdom? The rules don't quite apply to us, nor protect us either. What do a girl's bravery and righteousness count for, unless she is also *pretty*?" (*Poisonwood* 244, emphasis in original). Linked to the capitalist commodification of women,[5] Christianity in practice requires girls to be pretty as well as righteous so they may marry brave and righteous men who will protect them on earth and guide them to the kingdom of heaven. Through the lens of five-year-old Ruth May's thoughts, Kingsolver also links Christianity to white supremacy. In response to a Belgian doctor's summary of white offenses against the native population, Ruth May thinks, "I was glad nobody wanted to cut off *my* hands. Because Jesus made me white, I reckon they wouldn't" (121, emphasis in original). Because she is white, Ruth May is exempt from such mutilations, imposed by whites as punishment for Africans' perceived transgressions, and her childish wisdom implicates Christianity in facilitating a hierarchy that values one race above another.

Orleanna shows the oppressive imbrications of these master narratives more explicitly. As Trites points out, Alcott uses adolescent girls as the protagonists for her novel, because adolescence is a time of change and best demonstrates the moral growth she wants her characters to experience (34). Having reached adulthood, Marmee, although she admits to having conquered flaws as a girl, now embodies moral perfection and resides as the angel of the March house. Orleanna, however, changes, as do her children. Describing her first encounter with Africa as a missionary's wife, she states, "We aimed for no more than to have dominion over every creature that moved upon the earth. And so it came to pass that we stepped down there on a place we believed unformed, where only darkness moved on the face of the waters" (*Poisonwood* 10). The biblical language implicates their Christian mission, which encourages the missionaries naively to believe they have divine right to mold Africa in their own image. Reflecting on the experience more than thirty years later, however, she not only recognizes the white privilege that combined with Christianity and capitalism to rationalize Africa's exploitation but also recognizes her own guilt in that exploitation: "You'll say I walked across Africa with my wrists unshackled, and now I am one more soul walking free in a white skin, wearing some thread of the stolen goods: cotton or diamonds, freedom at the very least, prosperity. Some of us know how we came by our fortune, and some of us don't, but we wear it all the same" (9). Unlike Alcott, Kingsolver does not confine the moral lessons learned to childhood. Age and status do not exempt her characters or, by implication, her readers from the need for moral growth.

Alcott's *Little Women* gives a new voice to female identity, and Kingsolver reconfigures that novel to envision a new American voice that is female. She uses women in the text to link exploitation in Africa to exploitation at home. The same white, Christian, capitalist patriarchy that inspires and excuses African exploitation also oppresses the American Price women. Kingsolver has these women, like the Africans, recognize and rebel against this oppression. In refusing to perpetuate this exploitation, Kingsolver intends for the Price women to set an example for other Americans to follow.

Brooks, a native of Australia who now has dual American-Australian citizenship, also rewrites Alcott's *Little Women* in her 2005 novel, *March*. Brooks, however, focuses on Mr. March, the absent center of Alcott's novel. In *Little Women*, we learn that Mr. March is "far away, where the fighting was" (Alcott 3). Marmee and the girls receive occasional letters from him, and, more than halfway through the novel, Marmee is summoned to Washington, D.C., to care for him while he is gravely ill. Although he returns to the family home before the novel's close, the reader feels his presence little more than before, as he is usually relegated to his study and his private thoughts. The first two-thirds of *March* records Mr. March's first-person thoughts and experiences, punctuated by his letters home, as he serves first as army chaplain and then as a teacher to the "contraband of war," slaves freed by the Union Army and working for wages at an experimental plantation. The final third of the novel, up until its penultimate chapter, records Marmee's first-person thoughts and experiences as she nurses her husband at an army hospital in Washington and comes to terms with the changes wrought in him by war. The final two chapters return to March's voice as he reconciles himself to his loss of innocence and returns home to his family.

Like so many women, Brooks first encountered *Little Women* as a girl. Her fidelity to the female characterizations and relevant plot details of the original story, which she refers to as an "iconic" one (275); her epigraph from *Little Women*; and her reference to the earlier novel in her dedication[6] all suggest a respect for this American classic. However, Brooks's relationship with *Little Women* was never awe-filled. When her mother recommended the book to ten-year-old Geraldine, the author recalls, "[S]he also counseled that I take it with a grain of salt. 'Nobody in real life is such a goody-goody as that Marmee,' she declared" (280). To supplement the characters that Alcott gives her, therefore, Brooks used biographical information on Alcott's own family, particularly her father, Bronson Alcott, whom she says was "far less perfect, and therefore much more interesting, than the saintly Marches" (280).

These details make a believable supplement to the plotline and characters inherited from *Little Women* and allow Brooks, like Rossner and Kingsolver, to talk back to Alcott and to substitute her own sociopolitical concerns for those of her nineteenth-century predecessor. Although she appears to respect and to admire the literary classic, Brooks reconfigures it in ways that comment on the race and gender politics of the original, coupling the political commentary with thematic elements emphasizing miscommunication and misinterpretation. Just as Kingsolver also comments on her political concerns with Western imperialist interests in Africa, so Brooks, writing in the midst of the U.S. war in Iraq, uses Mr. March's involvement with the Civil War to offer a critical statement about war in general.

Also, like Kingsolver, Brooks foregrounds racial concerns that are conspicuously absent from *Little Women*, and Brooks's shared time frame with *Little Women* serves to further emphasize this topic's absence from the earlier novel. For example, in direct opposition to the classic novel's exaltation of the social and spiritual power of motherly love, Brooks emphasizes that such bonds were denied to many nonwhites in the nineteenth century. Mr. March remembers his first trip south as a young man of nineteen, when he becomes a house guest of a plantation family and befriends Grace, their well-educated, refined, young slave. When March comments that Grace's invalid white mistress loves her as a daughter, Grace pointedly responds, "Does she so? I wouldn't know. My mother was sold south by Mr. Clement before I was one year old" (24). The comforts of Marmee's wholesome bosom and Christian wisdom, so essential to the formation of little women, are inaccessible to disrupted slave families. During the Civil War, at March's first post as army chaplain, he again meets Grace at the now-ruined Clement plantation. Far from home and facing mental and physical hardship, he becomes sexually attracted to this woman with whom he shares his experiences. The pair never consummate their mutual attraction, even though such desires would not scandalize a twenty-first-century reader. When an army surgeon witnesses their embrace, however, and subsequently lodges a formal complaint against March, we glimpse a more predictable nineteenth-century response. Although the existence of mixed-race people clearly testifies that such liaisons often occurred, the affairs were expected to be hidden and were not discussed in polite society. For this reason, even though he is innocent of adultery, March's letter home explaining his resulting transfer is "shrouded in words meant to mislead" (73).

Through these letters home to his family, Brooks suggests a reason why Alcott, and in turn her characters, seems so isolated from or indifferent to the war and the racial struggles associated with it. On the novel's opening pages, Mr. March composes a letter to Marmee following a horrible defeat of his unit at the Battle of Ball's Bluff. Yet he reflects to himself that although he promised to write every day, he "never promised [he] would write the truth" (4). March intentionally omits the suffering of war from his letters, and he views the evasion as loving protection of his family. Rather than describe the bloodshed and torture, March describes the landscape: *"The clouds tonight embossed the sky. A dipping sun gilded and brazed each raveling edge as if the firmament were threaded through with precious filaments"* (3). Not wanting to burden his wife and daughters with the scenes he has witnessed, he repeatedly resorts in his letters to the most conventional and banal subject possible, the weather. When he is transferred from one post to another by boat, his words to Marmee compare the northern to southern climate and rivers, but his thoughts to himself dwell on "the federal ram-boat steaming into the enemy's vessel, staving its side like crumpled paper so that it sank in less than three minutes, with the loss of all hands" (90). As March's letters and corresponding thoughts demonstrate, unpleasant truths are deemed inappropriate for and withheld from women and girls. If such attitudes held sway in the nineteenth century, as Brooks and others suggest,[7] it is no surprise that Alcott's March women seem to be unaware of these details and of their effects on life at home. Even if Alcott herself, who published her first book, *Hospital Sketches*, about her experiences as a Civil War nurse, were knowledgeable about the horrors of slavery and war, the same conventions that prevent March from discussing them in his letters would have prevented her from depicting them in her novel written primarily for girls. These silences in turn affect her readers' understanding of their world and themselves and perpetuate a cycle of ignorance that lives on, as does the novel. Rather than reject the earlier novel, however, by emphasizing these silences, Brooks encourages readers to look for what has been left unsaid and to understand what the evasions reveal to us about ourselves.

Despite such sheltering silences, *Little Women* does argue for stronger than conventional roles for women by emphasizing the mother's authority, the girls' education, and their ability to work for and to support themselves. Brooks emphasizes this neofeminism through March's memories of his early courtship with Marmee, who longs for "the day I will be entrusted with daughters of my own. . . . I swear I will not see their minds molded into society's simpering ideal of womanhood. Oh, how I would like to raise writers and artists who would make the world acknowledge what women can do!" (64). Marmee does in fact raise a writer in Jo and an artist in Amy, just as Alcott's own mother did with Louisa herself and younger daughter May. However, like Kingsolver, Brooks also comments on the silencing of Jo's temper by having March remember his own efforts to curb his wife's temper: "The intemperance of her attack left me breathless. Angry women generally cannot be said to show to advantage, and to see that lovely face so distorted by such a scowl as it now wore was immensely shocking to me. Who could have imagined this gently bred young woman to be so entirely bereft of the powers of self-government? I had never seen such an outburst, not even from a market wife" (84). Here, he explicitly links the inappropriateness of her outburst to her gender and her class. March's words do not suggest that anger itself is inappropriate, just anger in a well-bred young woman. Conduct books of the time period illustrate a similar attitude toward women's outspokenness and independence. Catherine Lavender, for example, quotes from the nineteenth-century *Young Ladies Book*, which instructs, "It is certain that in whatever situation of life a woman is placed from her cradle to her grave, a spirit of obedience and submission, pliability of temper, and humility of mind are required of her" (qtd. in Lavender).

The fact that Marmee's outburst is in response to Emerson's lukewarm engagement with abolitionism rather than a trivial subject leads the reader to believe that Brooks disapproves of her silencing and, by extension, Alcott's silencing of Jo. Before her ultimate defeat, however, Marmee registers her own denunciation of this double standard: "You call our girls your 'little women'; well, I am your belittled woman, and I am tired of it. Tired of suppressing my true feelings, tired of schooling my heart to order, as if I were some errant pupil, and you the schoolmaster. I will *not* be degraded in this way" (Brooks 130–131, emphasis in original). Although a contemporary reader may share Marmee's outrage at such patronizing treatment, Brooks remains true to her predecessor's story and has March conquer his wife's temper. Apparently evasion, indirection, and repression were not only expected of correspondence to women but also expected of women's correspondence with others.

Brooks demonstrates that this lack of communication is damaging not only to women but also to men. Early in the novel, March sits down to write his letters to Marmee, as if seeking comfort and shelter in her from the chaos of war: "I find myself turning to this obligation when my mind is most troubled. For it is as if she were here with me for a moment, her calming hand resting lightly upon my shoulder. Yet I am thankful that she is *not* here, to see what I must see, to know what I am come to know" (4, emphasis in original). Rather than seeking comfort by confiding his experiences to his wife, he strives to shelter her. This isolation leaves him emotionally vulnerable and causes him to seek comfort in the one woman with whom he does share his wartime experiences, Grace. Later, having been ignominiously transferred, he wallows in guilt over his attraction to Grace and over the misfortunes of war that he can reveal to no one.

March suggests that such failure to communicate can lead not only to the destruction of a marriage but also to the destruction of war. When he first impulsively decides to join the war effort, in the midst of his words of blessing at a farewell rally for the troops, March makes eye contact with his wife in the crowd: "She knew, even before I did, that I meant it. She lifted her palms in a gesture of assent, as if to put wind beneath my wings" (183).

Reading her assent, he publicly declares his intention to go to war. Later, during Marmee's narrative, she recalls the same moment:

> I raised my arms to him, imploring him not to say the words that I knew were forming in his mind. He looked me full in the face, he saw my tears, and he ignored them and did as he pleased. And then I in my turn had to pretend to be pleased by my hero of a husband....
> I am not alone in this. I only let him do to me what men have ever done to women: march off to empty glory and hollow acclaim and leave us behind to pick up the pieces. (211)

March's words echo those of Orleanna, who indicts herself as silent onlooker in the deeds of her husband. Although women did not generally join the fighting during Alcott's time, they were affected by its ensuing destruction, and Kingsolver and Brooks implicate women in the violence of war. Even though one remains at home, Brooks suggests, one still bears a responsibility for war and its aftermath. Like Kingsolver, Rossner, and the other contemporary writers of reconfigurations examined in this study, Brooks emphasizes the varied interpretation of signs, in this case encouraging her readers to interrogate their interpretations of the Civil War, the war in Iraq, and texts that narrate the American experience.

Although the war-scarred March longs for a return to his prewar innocence and moral certainty, he has experienced too much and can never go back. Brooks's readers have also experienced too much, such as multiple wars, one of them atomic, and changes in race and gender relations, and therefore they cannot return to the moral certainty of *Little Women*, a book written for younger people during the nation's younger days. *Little Women* ends in a "day of frolic" (Alcott 447), with the united March family basking in the love and happiness that is the reward of virtuous lives. *March* ends after Marmee faces a dilemma similar to her husband's, when she searches for "a style of truth that would not dishearten" (Brooks 248) her family as she writes a letter home to reveal his condition. She ceases to blame her husband for his evasions and comes to think of them as "perhaps, a daily act of love" (248). By revealing Marmee's struggles to express herself, Brooks complicates her message and emphasizes the difficulties inherent in communication rather than simply condemning one character's actions. At Mr. March's ultimate reunion with his family in Concord, surrounded also by "the ghosts of the dead," he again remains silent about his experiences, but this time not due to an intentional evasion. As each loving daughter asks her father how she seems changed in the year since they were last together, Mr. March compliments in turn the growth of each. Then, Beth begins to play the piano: "All eyes were on her then, before anyone had thought to ask their father how a year at war had changed *him*" (273, emphasis in original). As safe haven from the outside world, the family unintentionally isolates those members whose most intense experiences lie elsewhere.

Stories, those we tell ourselves and those we read in books, create narrative unity and cohesion—a logical beginning, middle, and end—out of events that may be experienced as disconnected or random. Louis O. Mink notes that narrative is our "primary cognitive instrument . . . [for] making the flux of experience comprehensible" (131). The first-person narrators in the novels of Rossner, Kingsolver, and Brooks each struggle to understand their experiences by creating their stories, piecing together events, and imposing a logical order on them, although often not the same sense or order imposed by other narrators in the text. Like the other contemporary novels in this study, each novel also documents the characters' narrative search for unity and cohesion through a quest for missing origins, a quest figured in *His Little Women*, *The Poisonwood Bible*, and *March* through an absent father (emotionally absent in the case of Reverend Price) and the thwarted attempts to access him physically and through language. For example, in *His Little Women*, perhaps in an unconscious attempt to replay her relationship with her father and to create a different outcome, Nell pursues romantic relationships with much older men, acquaintances or friends of her father. When the first of these affairs ends, teenage Nell reflects, "I could not think of Hugo without pain and confusion. His vanishing echoed some event in a not-quite-remembered time when bliss ended in a similarly abrupt and incomprehensible way" (*His Little Women* 37). Literally, the "not-quite-remembered time" to which Nell connects her lover's vanishing is her abandonment by her father, a man of similar age and status. Nell longs for father figures to give her a sense of a beginning, of groundedness, and the relationships she has with older men are an attempt to rewrite the past in order to create one.

Yet as we have seen with the reconfigurations of Poe, Hawthorne, and Melville, Nell's longing for a "not-quite-remembered time when bliss ended" in an "abrupt and incomprehensible way" has many analogues in Western cultural history. The biblical story of Adam and Eve, cast out of the garden where they had experienced oneness with God, recounts a similar traumatic end to bliss. In "Beyond the Pleasure Principle," Sigmund Freud speculates that the trauma of birth and the end of the unity and fulfillment experienced by the infant in the womb later manifests itself psychologically in the "death instinct," through which we long for a return to intrauterine bliss and an end to struggle. Perhaps what the cultural narratives of Freud and the Bible reflect is the human awareness of the gap between perception and reality and the impossible desire to heal that split, a wish to reclaim the memory of the dawn of consciousness and language. According to the psychological concept of "theory of mind," as the mind develops between ages three and four, we gradually become aware of how we and other people think and how we manage information, a process known as *metacognition* (Doherty 3). The child becomes aware that not everyone views the world in the same way, that there is a gap between objective reality and one's consciousness of it, and that these differences can create misinterpretation. At around the same time, more complex communication skills, such as the ability to create three-dimensional story characters, develop (Sugiyama 189). Creating characters with beliefs and desires is a way to imagine the beliefs and desires of other people and also to enlighten others about our own beliefs and desires. As Michele Scalise Sugiyama puts it, "[S]torytelling may help build or strengthen theory of mind, which in turn enriches storytelling, which further enriches theory of mind, and so on" (189). Interestingly, this is about the same age, three to five years, that Freud designated as the Oedipal phase, during which a (male) child displays and then learns to repress his desire for unity with the mother, the desire for that bliss of perceived unity in mind and matter.

Freud's theory, the myth of expulsion from the Garden of Eden, and theory of mind all record a dawning of consciousness and an awareness of a disconnect among the self, the world, and others. Both Freud and the Bible tell stories of a lost bliss, but perhaps what they symbolically document is the lost illusion of oneness that comes with maturing consciousness. According to Ludwig Wittgenstein, "The *in*exactness, the impurity of our negotiations with language, is not . . . some secondary condition of a lapsed primary, not a quotidian deviation from some purer form of discourse or intelligence that we must always try to recover. 'Impurity' of this sort is on the contrary the working base of all verbal experience" (qtd. in Kroeber 171, emphasis in original). Coherent narratives combat this "impurity" by recreating the illusion of unity and coherence in life and by attempting to create a shared reality of experience.

Rossner's, Kingsolver's, and Brooks's desire to rewrite *Little Women* responds to a similar impulse, the desire for narrative cohesion. Narratives like *Little Women* are part of our culture's collective narrative that helps us understand who we are. By reshaping the past narrative, the authors create the illusion of shared experiences and perceptions with their society and of narrative cohesion in long-time. By revising *Little Women*, Rossner, Kingsolver, and Brooks rewrite a part of the American cultural narrative. Through their revisions, the contemporary authors suggest aspects of that identity that Alcott chooses not to reveal and ways that her portrayal is now obsolete. By emphasizing the uncertainty of language, however, through problematically mingled fact and fiction in *His Little Women*, through wordplay and errors in translation in *The Poisonwood Bible*, and through purposefully misleading correspondence in *March*, the authors emphasize that such narrative cohesion is an illusion. By revising the earlier narrative, they revise the collective narrative of American experience to provide a sense of cultural order and meaning that they recognize as their own, while acknowledging that this cultural order is a construction, subject to revision and to reinterpretation.

5 The "Quintessentially American Book"
Reconfigurations of *Adventures of Huckleberry Finn*

Although *Adventures of Huckleberry Finn* is frequently taught in secondary school and college classrooms, the characters Huck and Jim and their river journey have pervaded American culture to the extent that even those who have never read Mark Twain's novel are familiar with them.[1] Readers identify with Huck's directness and lack of pretension and embrace the themes of freedom, independence, and acceptance found with Huck and Jim on the raft. As Frances W. Kaye points out, "For most of the twentieth century it has served as the book that defines the American language, the American place, and the spunkiness, independence, and resistance to authority of the American people" (16). Bernard DeVoto, one of the earliest critics to contribute to the canonization of *Huckleberry Finn*, wrote in 1932 that this novel "comes nearer than any other [book] to identify itself with the national life." While acknowledging that no one novel can fully represent the whole of American past, DeVoto asserts that "more truly with *Huckleberry Finn* than with any other book, inquiry may satisfy itself; *here*, is America" (314, emphasis in original). Janice McIntire-Strasburg echoes DeVoto's conclusion, but she focuses more on how this novel reflects an idealized vision of an American past rather than America as it truly was: "The character of Huck and the geographical space of the river allow us to celebrate characteristics of our national culture that we wish to project: independence from societal pressures, individuality, and independence of thought and action" (96). Regardless of the accuracy of its portrayal of American history, *Huckleberry Finn* reinforces many Americans' perceptions of national identity.

Despite the iconic status of the book and its characters, *Huckleberry Finn* has been the source of controversy since its publication. Panned first by librarians and educators because Huck's poor grammar and indecorous conduct set a bad example for the young, the novel has more recently met with criticism by educators and parents who object to its perceived overuse of the offensive word "nigger." Literary critics have also debated the artistic merits of the book. Perhaps most famously, Leo Marx's "Mr. Eliot, Mr. Trilling, and *Huckleberry Finn*" criticizes the novel's ending, where Tom Sawyer directs Huck in romanticized scenarios to rescue the captured Jim.

In this section, Jim loses the dignity that Huck and readers have learned to see in him and becomes instead a passive pawn in a boys' game. Gene Jarrett sees this ending, often referred to as the Evasion, resulting from "Twain's anxiety over confronting his own admirable creation," that creation being the sympathetically rendered Jim of the novel's beginning and middle (3). More recently, critic Jonathan Arac has commented on what he calls the novel's "hypercanonization," a process by which the novel has been identified as the "quintessentially American book." For Arac, "the identification of a book not just with a nation, but with the *goodness* of a nation" is politically and aesthetically troubling (782, emphasis in original). "We want the book to mean too much and to do too much"—more, according to Arac, than a close reading of the novel supports. Other critics have attempted to redeem Twain's ending by interpreting it as an allegorical representation of the de facto re-enslavement of African Americans during the reconstruction era in which the novel was published. As Shelly Fisher Fishkin puts it, "Is what America did to the ex-slaves any less insane than what Tom Sawyer put Jim through in the novel? . . . What is the history of post-Emancipation race relations in the United States if not a series of maneuvers as cruelly gratuitous as the indignities inflicted on Jim in the final section of *Huckleberry Finn*?" (199–200).

We can see that Twain's novel is more complex than most films and other popular culture references suggest, and these conflicting interpretations that the work has inspired mirror the conflicting influences that first inspired Twain's creation. For example, R.J. Ellis explores the connections between *Huckleberry Finn* and Harriet Prescott Spofford's long short story, "Down the River." Published in 1865 in the *Atlantic Monthly*, a magazine Twain read frequently, Spofford's story recounts an unusual friendship between a slave girl, Flor, and her young mistress. Like Huck and Jim, Spofford's fugitive seeks her freedom by rafting southward down a river, but Flor's journey culminates in the Civil War and the freeing of the slaves. Ellis identifies significant parallels between these works that end when Huck witnesses the feud between the Shepherdsons and the Grangerfords, scenes often interpreted as a symbolic representation of the Civil War. Significantly, after this point, Twain pauses in his novel's composition, perhaps, Ellis suggests, at a loss for how to continue without Spofford's inspiration (42). In contrast to Spofford's sympathetic fictional slave narrative, blackface minstrelsy, a racist but popular form of entertainment to which Twain was partial, also significantly influences the novel: "Convinced of the humanity and identity of American blacks, Twain seems nonetheless to have been haunted by their difference. Hence he returned over and over to the actual practice and literary trope of blackface, which hedges by imagining the Other as black only in exterior, still white inside" (Lott 140). In addition to these two influences, McIntire-Strasburg detects the "style and structure of both the travel book and the Southwestern humorous sketch" informing *Huckleberry*

Finn (83). Such a wide range of models lends support to DeVoto's claim that this novel best represents the breadth of nineteenth-century American experience.

Perhaps partly due to the novel's iconic status and partly due to the controversy over that status, several contemporary writers have reconfigured Twain's *Huckleberry Finn*. In "Mark Twain and Nation," Randall Knoper observes, "A standard practice of nation-constructing is the linking of the new entity to a past, fashioning stories and elaborating genealogies that explain the nation in terms of fathers who can be celebrated, or in terms of immemorial origins, sometimes of a primordial racial sort. History is rewritten as national history; the nation is narrated in this process of self-imagining" (4). The present study has been examining this same process of nation building at work in contemporary reconfigurations of American literary classics, where those classics become the celebrated origins to which the new works ally themselves. According to Knoper, "Twain repeatedly participated in and mocked this process" (4), but the four contemporary writers that I discuss in this chapter refrain from mockery. In John Seelye's *The True Adventures of Huckleberry Finn* (1970), James Dickey's *Deliverance* (1970), Nancy Rawles's *My Jim* (2005), and Jon Clinch's *Finn* (2007),[2] the authors pay tribute to *Huckleberry Finn*'s centrality in American culture by reworking themes, characters, and plot elements from Twain's novel. Through their revisions, however, they also add their voices to the critical debate regarding the book's flaws. The revisions allow them to offer new literary interpretations of the American cultural elements Twain invokes. As with other contemporary writers who reconfigure American classics, these writers overtly call attention to the fallibility of language and the variability of interpretation within their texts. Their emphasis on misinterpretation, reinterpretation, or willful deception through language forms an analogue to the many varied interpretations of Twain's text and underscores that all knowledge is based on subjective perception and is always subject to reevaluation and reinterpretation.

Twain also points to the unreliability of language and the variability of interpretation, aware that although identities, communities, and nations must be built, at least in part, on language, this is nevertheless a foundation of shifting sands. Twain uses this uncertainty for comic effect throughout the novel, such as in chapter XIV, where Jim and Huck debate the wisdom of the biblical King Solomon, and in chapter XXI, where the King and Duke recite butchered Shakespeare. In chapter XXXII, Aunt Sally Phelps asks Huck (who is pretending to be Tom) if anybody was hurt in the cylinder-head explosion he has invented to explain his lateness: "No'm. Killed a nigger," Huck answers. When Aunt Sally responds, "Well, it's lucky, because sometimes people do get hurt," (279), readers realize that they and Twain define "people" differently than do Aunt Sally and, perhaps, Huck. Early in the novel, Tom absurdly insists that, although they do not know what "ransom" means, the gang's victims must be ransomed nonetheless: "Don't

I tell you it's in the books? Do you want to go doing different from what's in the books, and get things all muddled up?" (11). The reader perceives Twain's ridicule of Tom's blind faith in the printed word, which Tom does not even understand, and the author's gentle implied censure here echoes the tongue-in-cheek warning to the reader that precedes the tale: "Persons attempting to find a motive in this narrative will be prosecuted; persons attempting to find a moral in it will be banished; persons attempting to find a plot in it will be shot." Although this warning is comically hyperbolic, the reader attempting to find motive, moral, and plot reaps frustration instead, because language and meaning refuse to cohere.

Despite Twain's warnings, readers continue to interpret his text. As graduate research professor of American literature at the University of Florida, Seelye's professional credentials testify to his expert knowledge of Twain scholarship, and it is to the scholars as much as to Twain that Seelye responds in his fictional reconfiguration of *Huckleberry Finn*. Through his novel's introductory chapter, Seelye gives an overview, in the voice of Huck Finn, of the critical response to Twain's novel and foregrounds the variability of interpretation, the possibility of misinterpretation, and the risk of linguistic deception. By naming individual critics in turn, such as Van Wyck Brooks, DeVoto, Leslie Fiedler, Lionel Trilling, Henry Seidel Canby, Marx, and James Cox, accompanied by each critic's praise or criticism of Twain's novel, Seelye reminds us that the novel's meaning is subjective and has changed over time. On the other hand, by titling his novel *The True Adventures of Huckleberry Finn* (as if Huck's other book of adventures were *not* true) and titling the introductory chapter "De ole true Huck," Seelye encourages us to doubt the authenticity of the Huckleberry Finn that Twain creates and suggests, no doubt ironically, that Seelye's version is somehow more authentic and realistic.

The opening lines of Seelye's novel echo the opening lines of Twain's but change them in such a way as to challenge the credibility of Twain's novel. Twain's *Huckleberry Finn* is narrated in first person by Huck. Famously, Twain's novel begins, "You don't know about me, without you have read a book by the name of *The Adventures of Tom Sawyer*, but that ain't no matter. The book was made by Mr. Mark Twain, and he told the truth mainly. There was things which he stretched, but mainly he told the truth" (1). Seelye's novel begins, "Some years ago, it don't matter how many, Mr. Mark Twain took down some adventures of mine and put them in a book called *Huckleberry Finn*—which is my name. When the book come out I read through it and I seen right away that he didn't tell it the way it was. Most of the time he told the truth, but he told a number of stretchers too, and some of them was really whoppers" (v). With these lines, Seelye simultaneously imitates and challenges the beginning of *Huckleberry Finn*. In Seelye's version, Huck refers to the earlier book by "Mr. Mark Twain"; only now, the reader is to believe, will Huck himself tell his own story. The device of presenting Huck as narrator is, Seelye's introduction suggests, one of Twain's "whoppers," but now the real Huck will straighten out all of Twain's lies. As Seelye's Huck explains to the reader, "Mr. Twain's book is for children and such, whilst this one here is for the crickets [critics]. And now that they've got *their* book, maybe they'll leave the other one alone" (xii, emphasis in original). By emphasizing that *Huckleberry Finn* is Twain's (rather than Huck's) book and is a children's book, Seelye challenges its authenticity and realism. Children's books, we assume, are light-hearted, often fantastic, moral tales with happy endings. On the other hand, the last sentence of the quotation above charges critics with unfairly expecting Twain's novel to be something that the author does not intend it to be. Lest the reader rest too comfortably with the truth of Seelye's *Huckleberry Finn*, however, the novel's title page, immediately below the title, reads "as told by John Seelye." Once again, the reader determines that this is only an interpretation of *Huckleberry Finn*, one filtered through the perceptions of Seelye.

After the introductory chapter, most of the rest of Seelye's book is nearly identical to Twain's, except that Seelye modifies the novel to address critics' most common objections. As Seelye's introduction points out, Brooks finds the lack of profanity in Twain's novel unrealistic.[3] Consequently, *The True Adventures* contains a modest sprinkling of "damns," "hells," and other swear words. DeVoto, Seelye tells us, says Twain strains credulity by portraying a fourteen-year-old such as Huck who never thinks about sex.[4] *The True Adventures* depicts Huck's age-appropriate sexual interest in a girl from St. Petersburg and in Mary Jane Wilks, the eldest of the three orphan girls whom the King and Duke try to rob. Seelye's most dramatic revisions of the original, however, appear at the end, where critics find Twain's novel most problematic.

In the voice of Huck Finn, Seelye's introduction paraphrases Marx's criticism of Twain's ending, mentioned above: "'Cording to him, that ending warn't moral, and it was all because Mark Twain couldn't face up to his own story—by which he meant mine. He said that Mark Twain couldn't measure up to the nat'ral ending the book deserved, that he just plain lost his nerve and had to cheat by tacking on a faint-hearted, immoral ending" (viii). Although Twain's novel ends happily, with Jim free and Huck lighting out for the territory, the series of coincidence (Jim's being captured by Tom's aunt and uncle, the Phelpses; Huck's showing up at their farm when Tom is expected to visit and being mistaken for Tom; Tom's showing up shortly thereafter and convincing the Phelpses that he is Tom's younger brother, Sid; and Tom's revealing, upon Jim's recapture, that Miss Watson had freed Jim two months earlier in her will) stretch the boundaries of realism. In addition, Tom's childish and selfish manipulation of Jim for the sake of adventure dehumanizes the black man and deprives the earlier bond between Huck and Jim of its redemptive force. As Daniel S. Traber points out, "Jim is forced back into assuming the mask of the deferential and docile slave, and Huck capitulates by allowing Tom, the representative of the dominant culture, free rein" (30).

Seelye removes Tom from the novel's ending and never allows Huck to set foot on the Phelpses' farm. Instead, upon learning that Jim has been captured, Huck paddles his canoe near the farm where he is held and meets Jim fleeing a posse of armed white men and dogs. "Weighted down with chains," Jim plunges off the riverbank to reach Huck's canoe (327), resembling the bloody, ragged, enslaved Samson in chains. Rather than the trivialization and dehumanization that Jim experiences at the hands of Huck and Tom at the end of Twain's novel, Seelye's Jim's walking out into the water, "a-coming on as best he could with all them chains on" (328), has a heroic bearing. Rather than a passive victim of a boys' game, he is an active agent in his escape, and Huck helplessly tries to reach him while dodging the posse's bullets. But because he is aiming at realism, Seelye cannot allow his book to end happily. By the time Huck has floated beyond the bullets' range, Jim is nowhere in sight: "There was nothing on the broad river but me, and I knowed then there warn't no sense looking further for Jim, because he was somewhere deep down under, weighted by them goddam heavy chains" (332). The oft-mentioned heavy chains form a symbolic reminder of the confines of realism and a literal reminder of the confines of slavery. The demands of both these structures determine Jim's fate. Seelye's ending indicts the brutality of a slave system that is willing to kill a man and a child rather than lose a $200 reward. It also offers a much darker vision than Twain's of the fate of the slave, most of whom did not, in reality, find their way to freedom, either by escape or manumission. Between 1831 and 1841, for example, slaveholders in the state of Maryland reportedly manumitted 2,342 slaves, .2 percent of the total (Whitman 203). The 1860 U.S. Census estimates the total number of slaves in the U.S. at nearly four million, and a National Park Service Special Resource Study estimates that approximately fifteen hundred slaves, or .0375 percent, successfully escaped to freedom each year (Kentucky and the Underground Railroad). By contrast, Twain's ending, as Seelye's introduction suggests, seems much more suited to the fairy-tale tastes of children.

Seelye, however, ultimately discourages the reader from viewing his portrayal of slavery as the best one. As Huck mourns the loss of his friend, he regrets not having listened to his conscience earlier when it told him to betray Jim. If he had turned him in sooner, he laments, Jim would still be alive today. No longer the heroic young man willing to risk damnation in order to save his friend, Huck wishes instead he had conformed to the expectations of his society. Of Twain's version, Trilling writes in the introduction to a 1948 edition of *Huckleberry Finn*, "[N]o one who reads thoughtfully the dialectic of Huck's great moral crisis will ever again be wholly able to accept without some question and some irony the assumptions of the respectable morality by which he lives, nor will ever again be certain that what he considers the clear dictates of moral reason are not merely the engrained customary beliefs of his time and place" (xii). According to Trilling, Twain's novel encourages self-examination and change. Through Huck's declaration ("All right, then, I'll *go* to hell" [283], emphasis in original), Twain conjures the voice of a people willing to risk the dissolution of the U.S. in order to end slavery. However unrealistic and flawed his portrayal, Twain leaves readers with the possibility of an enduring friendship between blacks and whites and of an unbroken willingness to endure sacrifice for the sake of integrity. The ending of Seelye's novel encourages readers to grieve over the empty spaces left by his revisions, for his ending deprives us of Tom, Jim, and, ultimately, Huck.

McIntire-Strasburg observes, "When Huck 'lights out for the Territory ahead of the rest,'" in Twain's novel, "he voices and confirms our belief that a mythical place exists free from the real danger, violence, and prejudice that also form a part of the American story; and this end to the novel offers us that hope, even though it seems clear upon reflection that no such place existed in the geographical space that constitutes America, even in Twain's time" (96). This quest for a mythical uncontaminated place is Twain's version of the quest for origins that so many of the works examined in this study have featured. The optimism suggested by Huck's plan, however, may be Twain's ironic commentary on the changing national landscape. Publishing his novel in 1884, although it is set around 1840, Twain knows that the region to which Huck plans to escape will soon be corrupted by gold-rush profit-seekers (Traber 32). Huck may be ahead of the rest, but not very far ahead; as McIntire-Strasburg suggests, Twain knows that such a quest is futile. And Twain's novel problematizes the notion of genesis in other ways, as well. Through Pap Finn, Twain suggests that one's origins are not always uncorrupt and restorative. Huck flees his origins in the shape of his father and essentially recreates himself on the Mississippi River with Jim. Seelye's ending denies readers even the dubious hope suggested by Twain. Instead of "light[ing] out for the Territory" (Twain 386), Seelye's Huck packs his scant possessions in the canoe, looks a last time at the raft "all shadows and emptiness" (337), and drifts aimlessly down the river. His final words are, "But dark as it was and lonesome as it was, I didn't have no wish for daylight to come. In fact, I didn't much care if the goddamn sun never come up again" (339). Although realistic, Seelye's novel ends with desolation and despair, as if to say to those "crickets" to whom he addresses his book, "Be careful what you wish for. You just might get it."

In *Deliverance*, Dickey reconfigures Twain's *Huckleberry Finn* more extensively than Seelye and in a contemporary setting.[5] Like Richard Powers in *The Gold Bug Variations*, Dickey updates the classic text in order to have his readers examine his present time through the lens of the past. *Deliverance* centers on men floating down a river, but in this twentieth-century version, the environment refuses to restore an uncorrupt identity. While drawing on themes, structures, and symbols found in *Huckleberry Finn*, *Deliverance* reveals a postmodern conception of society and the self, particularly with regards to gender and sexuality. Whereas Huckleberry Finn heads out to new territory in order to free himself of the scripts of his society (although perhaps a fruitless quest, as discussed above), Dickey's novel suggests that there is no free territory, and perhaps there never was.

In Dickey's 1979 introduction to a New American Library Signet Classic edition of *The Adventures of Tom Sawyer* and *The Adventures of Huckleberry Finn*, the contemporary author pays homage to Twain's genius, especially in *Huckleberry Finn*. After quoting Ernest Hemingway's famous tribute, "All modern American literature comes from one book by Mark Twain called *Huckleberry Finn*. . . . All American writing comes from that," Dickey responds, "This statement may not be *entirely* true, for the assessment of the influence of *Huckleberry Finn* is stated with an assertiveness that brings its judgment into question. . . . But the second part as to the *value* of the book probably *is* true" (v, emphasis in original). Particularly relevant to a discussion of *Deliverance* are Dickey's comments about Twain's Mississippi River: "The river in both these books [*Tom Sawyer* and *Huckleberry Finn*] is the greatest character in American literature, unsurpassed even by the character of the sea in *Moby-Dick*" (vii). Dickey adapts this great character and the journey upon it for his own novel. Manuscript evidence confirms that Dickey was thinking of Twain's novel as he composed his own river adventure. In a typescript early draft of *Deliverance*, then titled *The Deliverer*, Dickey writes the following description of the mapped image of the Cahulawassee River upon which his characters travel: "Images, confused, many rivers and pictures of rivers, all of them this map green." Above this line, the author writes by hand, "Huck Finn and the butterfly boats of the Nile" (see Figure 5.1). Fiedler, in his controversial 1948 essay, "Come Back to the Raft Ag'in, Huck Honey," sees Twain's river as a mythic conception of American identity as well as a metaphor for the Self.

Fiedler claims that in Twain's *Huckleberry Finn* and other nineteenth-century American classics, "the mythic America is boyhood" (5), but Dickey's novel presents middle-age men trying unsuccessfully to reclaim this lost authentic self.[6] In *Deliverance*, the four male friends plan to canoe down a Georgia river before it is dammed up to create a man-made lake. The lives of these city men provide few opportunities to commune with nature and few opportunities to commune freely with other men. The underlying purpose to the trip seems to be to buttress their diminishing sense of masculinity and their appreciation for the masculinity of their peers. As Ed Gentry says of the group's fitness-crazed leader, "I felt a great deal lighter and more muscular when I was around Lewis" (34). Early in the trip, as the men take a break from their paddling to swim naked in the river, Ed's homoerotic appreciation for Lewis becomes obvious: "I looked at him, for I have never seen him with his clothes off. Everything he had done for himself for years paid off as he stood there in his tracks in the water. I could tell by the way he glanced at me; the payoff was in my eyes. I had never seen such a male body in my life, even in the pictures in the weight-lifting magazines" (102). Ed emphasizes here the fact of Lewis's nakedness and his maleness. The

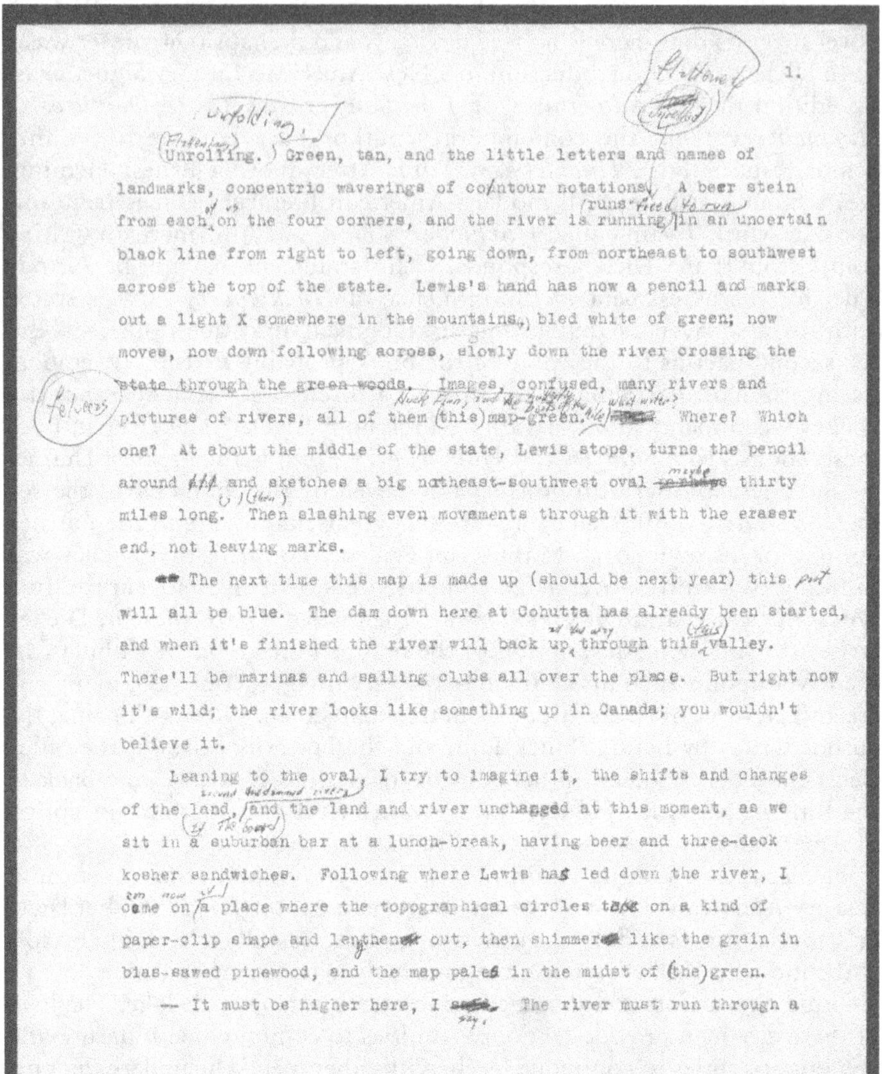

1.

Unrolling. Green, tan, and the little letters and names of landmarks, concentric waverings of contour notations. A beer stein from each on the four corners, and the river is running in an uncertain black line from right to left, going down, from northeast to southwest across the top of the state. Lewis's hand has now a pencil and marks out a light X somewhere in the mountains, bled white of green; now moves, now down following across, slowly down the river crossing the state through the green woods. Images, confused, many rivers and pictures of rivers, all of them (this) map-green. Where? Which one? At about the middle of the state, Lewis stops, turns the pencil around and sketches a big northeast-southwest oval thirty miles long. Then slashing even movements through it with the eraser end, not leaving marks.

The next time this map is made up (should be next year) this will all be blue. The dam down here at Cohutta has already been started, and when it's finished the river will back up through this valley. There'll be marinas and sailing clubs all over the place. But right now it's wild; the river looks like something up in Canada; you wouldn't believe it.

Leaning to the oval, I try to imagine it, the shifts and changes of the land, and the land and river unchanged at this moment, as we sit in a suburban bar at a lunch-break, having beer and three-deck kosher sandwiches. Following where Lewis has led down the river, I came on a place where the topographical circles take on a kind of paper-clip shape and lengthen out, then shimmer like the grain in bias-sawed pinewood, and the map pales in the midst of (the) green.

— It must be higher here, I say. The river must run through a

Figure 5.1 Page 1 of a typescript from *The Deliverer,* an early draft of *Deliverance*, with James Dickey's corrections. From Emory University's Manuscript, Archive, and Rare Book Library. Subseries 2.3, Box 142, Folder 22.

two men connect through this physical moment: Lewis observes Ed observing his body and appreciates Ed's appreciation of it.

As Fiedler points out, setting is all-important for this "Sacred Marriage of males," and in the nineteenth-century novels Fiedler analyzes, the setting is "Nature undefiled" (9). The river journey through nature in both novels invites a psychological interpretation, one that Fiedler explores in *Huckleberry Finn*. Wyman H. Herendeen notes the archetypal significance of rivers as "the thread joining the body and the mind," in that they are the geographic site of earliest civilization and, as such, the place in which myth and history began. Rivers, thus, provide a figurative link to our earliest selves (8–9). The journey down the river is symbolically a psychological one. The isolation from society and separation from daily concerns provides the opportunity for introspection, and the depths of the water represent those of the mind. In this reading, nature is a part of the self, the unacknowledged self that threatens the public self. Of course nature is not quite undefiled in *Huckleberry Finn*, as threatening steamboats and the King and Duke's intrusion onto the raft verify. Likewise, nature, at least at the beginning of the journey, is far from pristine in *Deliverance*. Just before the four men set off in their canoes, Ed discards his empty beer can in the water (75). Once they shove off, they see "rusted pieces of metal" and plastic containers lining the shore. Slightly farther down the river, they encounter what they suppose to be the waste of a poultry processing plant and observe "the river feathering itself," as if transforming into a creature of the air (77). The beginning of this trip certainly emphasizes twentieth-century industrial life's violation of nature and the tainted rafters trying to reclaim pristine nature. In *Deliverance*, if we read the river as a symbol of the internal psyches of the men who canoe its surface and are occasionally plunged into its depths, then the opening scenes suggest that the psyche has been violated and defiled.

The ostensible purpose of their journey is communion with nature (the self) and with other men. In *Deliverance* the others with whom the protagonists share their river journey and consciously or unconsciously confront hidden aspects of themselves are not African American, like Jim in *Huckleberry Finn*, but poor white mountain folk. The novel links these hillbillies to their natural setting; they are, in a sense, violated nature responding with violation. The violation the mountain men enact is a violent homosexual rape, suggesting that modern man has raped the land and is now suffering nature's retribution. However, extending the metaphor further with the aid of Fiedler, nature (including the hillbillies) becomes a part of the protagonist's self, a violated self responding with violation. The rape is the violent eruption of homosexual desire that, despite the protagonists' refusal to acknowledge it, underlies the trip from the beginning; *Deliverance*, therefore, presents a more overtly sexual dynamic that replaces the mainly homosocial bonds Fiedler[7] sees underlying *Huckleberry Finn* and other texts. *Deliverance* reveals that the psyche has been violated through the repression and denial of the homoeroticism that becomes glaringly obvious to readers but to which the characters seem either oblivious or openly hostile.[8]

Huckleberry Finn and *Deliverance* offer similar truths about the self through their symbolic journeys downriver. Both novels suggest to readers that identities of race, class, gender, and sexual identity are social constructions. In *Gender Trouble*, Judith Butler views gender attributes as performative, behaviors that we learn through imitation. Butler approaches the concept of gender from a theoretical, psychoanalytical perspective, but the same conclusions can be reached from an evolutionary perspective. Most children learn normative gender roles by observing a parent of the same sex or by observing other same-sex role models. These normative roles derive from and then in turn become the scripts and schemas that inform the narratives we receive from others and the self-narratives we compose. Adults often guide children by discouraging behaviors inappropriate for their genders and by making negative examples of others who deviate from gender norms. Gender-appropriate behavior is perceived to be necessary (1) because male-female sexual intercourse ensures the survival of the species; and (2) established social structures, which protect the cohesion and strength of a group, are often built around predictable gender norms. If we view gender in this way, we see that gender identity is not something innate to us as human beings, but a "regulatory fiction," an artificial system imposed on us by our culture. According to Butler, however, most of us fail to recognize the artifice, because the performance is so embedded in our culture and is necessary to maintain power structures and societal norms.

As she explains in her essay "Reading Gender in *The Adventures of Huckleberry Finn*," Myra Jehlen sees Huck's learning about the social constructions of gender through his encounter with Judith Loftus shortly after he and Jim have begun their journey together. Going ashore disguised as a girl in order to learn what the town knows about his and Jim's disappearance, Huck stops at the home of Mrs. Loftus, who easily sees through his disguise. As if to aid in future disguises, the woman instructs Huck on the differences between girls and boys: The former cannot throw, can thread needles, and will catch thrown objects in their skirts rather than with their knees. According to Jehlen, "Femininity, as Judith Loftus has here defined it, is something that women *do*, a composite activity made up of certain acts they perform well and others they as skillfully perform badly.... Masculinity is the equal and opposite condition.... What Huck learns from Judith Loftus ... is that the concealment [of masculinity] is not the issue but the projection [of femininity]: projection meaning construction" (513). Jehlen further argues that, although the connection is not explicitly stated by Huck, the insight he gains from Mrs. Loftus "sets the stage for the revolution to come in his sense of himself in the equally basic area of race" (513). In other words, seeing gender as a social construction allows Huck to reevaluate his conception of race and to defy society's expectations regarding his attitudes and conduct toward Jim. Although he has been taught to think of Jim as subhuman property, he learns to think of him as a friend.

Similarly, in *Deliverance*, Dickey suggests the constructed nature of gender. As Ed Gentry returns to his office after lunch, before the canoe trip, he notes that he is surrounded by women, a fact that generates in him a feeling of desolation. As if to assert his masculinity in contrast to these women, Ed looks for a "decent ass" among them but gleans no satisfaction here. To himself he says, "I am with you but not of you. But I knew better. I was of them, sure enough" (15). Ed's feminizing environment has made a woman of him, and he looks to the canoe trip to help him rebuild his masculinity. At the outset of the trip, Ed feels that here, too, he acts a part: "I was light green, a tall forest man, an explorer, guerrilla, hunter. I liked the idea and the image, I must say" (69). Even after their lives are threatened and one of them is perhaps killed by a hillbilly, at a time of crisis when Ed's idol Lewis believes that man is at his most natural, true, and powerful state, Ed still feels that he is merely playing a part written for him by others: "We were cast in roles, and first we must do something about them. . . . We were all acting it out" (173).

Humans learn the scripts and schemas that construct gender in large part through language, and Dickey reveals the fallibility of such language through explorations of its multiplicities and failures of meaning. At the novel's beginning, Dickey emphasizes the distance between representation and reality. As the four raftsmen, Ed, Lewis, Bobby, and Drew, look at a map before their trip, Ed, an advertising executive, thinks about the map as a stand-in for the real: "It was certainly not much from the standpoint of design. . . . Yet the eye could not leave the whole; there was a harmony of some kind. Maybe, I thought, it's because this tries to show what exists. And also because it represents something that is going to change, for good" (11). Although it tries to show what exists, the map is only a two-dimensional model rather than an exact duplicate, and Ed's attempts to find a deer's eye within the map's greenery fail. The map is a type of language, a signifier that represents an absent signified. According to Karl Kroeber, "[The] most significant attribute of discourse" is that "it allows us to *change* our apprehension of reality, thereby differentiating us from animals that are trapped within a given sensory situation. . . . Writing, it must be stressed again, enhances the capacity of oral utterance to go beyond itself in being understood, but that potency is always present in speaking, in which begins the human power to distance reality from itself" (42, emphasis in original). Although such distancing enables higher-order thinking, as Kroeber implies, Ed, like many of the contemporary characters examined in this study, longs to close that distance between reality and its articulation, seeking that undifferentiated state that more closely resembles nature. As the journey progresses, Ed repeatedly compares the reality of his experiences to artistic representations with which he is familiar, such as Lewis to an archer on an urn (*Deliverance* 134) and a vertical cliff to a drive-in movie screen (147), but the compared items frustratingly refuse to merge with the real. At the height of his physical and emotional exhaustion, as he climbs a vertical cliff to the top of the river gorge, Ed suggests that his image of reality and reality itself finally do fuse: "What a view. *What* a view. But I had my eyes closed. The river was running in my mind, and I raised my lids and saw exactly what had been the image of my thought" (170).

Dickey suggests this union of perception and reality is an illusion, however, for despite Ed's believing that his thoughts are one with his surroundings, including the mountain man he stalks, the plot reveals that much of it remains hidden from him. He does not know, for example, whether his companion Drew has really been shot, a crucial piece of information on which he bases his subsequent actions, and he is not certain whether the mountain man he eventually kills is the same one who has attacked Ed and Bobby earlier. Near the novel's end, Ed thinks about the story he will tell the authorities and how it differs from what really occurred: "I sat down and tilted back in a chair and was perfectly still, getting my story together one more time, the most important time. But back of the story was the reason for the story, and the woods and the river, and all that had happened" (232). Representations, Dickey suggests, are never exact and are always vulnerable to individual perceptions and manipulations. Similarly, although their characters navigate different bodies of water (the Cahulawassee and the Mississippi), Dickey renders simply another version of the same symbolic river that Twain writes about a century earlier. The similarity reminds readers that Dickey's and Twain's rivers are fictional ones composed of language, not the real rivers, not the real nation.

Ed's recognition of the distance between reality and its representations, as well as his recognition of the performative nature of gender, affords him an opportunity to challenge conventional definitions of masculinity and femininity, an opportunity of which he does not avail himself. Despite the fact that Ed sees these constructions as constructions, he is unable to rise above them, as Fiedler believes that Huck eventually does when he vows to "go to hell" rather than turn Jim in. Rather than forcing his beliefs to conform to society or acting against his own beliefs, Huck decides to opt out of the system in order to save Jim. In this way, according to Fiedler, he reclaims a true, whole self that has been previously inhibited by his society. This interpretation reflects a Freudian view of identity, one in which an authentic self precedes learned social performances. The dark Other is a central part of Fiedler's thesis. The dark Other, according to Fiedler, is our shadow self, and love of this Other is figuratively love and acceptance of that darker part of our own natures: "Our dark-skinned beloved will take us in, we assure ourselves, when we have been cut off, or have cut ourselves off, from all others, without rancor or the insult of forgiveness" (11). Fiedler recognizes this portrait of acceptance as naive wishful thinking on the part of the authors. Ultimately, through the love of the Other, this bond that is outside the normal conventions of society, the authors reveal a desire to love and to accept the wayward part of the self, that part of the self that has sinned.

In *Deliverance*, instead of a dark-skinned companion for the four adventurers, the Other takes the form of two violent white mountain men. It is interesting that this novel that mirrors so much of *Huckleberry Finn*—including the all-male journey downriver, the blurring of gender distinctions, and the suggestion of homoerotic bonding—would present as dark, unacknowledged shadow figures characters who are of the same socioeconomic class as Huck, the narrator with whom readers should identify in the earlier novel. The mountain men also resemble the protagonists of *Deliverance* more closely than Jim resembles Huck in that the hillbillies and the Atlantans are of the same race. These similarities and the blurring of distinctions they invite suggest that the categories of Self and Other are themselves illusions, constructions, and that the Other is merely one of many available choices, a choice that was refused. However, these prohibited attachments are not entirely lost, if not consciously mourned. Butler posits that the bodily ego is "the archaeological remainder, as it were, of unresolved grief" (*The Psychic Life of Power* 133). Because we unconsciously grieve the loss of the forbidden attachments, we compensate by identifying with that prohibited object, and masculinity and femininity are formed.[9] The journey into the depths of the river resembles an archaeological dig to uncover these lost object choices. Significantly, a mountain man once told Lewis that the river is "rougher than a night in jail in south Georgia" (*Deliverance* 47), conjuring images of violent homosexuality and foreshadowing the homosexual rape that occurs on the river. For Ed and his companions, the sexual violence of their journey suggests the psychic violence of compulsory heterosexuality.

When Ed and Bobby Trippe first encounter the two mountain men in the darkened woods, Ed's first thought is that they are "escaped convicts" (108). Figuratively, perhaps these embodiments of guilty desires have escaped from the denied depths of the unconscious mind. Ed mentally challenges their intrusion with a more comforting image of their defeat at the hands of his friend Lewis: "Lewis' pectorals loomed up in my mind, and his leg, with the veins bulging out of the divided muscles of his thigh, his leg under water wavering small-ankled and massive as a centaur's" (110). Though Ed does not recognize it, his mental conjuring of Lewis is extremely homoerotic. He visualizes one leg rather than two, and it is hard, massive, bulging. He compares this leg to a centaur's, a mythic creature associated with rampant sexuality. Ed's defense against the overt and violent homosexual threat of the mountain men is the safer unacknowledged desire to which he is accustomed. Butler speaks of "the incorporation of the [lost] attachment *as* identification, where identification becomes a magical, a psychic form of preserving the object" (*The Psychic Life of Power* 134). The trauma of witnessing Bobby's rape causes Ed to identify uncomfortably with his experience: "My rectum and intestines contracted" (*Deliverance* 113). Ed is saved from similar violation when Lewis penetrates the body of his would-be rapist with a phallic arrow. Ed rejects the similarities between himself and Bobby, suggesting the foreclosure of prohibited desire; however, his more comfortable identification with the hypermasculine Lewis suggests the melancholic internalization of this lost attachment.

Although acceptance is problematic, repression is likewise difficult to maintain. Ed's response to the eruption of overt homosexuality through

Bobby's rape is to devote more energy toward its repression. The men bury the body of the slain rapist deep within the woods, comfort themselves with the knowledge that soon it will be buried even deeper under the man-made lake (the lake that will, importantly, eliminate the possibility of future river journeys), and vow never to speak of these experiences again. The coming lake will bury all evidence that it was briefly possible to explore these desires at all. In addition, as Pamela Barnett points out, "Most brutal among Ed's defenses is his repeated reduction of Bobby to 'ass,' the orifice that has become feminized through the rape. . . . [For example] When Bobby fails to follow an order that Ed has given him, Ed thinks to himself, 'Bobby, you incompetent asshole, you soft city country-club man' (201)" (8). Ed's humiliating cruelty to Bobby following Bobby's rape resembles what Eve Sedgwick describes as homosexual panic. According to Sedgwick, homosexual panic arises when the intense male social bonds that male entitlement demands become difficult to distinguish from the "most reprobated bonds" of homosexuality. The similarity of the two bonds, one socially mandated and one socially prohibited, causes confusion and fear that one's peer and perhaps even oneself may be a homosexual. The fear and confusion leads to violence against those perceived to be homosexual threats (185–186). Homosexual panic and the fear and violence associated with it are examples of the tools that Butler says our culture uses to regulate appropriate identity. By demeaning Bobby, Ed also strengthens the repression of the homosexuality that he fears in himself.

In *Deliverance*, the slain mountain man's companion returns, kills Ed's companion Drew, and attempts to kill the rest of them. As the men flee, they are spilled from their canoes when they encounter violent rapids. Unable to skim the surface, they are plunged into the depths of the water that threatens to hold them under: Those who plumb such psychic depths risk their lives. During this spill, Lewis's leg, previously associated with his masculine sexuality, is broken. Assessing the damage, Ed says, "I could tell by its outline that his thigh was broken; I reached down and felt of it very softly. Against the back of my hand his penis stirred with pain. . . . There was a great profound human swelling under my hand. It felt like a thing that was trying to open, to split, to let something out" (149–150). The previously sexualized leg wants to let something out, but Ed cannot let that happen. The stirring of the penis in pain suggests the outing of forbidden sexual desire. Unprepared to confront that which he has spent so much energy repressing, Ed's only alternative is to kill the mountain man who threatens them through his embodiment of homosexual desire. If we view the mountain man as a part of the self, as the unwelcome return of the negative impulses that the self has repressed, then Ed's stalking and killing of this man is an attempt to stamp out that which is horrifying in himself.

Like the hypermasculine Lewis, Ed stalks and then kills this man with a phallic arrow. During this pursuit, Ed engages in numerous types of penetration. Ed describes climbing the cliff wall as "fuck[ing] it for an extra inch or two in the moonlight" (177). Of calculating his prey's next move, he says, "For me to kill him under these conditions, he would have to be thinking as I had thought for him, and not approximately but exactly. The minds would have to merge" (185). And as Ed prepares the shot that will pierce his foe with an arrow, he thinks, "We were closed together, and the feeling of a peculiar kind of intimacy increased . . . and I just knew then that I had him" (191). Ed's thoughts reflect an uneasy blend of hatred, desire, and identification, an untenable psychic position. As he had before the rape, Ed deflects his homoerotic desire into figurative representations of it so that, in his annihilation of the threat of homosexuality, he may figuratively consummate his desire. Historically, being the penetrator in a same-sex union is less taboo or demeaning than being the penetrated. Because traditional masculinity involves dominance and control over the Other, and to be penetrated by another suggests submission or passivity, passive homosexuality and masculinity are at odds. If the (white) masculine body is that which possesses and penetrates, the black body, the female body, and the homosexual body are to be penetrated and possessed.

However, in the process of killing the mountain man, attempting to silence forever his troubling desires and to reassert his masculinity, Ed gravely wounds himself: "Something went through me from behind, and I heard a rip like tearing a bedsheet" (192). As Barnett points out, the language here suggests anal rape, as Ed is penetrated from behind. The physical wound is from one of Ed's own arrows that he has fallen upon, but the figurative wound is to Ed's psyche and sense of himself. Significantly, the wound, although unintentional, is self-inflicted, indicating the damage caused by the tremendous energy Ed devotes to repression. Here, his own penetration brings the suggestion of homosexuality dangerously close to the surface, where it threatens to reveal itself to the world: "[I]t was in me. *In* me. The flesh around the metal moved pitifully, like a mouth. . . . I put the knife against the flesh above the wound. Just cut right down, I said aloud. Cut down and cut it loose" (195). His response is to physically cut the offending arrow from his side, violently removing the evidence with yet another phallic symbol. The brutality of Ed's actions reminds us of the stakes involved. Indulging in forbidden desires results in pain and injury: better at one's own hands than at the hands of others.

In comparison with the ending of Dickey's novel, the ending of Twain's *Adventures of Huckleberry Finn* seems, if read straightforwardly, naively optimistic. By accepting the Dark Other, Huck challenges his and his community's construction of race, and he then finds that he can no longer live within that community's confines: "But I reckon I got to light out for the Territory ahead of the rest, because Aunt Sally she's going to adopt me and sivilize me and I can't stand it. I been there before" (362). As discussed above, Twain may have intended this ending ironically, but on the surface, Huck abandons the community that does not share his acceptance of the Other as part of the self. The linear structure of *Huckleberry Finn* contrasts with the cyclical structure of *Deliverance* and enhances this interpretation of the ending. Throughout Twain's novel, Huck and Jim move forward down the river, and Huck continues this forward movement beyond the novel's ending. The river likewise continues to flow after they leave it; for Huck and the river, this is a one-way trip.

In contrast, Dickey's characters planned their return trip from the novel's beginning, and this difference in the novels reflects two different models of identity construction. The four rafters from Atlanta pay local men to drive their cars down to Aintry so they can drive home in comfort after the canoeing is finished. Shortly after their trip, the river will flow no more; it is to be dammed forever to form a man-made lake. Just as "there is no 'I' who stands *behind* in discourse and executes its volition or will *through* discourse" (Butler, *Bodies That Matter* 225, emphasis in original), there is no free territory beyond civilization. Of course, the physical body and mind are present before discourse, but psychologists, philosophers, and anthropologists have long debated the role of language in conscious human thought. Psychologist Peter Carruthers, for example, claims, "[H]uman cognition is constructed in such a way as to require the presence of natural language if it is to function properly" (18). In order to engage in higher-order thinking and to recognize itself as an "I," the human mind needs language, and that language has been shaped by society. Because no human consciousness is free of social constructs, Butler argues that the most one can hope for is freer play among the options that have been socially constructed. Unlike Huck, Ed dutifully destroys that which challenges his own and his community's conceptions of gender and sexuality, and he finds comfort in his return to his community at the novel's close.

He returns from his nightmare experience to comfortable, if not passionate, heterosexuality. In his wife's words, "I'm right here with you. There's no more woods and no more river. Go to sleep" (*Deliverance* 273). Although Ed finds solace in this temporary sleep, Dickey suggests that submerged desire will one day wake. Ed reflects that the river is within him, and that it will be until he dies: "The river and everything I remembered about it became a possession to me, a personal, private possession, as nothing else in my life ever had. Now it ran nowhere but in my head, but there it ran as though immortally. I could feel it—I can feel it—on different places on my body. It pleases me in some curious way that the river does not exist, and that I have it" (275). Here, Ed's description of the river suggests Butler's "archaeological remainder . . . of unresolved grief" (*The Psychic Life of Power* 133). The more troubling suggestion of the novel's ending is that the repressed may one day return again and that bodies do not stay buried forever. We must remember the muddy little girl who informs Ed about a cemetery excavation in Aintry as he prepares to leave the hills and river physically behind him: "They're gonna move them people 'fore they finish the dam. They're diggin' 'em up" (*Deliverance* 266).

Reviewer Kim McLarin's description of Rawles's *My Jim* is apt: "Rawles's book is not meant so much as a repudiation of *The Adventures of Huckleberry Finn*, but an illumination of that great work, a widening." In an interview with Nancy Pearl, Rawles says that in the hands of the right teacher, *Huckleberry Finn* is a "wonderful book" because of the important issues it raises for American history and literature. Although she writes the book to stand alone, Rawles acknowledges that a "richer read" results from having read *Huck Finn* (Pearl), and her novel remains true to the letter of Twain's book in the areas in which the two overlap. Rawles's Jim does indeed love his family; he runs away with the white boy Huck when his mistress, Miss Watson, plans to sell him; he hopes to one day buy his family's freedom; he guiltily recalls punishing his daughter 'Lizbeth for a failure to listen, only to realize she had been rendered deaf by scarlet fever; he receives money from another white boy (Tom); and he is freed by Miss Watson's will. Such details, however, remain on the periphery of Rawles's narrative. Her primary focus is the life of Sadie, Jim's wife, who remains behind in slavery with her children when Jim joins Huck on their river adventures. Yet even though the main character and plot differ greatly, Rawles still honors the spirit of Twain's novel by portraying the inhumanity of slavery and the slave's hunger for freedom.

Rawles widens Twain's focus by drawing on other nineteenth-century works about slavery, including slave narratives, such as those by Frederick Douglass and Harriet Jacobs, and including the famous antislavery novel *Uncle Tom's Cabin* (1852). Rawles also shifts the focus away from black and white relations, as it is in *Huckleberry Finn*, to show instead the perspective of the black family left behind. From that family's perspective, Rawles creates a somber, uncertain ending that pointedly contrasts with the slapstick and deus ex machina plot points of Twain's final chapters. The uncertainty at the novel's end and the novel's overall foregrounding of the function of memory and language cause the reader to question the absolute authority of any single text and to embrace fluidity of expression and interpretation.

My Jim uses antislavery tropes that were common in the nineteenth century, some of which are also used by Twain. One of the most commonly depicted evils of slavery was the separation of black families. Douglass's 1845 narrative recounts his early separation from his mother and grandmother, and Harriett Beecher Stowe depicts Eliza's daring escape to avoid losing her son to a slave trader. Twain also shows his Jim lamenting the separation from his family: "He was thinking about his wife and his children, away up yonder, and he was low and homesick. . . . He was often moaning and mourning that way, nights, when he judged I was asleep, and saying 'Po' little 'Lizabeth! Po' little Johnny! It's mighty hard; I spec' I ain't every gwyne to see you no mo', no mo'!'" (201). Likewise, Rawles shows Jim's wife, Sadie, crying for her lost loved ones after almost a lifetime of separation: "I cries thinking bout how they force me to leave my husband. How they tear my children from me. All them years ago. I wants to stay and they aint let me. . . . My Jim she whisper. My Lizbeth. My Jonnie. Been years since I calls they names" (15). Here, Rawles remains true to the spirit of *Huckleberry Finn* but "widens" the perspective to show the lifelong pain resulting from the separation of families.

The corruption of religious beliefs in support of slavery is another common antislavery theme adapted by Rawles. Douglass, in his 1845 narrative, pointedly distinguishes between the "slaveholding religion" of the South, with its "men-stealers for ministers, women-whippers for missionaries, and cradle-plunderers for church members," and the "Christianity of Christ" (120). Similarly, Huck reveals the hypocrisy of the religion he has been taught when, in rejecting that religion in order to help Jim, he unwittingly does the truly Christian thing. Along these same lines, Rawles reveals that the slaveholders' economic concerns supersede their spiritual ones: "We gots Sunday service in the smokehouse when the tobacco aint drying. Harvest time Mas Watson don't say nothing bout Jesus. We aint got souls when the tobacco curing" (35). Unlike Twain's naive Huck, Sadie recognizes and names the religious hypocrisy and exploitative practices of the whites in charge.

Rawles also responds directly to Stowe's portrayal of religion, and she is more critical of Stowe than she is of Twain. Unlike Twain or Douglass, Stowe shows the positive power of religion in a slave society. Little Eva, from *Uncle Tom's Cabin*, the almost angelic child who is too pure for this world, converts slaves to Christianity and invokes the name of Christ to convince her father to free his slaves. Tom, the Christ-like figure of the novel, endures physical torture rather than rise up against his master, knowing that his true reward awaits him in heaven. Rawles names the black preacher in *My Jim* after this famous nineteenth-century author in order to comment on Stowe's portrayal of religion: "Stowe all the time talking bout heaven. Getting to the other side and resting in the Lord. I so sick with wanting my freedom I cant stands to hear no sermons. Folks all the time singing bout campground. I just want to lay my head down on Jims chest and never gets up. Nobody to bother us. Thats my heaven" (80). Rawles recognizes that the promise of paradise was often used as a ploy to convince slaves patiently to obey their earthly masters. For Sadie and for Rawles, the hope of heavenly reward does not compensate for a lifetime of suffering.

Beyond augmenting Twain's points, part of the "widening" perspective that Rawles creates in *My Jim* involves talking back to Twain's novel and underscoring its omissions. At times, Twain emphasizes Jim's superstition and ignorance for comic effect, and the Tom-inspired hijinks of the novel's last chapters, aimed at parodying Romantic literature, deprive the ending of moral seriousness. Readers come to know Twain's Jim after he has fled his captivity, and although Jim does long for his absent family, from Huck's perspective, at least, his and Jim's life is "mighty free and easy and comfortable on a raft" (155). A careful reader might understand that the situation likely is not so comfortable for Jim, but Rawles's point is that we do not have access to Jim's thoughts in Twain's novel. In interviews, Rawles states that she "hope[s] readers [of her novel] will take away some knowledge of what slavery is like for ordinary people who don't have a chance to escape" (Johnson 178). She adds that Sadie is a composite of such people who "spent their lives in slavery," and *Huck Finn* "is not a book to read if you want to learn about slavery" (Pearl).

Rather than departing on a quest for freedom, Sadie and her children are forced to survive in bondage. And where Twain uses humor to draw his reader in and to make his moral message more palatable, Rawles confronts the emotional pain of slavery directly. For example, when Sadie is beaten in an effort to extract information about Jim's whereabouts, Rawles describes her physical and emotional condition: "My arms pull back behind me. My bones stretch long like the limbs on a sycamore. Lord I be pain. And what they doing with my children. . . . My throat so parched I cant cries out if I wants to. The blood from the beating sticking to my back. The mud still on my face. I tries to hold on cause I cant leaves my children. Not like this. I wants them to see me strong again" (98). Not only does Rawles emphasize the physical abuse with concrete details, such as Sadie's thirst and her strained limbs, she also emphasizes the emotional pain of worry and Sadie's strength to persevere. Like Jacobs, Douglass, and Stowe, she draws readers' attention to the physical and psychological abuse of slaves, including the sexual abuse of slave women, and like them she taps the readers' emotions to promote change, in this case a change in understanding or attitude. Yet Rawles makes the emotion seem more authentic and realistic than the sometimes overly sentimental narratives of Jacobs, Douglass, and Stowe by taking a page from Twain's book. Instead of the educated, formal first-person prose of Jacobs and Douglass or the educated, formal third-person narrator of Stowe, Rawles uses first-person dialect, as does Twain, to animate her narrator. The reader imagines listening to a real oral narrative told by a former slave, making her experiences more believable. And because of the integral connection between self-narration and identity construction, hearing Sadie's autobiographical narrative conjures a seemingly real person in readers' imaginations. Through the emotional impact of such scenes, Rawles also encourages a new reading of Twain's Jim. When we witness the suffering of those Jim leaves behind, his flight from slavery appears less noble and brave.

Rawles also emphasizes gender issues that are nearly absent in Twain's novel. For many, *Huckleberry Finn* is a boy's adventure book, a story of male bonding,[10] or a quest for racial unity. Women, for the majority of the novel, are absent. By telling Sadie's poignant and convincing story, *My Jim* highlights an absence in Twain's book, which does not even give Jim's wife a name. According to Patrick Colm Hogan, this is a process that all readers go through when interpreting a work of literature, and Rawles, like the other contemporary writers examined in this study, was a reader of a classic text before she wrote its reconfiguration. A story activates a reader's own "memory fragments" that "become part of that literary synthesis, contributing to our understanding of characters, our concretization of scenes, our inference to the unstated causes of events" (162). As a black woman and a feminist, Rawles interpolates a version of herself into Twain's narrative and creates her own novel to articulate her interpretation of the earlier work, for, as Kroeber suggests, "[T]he only adequate fashion of interpreting a story is through more narrative discourse" (63). Through her focus on a female slave, Rawles echoes Jacobs's *Incidents in the Life of a Slave Girl*, which emphasizes that slavery can be worse in some ways for women than for men due to their greater sexual vulnerability to white men and their maternal attachment to children who are treated as another's property. But Rawles also lays partial blame for black women's suffering on black men. In doing so, she again changes the reader's view of Jim and colors the way we read this character's escape in *Huck Finn*.

The Jim that Rawles creates, though loving, kind, spirited, and well-intentioned, is also full of empty promises. After Sadie is sold to another plantation and Jim visits her for a day, the two pledge their love as they say a temporary good-bye: "You got my heart belong to me I [Sadie] says. You aint never gonna lose me he [Jim] say" (95). Shortly after that Sadie learns that Jim has run away without her and the children. Hearing nothing for months, Sadie fears that he is dead, but Jim finally sends word that he is alive and will come for her and the children: "You ain't got to worry none" (109). Unfortunately, Jim comes too late. Master Stevens has already seduced their daughter, Lizbeth, sold their son, Jonnie, out of spite, and blinded Sadie in one eye before selling her to a slave trader headed downriver, her punishment for setting the tobacco barn on fire. Jim finds his wife waiting with the rest of the coffle for the journey south. Fresh from his adventures with Huckleberry and rich with the money given him by Tom, Jim is still powerless to help his physically and emotionally shattered wife. Thinking of his broken promises, the reader compares his river journey in *Huckleberry Finn* to the one for which Sadie is destined, and Jim suffers by comparison. Although Master Stevens is the true villain, Jim might echo some readers' thoughts as he says, "Gots my freedom but I loss my family. What kind a man I be" (130). Still, he makes Sadie one more promise: to come back for Lizbeth to buy her freedom. Years later, Sadie learns that Jim returns for Lizbeth after the Union has already freed her and the other slaves in Hannibal, once again too late: "But her [Lizbeth's] heart broken and she die in the refugee camp. Next day I comes and she aint there" (158). In contrast, Sadie refuses to leave her family even in freedom, although doing so would be a dream come true: "Jimmy you know I loves you. Loves you from the moment you born. I waits all my nights for the day when you come back to me. But now I gots another. I gots two sons and a daughter living and none of them Dubans. But he father them all and my granbabies too. So him I cant think of leaving" (159–160). Rawles's Jim is not a bad man, but his decision to run without his family appears selfish and negligent, especially when compared to Sadie's decision to honor her responsibilities when her heart longs to do otherwise.

Sexual and gender oppression is a recurring theme in *My Jim*, and Rawles shows that it extends beyond the confines of slavery. As in Louis Bayard's *The Pale Blue Eye*, Sena Jeter Naslund's *Ahab's Wife*, and Bharati Mukherjee's *The Holder of the World*, readers may detect in Rawles's attention to gender issues a presentist bias, interpreting a nineteenth-century novel through the lens of twenty-first-century social norms. For example, Miss Douglass, Jim's owner, spends her youth constantly asking Jim, a seer, whom she will marry, and Sadie surmises, "Thats all she got to look forward to" (35). And Sadie's daughter (born of another father after Jim has left) is dismissed from the reconstruction school when she becomes pregnant. As Sadie tells her granddaughter, Marianne: "Your mama love school more than anything else but you the end of school for her. Your daddy stay in school" (144). And Andrew, the black man used as a stud by his master in Louisiana, tells Sadie that the only person he ever loved was not one of his female partners, but a boy named Lemuel. In her implied critique of nineteenth-century gender norms, Rawles treads territory that Twain never approaches, and Sadie registers the stifling of identity for the reader. Yet Rawles is not overly simplistic in her characterizations of men and women. Through Papa Duban, Sadie's husband in her old age, she shows a man who is loving and reliable, and through Marianne's mother, who eventually abandons her young daughter to find a new life, she shows a woman who is neither.

Like other contemporary reconfigurations, Rawles also explores the subjective nature of truth and the effect of perspective on meaning by emphasizing the malleability of language. In an interview with Sarah Anne Johnson, Rawles says, "I was also intrigued by the similarities between the language of love and the language of slavery—possession, belonging, mine, we are bound. I came to the conclusion that you can't possess what you don't love (you can only use it) and when you seek to love, you seek not to possess but liberate" (176). The paradoxical nature of the statement above—that you can't possess what you do not love, but love seeks to liberate—is echoed by the language with which Sadie describes her loved ones: "My Jim, my Lizbeth, my Jonnie" (15). The same words could be used by a master to describe his or her slave. These seemingly opposite relationships, a slave owner versus a wife and mother, employ identical language to refer to property and loved ones. In addition, as Jim and Sadie speak of their love, they often say that they belong to each other or are bound together, again using the language of possession.

Slaveholders also manipulate language as a means of control in the novel. Sadie complains, "Whites always telling us dont steal dont lie dont cheat. And here they come stealing us and lying to us and cheating us out our freedom. They beat us with the word just as sure as they beat us with the whip" (36). Language is a powerful weapon, most often wielded by people determined to maintain their power. The meanings of words, such as freedom, can be ignored or changed to suit their needs. At another point, Sadie explains to Marianne why Jim does not stay in Missouri after he has been freed by Miss Watson's will: "Jim a free man then but that aint mean nothing in Missouri. . . . Any no count patroller come snatch you and sell you to slavers no matter how many papers you got" (23). Although the papers—writing—should suggest truth and legitimacy, this meaning can be dismissed when expedient. Some texts convey power while others do not, and those in power decide which ones are which. By extension, some books, or stories, become canonical while others do not, and again, those in power decide which is which. By calling attention to the manipulation of meaning, Rawles undermines the authorities within the text, just as her reconfiguration weakens *Huckleberry Finn*'s exclusive claim to Jim.

Rawles emphasizes the subjectivity of Truth and the reader's/listener's role in making meaning of a story through the structure of the novel as well. Marianne tells the reader that she writes down everything her grandmother says (18), but her grandmother says that such transcription is unnecessary: "Everything I tells you happen long ago. Me I remembers it just like this morning. You want to know bout my things and why I keeps them close to me. I tells you if you listen. No need to write it down" (58). But contemporary cognitive psychology tells us that such accurate recall is unlikely. According to Kay Young and Jeffrey L. Saver:

> Modern neuroscience has demonstrated that retrieving memories is not the simple act of accessing a storehouse of ready-made photos in a stable neural album, preserved with complete fidelity to the moment of the formation. Rather, each act of recall is a re-creation, drawing upon multiple, dynamically changing modular fragments to shape a new mosaic. . . . All memories are suspect, at the neural level. Fidelity-stable recall and self-interpretation of the past is not a property of the human brain and mind. The varied subjectivity of literary autobiographic productions has its root in the inescapable subjectivity of the brain's narrative and memory system. This variability of memory, however, does not detract from the primacy of narrative recall in organizing human experience. (79)

The mosaic into which the memories are shaped in Young and Saver's description above resembles the quilt that Marianne and Sadie construct as Sadie remembers her life. Each significant object that she has saved from her past, such as a fragment of pottery or a button, generates an associated story, which then becomes a pattern reflected in the quilt. The memory fragments are pieced together to form a cohesive narrative, which is as much an act of creativity as the finished quilt itself. Because memories are inaccurate and influenced by current situations, the construction of an accurate narrative of her past is not possible, but storytelling, narrative construction, is still an important part of human attempts to understand our experience. Accurate recall seems less important, though, if we consider that stories often have more to do with the storyteller's present than with his or her actual past. As Hogan puts it, "'[R]etrieving' a memory is a highly elaborate and constructive process. . . . In other words, we do not really remember the past, we reconstruct it—often in a way that reflects our present concerns as much as our past experience, sometimes in a way that does not reflect our past experience at all" (161). The objects that Sadie and Marianne look at, discuss, and represent in the quilt, then, prime the memories and anchor the narrative, and around them they embellish with details. The resulting cohesive, nonlinear, narrative of memory fragments and the quilt pattern born of scraps are both artistic creations.

Finally, the troubling evasion sequence of *Huckleberry Finn* disappears from *My Jim*, as it does from Seelye's and Dickey's reconfigurations. Rawles creates a somber, uncertain ending that shuns closure and naive optimism, pointedly contrasting with the minstrel-show antics of Twain's final chapters. Because she devotes several chapters to Sadie's postwar experiences, she emphasizes that suffering does not end with slavery. As Sadie puts it, "The only ones free the spirits" (160). The novel begins with Marianne, Sadie's granddaughter, pondering a marriage proposal from a young man who plans to move to Oklahoma. Unsure whether she is ready for marriage and whether she can leave her grandmother, Marianne asks for Sadie's advice. As Marianne says at the end of chapter 1, "For more than a week Nanna tell me what grown folks scared to talk about. . . . And at the end of the telling I knows what to do" (18). Sadie's life story inspires her granddaughter's decision, but the reader never learns what that decision will be. Does Marianne abandon her elderly, half-blind grandmother, as Jim does so many years earlier? Does she deny herself marriage and happiness because of a sense of duty and the fear of change? Which is the better alternative in this case? The ambiguous ending encourages readers to think about what they would do in Marianne's situation, but it also encourages us to think about the perspectives of Sadie and of Jim. Should Jim have stayed with his wife and children and risked being sold away by Miss Watson? Should he have taken them with him and increased the risk of capture for them all? Was his decision to run alone the only viable alternative? Rawles raises these questions but refuses the false comfort of easy answers. The ending's ambiguity coupled with Sadie's life-story in contrast to what we have previously known of Jim suggest the subjective nature of truth and the effect of perspective on meaning. The ending also implies that in any story, such as Jim's from *Huckleberry Finn*, there is much that readers and listeners cannot know. Twain's novel is told from the perspective of Huck, and Jim never has control of the narrative, never has his own voice. Although Rawles's novel is called *My Jim*, Sadie and Marianne control the narrative, and Jim still has no voice. His perspective is yet to be written.

When Sadie and Marianne finish the quilt that they have pieced together throughout the unfolding of Sadie's narrative, they read it together, much as one would read a work of literature. But for Marianne, the quilt tells a new story: "Lets put up this quilt and look at it. You call off what you see. I believes we gots everybody up there. . . . All them watching over you. Folks you aint even know wishing you well praying right now for your soul. If you let the spirits near you they guide you along. All them Africans. They spirits never settle till the last of they children come home" (161). For most listeners, the story heard becomes a composite of their own stories and the speaker's story (Schank and Abelson 14; Hogan 162). In this case, the narrative of suffering and loss that Sadie pieces together has become, through Marianne's listening, signified by her active participation in the quilt-making, a tale of comfort and protection. In part, the comfort and protection stems from the fact that the story emotionally binds Marianne to her grandmother, enhancing their sense of a shared identity. In accepting the quilt, accepting the story, and making both her own, Marianne does not diminish her grandmother's experiences or her story. Similarly, in revising Twain's novel, Rawles memorializes *Huckleberry Finn*, binding her contemporary tale to the American cultural narrative, commenting on it, and making it her own.

Clinch makes chapter 9 of *Huckleberry Finn* the jumping-off point for his novel *Finn*. In that chapter, an excerpt of which Clinch quotes for an epigraph, Huck and Jim see a dead body in a house floating down the Mississippi River. Jim later tells Huck that this dead man is his father. Twain never explains who has killed Pap Finn, why he has been killed, or how the house has come to be floating downriver; the answers to these questions form the disturbing conclusion to Clinch's novel and appear to create a backstory that predates Twain. Through this reconfiguration, *Finn* changes our understanding of *Huckleberry Finn*. Like Rawles, Clinch challenges the truth we once thought we understood about this classic novel and about our culture, and, like Dickey, he challenges the existence of a pure Edenic origin that may somehow be reclaimed.

As with most contemporary writers who reconfigure classic American texts, Clinch's desire to reconfigure *Huckleberry Finn* appears to have sprung from mixed motives: part homage and part critique, part bid at literary greatness and part marketing strategy. In his essay, "Dangerous Words, Dangerous Ideas: A Prescription for Literature That Lasts," Clinch speculates about the educational opportunities that a classroom pairing of his book and Twain's might afford. Clearly, being paired with the "quintessentially American" book in literature classes would be a tremendous honor for an author of only one published novel, and it would also be tremendously profitable. At a talk at an Oxford, Pennsylvania, public library in 2008, Clinch mentioned that he and his agent twice rejected a publisher's financial offer before finally accepting the satisfactory third offer. Simultaneously commercializing and idealizing canonical literature, the reconfiguration manifests the postmodernism's general blurring of high- and low-culture distinctions.

Finn is a complex postmodern response to Twain's work and also an homage to its status as American icon. In a radio interview, Clinch remarks:

> A lot of people have said I had a lot of nerve to take on what everybody agrees is the greatest centerpiece of all American literature and to find something new there, to dare to muck about with Huck Finn, with Mark Twain. For my part, I set out to be as true and as honorable to that material as I could because I respected it so, and, therefore, when I was working up this underlayment to it, it was more a matter of honor than of daring, I think. (Moss-Coane)

Clinch also states that to "write a book that's challenging enough and important enough and, above all, *true enough* to be banned by more than one generation . . . for more than one reason" was a worthy goal for novelists everywhere ("Dangerous Words"). Of course, Twain does just that with *Huckleberry Finn*, and Clinch says that he would be honored to follow in those footsteps.

However, by reconfiguring Twain's work, telling the life-story of Huck's racist, abusive, and alcoholic father Pap Finn, Clinch also echoes the criticism of Arac, Marx, and others. Specifically, through the creation of Mary, Huck's black slave mother, Clinch seems to agree with critics who suggest that the bond between Jim and Huck created by Twain is not as epiphanic and zeitgeist-altering as many believe. As previously discussed, the climactic scene in the middle of chapter 31, when Huck abandons his plan to tell Miss Watson Jim's location, is traditionally read as a noble moment of enlightenment. Arac, however, undercuts the significance of Huck's decision: "Twain deliberately simplified and restricted Huck's resources by eliminating from his consciousness the languages of Christian love and republican equality. . . . Twain achieves tremendous comic power, but only by omitting the actual means by which individuals in American history came to act against the system of slavery." Arac also argues that idealizing the relationship between Huck and Jim, which thrives only in isolation from society, invites complacency: "Liberal white American opinion identifies with the wonderful boy Huck. Even though his society was racist, he was not, and so 'we' are not" (779).

Clinch's creation of Huck's mother suggests how much further Twain could have gone to reveal the unspoken intricacies of race in America. Clinch has said that the character of Mary arose after he asked himself, "What kind of woman would have a child with that man?" (Reading and Book Talk). The answer, he decided, would be a woman with no options, so he imagines her as a slave captured by Finn during her attempt to escape from her master. Of course, the Pap Finn that Twain creates is "a Niagara of bigotry" (Clinch, "Dangerous Words"), and so, too, is the character that

Clinch creates, despite his relationship with a black woman. Finn's father, known only as The Judge, has a deep-seated racism along with social respectability, and he passes down only one of these two traits to his son. Pap Finn recounts to Huckleberry a threatened punishment remembered from his own youth with The Judge: "Said I'd get more than a whipping. Said I could count on being buggered up the ass if it come to that. Buggered up the ass by a filthy good-for-nothing nigger" (*Finn* 77). The Judges combined threats of sex and violence, racial hatred and parenting, unsettle the reader, as well as Finn. The conflict between this learned racism and his sexual attraction to black women, linked from his childhood, unhinges Finn. His relationship with Mary, whom Clinch says he loves in his own way, leads to guilt and shame at his own behavior, and his hatred of her becomes also a hatred of himself: "Finn despises himself upon arising, both for that which he has done and for that which he has not done" (271). Clinch suggests the complexity of racial enmity in America, acknowledging that our feelings about the racial Other are often conflicted and often more about ourselves.

Through this family structure—white father, black mother, and mixed child—Clinch suggests the intimate closeness of races living in America even in the nineteenth century and points to the reality of interracial relationships that were often unacknowledged. In her book *Was Huck Black?*, a source that Clinch read while researching his novel (Reading and Book Talk), Fishkin argues that Huck's voice is influenced by the dialect of black people whom Twain knew and black characters he had created in earlier works. As Fishkin explains, "[T]he voice of Huck Finn, the beloved national symbol and cultural icon, was part black" (144). Because *Huckleberry Finn* is "the novel that we have embraced as most expressive of who we really are" (144), Fishkin argues that her findings underscore the extent to which the nation is also part black, a fact that has been all-too-often erased from canonical literature. Building on Fishkin's assertions, Clinch makes Huck's mixed-racial heritage literal. Biracial individuals were common enough in the nineteenth century to necessitate laws defining who was black and who was white, and Paul R. Spickard estimates that in 1850, approximately two hundred thousand mixed-race persons lived in the upper South (including Mark Twain's Missouri) (247). Of course, Clinch's novel could not have been written in Twain's time, or, if it were, it would not have been widely embraced. Clinch says that he "set out to reflect on the shifting states of race relations in America" ("Dangerous Words"), updating Twain's narrative of American life to more closely reflect the vision held by Americans today.

In Clinch's rendering, Huckleberry Finn, "one of the most famous characters in the literary gallery of American individualists" (Traber 18), is half white and half black. Through repeated image patterns, Clinch suggests that both black and white are also figuratively part of Finn himself. For example, Finn is sentenced to a year at Alton Penitentiary after nearly killing a man in a bar fight, a man who has derisively commented on Huck's racial background. Clinch explains that Alton was a real prison, open during the appropriate time period, that the author had discovered while researching the book:[11]

> First thing they did when you went there was they shaved half your head to make it more difficult for you to escape. . . . So Finn is there for a year; he works outdoors; he works in the fields; he does what the prisoners would have done. At the end of the year, the prison barber comes and he shaves the other half of his head, and here we have in the middle of this book, which is about race, it's about black, it's about white, it's about the conflicts, about overlap, we have this guy with half of his head white and half black. And that was just a gift from the gods of research. (Reading and Book Talk)

Upon being released from prison, Pap Finn's head is both brown and white, representing the mental conflict between his father's white supremacist teachings and his wife's acceptance and love. In *Playing in the Dark*, Toni Morrison comments on a "dark, abiding Africanist presence" unacknowledged in canonical American literature (5). This presence, according to Morrison, marks the influence of African Americans and of slavery on the white imagination. In a similar vein, Clinch's novel, by documenting Huck Finn's parentage, seemingly uncovers a formerly hidden black presence in American literature, and the biracial identity of an American icon suggests a dual heritage for us all. Clinch suggests a complex national origin that is often elided by history and literature. Not only are we racially mixed, but our heritage combines the violent hatred and abuses of Huck's father with the nurturing acceptance of his mother. The novel encourages readers to see white and black, with all the associations the two colors entail, within themselves, just as they see them in these iconic fictional characters.

Like Seelye's, Clinch's novel also seems to address critics' concerns about Twain's overly glib ending. By focusing on Twain's most despicable character and, if not making the reader like him, at least making us care right up until his well-deserved but witheringly dark end, Clinch manages to exorcise some of his novel's hatred and racism while also helping us see them in ourselves. In Twain's novel, a black man and a white boy, two people separated by a seemingly unbridgeable social barrier, form a bond of love and friendship in their several weeks' journey on a raft. Through unlikely plot contortions, Twain manages to end with both characters contented without destroying the society in which they lived, but they cannot remain together. Huck lights out for the territory, and Jim enters his freedom in a manner undisclosed to the reader. Clinch's Finn, on the other hand, despite more than a decade of intimate contact, does not unlearn his racism: "[D]ay by day . . . he finds himself pursuing her degradation as if by diminishing her he might diminish his own wrongdoing" (272). One does not so easily shake free of such a confused tangle of emotions, the ends of which are firmly held by family and friends. Likewise, as Rawles also emphasizes, the country's racism did not end with slavery and reconstruction. Despite overt promises of equality, racial discrimination plagued the U.S. in very obvious ways through the Civil Rights movement and continues to a lesser extent today.

In an attempt to rid himself forever of his dual attraction and hatred for Mary and to erase what he perceives to be the sin of their union, Finn murders her and skins her body:

> Thus with brutal thrust and tender prod does he remove all trace of skin. . . . Fastidious in his methods, he arranges each portion upside down or inside out, its inner surface made outer to show red and slick and fibrous but never allowed to reveal the dark curse of its hidden face. He arranges the pieces thus to speak of death and death only without particulars, as if by such transformation he can alter all that has gone before and begin anew, clean and pure and washed in the indiscriminate blood. (42)

Finn's obsessive removal of Mary's skin mirrors his country's obsession with skin color and race. Mary becomes a sacrificial victim, by whose blood Finn hopes to wash himself clean, or white. Likewise he whitewashes the room in which the two had slept and tells Huck that his real mother had been a white woman who died in childbirth. But the bloodstains show through the painted walls, and Clinch's novel reveals the truth about Huck's—and America's—biracial heritage as well. As in Dickey's *Deliverance*, repressed aspects of the self always return. Finn's forbidden desires return as he seduces another black woman and plans to kill her as well.

Clinch's revision encourages readers to feel that they understand more about Twain's novel than the narrator himself, young Huck, does. Early in *Huckleberry Finn*, many of St. Petersburg's residents are convinced of Pap Finn's death by drowning when a decayed corpse floats down the river. Twain suggests Huck's savviness by revealing the boy's knowledge that the corpse could not be his father's, because "a drownded man don't float on his back, but on his face" (14). Clinch's revision, however, undermines the boy's knowledge by opening with this same scene and later revealing the body to be Mary's. Although he is not fooled like the rest of St. Petersburg into believing his father has died, Huck also does not recognize his own mother. Clinch's version further unsettles the reader's faith in Huck's narrative reliability when we reflect on the scene in which Huck and Jim discover the dead body in the house floating down river. In *Finn*, we see that the house on the river is Huck's own boyhood home, and the baby bottle and dress that he and Jim find belonged to Huck and his mother. Twain's Huck does not recognize his father's body, the face of which is turned toward the wall, but after reading *Finn* and superimposing Clinch's fictional world onto Twain's, we see that he also does not recognize his own house. Near the end, when Clinch's Huck naively believes his father's lie about his mother's identity, we see that Huck does not even know himself; his origins have been obscured by time and by lies.

Finally, by incorporating a symbolic act of writing and reading, through the nearly illiterate Finn's insane scrawls on the walls of his house, Clinch reminds us that the attempt to define and to understand experience through language, including understanding a nation's identity through its canonical literature, is at once an innately human and innately flawed endeavor. After Finn has whitewashed the walls of his and Mary's bedroom, he feels compelled to write upon these white walls, first with his dirty fingers and then with burned charcoal, the reblackening again suggesting that what he loathes and despises springs from within: "Something inexorable within him stirs. . . . [H]e climbs the stairs to the bedroom, and there upon the wall in anguished word and picture he describes the story of his urge and of his longing and of his despair over the fate of his poor doomed immortal soul" (135). The black and white in connection with writing also suggests that both races, and the turmoil they share, are necessary to create the meaning Finn desires, a meaning that records in microcosm the racial strife of America. Finn documents his deeds, but also his suffering, his ambivalence, and his feeling of powerlessness before the will of others and before his own desires. By writing, he attempts to exorcise his demons. Similarly, narrative helps us understand ourselves and make sense of reality, but that reality is in turn shaped by what we write. Narratives help us understand and define our culture and history, and by reshaping classic narratives, contemporary writers attempt to make them better fit their own understanding of identity.

Clinch also reminds readers that interpretations are always influenced by the perception of the interpreter and are always under construction. When another black woman, whose husband Finn has also killed, unbeknownst to her, visits his home and reads his walls, she sees only his crimes recorded there in black and white and shoots him as he sleeps. The reader familiar with Twain's *Huckleberry Finn* knows that days later, but also a century and a half earlier, Huck sees the writing on these walls and finds no meaning in it at all: "[A]ll over the walls was the ignorantest kind of words and pictures, made with charcoal" (61). Just as humans project their own anxieties and desires onto others, so, too, their desires, fears, and circumstances affect the meaning they see or fail to see in a text, whether it be a scrawled message or a novel like *Huckleberry Finn*. The nonlinear structure of Clinch's novel also suggests the unending layers of interpretation and the reshaping of identity through experience. *Finn* begins near the story's chronological ending, jumps back to reveal those events' origins, and ends up shortly past the events with which it begins, the same events that occur near the beginning of Twain's novel written 120 years earlier. With each cyclical reiteration, the reader learns new information and pieces together a coherent narrative. The linear structure of Twain's novel suggests an illusion of progress, continually moving forward in a literal and a figurative sense, but Clinch's structure emphasizes that humans constantly revisit and reshape the past, similar to the way contemporary novelists reconfigure classic works to reflect the cultural identity of their own time.

Through their revisions of Twain's "quintessential American book," Seelye, Dickey, Rawles, and Clinch attempt to revise the narrative of America itself. The narrative reinterpretation acknowledges the centrality of this classic narrative to America's self-definition, but it also attempts to better understand the past and the culture from a contemporary perspective. The contemporary novels' postmodern hyperawareness of the separation between signifier and signified and between perception and reality encourage readers to see that their versions of American culture, as well as Twain's, are influenced by their own perceptions. They suggest that this process of exploring and shaping experience through narrative is psychologically and culturally necessary, recurring, and inevitably inaccurate.

6   Life after Awakening
Anne Tyler's Revision of Kate Chopin's *The Awakening*

Published in 1899, Kate Chopin's *The Awakening* was excluded from the American cultural narrative until nearly sixty years later. Contemporary reviewers censured the heroine's immoral conduct and the narrator's failure to condemn her for it. As one reviewer says, "It is not a healthy book; if it points any particular moral or teaches any lesson, the fact is not apparent" (Culley 146). One particularly harsh reviewer vividly conveys the danger he perceives in Chopin's novel, branding it "too strong drink for moral babes, and should be labeled 'poison'" (qtd. in Menke 83). After its initial condemnation, the novel was banned in some locations and sold poorly in others. For many years, the novel was neglected or forgotten, but as early as 1956, Robert Cantwell praised *The Awakening* as one of "the world's masterpieces of short fiction" (qtd. in Sullivan and Smith 147). Then, Per Seyersted reintroduced the work to a wider readership in 1969 when he published Chopin's biography and a complete edition of her works. Since then, *The Awakening*'s place in the American canon has been generally acknowledged. Pamela Glenn Menke, for example, notes that *The Awakening* was "anthologized in its entirety in the first edition of *The Norton Anthology of Literature by Women* (1985)" (81) and has "become the major work by a woman author in the canon of American literature" (84). Similarly, Elaine Showalter views *The Awakening* as "a revolutionary book. . . . Generally recognized today as the first aesthetically successful novel to have been written by an American woman, it marked a significant epoch in the evolution of an American female literary tradition" (34). Clearly, these critics suggest, today's American cultural narrative contains the voice of Edna Pontellier, Chopin's heroine.

Contemporary novelist Anne Tyler reconfigures Chopin's narrative in *Ladder of Years* to add a more mature female voice to that of Edna, who commits suicide at the age of twenty-nine. In many ways, Tyler's heroine, Delia Grinstead, is like an Edna who survives into middle age. Tyler's work has been criticized for being too traditional and old-fashioned in its portrayal of American life. For example, Brooke Allen says, "Delia is strangely anachronistic, seemingly belonging more to the generation brought up on Doris Day and Rock Hudson than on the Rolling Stones" and that Tyler's characters seem "eerily untouched by any of the revolutions, be they sexual or feminist, of the last forty years." Joyce Carol Oates quips that Delia seems never to have heard of Betty Friedan or Germaine Greer. Yet by transporting this Edna-like character nearly a century ahead in time, to the 1990s, Tyler suggests that for many women, not much has changed since Edna's death. Like Edna, Delia struggles to give birth to herself after her family and social roles have combined to stunt her sense of personal identity. Despite Allen's and Oates's criticism, however, Tyler does update Chopin's narrative to reflect the value of work for women—something that became more important in the late twentieth century—and to call attention to the lack of literary models for older women that continues to this day, a problem unmitigated by the early death of feminist heroines, such as Edna. Like the other contemporary writers of reconfigurations in this study, Tyler emphasizes the importance of narrative to identity and self-definition. Her reconfiguration adds a new voice to the American cultural narrative, and her novel's ambiguous ending suggests that this narrative must continue to evolve.

Tyler incorporates many aspects of *The Awakening* into *Ladder of Years*, including plot and character elements. Paul Christian Jones, the first critic to discuss the connection between these two novels, identifies several parallel features in the texts. First, both protagonists feel stifled in marriages to significantly older men, and their husbands' treatment of them underscores the lack of equality in their relationships: "The scene at the beach in which Sam lathers an 'obedient' Delia with sunblock lotion recalls a similar beach scene early in *The Awakening* when Léonce scolds his young wife Edna for being 'burnt beyond recognition'" (Jones). Jones also points out that in each case a younger man, Robert in *The Awakening* and Adrian Bly-Brice in *Ladder of Years*, serves as catalyst for the protagonist's quest for liberation. Chopin represents Edna's first moments of awakening as beginner swimming strokes. For Delia, who hates the water, her first steps toward freedom occur as she walks down the sandy beach alone (Jones). Another significant similarity that I would like to add to those Jones has noted is the independent residence each woman establishes. As she searches for herself, Delia resides in a "satisfyingly Spartan" (Tyler 110–111) boardinghouse room that echoes Edna's modest "pigeon-house." Finally, the two women also share similar backgrounds: Each grew up with two sisters, a father, and no mother. Delia's mother, like Edna's, died when Delia was very young, leaving her with only the parental influence of her doting father. Although he seems more sympathetic than Edna's father, who had "coerced his own wife into her grave" (Chopin 71), Delia's father was also controlling, discouraging her from attending college in order to serve as his receptionist. Again, according to Jones, "both Chopin and Tyler use the figures of the absent mother and overpowering father to suggest male oppression that dominates these women's lives."[1] Although these novels are set nearly a century apart, Delia and Edna struggle with some of the same issues, particularly in how to develop an individual identity rather than being subsumed by the family.

The two novels also share a similar circular structure. In an analysis of Guy de Maupassant's influence on Chopin, Elizabeth Nolan describes the "sinusoidal structure" identified by critic Richard Fusco in the French writer's work:

> Typically, these tales are "tripartite" and involve movement between locations. In most cases, an interlude in a "Romantic" landscape during which a character escapes from the reality of their existence to achieve "a transcendent grasp of his plight", is framed by a beginning and end located in the realms of grim reality. The narrative progression . . . is from pessimism to possibility with a return to pessimism more keenly felt. (128)

Nolan explains that Chopin adapts Maupassant's tripartite form so the romantic and liberating setting of Grand Isle frames the realistic and confining setting of New Orleans. Tyler in turn adapts Chopin's structure, returning it to a pattern that more closely resembles Maupassant's. Delia's story begins in her family home in suburban Maryland, where she has lived her entire life. When she married at eighteen, her husband moved into her father's house, with whom he shared a medical practice. It is in this setting that Delia has begun to feel unappreciated and unfulfilled as she faces the grim reality of her empty days. On a family beach vacation, Delia responds to a minor argument with her husband by walking away alone, hitching a ride with a repairman to Bay Borough, a small town where she knows no one, and beginning a new life. Although the town itself is far from romantic, it is here that Delia, at least for a time, transcends her plight and begins to find her own adult identity. Another brief, solitary seaside vacation precedes Delia's return home to reality and its disappointments.

In addition, Edna and Delia struggle against the role of mother-woman, although they are at different stages of life, and Delia's being older is one of the important adaptations that Tyler makes to Chopin's message. Chopin's imagery in *The Awakening* suggests the conflict between the demands of childbirth and childrearing and the desire to give birth to one's self. Gail Lippincott analyzes the image patterns in *The Awakening* to argue convincingly that "Edna is . . . pregnant—metaphorically—with her own individual self" (55). In contrast, Adèle, the ideal mother-woman of Chopin's novel, is newly pregnant with yet another child at the beginning of the book, and Edna witnesses her giving birth near the end. To this event, Edna responds with "a flaming, outspoken revolt against the ways of Nature" (Chopin 109), rejecting the claims of motherhood that impede her self-development and self-determination. Bert Bender interprets the emphasis on motherhood in the novel as a manifestation of Darwinian influence on Chopin's thinking and writing (465). According to Bender, Chopin carefully read *The Descent of Man and Selection in Relation to Sex* (1871), and she agrees with most of Charles Darwin's theories, except that she sees the female role in this process as less passive than Darwin suggests. Yet Bender sees in *The Awakening* a sense of despair, as evidenced by Edna's suicide, resulting from this influence: "[H]uman sexuality as presented in *The Descent of Man* denies the myth of constant love" (464). In Chopin's novel, Dr. Mandelet suggests that love is no more than an "illusion" when, after the birth of Adèle's baby, he tells Edna that "It [love] seems to be a provision of Nature; a decoy to secure mothers for the race" (Bender 465; Chopin 109–110). Shortly before her suicide in the ocean, the origin of all life, Edna thinks of the fleeting quality of love—"To-day it is Arobin; tomorrow it will be some one else" (Chopin 113)—and, more importantly, of her children: "The children appeared before her like antagonists who had overcome her; who had overpowered and sought to drag her into the soul's slavery for the rest of her days. But she knew a way to elude them" (113). As Bender points out, the children are antagonists, because "they are nature's cause in natural and sexual selection" (473). The illusion of love is an evolutionary adaptation, a trap in Edna's eyes, that ensures survival of the species. Having seen through the illusion, Edna escapes her entrapment through death.

Earlier in *The Awakening*, Edna tells her friend Adèle, "I would give up my life for my children, but I wouldn't give up myself" (Chopin 48). However, Delia, a forty-year-old mother, did give up herself for her husband and children. Now that they are grown, or nearly so, having turned into "semi-strangers" (Tyler 260), she finds that she has nothing left. If Edna had lived to rear her children, would she share Delia's position, lacking an identity when her children are grown? Having secured a mother for the race and no longer needing her, nature, embodied here by Delia's family, emotionally casts her aside: "Sometimes she felt like a tiny gnat, whirring around her family's edges" (24). Like Chopin, Tyler also suggests that illusion or trickery helps secure mothers for the race. At a makeshift Thanksgiving dinner in Bay Borough with people she barely knows, Delia listens to a woman complain about marriage:

> Everyone pushes it so, especially the women. Your mother and your aunts and your girlfriends. Then after you're married and you see how he's always so full of himself. . . . And if you mention this to your mother and your aunts and so forth, "Oh," they say, "marriage is a pain, all right." "Well, if that's the way you feel," you want to ask them, "why didn't you speak up before? Where were you when I was announcing my engagement?" (191)

Here, Tyler blames society, particularly other women, rather than biology for entrapping women in family roles. In a later passage, Nat, an elderly man, views life in a way that echoes Chopin's Darwinian outlook: "I've always pictured life as one of those ladders you find on playground sliding boards—a sort of ladder of years where you climb higher and higher, and then, *oops!*, you fall over the edge and others move up behind you" (241). The goal of Nature is survival of the species. The older individuals must make way for the young, who can have their own children and then ultimately step aside for them to take their own turns.

Like *The Awakening*, *Ladder of Years* explores the burden of reproduction, but the contemporary novel concentrates on a woman at the later end of her reproductive cycle. Virginia Schaefer Carroll reads Tyler's novel as "an intimate account" of a middle-age woman making the difficult transition into menopause. Although Delia is only forty and therefore probably too young for menopause when the novel begins, Carroll points out that Tyler herself was fifty-three when the novel was published. Also, Delia, who was married at eighteen to a man fifteen years her senior, experiences in other ways, such as having grown children and an ailing husband, a stage of life that most women encounter closer to fifty. To cope with her feelings of uselessness and emptiness, Delia must, like Edna, metaphorically give birth to herself. To do so, she leaves her family behind and creates a new life for herself in Bay Borough, becoming Miss Grinstead instead of Delia or Mrs. Grinstead, wearing a new style of clothing, and "chang[ing] into someone else—a woman people looked to automatically for sustenance" (227). The choice of words here is interesting. Delia enjoys others' perceptions of her efficiency and usefulness, something she has missed at home. However, providing sustenance was one of her primary duties when her children were young. Has Delia found herself or merely a new set of others for whom to sacrifice herself? Later, when two of her children visit her in Bay Borough and then angrily depart, she thinks of her interrupted lunch as she watches them drive away: "She felt the most amazing hunger, all at once. She felt absolutely hollow. You would think she hadn't eaten in months" (259). Is her appetite a healthy sign that Delia has escaped guilt and learned to live for herself, or is the hollowness a mournful reminder of the children she once carried and the difficulty of giving birth to oneself in midlife? Tyler leaves these questions unanswered, but by exploring the concerns of a woman at this stage of life, she adds a voice that had been previously underrepresented in the American cultural narrative. Throughout *Ladder of Years*, Delia reads novels and short stories, and, as Carroll points out, "a well-crafted, moving story from another middle-aged woman may be the reading Delia Grinstead wished she could have found."

Another of Tyler's supplements to the narrative of female awakening pioneered by Chopin is a representation of the value of work. Because Edna's life is so materially comfortable, some readers find her complaints unmoving. With a nanny to care for her children, a cook and maid to do housework, and the freedom to use most days as she pleases, Edna may seem to have little to rebel against. A woman of a lower economic class may have had more legitimate complaints but fewer opportunities to indulge them.

Even if Edna had wished to pursue work, however, she would have found it difficult. Although men frequently defined themselves and found fulfillment through their work, a nineteenth-century woman of middle or upper class was discouraged from work outside the home due to the unhealthy moral and physical strain such efforts were believed to place on her. Instead, her job was to make the ideal home for her husband and children (Lavender). Women's work in the home, however, is usually unpaid and, therefore, devalued in a society that frequently measures status by wealth. Although more women began to work outside the home in the second half of the twentieth century, the United Nations Development Report from 1995, when *Ladder of Years* was published, still cites the lack of pay for women's work as a hindrance to women's equality in society. In industrialized societies, such as the United States, "men receive the lion's share of income and recognition for their economic contribution—while most of women's work remains unpaid, unrecognized and undervalued" (88). The report goes on to state, "[B]ecause status in contemporary society is so often equated with income-earning power, women suffer a major undervaluation of their economic status" (97). Key to Delia's developing identity is a paying job by which she supports herself.

Although she has worked for years as her father's and then her husband's receptionist, this work was unpaid, took place in the doctors' home office, and often blurred into her household duties when patients went in search of Delia and the children in their living quarters. In Bay Borough, however, she reinvents herself. Because she leaves the beach in only her bathing suit, her husband's beach robe, and a pair of espadrilles, her first act is to buy underwear and a new dress, one that is "not Delia's style at all" (Tyler 106). Turning to face herself in the dressing room mirror, she finds "someone entirely unexpected": "She might be a librarian or a secretary, one of those managerial executive secretaries who actually run the whole office behind the scenes" (107). That same afternoon, she hears of a lawyer in need of a secretary, and she applies for and gets the job. It is not surprising that Delia takes great pride in her position, cashing her "first real paycheck" at age forty: "[S]he carried her head high and set her feet down with precision. She might have been the heroine in some play or movie. And her intended audience, of course, was Sam" (146). She imagines her husband, who has previously thought of her as childish and silly, visiting as she walks home with the sensible purchases made with her paycheck and offering to carry her packages: "Thanks. I can manage," she says (147). And Delia can manage. "Miss Grinstead," the legal secretary, is competent and professional. Later, she imagines her sister, who has paid a brief visit to Delia in Bay Borough, describing her appearance to Sam: "'Delia's employed by a lawyer,' Eliza might have said. 'She handles every detail for him. You should see her all dressed up for work; if you met her on the street, you wouldn't know her.'" (167). Her job, she believes, transforms her identity, making her over into someone her family would not recognize. Unfortunately, as the passage above indicates, Sam's approval is still an important component of her self-esteem. Now, though, Delia has evidence of her capabilities, whereas previously she has had only resentment of his doubts.

The quotations above also underscore the importance of narrative, the stories we tell ourselves and the literary narratives that we inherit with our culture, to developing and understanding identity. When writing *The Awakening*, Chopin lacked narrative models to help her define and to understand the person Edna wishes to become. Rebecca Dickson points out that in the mid–nineteenth century, American female writers whom Chopin would have read stress the importance of virginity for young, single heroines and view married women as uninteresting subjects for literature (39). Later nineteenth-century female writers, such as Sarah Orne Jewett and Mary Wilkins Freeman, whom Chopin admired, write about different types of female characters, but they generally ignore female sexual desire (40). Edna, for whom free sexual expression is an important component of her awakening, and Chopin, who creates this heroine, have no American models.

The absence of literary models makes Chopin's and her heroine's task of discovery and understanding more difficult. Jerome Bruner, investigating autobiographical writing, "claims that individuals make sense of their personal experience by articulating it along the lines of consecrated literary genres. . . . Such genres provide a foundation for our sense of identity, while at the same time making us members of the community that created them" (Ritivoi 233). Established genres, then, influence future narrative endeavors, including fictional creations and autobiographical ones. Without close American literary models, Chopin borrows elements from French writers, such as Maupassant and Gustave Flaubert, and British scientific writers, such as Darwin, Thomas Henry Huxley, and Herbert Spencer, and combines these with the female local color tradition that was more readily accessible at home. Chopin, however, explicitly represents this lack of an appropriate language to express ideas through her heroine, Edna. Repeatedly in *The Awakening*, Edna is unable to articulate her developing thoughts and desires. After a typical argument with her husband, she sits up crying, but "she could not have told why" because the "oppression" she experiences is "indescribable" (8). Later in the novel, in a conversation with her lover, Alcée Arobin, she expresses her confusion: "'One of these days,' she said, 'I'm going to pull myself together for a while and think—try to determine what character of a woman I am; for, candidly, I don't know. By all the codes which I am acquainted with, I am a devilishly wicked specimen of the sex. But some way I can't convince myself that I am. I must think about it'" (82). Gerri Brightwell contends that such lines demonstrate Edna's difficulty of voicing her feminist views in a patriarchal society. Citing Ferdinand de Saussure's assertion that "what is unnamed cannot be recognized or defined," Brightwell convincingly argues, "Without words to label her desires, they exist only as what Saussure described as 'vague, uncharted nebula' of thought without language."[2] Edna's difficulty with self-expression mirrors Chopin's own struggle to narrate a new type of heroine as well as her readers' difficulty in accepting this heroine.

Significantly, just as Chopin succeeds in narrating Edna's story in *The Awakening*, her character Edna does succeed in narrating a story that expresses at least some of her nascent impressions. At the dinner party in honor of her birthday, she entertains her guests with a story "of a woman who paddled away with her lover one night in a pirogue and never came back. They were lost amid the Baratarian Islands, and no one ever heard from them or found trace of them from that day to this" (70). Her story is well-told, captivates her listeners, and partially expresses Edna's new-found passions inspired by Robert Lebrun and by the sea. Yet, it is "pure invention," not related to her by anyone (70), and, like the lovers in her story and like Chopin, whose purely original narrative creation, *The Awakening*, was silenced, Edna's attempt at narration is never heard again. Shortly after this dinner party, Edna is traumatized at Adèle's birthing chamber and rejected by the well-meaning Robert. Once again, her thoughts become inarticulate—"Oh, I don't know what I'm saying" (112)—and she dies with the knowledge that she has been misunderstood (114).

In *Ladder of Years*, Tyler foregrounds the importance of narrative to identity formation through Delia's reading of literature, Delia's reliance on cultural scripts to narrate her own life, and Delia's suggestion that language must evolve to facilitate the articulation of new ideas. At home in Roland Park, Delia reads mass-market romance novels that Tyler seems to ridicule but Delia seems to relish. The heroes utter declarations of love in "uncontrolled" voices, and the "slender" heroines wear "ivory satin" negligees (33). Delia has a habit of reading these books in the waiting area of her husband's office, manifesting her lack of professionalism as his receptionist. Because the men are always rich, "Never again would the women they married need to give a thought to the grinding gears of daily life—the leaky basement, the faulty oven, the missing car keys" (31). The reader notices the lack of realism in these details, but to Delia they "sound wonderful" (31). These romance novels fuel her fantasies of a different life without empowering her to create one, and Heidi Slettedahl Macpherson suggests that when Delia walks away from her family at the beach, she attempts to play out a romance plot: "The boy-meets-girl, boy-loses-girl, boy-gets-girl-back plot outline is an implicit one in *Ladder of Years*, and while the novel somewhat follows this trajectory, its unsatisfying resolution, and the failure of the men in the novel to conform to their expected roles, renders the romance frame impotent by the end" (134). In a romance plot, Sam should suddenly realize how much Delia means to him, pursue her to declare his undying devotion via grand gesture, and sweep her up in his manly arms. Instead, he gives Delia her space, and she finds herself alone in a thoroughly unromantic location.

Delia, however, selects more serious reading material in Bay Borough, mainly because the small-town public library lacks newer books, but the change also matches her new professional demeanor. The reader learns of three classic American novels she reads—*The Great Gatsby*, *The Sun Also Rises*, and *Daisy Miller*—but none of these books seems to make an impression on her. Key contributors to the American cultural narrative, these books do not reflect Delia's presence in American society. Created by men, the novels' female characters are much younger than Delia and are characterized as flirtatious and possibly sexually dangerous. Self-definition, in these novels, is the privilege of men, and women serve as part of the surrounding world against which or through which the men understand themselves. The last novel, *Daisy Miller*, features a protagonist who dies very young, much like Edna, for her failure to conform to the sexual mores of the society in which she lives. Yet even here the reader never glimpses Daisy through her own eyes. We see her only through the eyes of her admirer, Winterborne. Because these books do not fully capture Delia's interest (distracted, she never even finishes *The Sun Also Rises*), she begins reading short stories. One, the only serious literature that Delia discusses in depth, is the Carson McCullers story "A Tree, a Rock, a Cloud," in which an emotionally scarred man proposes that people should begin by loving "easier things," such as a tree, rock, or cloud, before "they worked up to another person" (Tyler 177). The character's pain and emotional repression resonate with Delia's disappointments and help her understand her current need for isolation.

Delia's new experiences and her more serious reading do help distance her from the illusions fostered by her romance novels. Because the library is unexpectedly closed one Saturday, she spends part of her meager salary on a paperback romance, *Moon above Wyndham Moor*. She finds that her tastes have changed, however, and the book is a "disappointment": "It just didn't seem very believable, somehow" (150). This recognition of falseness where she had earlier seen dreams-come-true leads her to recognize the illusions in her own life. Immediately after the paragraph in which she rejects *Moon above Wyndham Moor*, she abruptly thinks, "Is he not going to come at all, then?" (151), meaning that Sam, she knows, will not be chasing after her. Although she has been in Bay Borough for several weeks, she has been expecting Sam to come for her all along. Realizing that he is not coming frees her to focus on more serious introspection.

Conspicuously absent from her reading list is *The Awakening*, a female-authored novel that, as discussed above, more closely addresses Delia's own experiences. If she had found this book in the Bay Borough Public Library and recognized its echo of her life, she might have found a language more suited to articulate her unhappiness, but it would still serve as an ultimately unsatisfying model because the only solution it offers is suicide. Although other contemporary novels besides Tyler's address this topic, the accepted American literary canon offers few openly estranged wives who survive, the best known being Hester Prynne. Likewise, the canon features few if any female protagonists over forty.[3] For this reason,

Delia longs for "an etiquette book for runaway wives" (206), one that would help her come to terms with her new identity and help her know how to behave in new situations.

When Delia settles in Bay Borough, one of the few people who seems sympathetic to her discontentment with her old life is her mother-in-law, Eleanor. Instead of recrimination, Eleanor sends comforting notes and a gift of a reading light: "On the few occasions when I've traveled myself, the reading light has generally been miserable. Perhaps you're having the same experience" (166). Knowing Delia's habit of reading in bed, or perhaps understanding that self-discovery and reading go hand-in-hand, Eleanor sends a light to facilitate this process. As an older woman, she has experienced the phase of life that Delia now struggles through, so the light she sends is figuratively her own example as guide. Carroll points out that Eleanor's note links her experience to Delia's, for "she too has 'traveled.'" When Delia flips over Eleanor's card, looking for the expected reproaches, all she sees are the repeated words "RECYCLED PAPER" (166). The words suggest the accumulated literary past behind all new efforts at writing, but we must recycle these efforts to accommodate our own words. Chopin's narrative serves as a template for Tyler's, but Edna, who dies so young, cannot fully voice Delia's struggles. New perspectives must be added.

Because of her lack of more suitable narrative models, Delia becomes stuck in scripts that lead her on a circular path. As used here, a script is a sequence of events that one expects to happen or a role that one expects to play in a given situation.[4] Like all human beings, Delia is a consumer and a producer of narrative. We learn scripts over time from our experiences, our observations, and our consumption of narratives in books, movies, and television. Repeatedly, Delia mentally narrates events or describes people around her as she perceives them, informed by the trite plots and stereotypical characters of romance novels and television. Before she leaves her family, for example, the unexpected ringing of the doorbell conjures a narrative featuring the younger Adrian Bly-Brice, a man to whom she is attracted but hardly knows: "A whole scenario played itself out rapidly in her mind—her family's bewilderment as she allowed herself to be led from the house, her journey through the night with him (in a horse-drawn carriage, it seemed), and their blissful life together in a sunlit, whitewashed room on some Mediterranean shore" (73). The description is humorously cliché, just a ripped bodice shy of a romance novel, and Tyler immediately undercuts it with the elderly, "doughy" woman who walks through the door. In Bay Borough her narratives become more practical, but no less clichéd. Seeing herself in her new gray dress for the first time, she imagines a conversation with a hypothetical boss: "'You'll find it in the Jones file, Mr. Smith,' she imagined herself saying curtly. 'And don't forget you're lunching with the mayor today; you'll want to take along the materials on the—'" (107). Like the familiar romantic details of the "journey through the night" and the "Mediterranean shore" above, the elements of her new self-narrative come readymade from popular culture. Rather than helping her understand experience and define her true, complex, unique self, Delia's self-narrative contains stock characters and plots. The scripts shape Delia into a familiar type: "Here is the secretary, Miss X, speeding back to her office after lunch. Preparing to type up her notes for the board of directors" (108). In contrast, more complex, subtle, and numerous literary models might help her find the language to shape and to understand her own identity.

Tyler also demonstrates how these narrative scripts can shape one's understanding of cause and effect in limiting ways. After becoming dissatisfied with her secretarial job, Delia takes a new position as a live-in housekeeper for a recently divorced man, Joel Miller, and his preteen son. Her duties consist of cooking, cleaning, looking after the child, and, once, helping entertain her employer's party guests. As Joel develops a romantic interest in her, the reader sees the similarity between Delia's current situation and the one she abandons in Roland Park, but Delia avoids such recognition: "In retrospect she saw all the events of the past year—her father's death, Sam's illness, Adrian's arrival—as waves that had rolled her forward, one wave after another, closer and closer together. Not sideways, after all, but forward, for now she thought that her move to the Millers' must surely represent some kind of progress" (232). Steeped in familiar narratives of progress and happy endings, Delia does not interrogate the possibility that she has retreated back to a comfortable trap, that instead of moving forward, she has merely retraced her steps. Tyler suggests the circularity of Delia's experience when, on a solitary beach vacation from her job with the Miller family, Delia begins reading, without realizing it, the same romance novel she had been reading on the day she left her family the year before. When Delia notices the repetition, she buys a new book to read, "not a romance but something more serious and believable" (310).

The ocean imagery in the quotation above—the "waves that had rolled her forward"—as well as Delia's return to the beach reminds us of Tyler's literary ancestor, *The Awakening*. Tyler's reconfiguration pays tribute to the first American feminist novel and, importantly, adds a new chapter to it, for those waves that first awaken Edna eventually destroy her. As John Glendening reminds us, Edna's seaside experience "reflects the oceanic origins of life itself" (41),[5] and in her return to the ocean at the novel's end, we see an echo of the quest for origins that appears in many classic American novels and their literary reconfigurations. Edna's death in the sea emphasizes that a reclamation of origins, of "the completeness of the maternal embrace or womb" (52), is impossible. Through Delia's cyclical return to the sea, Tyler reclaims her literary origins, but her heroine avoids the self-annihilation of Edna by resisting the seductive voice of the sea. Perhaps Edna, awakened feminist of 1899, is so far ahead of her time that she cannot live as herself in her society. Delia's times, however, are different, and if anything, Delia seems to be behind them. Or, as Bender argues, perhaps Edna recognizes the Darwinian lures that trap her in an unfulfilling cycle of reproduction, care of offspring, and death and opts out. Delia, however, finds herself in that relatively free time when children are grown and death is not so near. Edna's story is a valuable component of the American cultural narrative due to its unique perspective, but to fully reflect a changing culture, the narrative must evolve.

Tyler voices this need for change by undercutting Joel's conservative view of language. A high school principal, Joel frequently corrects his son's grammar and laments his son's and others' improper or nonstandard word usage, objecting particularly, as Delia points out, to new words and phrases, such as "'input' and 'I'm like' and 'warm fuzzies.'" (330). As Delia explains to him, these changes are necessary and never ending: "Probably half your own vocabulary was new not so long ago.... These terms pop up for good reason. 'Glitch.' 'Groupie.' ... Don't you sometimes *wish* for new words?" (330–331). Delia herself has wished for new words in the form of an etiquette book for runaway wives. Just as the language of speech evolves, the language of our cultural narrative should evolve to reflect contemporary society. One way this evolution occurs is through contemporary reconfigurations that adapt their literary ancestors, thereby not only reflecting the present but also linking the present to history and to American cultural identity.

The canon grounds the cultural narrative in historical time but must be flexible enough to withstand this evolutionary process. Tyler, like the other postmodern authors examined in this study, demonstrates the uncertainty of interpretation to indicate that this artificial product, narrative, reflects individual perceptions rather than objective reality. Tyler's first demonstration of how differently people perceive the same events occurs in the newspaper article on Delia's disappearance, which appears as a preface to the novel. The reporter has apparently consulted Delia's family regarding her description, but they cannot seem to agree on her most basic characteristics: "A slender, small-boned woman with curly fair or light-brown hair, Mrs. Grinstead stands 5'2" or possibly 5'5" and weighs either 90 or 110 pounds. Her eyes are blue or gray or perhaps green" (1). Reading the description in Bay Borough, Delia wonders if her family has ever looked at her. Tyler's point seems to be that they have looked at her and all seen different things. The article also offers a glimpse of her sister's narrative of Delia's life, in which she "alleged to reporters that the missing woman 'may have been a cat in her most recent incarnation'" (1). To Delia, this comment is absurd, but her first boss, Mr. Pomfret, after having read the newspaper article, wryly adds this same detail to his description of her (172). Individual perception influences narratives of experience, but narratives also become experiences that influence future narratives.

A similar example in the text, which describes Sam and Delia's differing memories of their first meeting, reveals the root of their marital problems. Delia remembers that she had encountered him alone earlier in the day, but Sam recalls meeting Delia with her two sisters later that evening: "Now she understood why Sam had forgotten his actual first glimpse of her. He had prepared to meet the Felson girls as a boxed set, that was why. It had not figured in his plans to encounter an isolated sample ahead of time. What *had* figured was the social occasion that evening, with marriageable maidens one, two, and three on display on the living-room couch" (44–45). Sam's memory of their meeting seems influenced by a predetermined script, formed by expectations that are shaped in part by previous experiences with narrative. The memory of the three virgins waiting for the handsome young bachelor to make his choice flatters his masculine pride. Sam's version of events diminishes Delia's individual importance and makes Sam's marriage to one of the daughters an inevitable conclusion. Delia's version is more romantic, for she has believed Sam had unexpectedly fallen in love with her at first sight.

Tyler does not claim that either version is more accurate, only that they differ, and the differences speak to their individual perceptions. Likewise, Chopin's Edna, although she is nineteenth-century American literature's only feminist, is not *the* voice of American feminism, but *a* voice. Tyler's reconfiguration adds a new chapter to Edna's story, but by leaving the ending of her novel ambiguous, Tyler makes it clear that other chapters have yet to be written and that the meaning of Delia's experience is subject to individual interpretation. One of the most positive aspects of the novel's end is that Delia survives. When she visits Delia in Bay Borough, older sister Eliza warns her, "Never do anything you can't undo" (144). Obviously, death is something that cannot be undone, and in Delia's depressed and erratic state of mind, particularly if the reader notices the parallels to *The Awakening*, suicide may seem a possibility. Nearly a century after Edna's death, Delia can abandon husband and children, temporarily at least, without facing the same social censure. As Eliza tells Delia, and Tyler tells her readers, she can leave and live through it. Another potentially positive aspect of Tyler's ending serves as a counterpoint to Edna's awakened passion and subsequent disillusionment that love may be only an evolutionary trick to secure mothers for the species. Delia, in contrast, discovers mature love in her marriage that is more satisfying than passion: "No hope of admiring gazes anymore, no chance of unremitting adoration. Nothing left to show but their plain, true, homely, interior selves, which were actually much richer anyhow" (403). Although the passion in a marriage fades, Tyler seems to say, deeper knowledge and love of one's partner compensates for its loss.

But does an awakened Delia manage to change her old life in ways that will make it more satisfying? According to one interpretation of the ending, she does. Jones concludes, "Tyler's book [is] engaged in a 'post-feminist' revision of Chopin's text, one that posits a feminist trajectory for women that does not necessitate a complete flight from the domestic sphere." Ostensibly as a guest at her daughter's wedding, Delia returns to her family in Roland Park; for reasons not clearly specified, she ends up staying on permanently and resuming her position as wife and mother.

Jones believes that Delia returns home as an empowered woman to a family who has also matured during her absence. For example, rather than accepting Sam's suggestion that she should be "doing something" about their daughter's desire to cancel the wedding, Delia lets her family members direct their own actions, but not hers: "She had never realized that worry could be dumped in someone else's lap like a physical object" (359). Delia's thoughts imply her awareness that family members have manipulated her in the past; she now has the power to resist their control. In another conversation between Delia and Sam, he explains why he married her: "You were so shy and cute and fumbly, smiling down at your little glass eyecup of sherry. You were so wavery around the edges. You I'd be able to handle, I thought, and I never stopped to ask why I needed to believe that" (381). Sam's words reveal a deeper level of introspection and communication than the reader and Delia witness before she leaves, which suggests that her absence has inspired his growth.

Other aspects of Tyler's ending support a less favorable interpretation of Delia's actions. Perhaps instead of returning home an empowered woman to a more mature family, Delia has merely capitulated to fear, guilt, and her programmed scripts to end up "back where she'd started" (406). As discussed above, a discovery of sexual passion is a major component of Edna's awakening, and this passion is symbolically linked to water in *The Awakening*. Bender argues that Mademoiselle Reisz's avoidance of water indicates her "essential sexlessness," which makes her an unacceptable model for Edna (471). And according to Menke, for Chopin, land "represents the entrapping results of . . . social control" and water "erodes the certainties of conventional landed society; its fluidity challenges land's structured roles and expectations" (79). So, water in *The Awakening* seems to represent social freedom, including free sexual expression. Unlike Edna, however, Delia has a catlike fear of water and an accompanying avoidance of sexual passion. She tactically evades sexuality by changing the topic in conversation (Tyler 17), pretending to sleep when Sam enters the bedroom (83), and dodging the sexual advances of Adrian (57) and Joel (331). Her family jokes about her dread of water just as they laugh at the possibility that Delia could be having an affair with Adrian. By incorporating the beach and other scenes that parallel *The Awakening*, yet limiting Delia's access to water and sexuality, two essential components of Edna's awakening, Tyler seems to hint that Delia's transformation is incomplete. Most tellingly, during Delia's second, solitary beach vacation, when she returns to the hotel room and strips off her bathing suit, "a second suit of fish-white skin lay beneath it" (310). Unlike Edna, she does not stand before the waves naked like a newly born woman; parts of her remain untouched by the sun and the sea, with its liberating associations.

Finally, her daughter Susan's wedding, which brings Delia back to Roland Park, reinforces the other cyclical aspects of the novel's structure and suggests that the novel's end point is the same as its beginning. When she arrives at the family home where the wedding is to take place, Delia realizes that in its music and choreography, Susan's wedding has "been planned to duplicate her own" (359). Here, the reader is reminded of the earlier Thanksgiving dinner conversation in which the young married woman complains of being pushed into marriage by the older generation, only to discover after marriage that they, too, see the institution's flaws. Will Susan's marriage duplicate Delia's in more ways than one? The question becomes more important when Susan, on the day of the wedding, declares that she will not marry her fiancé because of his insensitive treatment of another person. Delia does not encourage Susan to go through with the wedding as planned, as do the other adults in the family, but neither does she discuss her own misgivings and dissatisfactions with marriage. After a few days' delay and her fiancé's efforts to set things right with the injured party, Susan does proceed with the wedding. Should the reader see Susan as a modern empowered woman who will marry only on her own terms, or is she, like an earlier Delia, caught in the romance script—"The boy-meets-girl, boy-loses-girl, boy-gets-girl-back plot outline" (Macpherson 134)? The latter interpretation would mean that Delia and her daughter have failed to sustain an independent, awakened existence within their society, and the legacy of Edna lives on.

Showalter argues that the suppression of *The Awakening* in the first half of the twentieth century delayed the development of American women's literature and feminism, because "literary genres, like biological species, evolve because of significant innovations by individuals that survive through imitation and revision" (34). The fact that Tyler's heroine struggles with many of the same concerns that Edna faces a century earlier supports Showalter's claim that a delay occurred in literary and cultural development. Furthermore, Tyler's reconfiguration of *The Awakening*, like the other reconfigurations examined in this study, supports Showalter's view of literary evolution. The contemporary author takes that which is relevant to the new environment, builds on it, and passes it on to the next generation of readers and writers. As a reconfiguration of *The Awakening*, *Ladder of Years* reinforces the position of Chopin's novel as a literary ancestor, part of the American canon. Tyler adapts Edna to show a mature woman who survives rearing children and survives leaving them. Using the evidence of the subjectivity of perception and Delia's overt comments, Tyler explicitly asserts that language must evolve, and, through the ambiguity of the novel's ending, she suggests that this evolutionary process is unending.

7 Plundered Narrative
Contemporary Rewritings of Faulkner's *Absalom, Absalom!*

Although all of William Faulkner's work was published in the twentieth century, rather than in the nineteenth century as were the other American classics examined in this study, he still serves as an American literary forefather to many contemporary writers and as the inspiration for some contemporary reconfigurations. During the Cold War, critic Lawrence Schwartz points out, "[T]here was a general revival of interest in the classic American writers—Hawthorne, Poe, Melville, and James," and Faulkner was viewed as the modern heir of these classic writers (201–203). Faulkner's influence over readers and writers of American literature is unquestionably significant. According to Michael Kreyling:

> "Faulkner" is the divine icon of a literary religion, establishing both Southern literature and modern American literature canons. His works redeem the South from its Nazarene inferiority and American literature from the banality of mere victory in the material culture of the postwar twentieth century.... Hundreds of the faithful pilgrimage to his home in "Yoknapatawpha" each August, study and teach his word, promulgate the story of his life in biographies. Faulkner has become "Faulkner"; shrines to his name crowd the literary terrain. (153)

Although Kreyling's language may be exaggerated for effect, by placing Faulkner's name in quotation marks, he indicates that the novelist's work has become a literary institution in its own right. Kreyling's comments echo those of many earlier critics who stress the importance of Faulkner's work to the American literary canon and to American identity. In a 1949 essay titled "William Faulkner and the Social Conscience," critic Dayton Kohler writes, "His Yoknapatawpha County is a part of the present world, his Jefferson the geographical center of a moral universe.... His Yoknapatawpha County is more than a microcosm of the South; it is a compass point in the geography of man's fate" (qtd. in Schwartz 195). Kohler's comments emphasize that Faulkner's influence transcends the merely regional.

In his 1988 study *Creating Faulkner's Reputation: The Politics of Modern Literary Criticism*, Schwartz argues that Faulkner's body of work was claimed in the service of American literary nationalism by critics in the 1940s and 1950s. The New Critics and New York intellectuals adopted Faulkner's work, with its "inherent textual difficulties," as a Cold War "symbol of resistance to Fascism and to delimited individual freedom, and as a symbol of the importance of stylistic innovation and personal perceptions over socially conscious art. When the dominant ethos of the postwar period was the moral superiority of the United States, it was not surprising that Faulkner came to be regarded as its most important literary voice" (199).

Faulkner's novel *Absalom, Absalom!* (1936), set in the nineteenth and early twentieth centuries and often viewed as his greatest work, is, not surprisingly, of key interest to critics and contemporary novelists alike. Focusing on the familial and social traumas associated with racism, slavery, the Civil War, and the war's aftermath, the novel documents a climactic point in America's cultural narrative. Illustrating the literary nationalism associated with this work, critic Eric Sundquist reads *Absalom*, which depicts the rise and fall of the Sutpen family, as an allegorical embodiment of President Abraham Lincoln's famous warning that "[a] house divided against itself cannot stand" (96–130). Still associating the work with American identity, some other critics read it as a critique of American nationalism. Barbara Ladd, for example, sees Faulkner's central concern in this novel as the capacity of history to "undermine official U.S. innocence" (*Nationalism* 144). By innocence, Ladd refers to the nation's tendency to "define itself as the working out in a New World wilderness of a Providential design impossible in the corrupt atmosphere of Europe" ("Direction" 539) as well as the country's amnesia about its crimes of exploitation and persecution. *Absalom*, however, forces our historical remembering. Through its complex exploration of race, gender, and blood in American historical identity, the novel destabilizes the myth of innocence.

Like many of the classic and contemporary novels examined in this study, *Absalom* associates its examination of history with quests for origins within the narrative, in this case through the present-day narrators' attempts to uncover buried secrets, through Thomas Sutpen's efforts to understand his past, and through Charles Bon's bid for paternal acknowledgment. As André Bleikastan points out, in the narrative revealed by Rosa Coldfield and then Quentin Compson, Sutpen appears "Jehovahlike . . . creating his domain *ex nihilo* . . . a fabulous founder figure—so much so that as late as chapter 7 Quentin reflects that 'maybe [it took] Thomas Sutpen to make all of us'" (139). Sutpen, at certain points and to certain narrators within the novel, seems to be the origin of the South itself. J.G. Brister similarly attributes to Sutpen "the Adamic power of signification. . . . Most importantly, he has the power to deny signification, as his refusal to acknowledge Bon as his son attests" (45). Here, by linking the quest for origins to signification, Brister sees in Faulkner's work a connection similar to that which I have identified in other novels within this study. The quest for mythic origins

(Sutpen as Adam) is associated with a longing for cognitive wholeness in which perception and reality invariably match up, and signifier and signified are irrevocably paired.

However, once suggested, Sutpen as origin is anteceded when readers learn of this character's own origins in West Virginia. By offering one tale of origin only to have it trumped by a yet more distant point of origin, Faulkner suggests that the origins that humans seek are forever out of reach. Any originary tale is an after-the-fact fabrication, a narrative constructed from the point of view of "now" rather than from the point of view of "then." As recounted through General Compson and then Mr. Compson, Sutpen's "earliest childhood memories are of a prelapsarian primitive paradise. . . . His family's move down from the mountains to Tidewater Virginia parallels the rise of human civilization. . . . Most significant, Sutpen's birth of consciousness occurs with the confrontation of his ape-like self in the shape of the master's well-dressed 'monkey nigger' butler" (Vernon 119). The dawning of Sutpen's consciousness and its concomitant loss of prelapsarian innocence occurs at the moment of his recognition of racial and class difference. Alex Vernon refers to this scene as a "concise literary rendering of the collective reaction to Darwin's *Origin*" (119), linking Faulkner's construction of Sutpen's response to the servant with cultural anxieties about human origins, exacerbated in the 1920s South by the Scopes Monkey Trial. Yet Sutpen's dawning consciousness resonates not only as a reminder of human origins but also as a reminder of American national origins with its sense of innocence lost due to racial and class conflict leading to the Civil War.

Absalom's canonical status and its thematic concern with origins suggest why contemporary American writers would choose to reconfigure it. The impulse to reconfigure a classic text is the writer's attempt to connect to his or her literary origins and to add his or her voice to the ongoing cultural narrative. The most recent of the classic American texts featured in this study, *Absalom* anticipates the contemporary texts' attention to revision and to the frustrating malleability of language and meaning. Instead of reshaping and retelling earlier works of American literature, however, this novel, through the characters' preoccupations with cultural and personal history, rewrites itself. According to Hortense J. Spillers, "The work plunders and reworks itself as narrators not only elaborate what they cannot have known, but also correct passed-down information, fill in gaps, piece together disparities, disprove or improve inherited conclusions, assume identities, even invent new ones, that the novel has not yet embedded" (328). For each of the narrators in *Absalom*, the Sutpen legend becomes a heightened moment of human experience that can be shaped to help the narrators define and understand their own experiences. For Rosa Coldfield, labeled bitter and outraged by Faulkner, Sutpen becomes the demon responsible for her misery as well as for that of his entire family. For the stoical Jason Compson, Quentin's father, Sutpen becomes the misguided would-be cavalier, unable, due to his own naivety, to achieve an ideal that was always already unworthy of the struggle. For Shreve, the Canadian observer, the legend is a dramatic tale of star-crossed lovers and of the absurdity of Southern society. For Quentin, a youth obsessed in *The Sound and the Fury* with his sister's virginity and with Southern codes of honor, it is a tale of incest, miscegenation, and the reluctant deterrence of both.

The contemporary reconfigurations analyzed in this study operate analogously to the way Spillers sees *Absalom*'s narrators operating. However, instead of using a (fictional) historical figure as a point of reference for their tales, as Faulkner's characters do, the contemporary writers use a classic American literary work as a point of reference for their novels. Faulkner's narrators and the contemporary novelists reshape their points of reference so the outcomes resonate more closely with the identities (cultural or personal) of their creators. These reshapings of experience (including the experience of narrative) through narrative help us make sense of that experience. In this way, not only do the past texts influence the contemporary ones, but the contemporary ones also influence our interpretations of their antecedents. To pursue the analogy with *Absalom* further, not only does the kernel of objective facts about the Sutpen family influence the narrative embellishments of each of the novel's narrators, but their narratives also influence the reader's interpretation of those initial facts about the Sutpen family. Whether reading a classic text or a contemporary one, readers approach texts from their own perspectives; their experiences shape the narratives they perceive, and the narratives they perceive in turn help them process their experiences. As the introduction to this study explains, the practice of self-narration helps humans develop higher-order thinking and understand events. Yet our brains do not simply mirror what our senses perceive. According to Oliver Sacks, "Experience itself is not passive, a matter of 'impressions' or 'sense-data,' but active, and constructed by the organism from the start" (44). And David Sloan Wilson describes the relationship between individual narratives and external reality by pointing out that narrative "organizes perception, making certain things obvious, others worthy of attention, and still others invisible" (34). This process is very similar to the way Toni Morrison describes memory: "Memory (the deliberate act of remembering) is a form of willed creation. It is not an effort to find out the way it really was—that is research. The point is to dwell on the way it appeared and why it appeared in that particular way" (qtd. in Rushdy, "Daughters" 567). Likewise for Faulkner's narrators in *Absalom*, the telling of the story is a matter of "hearing and sifting and discarding the false and conserving what seemed true, or fit the preconceived" (253).

Although Faulkner does not suggest his characters' awareness that their narrative engagement always manipulates meaning, Faulkner himself is very much aware of this effect of language and perception and makes it explicit in the novel. Masami Sugimori points out that Faulkner's attention to paradox and inconsistency in the different versions of Sutpen's story emphasizes that "language in its differentiating/distancing operation enables one to order the essentially 'chaotic' world (exemplified by the endlessly obscure line between white and passing white) into comprehensible units *and* denies him/her access to the same world through inevitable reduction and distortion" (6, emphasis in original). In other words, the same language that enables us to process and to make sense of experience inevitably alters that experience by ordering it. Having had the experience of reading Faulkner as well as a postmodern sensibility that in general blurs the boundaries between and among experiences and ways of knowing, David Bradley and Morrison likewise explore the dissonance between language's essentialness for processing and communicating events and language's distancing effect on experience; paradoxically, these contemporary reconfigurations seek the stability of an ongoing American cultural narrative while simultaneously pointing out the unreliability of the language with which that narrative is constructed.

Bradley in *The Chaneysville Incident* (1981) and Morrison in *Beloved* (1987) reconfigure *Absalom, Absalom!* in significant and obvious ways. Bradley tells Mel Watkins, a *New York Times Book Review* interviewer, that *The Chaneysville Incident* was influenced by Faulkner's *Absalom, Absalom!* Specifically, Bradley says he is indebted to Faulkner for the "device of having the tale told to another character" (21). Morrison has commented many times on her appreciation of Faulkner. On the other hand, she has also asserted, "I am not *like* Faulkner" (McKay 152, emphasis in original), voicing a fear and resentment of being labeled as unoriginal. Because her reconfiguration is perhaps less conscious than Bradley's and because it has been the subject of many critical analyses,[1] this chapter explores in detail the ways that Bradley responds to Faulkner and then only briefly examines how Morrison's reconfiguration fits with the other contemporary reconfigurations discussed in this study. Bradley and Morrison reconfigure *Absalom* in ways that comment on Faulkner's depiction of race and gender. These contemporary texts also reflect the authors' views of language as indeterminate and of storytelling and interpretation as interminable. The unending yet unreliable narratives create in all three works what Phillip Novak describes in *Beloved* as an "acute sense of longing, this experience of the present as being marked by an absence, [which] leads both the novel and its characters inexorably to the past, to a kind of continuous reproduction or reliving of the trauma from which this sense of divestiture seems to spring" (205).

A common element in Faulkner's, Bradley's, and Morrison's novels is a thematically significant haunting, ghostly presence. Speaking about the ghostly presences in *Absalom* and in *Beloved*, Peter Ramos notes, "Absent and present, these ghosts arise from and point toward some violent, unjust, unfinished history" (49).[2] For Faulkner, the unfinished story is that of Sutpen, with its multiple interpretations and repercussions, and although he extends and explores these interpretations and repercussions, Faulkner refuses, in the end, to provide the last word, to give closure. The narrative refuses to yield Truth, and the ghosts refuse to lie still. Through their revisions, Bradley and Morrison add voices that are silent in Faulkner's narrative, but their unwillingness to provide ultimate Truth and to silence their ghosts suggests an acknowledgment that the history is still unfinished. Subsequent readers may want and need still other voices.

A careful reader who compares *The Chaneysville Incident* to *Absalom, Absalom!* cannot help but notice many significant parallels. In both novels, an insider tells a community legend to an outsider, and other secondary storytellers emerge as the tales progress. In both novels, the community legend concerns a larger-than-life man with a design, and both writers suggest that the past lives on in the present. In *Chaneysville* and *Absalom*, the primary narrators resort to imagination to complete their tales when the facts have run out, and nine chapters of development finally give birth to their narratives. Both novels deal with interracial romance, liaisons that Faulkner and Bradley refer to as *miscegenation* (Blake and Miller 29), and the female participant in each liaison is named Judith.

Despite the numerous parallels, the two novels have striking and pointed differences. Published in 1936 by a white Southerner, *Absalom* is set in late-nineteenth and early-twentieth-century small-town Mississippi and in a Harvard dorm room. Published in 1981 by an African American Northerner, *Chaneysville* is set primarily in twentieth-century rural Pennsylvania. Whereas in Faulkner's novel the black man is the subject of the narration, in *Chaneysville* the black man is the narrator (Benston 160); and although in *Absalom* a woman's hysterical utterances incite the male narrators' struggle to master the narrative, in *Chaneysville* a woman's careful and compassionate contributions fill holes in the tale. Examining a common symbol in the two works reveals how Bradley's novel clarifies and critiques the racial and gender dynamics depicted in Faulkner's work. In both novels, recurring references to snow form a symbolic pattern that suggests the oppressive, repressive, and obscuring potential of white historical master narratives. Recognizing this negative potential, Faulkner leaves Quentin shaking and numbed by the harsh cold without offering the warmth of a resolution. Bradley, however, allows his characters to dig through the snow, to counter its effects with empowering fire, and ultimately to create a liberating, if not final, counter-narrative.

John Washington, the narrator of *The Chaneysville Incident*, is a historian by profession and a hunter by early training. The novel begins as he is called home to the deathbed of his estranged childhood mentor, Old Jack. As he sits at the old man's bedside, he "began to think about what a man's dying really means: his story is lost. Bits and pieces of it remain, but they are all secondhand tales and hearsay, or cold official records that preserve the facts and spoil the truth. . . . Funeral eulogies become laudatory biography, which becomes critical biography, which becomes history, which means everyone will know the facts even if no one knows the truth" (Bradley 48). These thoughts serve as a challenge to John as hunter and historian. Klaus Ensslen says, "For black Americans the countermanding of official versions of their history through authentic self-representation is as old as the story-telling impulse itself" (281). But the surname Washington underscores that John's history is America's history, a part that must be recognized for the nation's history to be complete. John therefore begins a quest to uncover the interconnected stories and truths about Jack; about his father, Moses Washington, who died more than twenty years earlier; and about a group of escaped slaves who died long ago in Chaneysville rather than be captured and returned to slavery. John quests not only to discover his own origins, in the form of his father, but also to discover his cultural origins, in the form of strong African Americans seeking freedom.

But like the "official records that preserve the facts and spoil the truth," the blanket of white snow impedes John's quest for physical clues and separates him from the Truth he seeks. Gaston Bachelard explains the symbolic resonance of snow in *The Poetics of Space*: "[S]now covers all tracks, blurs the road, muffles every sound, conceals all colours. As a result of this universal whiteness, we feel a form of cosmic negation in action" (Kelman 71). Literally, the falling snow prevents John from taking Jack out of his remote cabin, over the steep hill, to a hospital where medical treatment might save his life, but before the snow gets heavy, it is Jack's experience with the white race that makes him unwilling to go: "I ain't sayin' they'd kill me, now, but they sure as hell would let me die" (Bradley 67). White snow and white racism are similar obstructions. Bradley's link between white racist oppression and snow echoes Richard Wright's symbolic use of snow in *Native Son*, in which a raging blizzard bombards Bigger Thomas as the white police surround and capture him. The blizzard makes visible the white control and oppression that has battered Bigger his whole life.[3]

When John's two worlds—that of his black family and community and that of his white Western education—collide, violence results. Early in the novel, John tells us that he once raped a white woman as a displaced form of retribution against women and whites; he believes that his mother and the white establishment had facilitated his brother's death in Vietnam. In a later scene, the snow forms a concrete representation of this human conflict. As Judith, John's girlfriend, tries to force him to open up to her, John again retreats: "I threw the rest of the coffee out into the whiteness and watched it stain the snow. It steamed for a moment, and then it froze" (262). The angry act of throwing the black coffee onto the white snow makes visual John's violent bitterness toward whites. The fact that the coffee only steams for a moment then freezes in the vast whiteness displays the futility he fears for blacks in this racial struggle. The black coffee on the white snow also forms a visual analogue to black ink on a white page. The written record is a fixed and frozen representation in contrast to the nuanced and changeable living experience.

When Jack asks if his girlfriend is white, intuiting information that John has been guarding, John escapes further disclosure by leaving the cabin: "Then I got out of there, and went to stand in the falling snow" (69). This line is immediately followed by a flashback to a question from Judith: "Why don't you ever talk about home?" (69). The juxtaposition of these two conversations makes clear that John keeps his two lives—ostensibly his past and his present, but also black traditions and the white dominant culture—separate; the snow that he retreats to represents the barrier between them as well as John's barrier within. As a hunter, John is familiar with this obscuring potential of snow: "[T]he air was full of fog and falling snow, and it was all too thick for any real vision. I could easily have been lost, for all the landmarks were shifted and changed by the grayness" (243). The snow can "obliterate a trail in minutes" (243), just as official history appropriates the facts and creates its own version of the Truth. Official history blankets over many inconsistencies and alternate versions, just as the snow blankets over the uneven ground beneath; however, because official history is all that most of us see, it becomes accepted as Truth, and we forget that other possibilities exist, just as we forget the nuances of a buried landscape in winter.

Snow figures prominently when Jack first tells John the legend of the escaped slaves. He says that he can hear them if the circumstances are right: "I never heard 'em anytime when there wasn't snow on the ground, for instance. An' I ain't never heard 'em when I was listenin' for 'em special. Now I think on it, I only ever heard 'em when I was on the trail a somethin' else, an' I'd be listenin' for whatever I was after, jest settin' there lettin' the sound come to me, an' then I'd hear 'em. . . . They're jest runnin' along. An' the sound you hear is the sound of 'em pantin'" (63). Jack only hears the slaves through the snow, suggesting that he only hears them through the distorting filters of official history. Symbolizing white oppression and master narratives of history, snow covers the whole landscape, obliterating detail and nuance. Paradoxically, although it can hide what lies beneath it, snow also creates tracks if one walks through it, making capture by the slave hunters more likely. In this slave legend, influenced as all slave narratives are by master narratives, these African Americans are forever running from slavery, panting with fear and fatigue. Similarly, Jack and the reader, both influenced by official narratives, assume that these fugitives are all male, because no woman could survive such harsh conditions. Although the slaves' stories are, as John and the reader later come to believe, muted and misunderstood by official history, they can never be completely silenced. Their quiet voices emerge when they are least sought after and least expected.

We see a similar use of snow as a symbol in *Absalom, Absalom!* After he has left Mississippi, Quentin is plagued by memories of the Sutpen legend that he cannot repress: "*I have heard too much, I have been told too much; I have had to listen to too much, too long*" (*Absalom, Absalom!*

168). He escapes temporarily to the "strange iron New England snow" (141), hoping to forget the atrocities of race and gender that he learned in the South; he wants to bury the truth under the blanket of whiteness, but the story follows him in the form of his father's letter. As Quentin and Shreve delve further into the past in their "tomblike" room, the repression becomes harder to maintain: "Then the darkness seemed to breathe, to flow back; the window which Shreve had opened became visible against the faintly unearthly glow of the outer snow as, forced by the weight of the darkness, the blood surged and ran warmer and warmer" (288). Quentin's surging blood, the turmoil within, competes with the numbing white snow on the threshold of the window. Outside is undifferentiated, pure white snow; inside is confusion regarding race, gender, and desire.[4] The window's threshold represents the familiar boundaries between our culture's definitions of black and white, male and female, masculine and feminine, a liminal space that, as evidenced by his repeated references to it, obsesses Quentin almost as much as the Sutpen tale. The white snow symbolizes official history's repression of personal and cultural conflicts that result from racial and gender oppression.

In *The Chaneysville Incident,* the blanket of snow and the white history it symbolizes function similarly to the white sheets worn by Ku Klux Klan members in an attempted lynching of Jack's friend Josh. Although this incident occurs in the 1920s, Jack tells the story to John in the novel's present. Klan members wear the sheets to suggest that all whites support their actions and to give the crime the official air of ceremony: "[H]avin' Parker Adams there, dressed up in a sheet, was 'bout the same thing as havin' a speech by the mayor, an' the Presbyterian preacher handy to lead the prayer. Whatever they was gonna do to Josh . . . it was gonna be damn near as official as the Fourth of July" (Bradley 98). Linking the lynching with the holiday that celebrates America's freedom suggests the American power structure's tacit approval of racial atrocities.[5] The sheets are also meant to conceal the white men's individual identities, "but," says Jack, "I knowed 'em all. Knowed 'em by their boots. I'd shined every damn pair, that very day" (105). Shined for this special occasion, their boots, or metonymically their tracks, help Jack discover the truth of their identities.

Just as Jack's position as the black shoeshine man gives him the ability to penetrate the disguise of the white robes, the traditional hunting skills, "the old tracking sense" (246) John learned from his father and from Jack allow him to intuit what lies beneath the snow. In order to find the trail of the lost stories he seeks, John must bridge the gap between his professional training, through which he has been indoctrinated into the white official narrative, and his early training. According to Jack, John has distanced himself from his origins through his university education. Here, white education or "book learning" functions similarly to the snow; white education is the official history that obscures the identities of African Americans whose truths differ from it or who are not thought to merit a place within it. After the mayor says that the college-bound John is a "credit to his race," Jack comments, "I didn't correct him, an' tell him that you wasn't colored no more, on accounts you read enough a them damn books to turn your head clear white" (135). Out of spite, but also confirming Jack's accusation, John responds by climbing up on his mentor's stand for a shoeshine.

In this conflict between John and Jack, we see the tension between the oral and the written tradition. Jack embodies the oral traditions of many African and African American communities, and he functions as a griot, or ritual storyteller, who passes on the community's values and history through his stories. Jack recounts tales about John's father in a ritualized fashion: "You want a story," he asks John before each installment, and without waiting for a reply he adds, "Then fetch the candle" (77–78). And the stories Jack tells are the stuff of legend, about a larger-than-life man who defies a white power structure and risks his life to save his friend's. Throughout most of the novel, John embodies a written tradition. As a historian, his profession involves recording, explaining, and sharing the past in writing. We learn through Judith's comments that he is good at what he does; however, his skill with written analysis fails him when it comes to the mystery of his father's life and death. John has written everything he knows about his father on note cards, but no matter how often he reads them, he cannot discover the key to the mystery. The snow that figures so prominently in the novel also suggests the white page, the blank page, linked to the European written tradition that fails John as he tries to understand his African American ancestors, as if trying to decipher his history through a lens of whiteness.

Faulkner also explores this tension between an oral and written tradition in *Absalom*, where written and oral narratives often vie for authority. According to Vernon, "Like the unnamed slaves upon whose backs Sutpen's dynasty rests, the unnamed narrative tradition upon whose structure the novel rests is that of African American oral storytelling" (123). Although written texts seem more imposing to Faulkner's characters, they never seem sufficient to convey their stories. Although she is herself a published writer, Rosa is compelled to tell her story to Quentin, ostensibly so that he might someday write it down. Instead of writing the story, Quentin himself retells it to Mr. Compson and Shreve. Mr. Compson's letter, which serves to officially transport the Sutpen tale from Mississippi to Boston, must be set aside in mid-reading while the two young men complete the story orally. Significantly, it is the distance "up from Mississippi and into this strange room, across this strange iron New England snow" (*Absalom, Absalom!* 141) that makes it possible to capture even part of the tale in writing. Speaking of Faulkner's novel, Vernon notes that the narrators' "struggles to understand the story they are severally trying to tell" mirrors the reader's "struggle to wrest meaning from the fractious and refractory materials of the text" (207), and readers encounter this same parallel struggle with Bradley's novel.

In *Chaneysville*, John's internalization of the dominant white culture plagues his adult life in the form of a recurring dream:

> There, at the bottom of it all, there was only one dream. Not even a dream; just an all-encompassing sensation of icy coldness, and a visual image of total white. No sound. No smell. No feeling really; just the cold. That was the dream, the coldness and the whiteness growing to envelop me, like an avalanche of snow, deceptive in slow motion, covering me, smothering me. And I could not stop it. I could not free myself. I could not wake up. (Bradley 149)

The snow here is the official history that envelops him, smothering the identities of his ancestors and his past. Perhaps unconsciously, he fears that he has so internalized white culture that it threatens him from within.[6] As he reacquaints himself with the woods and picks up the scent of a trail, John begins to separate himself from the identity given him by his formal education: "I thought I knew how he died; I wondered if I was ever going to figure out why. I wondered if I—not the historian, but I, whoever I was—really wanted to know" (223). The process of discovering his past through self-narrative appears essential to John's understanding of "whoever" he is.

Before he can successfully track down the stories he seeks, however, he must recognize that the knowledge he gained from his white Western education and the knowledge he gained from his black family and traditions are both parts of his identity and both useful resources on which to draw. The person who helps him do this, it turns out, is a white woman. Her contributions to his narrative also compel him to recognize the positive contributions of women to both traditions. Judith, a psychiatrist, first helps John understand Jack's background by explaining the progression of epidemic typhus, a disease that wiped out most of the community in which Jack grew up. Later, John reconsiders his earlier impulse and decides to take Judith with him on his search for Moses Washington's grave. Here, beneath the snow, they make the most significant discoveries of their hunt: a group of stones marking the graves of the twelve escaped slaves and of John's great-grandfather, C.K. Washington, who had tried to aid their flight. John "reads" the burial ground to discover the connection between the twelve buried slaves, his own family, and the white Iiames family, but before he makes this discovery, he must uncover the stones. The burial markers lie hidden beneath the snow, just as the circumstances and motives for these people's deaths are obscured by official history. But together, John and Judith kick away the snow until they find all the graves and understand the order of their arrangement.

A similar hunting trip occurs in *Absalom*. While in his Harvard dorm room with Shreve, Quentin remembers a hunting trip with his father in which they wander into the Sutpen family graveyard before Quentin is aware of their location: "It was dark among the cedars, the light more dark than gray even, the quiet rain, the faint pearly globules, materializing on the gun barrels and the five headstones like drops of not-quite-congealed meltings from cold candles on the marble" (*Absalom, Absalom!* 153). Like the discovery of the graves in *Chaneysville*, examining these headstones prompts a greater understanding of the lives of the people who now lie buried beneath them. It also leads to knowledge of their descendants, to the realization that the feeble-minded boy, Jim Bond, who lives in the decaying mansion with the former slave Clytie is the grandson of Charles Bon, the Romantic hero of the tale who obsesses Quentin and Shreve. Faulkner, however, does not narrate this hunting trip that occurs in Mississippi until the second half of the novel, when Quentin is in the icy coldness of Massachusetts. Like snow on a landscape, official history has the benefit of hiding what we do not wish to see. The distancing snow of New England provides the safety that enables Quentin to interpret the tale begun back in Mississippi and to consign it to a safe cultural and temporal space: "Now he (Quentin) could read it [his father's letter], could finish it—the sloped whimsical ironic hand out of Mississippi attenuated, into the iron snow" (301). Whatever Truth Quentin might glean from this sloping hand of Mississippi is attenuated, temporarily at least, by the cold, obscuring, distancing whiteness of the snow. He attempts to repress his knowledge of the tragedies and injustices of the Southern racial hierarchy, but the buried emotional turmoil displays itself in the hysterical trembling of his body and in his frantic denials that he hates the South.

In *The Chaneysville Incident*, the last gravestone that John and Judith find is that of Moses, John's father. Significantly, it is Judith who stumbles on this marker. Throughout most of his life, John has had difficulty trusting whites and women, but it is Judith who helps bring him closer to his ancestors. At this point, John shares with Judith the entire hidden life of Moses as he understands it. Moses had lived and then shot himself in order to follow his grandfather C.K., believing, as did his African Ancestors, that "black people did not die. . . . He simply took up residence in an afterworld that was in many ways indistinguishable from his former estate" (Bradley 208). Death, in his view, is not an ending of life as we know it but a continuation in a different realm.[7] Bradley suggests that this traditional view of death has been a repressed alternate narrative as well. He recounts a myth in which whites intercept a message from the sky god and purposefully misinterpret it to better suit their own interests: "And then they [whites] told the other men [blacks] that the Sky God said that when the Stillness came on men that they would cease to be; that their bodies would turn to dust and ashes, and that their spirits would be cast into a lake of fire to burn in torment forever—unless they did exactly what the pale men said" (429). Like the myth, official history favors those who have the power to write it and to tell it.

In the letter he writes to Quentin, Mr. Compson in *Absalom, Absalom!* also suggests these two ways of seeing death. Mr. Compson first posits Rosa's death as *"the ultimate escape from a stubborn and amazed outrage"* (142), but later in the same letter wonders if *"perhaps she has escaped not at all the privilege of being outraged and amazed and of not forgiving but on the contrary has herself gained that place or bourne where the objects of the outrage and of the commiseration also are no longer ghosts but are actual people to be actual recipients of the hatred and the pity"* (301–302). As in the traditional West African view recorded by Bradley, the dead simply move to another dominion, where they carry on with life much as they had before.

In finally sharing his story with Judith, John takes part in the oral tradition, even repeating the words that Jack has used before beginning a tale:

> "You want a story, do you?" I said.
> "What?" she said. "I don't understand."
> "Fetch the candle," I said. (Bradley 393)

As Matthew Wilson notes, "In repeating exactly the words that Old Jack used to say to him, John not only recreates a ritual out of his childhood, but he also takes the position of Old Jack, his mentor. . . . Taking Old Jack's role, John becomes almost a ritual storyteller, a bearer of collective wisdom, while Judith, conversely, assumes the role of John when he was young, a neophyte, an initiate" (102). In return, Judith has helped John "read" the blank page of snow in the graveyard—helped him integrate written tradition with his family's story. As John opens up to Judith, bridging the gap between his two lives and two traditions, he simultaneously gains greater access to his African ancestors. He now hears the twelve escaped slaves whom Jack has told him of long ago, whose graves he and Judith have just discovered, but now instead of running and panting through the snow, they are singing.

As John tries to complete the buried narrative, to understand why C.K. was with this group and why Moses followed them, he loses the trail: "There *aren't* any more facts," he tells Judith. And she tells him to "forget the facts" (Bradley 391). In John's mind, her words echo Old Jack's advice when John had lost the trail of a buck: "'You figure too much, Johnny,' he had said. 'You ain't lost him. You jest lost your feel for him. He's still there. Quit tryin' to figure where he's at an' jest follow him.'" (393). The association of Judith's and Jack's words in John's mind show that he is drawing on his black and white, his male and female cultural influences to complete the narrative. He follows his instincts and is able to bring imaginative closure to the tale. His completion of the legend is similar to that of Quentin and Shreve, who fill out the Sutpen legend with details and motives that they cannot verify, but which Faulkner tells us were "probably true enough" (268). Any version of history will be influenced by the historian; in order to understand the history and to understand themselves through history, Quentin, Shreve, and John must add their own voices to it.

In the tale that John completes, the twelve escaped slaves with C.K. as guide kill themselves rather than return to slavery. Judith's influence can be seen in the fact that C.K.'s love, Harriette Brewer, becomes a heroic figure in the final narrative (Egan 286). Harriette inspires the escape and leads the slaves until they meet C.K., and together they lead the slaves in their final escape: "[T]hen he saw Harriette Brewer take her knife from beneath her shawl and hold it high, and then he heard her, heard her singing softly, then louder, heard the others join in, the words of the song growing, rising from the hilltop, floating down the incline, the words sharp and clear against the night: 'And before I'll be a slave I'll be buried in my grave, and go home to my God, and be free'" (Bradley 430). Like Faulkner, Bradley exposes the alternate narratives of history that reveal the atrocities committed against women and blacks in the nineteenth century, but whereas Faulkner's women and blacks remain defeated and outraged, Bradley exposes still other narratives—those buried deepest—in which they emerge triumphant even in death.

As Quentin tries to complete the narrative of the Sutpen family in *Absalom*, he becomes lost within it. As Faulkner discloses in *The Sound and the Fury*, Quentin's inability to escape the past eventually leads to his suicide at the end of his freshman year at Harvard.[8] As John completes the tale of his ancestors in *Chaneysville*, Bradley suggests a more optimistic ending. John joins the narrative, continuing it with his own life, and in doing so he melts the obscuring blanket of snow that represents official versions of history:

> I gathered up the tools of my trade, the pens and inks and pencils, the pads and the cards, and carried them out into the clearing. I kicked a clear space in the snow and set them down, and over them I built a small edifice of kindling, and then a frame of wood. I went back inside the cabin and got the kerosene and brought it back and poured it freely over the pyre, making sure to soak the cards thoroughly. I was a bit careless, and got some of it on my boots, but that would make no difference. (431)

Some critics read this scene as John's effort to free himself of the past. These readers believe that John will destroy his notes and then head back down the hill to join Judith in a healthy and happy future together;[9] in fact, Bradley refuses to tell us the main character's ultimate fate, leaving this history still unfinished, with the possibility of other versions to be told.

Especially in light of the earlier episodes with Jack, it makes sense to read this final scene as John's preparation to take his own life, as Moses and C.K. Washington have done before him. Paradoxically, John's death does not suggest finality to his tale. When Jack dies earlier in the novel, John's preparation of the body is influenced by traditional African views of death. In his coffin, John places new overalls, boots, rifle, and pipe tobacco, providing this old hunter with the supplies he will need in the afterworld. Near the end, as John sets the fire, he tells us that the kerosene on his shoes will make no difference, perhaps because they, too, will be consumed in the fire. John refers to the structure he builds as a pyre, suggesting that his body will be consumed in the fire he sets there and that his actions constitute a funeral rite. He intends to burn the tools of his trade, the things he might need with him in the afterworld. In the symbolic patterns the novel establishes, fire signifies the opposite of snow. Literally fire melts the obscuring, icy whiteness of snow, and figuratively its power is what gives a man a voice. When John was a young boy, Old Jack had taught him how to build a fire anywhere, because, Jack said, "[Fire] gives a man say. Gives him *final* say. It lets him destroy. . . . A man with no say is an animal. So a man has to be able to make a fire, has to know how to make it in the wind an' the rain an' the dark. When he can do that, he can have some say" (42, emphasis in original). Giving a voice to the oppressed provides counter-narratives to official history. Building this fire gives John a say in the story of his ancestors, allowing him to join them in the afterworld, and it gives him a say in the master narrative of history. John's statement, his "say," counters the "blank page" of snow, the absences in the accepted historical narrative. John clears a space in the snow in order to build this fire, and through his self-immolation he ensures that the story of the escaped slaves, C.K., Harriette, and Moses can no longer be lost and buried.

The fire at the end of Bradley's novel echoes the one at the end of *Absalom*. Clytie, the daughter and former slave of Sutpen, and Jim Bond, the grandson of Charles Bon and great-grandson of Sutpen, use kerosene to set fire to the mansion when they believe the authorities have come to arrest Henry for the long-ago murder of Charles. Just as Old Jack has told John, this fire gives Clytie power, allowing her to control her own narrative rather than surrender it to white authorities. But Clytie's say is not a final say. Faulkner allows Shreve a final mocking interpretation of this tale: "You've got one nigger left. One nigger Sutpen left. . . . I think that in time the Jim Bonds are going to conquer the western hemisphere. Of course it wont be quite in our time and of course as they spread toward the poles they will bleach out again like the rabbits and the birds do, so they wont show up so sharp against the snow. But it will still be Jim Bond" (302). Faulkner suggests a meager victory for the descendants of African kings if their representative is this feeble-minded heir, and even he will become whitened to blend in with the oppressive backdrop of history. Quentin, likewise, has become enfeebled by the history he recounts, and even the cold white snow of New England is unable to hide the emotional distress he so adamantly denies. When Shreve asks him why he hates the South, Quentin responds, "'I dont hate it,' . . . *I dont hate it* he thought, panting in the cold air, the iron New England dark: *I don't. I dont! I dont hate it! I dont hate it!*" Faulkner allows his characters to reinter the horrors they have uncovered, even though Quentin's hysterical symptoms reveal the cost of such repression.

Of course if John dies at the end of *The Chaneysville Incident*, the final interpretation of his actions will also be in the minds of others: "As I struck the match it came to me how strange it would all look to someone else, someone from far away. And as I dropped the match to the wood and watched the flames go twisting, I wondered if that someone would understand. Not just someone; Judith. I wondered if she would understand when she saw the smoke go rising from the far side of the hill" (Bradley 432). Although Bradley does not give his readers ultimate closure, his ending does leave them with more hope than Faulkner's. Because they have shared at least part of this journey and created part of this story together, John hopes that Judith will understand his final act and correctly interpret it for others. John's actions also suggest that he hopes someone may follow him, as Moses followed C.K. and as he has followed Moses. Before he sets the fire, he puts "the books and pamphlets and diaries and maps back where they belonged, ready for the next man who would need them" (431). Perhaps he intends for these documents to serve as trail markers for someone in the future, just as Moses left them for him. Missy Dehn Kubitschek points out that, although John has earlier told Judith that he will leave her if she becomes pregnant, "by the time he re-imagines his familial history . . . a baby has become one of the fugitives—and it belongs to a woman named Juda. The history would seem to prophesy a child [for John and Judith]" (10). This child, of course, will be half white. If we are to believe that the child will someday follow John's trail into the afterworld, then Bradley is truly bridging the racial gap and uniting the white and black histories into one. Not only will John and Judith's child physically combine their two racial bloodlines, but by possibly following John into the afterworld, he or she also represents a spiritual union of African and European traditions.

Like *The Chaneysville Incident*, Toni Morrison's *Beloved* displays some obvious parallels to the plot, characterization, and structure of *Absalom, Absalom!* Instead of the two sons, Charles Bon and Henry Sutpen of *Absalom*, *Beloved* features two daughters, Beloved and Denver, the eldest of whom returns from a type of exile to receive the mother's acknowledgment and affection, just as Charles Bon appears at Sutpen's Hundred hoping for his father's acceptance. Like Charles Bon, Beloved is finally banished forever from the home, in part due to the will of the younger sibling who once adored her, just as Henry adored and then murdered Charles. The larger communities in both novels view the main characters, Sethe and Thomas Sutpen, with suspicion because of their unconventional actions and aloof demeanors. Novak notes another important parallel between the two novels: *Absalom* and *Beloved* "elucidate a central traumatic event—the killing of Sethe's 'crawling-already? baby' mirroring, in this structural sense, the killing of Charles Bon" (208). For both works, this traumatic experience occurs in the past, and both approach it through memory and hearsay without ever fully disclosing the event to the reader (210). The attempt to understand past trauma through narrative becomes a focus of *Absalom*, *Chaneysville*, and *Beloved*. In this way, the authors underscore the importance of narrative in cognitive processing, and within these reconfigurations, *Absalom* becomes a part of the experience that the contemporary novels attempt to assimilate. In other words, the narratives of Morrison and Bradley not only recount their characters' attempts to understand the past by telling their stories but also recount their authors' and the culture's attempts to understand Faulkner by retelling his story.

Morrison, however, introduces important differences to Faulkner's template that offer at once a more revealing portrait and a more damning indictment of the racism and sexism of the slave system. Here I do not suggest that Morrison's novel is superior to Faulkner's, but only that her authorial intentions and perspective differ due to the differences in the two authors' identities and their places in history. In his essay "The Fall of the House of Sutpen and the Rise of the House of Sethe," Michael Hogan reads Sutpen's Hundred as a "patriarchal site" and Sethe, Denver, and Beloved's home at 124 Bluestone Road as "a matriarchal one": "Sutpen's mansion, an icon of patriarchy and slavery, burns; 124 Bluestone Road, an emblem of female strength and freedom endures" (169). *Beloved*'s outcome reveals a more triumphant and empowering attitude toward the abuses of slavery than *Absalom*'s, and, as Hogan points out, a comparison of the two works suggests the privileging of a matriarchal paradigm over a patriarchal one. Faulkner does shine a denunciatory spotlight on the racism and sexism of the slave system through the (possibly) mixed-race Charles Bon; through the perpetual virgin, Rosa; through Judith, the daughter widowed without having been a bride; and through the inevitable self-destruction of Sutpen's design. But like Bradley's, Morrison's novel makes central those who are relatively voiceless and powerless victims in *Absalom*, the woman and the African American. Through the eyes of Sethe, readers experience the pain of physical and sexual abuse as she recounts having her breast milk stolen by boys with "mossy teeth" and then being beaten by those same boys, while pregnant, for having told the plantation mistress on them (*Beloved* 16–17). Like Bradley in *Chaneysville* and unlike Faulkner in *Absalom*, Morrison portrays a detailed account of a slave's flight to freedom and the desperate response to imminent recapture. Yet unlike Bradley, Morrison's central woman and slave are one and the same. Philip Goldstein notes the influence on *Beloved* of female slave narratives, such as Harriet Jacobs's *Incidents in the Life of a Slave Girl*. However, as the preceding example illustrates, Morrison makes explicit the sexual abuse and maternal torment that Jacobs reveals through veiled reference (Goldstein 143).

As with *Absalom* and *Chaneysville*, *Beloved*'s obsession with the past, with what Sethe calls "rememory," becomes a quest for origins, and part of gaining access to that origin involves repossessing a piece of America's literary past through *Absalom*. Slavery is as much a part of American history as the Declaration of Independence, and although many say that America was founded on the principles of freedom, they might also say that America was founded on the practice of slavery. But, as Morrison has noted, much of slave history, through a "deliberate, calculated, survivalist intention," has been forgotten ("Interview"). Morrison bases her novel in part on a piece of real African American history, the story of Margaret Garner, an escaped slave who killed her own daughter rather than see her re-enslaved when recapture was imminent. Ashraf Rushdy quotes the abolitionist Lucy Stone, who "describe[ed] Garner as a quintessentially American hero: 'I thought the spirit she manifested was the same with that of our ancestors to whom we had erected a monument at Bunker Hill—the spirit that would rather let us all go back to God than back to slavery'" ("Daughters" 573). Morrison's novel reclaims this episode of the American past, but her portrait of Sethe is more complex than Stone's portrait of Garner. Just as she forces Sethe to face the positive and negative aspects of her own past, Morrison encourages readers to remember the brutality of American history alongside its heroism.

Morrison directly connects this desire to reclaim parts of American history to her appreciation of the writing of Faulkner. She has said that what appeals to her in Faulkner's work "had something to do with my desire to find out something about this country and that artistic articulation of its past that was not available in history, which is what art and fiction can do but sometimes history refuses to do" ("Faulkner and Women" 296). Faulkner's *Absalom*, a canonical piece of American literature that explores as its subject the American past, provides Morrison a vehicle through which to access the canon and to interpolate her story back into American history. Just as the exploration of the past in *Absalom* involves a quest for the father, Morrison's character Beloved, embodiment of the repressed past, hungers for reintegration with the maternal. Other characters within the novel also seek a similar blissful union that, like all quests for origins, is ultimately impossible. As Novak points out, "Denver fixates on the story of her own rather harrowing and improbable birth and dotes on Beloved, the embodiment of her feelings of loss and isolation. . . . Sethe and Paul D are drawn, despite their best efforts at resistance, to memories of Sweet Home" (205). These characters seek to reclaim that lost something that will once again make them whole.

Morrison emphasizes that the recovery of lost innocence and the direct access to the past are, like the complete healing of deep wounds, impossible. Some barrier always intercedes, whether it be the unreliable memory, the ambiguous word, or the physical or emotional scar. Like Faulkner and like the other contemporary writers in this study, one way that Morrison reveals this barrier is by emphasizing the indeterminacy of meaning through language, by frustrating the readers' and characters' need to "see" through language. Like *Absalom*, *Beloved* refuses to provide direct access to the core "something" that has been lost. According to Novak, Morrison's novel, like Faulkner's, "never quite manages to arrive at its destination, insists in fact that the origin/aim of the discourse lies outside the realm of narratability" (208). For example, after chapters of suspense and uncertainty, readers finally see Sethe running to the shed at 124 Bluestone Road, but when we enter the shed, Beloved is already dead (210). Novak continues, "As is the case with *Absalom, Absalom!*, we are always already located in the aftermath of the killing, always already struggling with a series of consequences whose cause remains obscured, absented" (210). Both novels emphasize this limit of language at climactic moments of the text. When Sethe finally recognizes Beloved as her lost daughter, the mother and two daughters speak in fragments of language:

> I loved you
> You hurt me
> You came back to me
> You left me
> I waited for you
> You are mine
> You are mine
> You are mine (*Beloved* 217)

The rapid exchange, the disconnection of ideas, and the lack of punctuation emphasize a desperate yet unsuccessful attempt to articulate thoughts and emotions. This scene echoes the moment of Quentin's encounter with the ghostly Henry Sutpen at Sutpen's Hundred (Novak 206):

> *And you are—?*
> *Henry Sutpen.*
> *And you have been here—?*
> *Four years.*
> *And you came home—?*
> *To die. Yes.*
> *To die?*
> *Yes. To die.*
> *And you have been here—?*
> *Four years.*
> *And you are—?*
> *Henry Sutpen.* (*Absalom, Absalom!* 298)

Both Henry Sutpen and Beloved represent past trauma within the novels. Although Quentin and Sethe attempt to understand this trauma through language, when they actually confront the embodiment of it, they are all but speechless, emphasizing the inadequacy of language to fully capture experience.

Without such walking ghosts as Beloved and Henry Sutpen, however, language is our only means of accessing the past and sharing experience with others. Literary texts such as *Absalom, Absalom!* that record a cultural narrative, then, are similarly a culture's primary means of accessing its past. By reconfiguring a cultural narrative, Morrison and other contemporary authors reinforce the canonical text as part of the cultural narrative, claim space for the new text within that narrative, and, by pointing out language's inadequacy, paradoxically destabilize the authority of the original canonical text. Catherine Gunther Kodat "borrow[s] terms from digital audio technology" to explain Morrison's relationship to this particular canonical work: "Morrison samples and remasters Faulkner's text both by critically redeploying its method and by reinhabiting the history it simultaneously evokes and abandons—and thus places into question the very notion of literary mastery" (194–195). The solution to the problem of a text's inability to fully capture the past is to have multiple attempts, multiple narratives that express the past from many perspectives and in many words, similar to what Faulkner does through the multiple narrators within *Absalom*.

Faulkner's *Absalom, Absalom!*, Bradley's *The Chaneysville Incident*, and Morrison's *Beloved* refuse narrative closure by embedding multiple answers to the texts' questions. At the end of *Beloved*, Denver at times thinks the mysterious girl was her sister and at times thinks she was "more" (*Beloved* 266). The community tries to forget her, but still "her footprints come and go, come and go" (275). The intentional forestalling of overall authoritative meaning mirrors the indeterminacy of language within the text and invites other bids at clarity. The American cultural narrative that these and other reconfigurations of classic texts compose is not a single authoritative text or a small core of authoritative texts, but a multivoiced and evolving continuum of stories.

Conclusion
The Future of Origins

Noting the "primordialness of languages," Benedict Anderson states, "No one can give the date for the birth of any language. It looms up imperceptibly out of a horizonless past" (*Imagined Communities* 144). As noted earlier in this study, the inaccessibility of language's origin mirrors the inaccessibility of human origins generally and the inaccessibility of individuals' memories of personal origin. Yet our points of origin are nonetheless a human preoccupation. Gillian Beer' assessment bears repeating, "In a world jostling with multiformality fissured by incomplete meaning, the dogged and dedicated search for the single solution, the recovered origin, becomes one pressing narrative response" (23). Recovering one's origin and adding it to a narrative of experience creates the illusion of control; it helps one process and understand experience as something manageable with the logical sequence of cause and effect.

Shared narratives, furthermore, create at least the illusion of shared experience and foster the formation of human connections. Perhaps because language seems to have always existed, Anderson continues, "There is a special kind of contemporaneous community which language alone suggests—above all in the form of poetry and songs" (*Imagined Communities* 145). The culture's literary canon, then, becomes the shared narrative that helps bind individuals into larger groups. The American literary classics discussed within this study by Edgar Allan Poe, Nathaniel Hawthorne, Herman Melville, Louisa May Alcott, Mark Twain, Kate Chopin, and William Faulkner form a key part of America's cultural narrative from its inception into the twentieth century. These classic works help define what Americans understand themselves and their land to be. For example, in Poe's "The Gold-Bug," we see America's uneasy yoking of capitalism and democracy, and in Hawthorne's *The Scarlet Letter*, we see America as imperfect Eden. Melville's *Moby-Dick* displays the celebration of open spaces and exploration associated with America's beginnings, and Alcott's *Little Women* links the Puritan quest attendant with American origins to secular middle-class domesticity. Twain's *The Adventures of Huckleberry Finn* dramatizes the country's racial conflict and celebrates independence as a means to triumph over it, while Chopin's *The Awakening* embodies that same spirit of independence in a woman whose fate is not so happy as Huck's. Finally, Faulkner's *Absalom, Absalom!* shows America confronting its racist and sexist transgressions without rejecting its sense of national identity. Through exposure to these narratives, either directly through reading or indirectly through absorbed cultural references, a community of Americans solidifies. The existence of such groups as Young America, with which the earlier classic writers within this study were affiliated, attests to the writers' conscious intentions to create such a national narrative.

I contend that the contemporary writers' emphasis on metatextuality and their choices of American classic texts for reconfiguration attest to their conscious intentions to revise this national narrative. By accessing these classic American texts, contemporary writers tap into the cultural narrative, reaching back to its origins as a way of establishing continuity and creating the illusion of narrative progression. Understanding the need to fulfill certain expectations for a reader and to access common ground, contemporary authors evoke familiar cultural schema in the form of canonical literature. The schema-reinforcing quality of canonical literature references a shared core of norms about literature and about our society, but individuals read and understand aspects of these canonical works differently. Therefore, contemporary writers, like all readers, do not simply absorb the inherited narrative without change. As Liedeke Plate notes, "This [literary] 'heritage' . . . is not simply a corpus of texts inherited, received, and passed on. Rather, it is to be understood as a field of negotiation, an arena of dispute and contest over the texts' meanings and their eventual place in literary history" (31). The reconfigurations of American literary classics add their voices to these ongoing negotiations, reinforcing the classic work's place in literary history, but at the same time shaping that work's meaning better to align with the evolving narrative of American culture.[1]

In reading the contemporary reconfiguration, a reader also (re)reads its antecedent and the contemporary author's reading of that antecedent, all of which combine to form a new narrative of cultural history in the reader's mind. Readers form interpretations of the contemporary works that alter the readers' existing schema but also, because they are colored by readers' perceptions, differ from the writers' interpretations. Patrick Colm Hogan explains that a reader's "personal primed memories" evoked by a work of literature fill in gaps in the literature and help the reader "concretize" or more fully connect with the work (161–2). A reader connects with a literary reconfiguration through his or her personal memories, through the reader's associations with the classic text, and through other texts, including scholarly interpretations, making the reader's relation to the reconfiguration more complex. As Karl Kroeber puts it, "Each retelling of a story permits the articulation of deeper possibilities that exist because they were *not* explicitly expressed in the original telling" (48, emphasis in original). Jon Clinch's retelling of Twain's novel, then, permits the articulation of Pap Finn's internal hell, and Sena Jeter Naslund's retelling of *Moby-Dick* permits the articulation of Una's physical, mental, and spiritual quests. Such articulations invite future retellings for still unexpressed possibilities, as with Nancy Rawles's *My Jim*, which reveals the life of Jim's enslaved wife but, perhaps intentionally, leaves Jim's perspective unvoiced, calling readers' attention to its absence.

Of course, this study has not examined all examples of contemporary reconfigurations of American literary classics, and new ones are written each day. As suggested above, because reconfigurations invite future retellings to support the continued evolution of the American cultural narrative, a fruitful area of inquiry might be the nature of second-generation retellings. One such work that exists within American literature is Charles Johnson's *Middle Passage*, which reconfigures Herman Melville's *Benito Cereno* (1855), which retells Amasa Delano's *Narrative of the Voyages and Travels in the Northern and Southern Hemispheres* (1817). Ashraf Rushdy, in *Neo Slave Narratives: Studies in the Social Logic of a Literary Form*, and Helen Lock, in "The Paradox of Slave Mutiny in Herman Melville, Charles Johnson, and Frederick Douglass," among others, discuss Johnson's revisions of Melville's text, and a number of other critics have examined Melville's revision of Delano's earlier work.[2] A space exists for a single, critical examination of the evolution of this tale from Delano to Johnson as well as examinations of other second-generation retellings.

In addition, other media might lend themselves to reconfigurations, and below I suggest many questions that have yet to be answered about American reconfigurations in film and television. As our culture focuses more on these media in the twentieth and twenty-first centuries, do we rely more on them to record our cultural narrative? Examples abound of films that reconfigure by updating a work of Shakespeare (*West Side Story* [1961—adapted from a Broadway musical] reconfigures *Romeo and Juliet*), Jane Austen (*Clueless* [1995] reconfigures *Emma* [1815]), a classical myth, or a fairy tale, and there is no shortage of critical studies that examine them.[3] We have fewer examples of contemporary films that *reconfigure* (not to be confused with *adapt*[4]) an American literary classic, such as Sam Raimi's *Army of Darkness* (1993) reconfiguring Twain's *A Connecticut Yankee in King Arthur's Court* (1889), or *The Bedford Incident* (1965) reconfiguring *Moby-Dick*. Why are American literary classics a less common source for these contemporary film reconfigurations? Room also exists for a study of contemporary American cinema that reconfigures an American film classic, such as *Thelma and Louise* (1991) and *Easy Rider* (1969) or *Brokeback Mountain* (2005—itself based on a short story by Annie Proulx) and the classic Western.

One might also examine the contemporary television program that reconfigures a classic show, such as *Will & Grace* as a rewrite of *I Love Lucy*. To what extent does the serialization and syndication of such programs affect their ability to record a cultural narrative or affect that cultural narrative's likelihood to be reconfigured by a later show? Finally, classic American literary works sometimes have central roles in episodes of

American television programs, particularly animated programs. The first Halloween episode of *The Simpsons* ("Treehouse of Horror," 1990), for example, retells Poe's "The Raven" (1845), and an episode of Disney Channel's *Phineas and Ferb* ("The Belly of the Beast," 2011) comically rewrites *Moby-Dick*. Why do these programs reconfigure classic works that their intended audience has likely never read? Do those who have not read the original works still comprehend the references? Like the contemporary literary reconfigurations, the references to earlier texts within these television programs assume a sophisticated awareness of the construction and manipulation of language and narrative. Are these reconfigurations merely an indication of the writers' lack of new ideas? Or are they an attempt to ground the television programs in an American cultural narrative, a means of community building and cultural education? Conversely, do the comic approaches to the classics suggest the shows' attempts to undercut that tradition? I believe these reconfigurations suggest a dual conservative and radical impulse similar to that which I identify in literary reconfigurations: the desire to connect to a tradition and a simultaneous desire to revise that tradition to better fit an evolving cultural narrative. Further study could better explain the function of reconfigurations in connection to cultural narratives within film and television.

This study has explored the connection between narrative and identity formation at individual and cultural levels. In addition, it has explored the role of cognitive development and narrative construction of identity in the recent proliferation of narrative reconfigurations and their preoccupations with language and origins. John Paul Eakin's foreboding observation, quoted in this study's introduction, that "the regulation of narrative carries the possibility of the regulation of identity" (*Living Autobiographically* 33) hints at control of the individual by society, *à la* Big Brother. Contemporary reconfigurations of American literary classics, however, suggest that the direction of this influence can be reversed so that, through narrative, such regulation can also be exerted by the individual on society. Although the reconfigurations do not strip their antecedents of all their power, they do diminish the power of the original. By showing readers the evolution of stories, their shaping of and shaping by individuals and cultures, contemporary writers suggest that narrative in general evolves similarly. If all individuals shape and are shaped by narratives, and all narrative is shaped by other narratives, then the canonical standard bearer steps down to take its place among a series of stories constructed over time.

Appendix A
Stealing Promethean Fire: An Interview with Novelist Louis Bayard

On March 3, 2009, Washington, D.C.

Interviewer: Thank you for talking with me. What are you working on now?
Bayard: I am working on a book right now called *The School of Night*. It's about a reputed group of Elizabethan scholars who are rumored to dabble in the dark arts, and they included Christopher Marlowe and Walter Raleigh. The school may never even have existed, but there's a legend about them that they met at Raleigh's estate in the dark of night and talked about all these forbidden subjects. So I'm spinning a yarn out of that, with some modern-day segments.
Interviewer: You talked a little bit about the dark arts and witchcraft in *The Pale Blue Eye*. Is that something you're interested in, or did you become interested in it through this work?
Bayard: As a subject itself, I'm not particularly interested in it; I'm more interested in it as a device, honestly, to kind of get things in motion—the MacGuffin there. Do you remember that Hitchcock phrase? Hitchcock used the term *MacGuffin* to describe the thing that gets the plot in motion, and he used it, that word, because it almost doesn't matter what it is a lot of the time. It's *The 39 Steps*, you know, *North by Northwest*—it almost doesn't matter; it's whatever gets things in motion. So for me, in *The Pale Blue Eye*, the dark arts were more of a device to create some red herrings, just to get people looking in the wrong direction, when in fact the real central story was lying hidden inside.
Interviewer: *The Pale Blue Eye* is your second novel that in some way reconfigures an earlier text, in this case with Poe as a character and a lot of themes and references to Poe's writing. What's the draw of that type of novel for you? Why reconfigure an earlier text?
Bayard: You know, in my mind, I think of it as a kind of reader's debt. When I did it in *Mr. Timothy*, it was my debt to Charles

	Dickens, because he was really the writer I've been reading the longest and the writer who's been the greatest influence on my own work still today. It was a kind of homage; at the same time there was a subversive quality to it as well, because I took this character that's very saintly, the Tiny Tim character, and turned him inside out, and darkened him, and darkened the whole world in which he thrives, so it was my way of sort of applauding Dickens's original work but also critiquing it in kind of a way and modernizing it, making it more relevant to modern audiences. In terms of Poe, I think my debt to him is that he was the creator of the modern detective story, so it seemed to me a fitting homage to place him in one and have him fend for himself, as it were, and in fact I'm not the first, I'm far away not the first to have used Poe. As you probably know, he's figured in lots of mystery stories. It just seems a natural trope, or switch to make, but it stems from being a reader. I think of my books as books that kind of read other books, and that's really where it comes from.
Interviewer:	It's interesting that you say that, because that's a pattern that I've noticed in a lot of these reconfigurations, that they read other texts, but they also seem to incorporate reader and writer functions within the text, you know; characters who read and write focus on that fallibility of language, the variability of interpretation, and there's this impulse to give both homage and critique at the same time.
Bayard:	Yes, yes, which creates a tension right off the bat, and I very duly record that tension by writing in Edgar Allen Poe's own voice, sort of mimicking that voice, and using that, as you said, contrasting that with the very different voice of Landor's. I think of them as twin poles of the English language, in which you have Landor, with a very hard Anglo-Saxon tread, and you have this garrulous Latin that Poe uses, the kind of language that looks to us as rather purple, so I thought of them inhabiting these opposed areas of the English language. One of the reasons I like multiple narrators, multiple texts as you pointed out, is that they cast each other into question. When you open up the door to more than one narrator, you basically open up the possibility that you're not quite getting the full story from either one of them, and I love the way that multiple narrators question each other and question themselves at the same time.
Interviewer:	I really enjoyed reading your book. When I first read about it, I feared that it would be a little gimmicky, but as I was reading it, I did not find it that way at all. I liked the tension between the two characters, and the fact that I pretty much

	bought Landor until the end, you know, and then I was just kind of blown away by the fact that he was unreliable all along. That worked for me.
Bayard:	I don't know if you've read *The Murder of Roger Ackroyd*, but Agatha Christie pulled the same stunt, though now I've just ruined it for you, but it was I think maybe the first mystery book in the English language where the narrator turns out to be the murderer. By the way, I assume somebody's done dissertations on Agatha Christie as well, and actually, she was one of the most sophisticated readers there was, because as a writer who plots very carefully, she understands exactly what assumptions people bring to reading, and she very carefully undermines them. Every time you think you're smarter than her, you are actually [thinking], "Oh, I guess she was smarter than me." I wanted that to be the surprise. In fact, that was the twist I had in mind from the very beginning. So the task became hiding my traces, as it were. In fact, some people have complained, well, at least one person complained, anyway, that it was actually too hidden, that there was no way for the reader to figure that out.
Interviewer:	It was certainly a surprise as I read it, but then when I went back and read over it again, I felt like there were clues, but they were not transparent so that you knew what was going to happen. I think that the second time around you could see little clues.
Bayard:	That was my hope, that people actually would be inspired to read it a second time, because whole lines, sentences change when seen in the light of the truth.
Interviewer:	*Mr. Timothy* had an element of mystery in it as well; can you talk about the appeal of mystery writing for you?
Bayard:	Well, I'm an accidental mystery writer; I didn't really set out to be one, but *Mr. Timothy* was the person who was responsible for bringing me there, and it really came out of again that impulse to turn Tiny Tim inside out and scrape away all the sentiment and familiarity with which he'd been encrusted and see what was left. And I thought that the best way to do that would be to plop him in the middle of this Victorian thriller, because one of the things that I realized early on, what's great about that genre is getting characters in motion, sometimes literally in motion if they're running for their lives, and I like the fact that it pounds on the characters, again, sometimes literally they're being pounded on, and it forces them to reconfigure themselves, figure out who they are, and change, and grow. I guess having done that with *Mr. Timothy*, which didn't start out as a mystery, it occurred to me that

it'd be interesting to revisit the same genre with the man who originally created it, Edgar Allan Poe. Also, just a function of the publishing industry is that when you have some kind of success, critical success or otherwise, with one kind of book, it's expected that your next book will kind of be in the same vein, so that's really what happened. I wound up wandering into this niche which I didn't necessarily set out to fill but which worked out, and it intrigues me, it makes me realize that the mystery/thriller genre can accommodate really almost any theme, any subject. It's made me realize how flexible it is and makes me even question the whole notion of genre, because when a genre can accommodate writers as diverse as Dennis Lehane, or Elizabeth George, Tony Hillerman, it seems to me that calling it a genre after a while doesn't make sense anymore.

Interviewer: I think you make a good point about the flexibility of mystery writing; this is literary fiction, but also mystery fiction.

Bayard: Of course, one of the reasons that I thought it fitting for *Mr. Timothy* was that Dickens himself was a big mystery aficionado. *Bleak House* is essentially a detective story, and he wrote also some short stories that were mysteries. He was very good friends with Wilkie Collins, one of the great early mystery writers, so it was a very congenial form to him, and the *Mystery of Edwin Drood* was his last, and unfinished book. Dickens and nineteenth-century authors didn't look down on genres, and there wasn't that kind of bifurcation that we see now. They just saw it as another way to tell a story. Of course, for Dickens, who was a serialized writer, it was very important to keep readers excited and interested in the story. Mysteries are great for creating little cliff-hangers. In Poe's case, he wrote his gothic stories and his detective stories not only to make money, but they clearly represent and embody all the themes that possessed him in his poetry, and all the other things that he thought more highly of at the time, so it's very reflective of him as well, and his obsessions and concerns, his manias.

Interviewer: What is your opinion of Poe as a writer?

Bayard: You know, that's a good question. Because I was an English major myself, I mean, I don't think Poe was ever assigned in any course when I went to college. I went to Princeton, I graduated in '85, and I'm trying to think if Poe was even assigned. I have a feeling he wasn't, and so I think in my mind I assign him to the high school canon, and he's jumbled in there with Judy Blume and *A Separate Peace* and all those things that were considered appropriate for us to read, and God knows why Poe was considered appropriate, because sometimes he's deeply inappropriate and highly disturbing. Some of his lesser-known stories are even more disturbing than some of the better-known ones. I guess I've absorbed a kind of critical distaste for Poe; I think Henry James is very dismissive of him, T.S. Eliot as well, the intelligencia had written him off.

When I was putting together the concept for this book, Poe was coming back to me in sort of an involuntary way, and I couldn't quite figure out why, because I hadn't read him in something like twenty years, and I suddenly realized, well, not suddenly, but I gradually realized that he had been so absorbed into our cultural DNA that we no longer even recognize him, but he's part of our literature, and an essential part. Not just the fact that he created the mystery story, reinvigorated the gothic horror story, but he also laid the seed for science fiction with *Gordon Pym*, a wonderful book. The themes, the obsessions and monomania of a lot of his characters figure very prominently in modern fiction, in Pynchon and Nabokov, people like that, Joyce Carol Oates, Stephen King. I mean, I think he's everywhere, yet it gets so absorbed into it, that we don't necessarily recognize him anymore. I think he's one of the most important writers ever to come out of America.

Is he one of the great writers? I don't always know. There's a part of him that almost dares you to laugh at his work, because it is so extreme. There's a story about a man who's hypnotically arrested at the very moment of death, just before death, and is held in this hypnotic state for months at a time, and is observed, and then the hypnosis is lifted, and he explodes in this cloud of pustular flesh, and it's one of the most disgusting endings. So there are things that I've come to admire about him, that I learned about him, I suppose in the course of researching this book, and one was that I find him quite brave in a way, because he puts his own manias right out there. Maybe he didn't think he was, but it's pretty clearly his own obsessions with death and dead women who aren't quite dead, or stay dead, and lots of his maidens who are sort of half beautiful and half terrifying—he clearly had issues with women—all of these issues are out there, and there was no self-censoring going on. I remember when I first started the book, I questioned the project for myself because Poe's just too weird for me, that road is too strange, but I reread a section of *Mr. Timothy* where the hero is trapped in a burning coffin, very gothic moment, very Poe-esque. I reread it, and I'm already there; I've met Poe on his own turf. We all have that, we all have that darkness within us, and Poe was the way to really get that out there.

What limits him I think is the monomania of his work. It's very deep but not wide at all; it's just Edgar Allan Poe, nothing else really exists. The women are ciphers; there's really no sort of plausible women, they're all just maidens or objects either of sex or horror. The same for other people: There's only one character in all Poe's works, so I suppose it doesn't have the amplitude of Melville that has secured his reputation, but he plunges as deep into that narrow crevice as he possibly can go.

Interviewer: Yes, the psychological themes resonate with everyone, even though we don't admit it or don't want to admit it.

Bayard: Yes, that's the thing. I mean, I wouldn't kill a guy just because he had a pale blue eye, but maybe one little turn of the screw is all it takes. It's like when you see stories of child abuse. Well I don't abuse my kids, but you know what, turn my screws in one direction, make me an unwed mother, or someone who's experiencing this who's had a horrible life, and yeah, okay, I see it. There are times my kids enrage me, and again, to borrow that Henry James phrase, it's that turn of the screw, it's what he specialized in. Just flip the dial a little bit over, and suddenly it's a whole different set of rules.

Interviewer: You just talked a little bit about Poe's portrayal of women, and of course there's been a lot written about Poe and gender, and race; did you have any impressions about Poe's portrayals of race as you were reading and researching Poe?

Bayard: Well, he was clearly a man of his time in that regard, and the black characters are almost always caricatures; the one I remember best is the manservant in "The Gold-Bug."

Interviewer: Jupiter?

Bayard: Jupiter. Yeah, he's played almost entirely for laughs, as a kind of minstrelsy laugh show that was very common in that day. Poe was a Southerner, pro-slavery, and so his racial attitudes were very much of that period. That's the one part of "The Gold-Bug" that's a little tough to read now. It's still a wonderful story, but that caricature portrayal of a black know-nothing servant: He doesn't know right from left.

In The Pale Blue Eye I made a point in having a black character Caesar who actually is intelligent, although it's interesting I used the phrase intelligent. I refer to him as an "intelligent Negro" and a black friend of mine just sort of winced when he saw it, because he thought it was a standard portrayal. Oh an "intelligent Negro," oh my gosh, he actually knows right from left! So I wasn't so conscious of that, but

	that language was absorbed from Poe, and James Fenimore Cooper, and authors of that era. They would have definitely commented on a Negro who was intelligent.
Interviewer:	Which makes it authentic for the characters that you're creating.
Bayard:	Yes, and this is what I said to my friend. I couldn't pretend that Landor's attitude toward blacks would be the equivalent of somebody's today—that just wouldn't work. It would just be one of those anachronistic things that bugs me sometimes in some historical novels, when they bring their modern attitudes to bear in a way that doesn't seem plausible to me. I mean, we're talking 1830s. We're not that very far along in racial terms, and Poe certainly wasn't either.
Interviewer:	Caesar is a character I was interested in. He's obviously very different from Jupiter in "The Gold-Bug," but Jupiter has often been read symbolically by critics. Did you intend Caesar to be a symbolic character?
Bayard:	Well, not particularly, but again, this goes back to intention, and what a writer actually puts in there is not necessarily what he thinks he's putting in there. I don't think I intended any grand symbolic construct for him. I meant him to be someone who's more than he seems to be. Not just this steward, he's actually working as an agent, he actually has this double life, in effect.
Interviewer:	Caesar has an important role, but we don't see him very much in the novel.
Bayard:	Well that was also historically determined, because from what I learned, there wouldn't have been, certainly of course there wouldn't have been, any black cadets at West Point, and certainly none of the staff, the army officers, would have been black, because they were not allowed, so the only place they could have been would have been as domestic service.
Interviewer:	Right. And I guess Landor would have limited contact with him in the capacity of a servant. As I was reading, I detected references to "The Fall of the House of Usher," "The Murders in the Rue Morgue," "The Purloined Letter," "The Gold-Bug," "The Tell-Tale Heart," and "The Philosophy of Composition." Were there any others that I missed?
Bayard:	Let's see, there's a very obscure story—that's where Landor's name came from—it's called "Landor's Cottage," and it's actually a disquisition on landscape architecture, which is something that fascinated Poe. It's something that combined art and nature in some previously unimaginable scale, and he thought it was an exciting new discipline. He mentioned the cottage,

and I borrowed some of the details for Professor Pawpaw, the birds in cages hanging on the trees, and that combination of artifice and nature is kind of striking passion, that came from that story. There are also quotes from some poems, like "To Science," that's directly quoted, and "To Helen." What I wound up doing was I immersed myself in a lot of Poe and then in some cases I actually listed a phrase or a word and dropped it in. I'd say the Poe stuff is about 1 percent Poe and 99 percent faux Poe. Yeah, part of the fun for me was laying the seeds of all these later stories in a way that wouldn't necessarily scream at people. I didn't want to have anyone be called "Usher," for instance, but I make reference to the house of Marquis, and the heart of course refigures "The Tell-Tale Heart." That's probably the most obvious example, but a lot of people don't remember the pale blue eye, which was the thing about the old man that drove the narrator mad.

I was really just sort of plucking things here and there, if there was a particular phrase that struck me because it conveyed the period, a kind of antiquated phrasing that I thought would give it a period flavor, so I just sort of plundered, knowing that I couldn't be sued, so that was a nice benefit of that.

Interviewer: You mentioned the pale blue eye. That was something I was very interested in. In "The Tell-Tale Heart," the pale blue eye belongs to that hideous old man, but you give it to, well it's linked to, Lea Marquis. Cadet Poe actually says she has a pale blue eye. And then the poem that he composes was supposedly composed through him by Mattie Landor, so you link it to two beautiful maidens, whereas Poe had given the pale blue eye to the hideous old man. Why did you make this change?

Bayard: Well, I think because death and sex in Poe's world are completely linked. They're really almost the other side of each other, and so there're several stories where a beautiful maiden is physically the bringer of death or an embodiment of death. It gets back to that quote about the death of a beautiful woman being so poetic, and so beautiful women are really carriers of death in Poe's world. To me, the link between the hideous old man and the beautiful young women is all a subliminal link back to Poe.

It's interesting, the first thing I wrote was the poem itself, the pale blue eye poem. I just wrote the first stanza of it, and it's the very first thing that sort of got me into Poe's world. I used the rhyme scheme and the meter of "Ulalume," maybe, one of his better-known poems. And the connections occurred to me later on. So the pale blue eye just became an image as much as anything that I would then link to a particular character. And again with the idea of creating red herrings and throwing the reader off track, there are a certain amount of mechanics that go into this decision as well. I also love the sound of it, the name, The Pale Blue Eye. As soon as I heard that, I thought that would be a nice title, which is one of the few times I had kept my original title.

Interviewer: I was expecting from the title a different sort of reference in the novel, and that was surprising to see that the pale blue eye was that of a beautiful young woman.

Bayard: Again, I didn't want to make the refigurings superobvious. I didn't want to have some old man wander in with a pale blue eye. To me that's a thud, rather than a tickle. It slaps the reader with the allusion rather than creating a web of association and connection.

Interviewer: With the poem "The Pale Blue Eye," you said you wrote that first. Was that an exercise for you to write in a Poe rhyme scheme to create the poem?

Bayard: Well, there was an exercise to it; it's hard to explain exactly, there was a point at which I'd start actually getting excited by a particular idea, because there were lots of ideas floating around and there's also a complicated process that happens with my editor and publisher about what ideas they're excited about it, so we slowly converged around a particular idea, and the idea was Poe. And that's really where it started out, a mystery story about Poe. And then, from there, came West Point, because I wanted to find one avenue of Poe's life that hadn't been seized by some other author, and I couldn't find anybody who had written about his time at West Point. At the same time, I was intrigued by West Point, because it was at such odds with Poe himself. As a Romantic poet, what was he doing at this hypermasculine regimented environment? So that disconnect was interesting to me. And then, yeah, I can't tell exactly what came first. I thought, "Well, since Poe was a poet, since that was all he ever wanted to be really from an early age, [I thought] we need a poem in here." I read his poems, I used "Ulalume" just as a template, but as soon as I got to the ghoul with the pale blue eye, something just clicked for me. I was like, okay, this is going to work. I had a whole world of association open up inside my head. The story kind of grows out of that. There was no particular idea for a story other than Poe at West Point.

Interviewer: It's very Poe-esque, the poem. Did you intend it as a parody, a gentle poking fun at Poe, or more of an homage?

Bayard: Again, getting back to what we were talking about earlier, there may be elements of both in that. I think that the narration of Poe is definitely parodic; the poem may be less so. I really intended the poem to work on the level of a poem, not simply as parody, but [to] create the kind of chill that Poe's own poems do. The narration is definitely meant to, I mean, there's a satirical quality there, because Poe's excesses are out there, you know. The fact that he doesn't hear from Lea, and he's already pining away unto death—I mean, he has extreme reactions to everything; it just seems Poe's way. As I said, there is a quality to a lot of Poe's work that skirts laughter, just barely skirts it, but then sometimes plunges headlong into it. When I talk about his bravery, that's part of it; he was willing to look ridiculous, he was willing to be absurd and go into . . . people. I was chastised by some people for the extremity of the climax with Lea in the ice house cave and eating the own heart. They thought, "God, isn't that over the top?" and my response is always, "Have you read Poe?"

Interviewer: Like "The Fall of the House of Usher"?

Bayard: Yes, it's swallowed by the earth; it doesn't just tip over, the earth swallows it! That climax is much more melodramatic than I would have done myself, but I figured, having entered Poe's world, I had to be that extreme. I had to. There were a couple of reviews where people did think it was absolutely ridiculous, that climax, with eating the heart, and I said, well, then I've done my job, because that's how Poe's stuff affects you, and sometimes the laughter I think can be a defense against the disturbing nature of the work. Laughter is a kind of defense mechanism that can kick in. It's somewhat similar to the work of David Lynch, who I think in some ways is very close, an inheritor of Poe's work. *Blue Velvet* is a fascinating movie, and yet parts of it, I was laughing at; it's absurd, and yet very unsettling, and beautiful, and terrible, and everything that Poe's work at its best can be.

Interviewer: You said that he's willing to be brave, and put himself out there, and appear ridiculous. With the Poe you create as a character, I think that there's an uncertainty about whether he's willing to put himself out there or just unaware of his absurdity. I'm thinking about the scene where he went to dinner with Lea and disguised himself as an officer with the absurd moustache.

Bayard: Which of course refigures the moustache Poe would have later in life, because that's what people remember most about him; they remember the moustache.

Interviewer: And the way Landor's describing him, there, he's just performing, but he appears ridiculous, very much unaware.

Bayard: Well, that's true. When I talk about Poe's bravery, maybe I'm talking about sort of an unconscious quality, because

I'm sure he would have been the first to say, put in that disclaimer, saying that this is not biographical. I'm not like these people. I know he said he only wrote gothic stories because that was the trendy thing to write. He figured that would make money, and he adduced all these commercial reasons for a lot of the choices he made, but the fact that he kept coming back to certain themes shows that they really were important to him, they tapped something in him, so he may have given himself an out by saying, "Oh this isn't me, this is just a particular species of sociopathy that I find interesting." But at the same time he is exploring these things, and risking, again being repellent and risking abhorrence from his readers. This is early nineteenth century, so these are not the kind of sensationalized audiences that we have today. I mean, even my kids, it would take a fair amount to even just scare them, I think, but in those days, I think this was pretty strong stuff, and it's still strong stuff, I think in some cases.

Interviewer: This next question is on a little bit different track than what we were talking about: There are a few points in *The Pale Blue Eye* where you're hinting at a developing eroticism between Poe and Landor, but then it never develops, never goes anywhere, and you also have Poe wonder if Artemis was having an affair with Leroy Fry, but then it's just mentioned once and never developed. I was wondering why you chose to introduce some homoeroticism, but....

Bayard: Never actually resolve it? Well, the homoeroticism came out of two things: one was the setting itself, West Point, the fact that these young men were essentially living the way that priests do. They were living just with each other; they could have visits with belles on the weekends, but it was a very masculine environment. So it seemed to be highly natural that there would be homosexual or homoerotic activity going on in that kind of setting, and I'm sure less so now that West Point's coed, but there's these young, charged men alone with each other....

Interviewer: And nobody else.

Bayard: Yes, exactly, kind of a penitentiary setting, so that seemed natural. And, too, there does seem to be homoerotic elements in Poe's own work. I know Oscar Wilde put him on the list of famous homosexuals. There's no evidence to suggest that he had any homosexual relationships. I think he simply had a case of arrested sexual development. Arrested maybe at twelve, or something. Wasn't his wife thirteen when they married?

Interviewer: Yes.

Bayard: Maybe it's thirteen. And so it's simply there in the original detective stories, these two men, and that's really what the homoeroticism in *The Pale Blue Eye* is meant to mirror—the relationship between Dupin and the narrator. They're living alone. I think Cadet Poe makes reference to it, saying, "[W]e could go live in France." Again this is an allusion to "The Murders in the Rue Morgue" and to the kind of domesticity that exists between those two men. It's not explicitly, or even implicitly, described in sexual terms, but it's two men living together in a kind of domestic arrangement in terms of great physical and personal intimacy. I think that's as close as you can get in nineteenth-century literature to an advocacy of homosexuality. Is it Leslie Fiedler—"Come Back to the Raft Again"?

Interviewer: In Twain and Melville.

Bayard: Yeah, it's very interesting to me, because there is a great deal of at least homosocial things in all of that American literature of that time, James Fenimore Cooper and all those guys.

And I do think there's also an element of father/son in the relationship between Landor and Poe as well, and I didn't feel I had to either swing it one way or another. I felt again the web or cloud of associative impulses that leaves you always a little unsettled, unclear as to what their true relationship is. I was clear in my mind that they were deeply fond of each other. The nature of that fondness, whether it was filial, whether it was implicitly homosexual, I don't think I even resolved it in my own head, and I didn't feel like I needed to.

Interviewer: Why West Point? You said that this would be part of Poe's life that hadn't been already written about too much. As I was reading, I could tell that Gus Landor, for example, was pretty antimilitary, and obviously for him as a character, that links up with what happened to his daughter. Did you intend any antimilitary kind of message?

Bayard: Antimilitary? You know, not necessarily. Landor's sentiments are fully in line with what a sizeable number of Americans felt about West Point at the time. As I think it's made clear, or hopefully is made clear, there was a great deal of resistance still at the idea of a professional military academy, the idea of even a standing army, which goes back to the revolution, which was not so long ago. Americans were still very uncomfortable with the idea of a uniformed military, or even a uniformed constabulary. There was that, and I think Davy Crockett was one of the congressmen who tried to abolish West Point, and you had President Andrew Jackson who was quite opposed to it as well and managed to undo lots of Thayer's decisions. So they were in an oppositional atmosphere at that time, and the survival of the institution wasn't at all assured, so I tried to convey the different emotions through different characters, Landor being one of them, and in his case, he has a very personal reason for not liking West Point, because he feels that that system of keeping young men cooped up can create opportunities like rape, of which his daughter is a victim. That's part of the function of the system that keeps them pent up at the height of their own sexual energy. Again, West Point appealed to me for many reasons, as I said, partly because it was a relatively unexplored part of Poe's life, unexplored part because there's not much documentation of his time there. A few letters survived and his court-martial records are available in the archives. But also, what I mentioned before, that is the junction between Poe the poet and West Point, which was in fact America's first engineering school. Every time you tell someone that Poe went to West Point, it's just a head-scratcher. People go, "Why was he at West Point?" If you look at his biography, it makes sense that he was trying to curry favor with his foster father. This was kind of a last bid for affection with John Allan, who, by the way, never actually went to West Point. That's an invented encounter, but I wanted to have that kind of final showdown between them. So that was intriguing to me, and the setting itself, the Hudson Valley, was then considered America's wilderness. This was well before the West had been colonized, and the Hudson Valley was—well a whole school of painting came out of it, and of course it's also amazingly picturesque. I went to West Point for really just a day, an overnight stay, because there's only so much you can see, only so much of the original reservation that survives, but it's the most beautiful campus I've ever seen. It's actually stunning, the hills rising around it, the river winding through it, absolutely beautiful, so I love the picturesque and really romantic quality of it. A lot of people found the setting quite gloomy, because it takes place mostly in winter. I intended it to be sort of romantic.

Interviewer: I think there are certain parts of it where you make it sound very picturesque and beautiful.

Bayard: Yeah, that was really my intent. It is mostly taking place in winter, so you have that darkness, that grimness to it. So all these factors kind of blend into it. I think that Poe's sensibilities are essentially feminine in a lot of ways, and I was fascinated by him, trying to imagine what it would be like to drop him into this very masculine setting.

Interviewer: Earlier you talk a little bit about how Poe portrays women. How do you see your portrayals of women differing?

Bayard: Gosh, I hope they're more progressive! I realize that the main female does turn into a kind of ghoul at the end, and again I felt I couldn't stray too far from the Poe template and create this extremely well-adjusted modern, suffragette kind of character, but I like to think that she has a little more wit and independence and resourcefulness than Poe's women. He would allow his women to be brilliant, but he wouldn't necessarily give them much in the way of humor or. . . .

Interviewer: Or voice.

Bayard: Yeah, they had very little voice. They're acted upon, even when they wind up sort of coming back in some kind of horrible way, Madeline. . . .

Interviewer: Madeline in "Usher"?

Bayard: Yes, she's considered locked away in a tomb, and it's only after that she decides to act.

Interviewer: And Ligeia is brilliant, but we only know that through the narrator. We don't hear much from her.

Bayard: There's no conversation. Yeah, in fact I think I borrowed a couple of details from Ligeia just to convey Lea's intelligence, but the idea of somebody actually flirting and teasing and being saucy and then turning around and being very cold, the idea of her having her own identity apart, I think that that's not so much Poe, it's more my updating, because it wouldn't have interested me to create just another cipher maiden. I wanted to have somebody else. So I'm actually quite fond of Lea, and I mourn her loss, but of course she had to go. It was inevitable, the death of a beautiful woman is the perfect subject! Once that line comes out, some beautiful woman has to die. In fact, two beautiful women die.

Interviewer: What about Mattie? How do you see Mattie as a character?

Bayard: Well, in a way, she's more Poe-like, isn't she, in that we don't need her. She's almost purely a victim, and we don't get much sense of her other than these very almost-cryptic reminiscences from Landor. There was only so much I could do to make her a character, since she's a ghost really. She's spectral. She can only be heard through the channel of the poem. I guess there was only so much I could do to make her three dimensional. She's much more in the traditional Poe vein I think, although I don't know if any of his women were raped. They all had more mystical fates; they just wasted away, I think. I don't think there were any sexual crimes, at least, none that I can remember.

Interviewer: Only perhaps symbolically.

Bayard: Chilling and killing. In "Annabel Lee," it's just a cold wind, basically, that comes along and kills her.

Interviewer: I liked the way you played with the line "the death of a beautiful woman is poetic subject imaginable," because Landor challenges that at the end.

Bayard: Well, he challenges that, because he's seen it happen himself, and there was no poetry in it for him.

Interviewer: So I think that is one way that Mattie at least functions differently here than she might have in Poe.

Bayard: Well, that's true. She's a kind of reproach in a way to the effect that what she suffers is much more horrible, in some ways, than the kind of vague deaths of Poe's characters. She's sexually violated, raped, she's bleeding, there's actual blood, Poe's women don't bleed so much, and there's very earthly consequences for her, in addition to this afterlife. And by the way, part of it is that it would be a strange coincidence if Mattie didn't sort of write that poem, but I wanted the supernatural to be just on the edge of supernatural. I mean, Lea gets up again after having supposedly choked—to me, it's just on the edge of possible. I mean, maybe it's just a weird coincidence that it happened that way.

Interviewer: Possibly it's all in Poe's mind? I think you did make that ambiguous to some extent. But it's possible that Poe is creating the poem.

Bayard: Absolutely. That's again kind of a modern impulse, to kind of blur that line between the natural and the supernatural. Maybe Poe did it himself, supernatural pieces. I don't know. Is it possible that Madeline Usher would have been able to survive being walled away in a tomb? I guess it's possible.

Interviewer: I think even that story leaves it a little bit ambiguous. Was she still alive when they put her in the tomb? Or not?

Bayard: Oh yeah, he was obsessed with premature burial. In fact, that's the name of one of his stories, I think. That was apparently quite a common fear of that day. I don't know if this is true, but "saved by the bell" supposedly refers to the fact that they'd be buried with bell cords so that if in fact they woke up, they could signal.

Interviewer: I've seen drawings of those, little alarm bells tied with a string down into the coffin.

Bayard: It was a societal fear of being buried alive.

Interviewer: I guess it would have been possible, to some extent.

Bayard: And it happened often enough, well, just enough, that there'd be some story of it actually happening. I think in "A Premature Burial," he's in a bunker in a steamship or something. He's in a very narrow berth of the steamship, and it feels like a coffin, and it's all dark, and I think that's how it plays out. But for most of the story, he's convinced that he's been buried alive. Or it could be that he's epileptic. Again, epilepsy figures in Lea, because it also reconfigures more than one Poe story. He was probably very intrigued by the altered consciousness aspect of it. Dostoyevsky is definitely. . . .

Interviewer: Those were all the questions I had, was there anything else, or anything you wanted to go back to that I asked about?

Bayard: Well, the issue of the bravery thing. I wrote a little essay on it, I could send it to you, for the Edgar Awards Banquet that's coming up in March, or I'm not sure when. And I talk again about the issue of bravery. The mystery story to me is a kind of very courageous undertaking, because basically he was betting that the simple act of deduction and analysis would be interesting. The crime in "The Murders in the Rue Morgue" is grisly, but we don't actually see it; it's only recorded. And the rest of it is strictly armchair deduction, all of Dupin's stuff. I think in "The Purloined Letter," he actually goes to the apartment and finds the letter, but it's all armchair. And he was betting that just the act of watching someone's brain come to a conclusion would be interesting enough for readers; and it was. In a sense, the creation of the detective story was a bet at the time; there wasn't much of a literary precedent for it. The one that I'm aware of that's actually inspired my most recent book, *The Black Tower*, was *The Memoirs of Vidocq*, this real-life French detective, who may have inspired "The Murders in the Rue Morgue."

Interviewer: I had read that is one that is a possible precursor for Poe's detective stories.

Bayard: And in fact it probably is partly fictional, so it may in fact be a fictional story in which he embroidered or invented things. In fact, I think they were ghostwritten as well.

Interviewer: You mentioned the Edgar Awards; what are the Edgar Awards'?

Bayard: The Edgar Awards are given out by the Mystery Writers of America. It's the preeminent award for mystery novels, and *The Pale Blue Eye* was actually nominated for it, so they have an awards banquet once a year, and because it's the bicentennial of Poe, they're having a special booklet, and various people are writing about Poe's effect on their work.

One of the things I say in my piece is try to imagine Poe pitching the idea of "The Murders in the Rue Morgue," the Dupin stories, to a modern studio exec: There's these two guys, they sit around in a rotting house in the middle of Paris, and they don't go anywhere, and they just sit in their chairs; and the detective reads all the newspapers, all the stories about the particular crime, and figures out who did it. Then

	there'd be a pause: And then what? Where's the car chase? Where's the action here? It gets back to that notion that the internal action is just as interesting as what's going around them. Again, the crime was the MacGuffin, the orangutan stuffing the body up the chimney.
Interviewer:	That just got the whole thing rolling.
Bayard:	Yeah. I think that he was much less interested in the nature of the crime than by how it was solved.
Interviewer:	And one of the things that happens in your novel is that the reader is watching the working of the reader's own mind in addition to the watching the working of Lander's mind. You're watching your own processes at the same time you're watching his.
Bayard:	And then getting the rug pulled out at the end, hopefully. I don't know if anyone's figured out the ending. The one thing I do in this book, I hope that I do well, is that I understand, just as Agatha Christie did, the assumptions that people make. And the assumption that an old man that doesn't have any obvious connection to the crime, the idea that he could actually be the perpetrator of it doesn't even occur to people. And also because Landor is portrayed very sympathetically, again, I hope so. I think people find him very sympathetic: He's lost his wife, his daughter has supposedly run away, he's alone in the world, and people tend to think of him as the hero. And to have it turn around is shocking to them. It's the kind of shock I was after.
Interviewer:	Why do you think fiction that reconfigures earlier literature has become so popular in recent years?
Bayard:	You know, I'm trying to understand if it's really more popular than it was two hundred years ago, because every time we try to find the prototype of it, we keep finding one earlier. A friend of mine said we should just call it the *Wide Sargasso Sea* book. That was Jean Rhys's book about the mad woman in the attic from *Jane Eyre*—a brilliant reinvention of that story. Well, no, no, we'd have to go back to *Joseph Andrews*, which is Henry Fielding's satirical reworking of Samuel Richardson's *Pamela*. Joseph Andrews is actually Pamela's brother. Fielding borrowed this character for a very different and much more ribald story. So the impulse has always been there. Shortly after *Don Quixote* appeared, people were writing their own Don Quixote stories, much to Cervantes's chagrin. I guess it gets back to that feeling of being readers, because every writer, of course, began life as a reader, and those are some of our most seminal experiences, and maybe it just makes sense to go back to some of these old stories and

retell them in our own way—it's a kind of stealing of some of the original Promethean fire, I suppose.

There does seem to be a real efflorescence of these kinds of books in the last ten or fifteen years, and I don't know exactly why. But there are probably commercial considerations, too. If you tell people that this is a book about what happened to Tiny Tim, you're already halfway to getting people interested if they have fond memories of Tiny Tim or the story—and everyone knows A Christmas Carol. So you can already feel people go, "Oh, okay." They know where they are, or at least they know where they're beginning, because they have some underpinning. Commercially speaking, it gives you a platform that a story about just any nineteenth-century character wouldn't necessarily have.

Appendix B
Interview with Sena Jeter Naslund

March 13, 2009, Louisville, Kentucky

Interviewer: Thank you for letting me come.
Naslund: You're welcome. Thank you for your interest.
Interviewer: I guess where we might start is talking about what drew you to this type of novel. Because *Ahab's Wife* is your second book that reconfigured in some way a nineteenth-century novel. So what drew you to this type of book?
Naslund: Well, I was drawn to the two efforts, *Sherlock in Love* and *Ahab's Wife*, for different reasons. We won't spend much time on *Sherlock in Love*. I wrote that novel because I wanted to learn how to handle plot better. I had read a very entertaining companion book by Nicholas Meyer, whom I knew slightly at University of Iowa, called *The Seven-Per-Cent Solution*. I was very entertained by it. I was never very interested in Sherlock Holmes at that point. I read one Sherlock Holmes story when I was a high school student. But I was interested in it because Meyers, in *The Seven-Per-Cent Solution*, used the historic figure Sigmund Freud in the retelling of the Holmes story, and I was curious as to what Nicholas Meyer thought of Freud. I know his father was a psychoanalyst and had written a very good critical analysis of Joseph Conrad from a psychoanalytic point of view. So, I really just wanted to see what it would be like to imagine oneself inside the historical person, because Holmes himself was secondary to me, and I wanted that plot exercise. My stories before that had been more or less of the Virginia Woolf type. I really like it when nothing happens except in the interior. That's my natural inclination, but those books don't sell very well. So, it was a learning exercise, and I had gotten interested in Ludwig II partly because there was a mystery associated with his death. People didn't really know exactly what happened at his death in 1886, as I present it. There was also the fact

that scholars of Sherlock Holmes stories say that 1886 is the "missing year" for the Holmes series, and that gave me a sort of permission; I wasn't going to step on toes.

But how I got interested in writing Ahab's Wife is, of course, a different story. I have quite a lot to say about this, so feel free to interrupt if you have to. I think I first read Moby-Dick the summer before I was going to graduate eighth grade and go into high school (in Birmingham, we had K–8, then high school). By this time, I was pretty interested in literature and reading in general. I was often visiting the Birmingham library. I was just reading all the fiction I had ever heard of, and I had heard of Moby-Dick but I didn't know much about it. My theory was that if it was famous enough for me to have heard about it, ignorant child that I was, then it must be a pretty important book and that I should read it. I can remember plucking it off the shelf at the library. It was an edition with the Rockwell Kent illustrations on it, which were as mystifying to me as the text, because they were done in a stylized way, and I didn't know why one would want to do that. I was used to illustrations of children's books which were quite pretty or lyrical or heroic—the Wyeth illustrations, for example. That made the book all the more curious to me.

Anyway, I read it then, and I wrote my first high school book report on Moby-Dick, which I also remember well because the teacher, who was actually quite a kindly person, asked me in front of the class, "Are these your ideas or the ideas of some art critic?" That was the term she used, art critic. I was stunned by the question, and I sort of stammered out, "Oh, I wrote it myself." Her question was intriguing to me, because, first of all, there was some place where you could read things other people had written about books, and, secondly, since she mentioned an art critic, that meant that the novel was some sort of art. I had, up until that time, thought of art as pictures up on the wall. And I loved the idea that the novel may be an artful product. So, both of those ideas were important to me, and I read Moby-Dick not again until probably I was a graduate student. I don't remember reading it in undergraduate. Then I was traveling with my daughter, in 1993 or '92 (when she was twelve or thirteen). We were doing a lot of driving, and we had decided that we needed some rules of the road, so we could enjoy the many miles that summer while I was giving talks. I hadn't published a lot, but I had published enough that I was on the conference circuit. So, our first decision was that we would be well stocked with candy and that we would eat as much as we wanted. I liked that rule as much as Flora did. The other rule was that we would entertain ourselves by listening to audiotapes (I got to pick a lot out). So we did listen to more childish books, such as Little Women, Dickens, and Huckleberry Finn, and we also listened to Moby-Dick. The novel my daughter loved the most was Moby-Dick, and I knew this because she heard it more than once, and she memorized Captain Ahab's speeches. She would puff herself up and become Captain Ahab, and as a literary mom I thought, "This is great. She has a good ear and she can tell what good literature is."

And then I thought, "Too bad there is no important woman character in the book, one with whom she could identify and memorize her speeches." This came, too, because the Sherlock Holmes book was an effort to put a female figure into the predominantly male masculine landscape of the Holmes story. So I had that idea before, that I sort of wanted to invade that territory and give a woman a place to stand in that kind of story. I didn't say anything to Flora, but I did continue to think about Moby-Dick and Huckleberry Finn, because they informally are sometimes referred to as candidates for the great American novel, but also as boys' books. I never thought of them as boys' books; I never thought of that at that time. But scholars, mostly men, especially when I was coming through, had nominated them. So I asked myself, analytically, what do these books have in common that they would both appeal enough so that they would be mentioned in this context, and the first idea I hit upon was that they were both quest stories. I thought that was good—that's a great mythic subject—and they were both quests over water, furthermore, the great Mississippi and the oceans of the world. I was pleased with that. Also, in the second place, that both of these books had characters who had transcended barriers, cultural barriers of prejudice, especially racial barriers. Huck and Jim, and, of course, Ishmael and Queequeg, who was, of course, tattooed all over from the South Seas and also a pagan. Ishmael's transcendence has gone so far as to worship the little wooden idol that Queequeg had with him. And again I was pleased with this thinking, and I thought, "Yes, a good novel should push the thinking of the community that is going to read it. It should have the courage to exhibit independent thought about well-established prejudices." So, again, I was pleased. Then the third thing I thought of was that neither of them had important women in them. I was very upset at that thought. I thought, "So this is what you have to do to write the great American novel: Eliminate half the population." So, that's a somewhat outrageous idea. There are a few women in some of those books, but they are very minor.

So, that was the background thinking of this project. I knew I wanted to write a more ambitious book. And I knew that I wanted to write a book that was different from the Virginia Woolf sensibility pieces. My model and my own sense of a project was actually not Melville, but Charles Dickens, whom I had read a great deal of growing up. Dickens had been very popular in his own age. People who couldn't read paid a penny reader on the street to read out loud. And, you know, the vocabulary and the syntax in a Dickens novel is not a simple matter. The suspense and the story line and the characters were all fascinating enough so that even illiterate people wanted to be part of his audience. That was appealing success to me, his wide readership. But also, his work had been of lasting literary value to many people. Not everyone would agree with that. He certainly has his place in the canon and in the teaching of literature. I thought I'd like to be able to do that. To be able to write a book that has a wide appeal, accessible to a lot of different sorts of readers; also, one that can aspire to literary merit. So, I was, in a sense, looking for a subject that would help me do that.

Then the book itself, coming off that ambition and the experience with my daughter, came to me all of a sudden. I had gone up to Boston for the publication of Sherlock in Love. NPR gave it a great review, and my publisher, David Godine, was extremely nice to me and gave me a little party. It was a little taste of the big time. I had rented a little car that I was driving around in Boston, which is a big thing for me, because Boston is a big city, and I wasn't lost and I could manage the little car, so I was a little full of myself. I said to myself, "Oh, you are a competent human being after all." So, out of that good feeling, as I was driving the car, I had a visionary experience; I had a vision, and I heard a voice. The vision was of a roof walk and a woman looking out at the ocean hoping to see her husband's whaling ship coming in with the try-pots burning, which she could see at night. But as she looked, she realized, and I realized looking through her eyes and identifying with her, that, intuitively, he was not coming home, not then, not ever. With that realization, her gaze shifted from the dark ocean waves to the great starry sky, and she began to ask questions about herself: "Who am I in the face of all this glory, this vast glory of the heavens?" And really pondering the questions, or the answer to the question, "What's my place in the universe?" And the voice spoke right up and said, "Captain Ahab was neither my first husband nor my last."

People have asked me why I wrote about Ahab's wife. Well, that is what the voice gave me. It didn't say, "Captain Brown was neither my first husband nor my last." Something in my consciousness went back, I think, to frustrations about Moby-Dick and the relationship to my daughter. That was part of the gift of the muse. That sentence came, and I knew that that could be the first sentence to a very big novel. I knew that that visionary experience would be set deep in the novel and would be a turning point. So I had to get from the first sentence to the visionary scene. And the first sentence gave me a structure, because I didn't know who the first one was, and I certainly didn't know who the last one was. But I trusted the voice. So, I described this idea to a number of friends to see what they would think about it, because I knew it was going to be a huge project. And I didn't have an agent or a contract. I had published four books, but I didn't want to spend a lot of time futilely on a huge project, so I mentioned it to friends, and their faces always lit up when I spoke about this. In Moby Dick, Captain Ahab does have a wife, but she's given no name and no life, and it seemed like an opportunity. And their faces lit up. When I was at parties, I started describing this idea to strangers, and their faces also lit up. And I thought, "This idea has a lot of curb appeal," as they say in real estate.

So, I decided I would write it, and the first thing I would do is, of course, to reread Moby-Dick very carefully to get the facts straight; such as Ahab was much older than his young wife, that he lost his leg after his second voyage after his marriage. I had assumed she had married him one-legged, but that is not true. He lost his leg on the second voyage, and he lost his life on the third voyage after his marriage, and there was a child, a son. So, I wanted to be scrupulously true to what I considered the facts, and there are some other mentions of the wife. I quote all of them in the abstracts. One of them bothered me, because it described the character as a sweet, docile person, and I was not interested in writing about a sweet, docile woman. I wanted to write about a quester, someone who took control of her own life. So, I looked at those passages very carefully, and what I found was that this was an utterance of Captain Peleg, who, I came to decide, was a Polonius figure in the novel. There are a lot of references to Shakespeare in Moby-Dick, especially to King Lear; Pip is the fool or jester. Also references to Hamlet. And

Polonius is usually interpreted as a fool in Hamlet. He's a windbag and so is Captain Peleg, and he was, not only in this instance but in other places, full of ideas that didn't hold water. So, I thought, "If Captain Peleg says this is the way she is, then she is surely not that way." So, that was an important rationalization. I used my best critical skills and tried to be fair-minded and still arrived at that conclusion. That opened the door for me to write about a character that I would really be interested in.

Another thing that was very encouraging was Ahab's attitude toward her. He mentioned that he left but one dent in the marriage pillow before he set sail, so I set it up that way. But the passage that was particularly meaningful to me is just as the chase is commencing in Moby-Dick and Starbuck is trying to persuade Ahab not to chase Moby-Dick but instead to go home to Nantucket to his wife and child. Ahab says to Starbuck, "Come close Starbuck, come close to me and let me look into a human eye. 'Tis better than to gaze upon sea or sky. 'Tis better than to gaze upon God. By the green land by the bright hearth stone I see my wife and my child in thine eye." So there is this impulse toward humanism and certainly tenderness and valuing of his wife. I wasn't going to write the story if I thought this was a bad marriage. I wasn't interested in skewering Ahab for being a bad husband. I think Melville was a bad husband, in many respects, to his wife. Some people think he actually physically abused her. She came out bruised one time and said she had fallen down a set of stairs. I think they reconciled later on, but I think he was a very difficult person. I could have gotten away with making Ahab that kind of person, but if he was, I didn't want to fool with him. So, I think he is much in the tradition of Heathcliff and Mr. Rochester in a milder version. He is this dark brooding figure that has a romantic nature that certainly has a powerfully attractive soul that is imprisoned in a tormented psyche. I think he is in that tradition. I was very grateful for Melville giving him this expression that I just quoted of his longing for intimacy and closeness with his wife and child.

So, those were important points. Then in the research I read a lot about Melville; I read a lot about the sources. I went to the Nantucket Historical Society, and I discovered for myself the story of the sinking of the whale ship Essex. Soon after my book came out, Nathaniel Philbrick published a book called In the Heart of the Sea, which is about the sinking of the whale ship Essex. I knew that Melville had been inspired to write Moby-Dick not only by Shakespeare but

Appendix B 199

also by that story, which was very well known. Philbrick says it was as well known in Melville's time as the Titanic story is in our time. It was very much an element of popular culture. But I didn't have Philbrick's book then, although I had met him. We just met by accident at a lecture, and he made it possible for me to visit the Maria Mitchell house after it was closed for the winter. I used that in my descriptions, which I was very grateful to have. I like him; he's a very nice person.

I discovered quite on my own that Melville had chosen to only tell half the story. Once the sperm whale rammed the ship, Melville goes toward the end of the book. But the other half of the actual story was that a number of people did get into the small whale boat, and they did run out of supplies, they did vote to draw lots and to resort to cannibalism. The lot did fall to a cabin boy, and they were all appalled and asked him how he felt about this, and he said that "'Tis as good a fate as any." And they did eat him. So, this was a puzzle for me. Why hadn't Melville wanted to include that? He had already written a big book; maybe he was tired. That's the simplest reason, but you know, when he had moved to the Berkshires, he already had a complete draft of Moby-Dick. He read Hawthorne's work, and he reviewed his Mosses from an Old Manse and reviewed it very favorably and compared it favorably to Shakespeare. It was an anonymous review; Hawthorne didn't know he had written it at the time. But he became interested in the darkness in Hawthorne's work, and Hawthorne turned out to be a neighbor in the Berkshires, and they became friends. Then Melville totally revised Moby-Dick into the book that we have. I wondered why Melville hadn't wanted that part of the story. My theory, and I can't substantiate my theory, was that he had already written about cannibalism in Typee and Omoo so much so that in society at that time, he was known as the man who lived among the cannibals. I thought he wanted to escape being reduced to that. He didn't want to repeat what he had already done. So I think that was why he exited.

To me this is the darker part of the story, darker than having Ahab become obsessed with revenge. Melville calls him a monomaniac. And that intrigued me, because one of the things about deciding to write a companion novel, at least for me, is that while I want to be true to the facts, and that's very important, I also want to do something that's been left undone, that I see the potential for but the author had chosen to tell other stories. With Sherlock Holmes, it was his emotional side, his musical side. Conan Doyle gave him a

Stradivarius violin, doesn't say how he got it, and lets him play it whenever he's feeling melancholy or wants to shoot up with a 7 percent solution of cocaine. Doyle definitely gives Holmes an emotional side, but the rational side, the cold, impersonal thinking machine, is what really faces the audience. I wanted to rotate that figure a little bit. And so I was with Captain Ahab. Here is this side of him that really loved his wife and child, but nobody ever wrote about that to my knowledge or paid much attention to it. Most people don't even know there was a wife mentioned. That left me with something new about Ahab as well as giving me the female character, Una, which I especially wanted for the book. So I found something that was true to the book and yet had my own stamp on it.

The first of these companion novels I had read was The Wide Sargasso Sea, off of Jane Eyre. I read that book, because I was scornful of people that took other characters, and I wanted to see if it qualified as art and stood on its own legs. I thought it did, and that was a great relief to me. I had read it years ago. Of course I know, we all know, that Shakespeare rewrote other people's stuff all the time. We consider it quite original and very fine. But still, that was an important question to me, whether this was worthy art, whether a product could come out of this endeavor that I would have no embarrassment about. So, this story of cannibalism intrigued me as a way of going, as they used to say about Captain Kirk, going where no man had gone before. I wanted to go where Melville hadn't gone, and the main way in which I wanted to do that was for my character not to be so much a victim as Ahab was [a victim to the anger of the whale]. And he, of course, was filled with hatred and grief and bitterness over what had happened to him. But isn't it a more interesting psychological dilemma to push it further and make the person guilty, in some sense, of atrocities? Not the victim of atrocities, but the perpetrator or participant at least. And this tied into the fact that I knew some Vietnam vets who did have post-traumatic stress disorder partly because of what they had seen and sometimes, for some of them, because of what they had done themselves. I had such a strong feeling for those people and so much in a way wanted to help them, to say accept this about yourself and go forward; don't look back all the time.

And so I created a female character that had to accept some hard things about herself as well as losses that were just causes of grief but not guilt. So, I wanted to show a character who, if her life was weighted down by guilt, would be able to accept her own shortcomings and still want to go forward. If the life she wanted for herself was taken away from her, if she were a victim in that sense, then she would have the courage and creativity to create a new life for herself. And if it happened again, she would do it again. I very much saw this as a contrast to Melville. His novel ends in death and destruction. I wanted to write a novel about a woman quester and have it end in triumph, not defeat. I wanted to write a triumph instead of a tragedy, but I wanted it to be earned. I needed her to really be involved in some fairly appalling situations. Usually when people ask me how much of you is in that book, I start off by saying I'm not a cannibal.

So, all of these things were important to getting organized and thinking through what I was going to do. It was lots of discovery; it wasn't all thought through before I embarked on it. I did about nine months of research before I settled down to write. I had to read a lot about sailing—I knew nothing about sailing or whaling—and about how people lived inland. I went to historic recreations, and I read about other people in this era and other "at sea" books. I had read some Conrad and about Two Years before the Mast. So, I tried to think about it as thoroughly as I could and to ask myself a lot of questions about it, about the shape and the overall thing I wanted to achieve.

In the process of writing the book, about in the middle of it, I felt somewhat lost. To use Melville's language, "I could go neither forward nor backward. I existed in a confused sea." I think that's such a lovely term, "a confused sea." He also speaks of "devious sailing." The book seemed to be getting unwieldy. Then a process that had nothing to do with Melville came to my rescue. I was visiting a friend, Lucinda Sullivan, who is also a novelist and former student of mine, and she had a new little room that was a standalone unit next to her swimming pool that had a new telescope in it. She had made a tablecloth, a white tablecloth, and written, in her own handwriting in gold, some quotations that had to do with the starry sky, which she loved. One of these was by a mutual friend of ours, also a former student of mine, Maureen Moorhead, and Lucinda had written on her tablecloth, "One must take off her fear like clothing. One must travel at night. This is the seeking after God." And when I read that, I thought, "That's exactly what I want at the center of this book." This is the story of a character questing after spiritual life that suits her, that is not orthodox. That, in some way, is defiant. And I had already, by this time, written the scene in the beginning where her father insists automatically that she believe exactly what he believes or he will make her. He will hit her if he needs to, and he does. So those elements were already there, but I hadn't seen how the spiritual quest needed to be the organizing factor of the book. In a sense, one could say that it is the organizing factor for Moby-Dick, but it is read as a kind of spiritual quest seeking after reality. It wants to strike through the mask to get at whatever is essentially genuine, authentic experience. My Una's questing has more to do with engaging the imagination. There is not that demand that there be something that you can get to when you strike through the mask. One can create a sense of oneness with nature.

I see the book as partly about a quest for home, a local home but also a cosmic home. Again it's a triumph in that way. She comes to feel at home in the universe, and her name is Una, which means oneness. I chose her name, and I was a long time finding her name; it was a very important step. I didn't really think I could write the novel until I knew what her name was. I had tried Stephanie, Philipa; I don't know exactly where they came from, except that my mother had always liked the name Stephanie. They just wouldn't do. Then the idea of oneness came, and this book is so much about achieving oneness, a very Romantic idea in a way. I found this name partly in thinking of the nature of the whale, and the whale is like the dragon in Spencer's Faerie Queen, having the reputation of wrecking ships and doing all kinds of damage, just as the dragon ravaged England. In the Faerie Queen, the Red Cross night is accompanied by a woman whose name is Una. So I saw Una as the right name for her, as Ahab desires to slay the dragon of the seas. So, I thought that would fit together, but I didn't know if this was a name in common use at this time. Lo and behold, I discovered that Hawthorne had named his daughter Una, after Spencer's Faerie Queen. I came at it from the other side, but of course Moby-Dick is dedicated to Hawthorne. So, it seemed as though it was the perfect name and also it is very close to my own name.

Interviewer: It does seem to fit.

Naslund: It does seem to fit. So, why I chose to write this book is complicated. It's for my daughter at heart.

Interviewer: Do you recall the first time reading *Moby-Dick* as a girl in eighth grade going into ninth grade, did you feel a similar frustration at the lack of women characters?

Naslund: Not at all. I was used to identifying with male protagonists. It never gave me a moment's pause.

Interviewer: It's interesting how you can just get so used to it and not even notice. Why do you think this type of book has proliferated throughout the years? You call them companion books, and, for lack of a better term, I have been calling them reconfigurations of earlier texts.

Naslund: I don't know the answer. I suppose everyone who does it has as complicated a reason as I do. I'd have to be you—I'd have to study all of these books to really be able to answer that. Though I haven't read about her thinking, I think that Jean Rhys felt that an injustice had been done to the first Mrs. Rochester. She wanted to say this person had a life that was precious and valuable to her. She had feelings too. I think she was reacting against the treatment of women in general. If they're inconvenient or too forward, then they're insane and should be locked in the attic. I think she had both political and social-justice ideas in mind. That is in the background of my doings, too. I do think it's unjust that apparently you have to leave women out [in order to write what's considered a great novel], or at least this has been true in the past. Who is, in American literature, a woman figure who dominates the imagination? The closest person, I think, is Hester Prynne from *The Scarlet Letter*. Can you think of anyone more so than that?

Interviewer: Not more so, certainly not. The only other character that came to my mind right away was Edna from *The Awakening*, but I would say Hester is more of a dominant figure.

Naslund: I think so. And look at who she is. She is a person who lives in shame with an "A" branding her, whose life is not fulfilled. In *The Awakening*, the character commits suicide, because she's hopeless, she can't reform her world. Both of those figures as role models for American girls and women are lacking.

Interviewer: What is your opinion of Melville as a stylist?

Naslund: Well, the last time I reread *Moby-Dick*, which was after I had written *Ahab's Wife*, the book was very funny to me. I was laughing on almost every page. I think some of the descriptions of the sea and the passion in the book are wonderful. I admired it enormously. Some people complain about long sections on whales, and when I was twelve or thirteen, that part was a bit tedious for me, but it didn't become so; I became curious. I wanted to know all he did about whales. I think it's no doubt a brilliantly written book. He was playing with the big boys. He was playing with Shakespeare, and he felt that Hawthorne had bested Shakespeare with just a collection of short stories. I think very few people would agree with that. I don't certainly. But all the time I wrote *Ahab's Wife*, I would open *Moby-Dick* at random and put my finger down at a sentence, the way some people open the Bible and look for instruction, advice, or consolation, and I did that with Melville. I would look to learn something from it about Melville's style. I wasn't particularly concerned about writing like him; I wanted my own style, but I did want it to be in the period-piece tone of voice. So, I have utmost admiration. People have often asked me, "Weren't you intimidated coming after the great Melville?" The truthful answer is no; I was inspired, constantly inspired by him, led on by the glory of his writing. My daughter was right to memorize those speeches, because they are grand.

Interviewer: They are; they're beautiful. You have mentioned a little bit today, and in earlier interviews, how you felt about Melville's handling, or lack thereof, [of] female characters; and then today you mentioned a bit about race in a positive way, about him transcending his time with Queequeg. And you deal with both in *Ahab's Wife*, similarly transcending the time period with Una helping the slaves to escape and her involvement in abolitionism. . . .

Naslund: Right. You know, I did think it was a flaw in Melville that the book came out in 1851, and he really doesn't do anything about slavery at all, albeit he does so in some of his other books. This is a decade away from the Civil War. I wanted to do that, because I did think that not only were women left out of *Moby-Dick*, but the issue of race is also left out, in terms of the American scene. So I did want to do that. There is that wonderfully funny scene about Ishmael and Queequeg sharing a bed, so I had my two women characters [Una and Susan] share a bed, specifically writing with that scene in mind. That scene has its funny elements as well, but they're doing something that is quintessentially female, having a baby. So I wanted to say upfront, Melville, I hear you, and I'm coming along right behind you. Another place I did that, and it was such fun to write, was near the end where Ishmael and Una are getting together, and she asks him (and, of course, Ishmael is the pretend author of *Moby-Dick*, the narrator) do you mind that we're writing the same book? He says no, and the stuff he asks her about patience and cash and so forth, that's straight from Melville—that's in *Moby-Dick*. And also Melville had used the statement about the great cathedral at Cologne—how it was left unfinished for over one hundred years, and Melville will go on to say (he practically gave me permission), "True erections," and I'm sure he is punning, "great ones, ever leave the finishing to posterity."

	He was really holding out a hand, so I added, "Think of the cathedral at Chartres. Think of its two towers. They do not match at all . . . but without both spires, or Chartres not be Chartres." So that's self-referential and metafictive, and it's also fun; it's a lot of fun to weave those things together and be true to both of those characters the way I've used them and to be able to use Melville. When I told my daughter I was writing this book, she was thoughtful for a moment and said, "So you're having a dialogue with Melville then?" I said, "Yes, that is what I'm doing."
Interviewer:	That's great. There was another part where I felt you were just having a little bit of fun with Melville, though it's not a very funny scene at all, when Una first learns of Ahab's ship having sunk, and they're telling her there was only one survivor. She asks who he is and no one can remember his name. I thought you were referencing the opening of *Moby-Dick*, "Call me Ishmael."
Naslund:	Oh sure, absolutely. At one time, I used the line "Call me Ishmael" in one draft of the novel, but some of my pre-readers loved it, and some said I couldn't get away with it—it breaks the whole fabric of the book. So now I come close to saying it, but I don't. He says, "Let me proffer you a name, Ishmael."
Interviewer:	One other thing that you deal with rather overtly in your novel is sexual orientation. I was wondering if you could comment on Melville dealing with that. What is your opinion of the handling of homoeroticism in Melville?
Naslund:	Well, when you read that scene of Ishmael and Queequeg in bed, the language of the scene is the language of marriage. Marriage is used to describe it. I do think that Melville is trying to make a case for tenderness and closeness between men. Also, in *Moby-Dick* there is this chapter when they are squeezing the spermaceti, and before long they've gotten mixed up as to what the substance is and they're squeezing each other's hands.
Interviewer:	A very erotic chapter.
Naslund:	Yes, it really is. I thought that Melville was in love with Hawthorne, and I thought he broke Melville's heart. He just had his wife, Sophia Peabody, write a little note to Melville, and Melville had dedicated this work of genius to him, and he could hardly get around to reading it. I think Hawthorne felt threatened. That's one reason I decided to skewer Hawthorne in that chapter called "The Minister in the Woods" and let Una have a quarrel with him; because I had a quarrel with him. I thought it was terrible. After *Moby-Dick*, the next book Melville wrote was *Pierre; or the Ambiguities* dedicated

to Mt. Greylock, not even to a person, but to a mountain he could look out his window and see. I think surely Melville knew he had written a great work, and it received some good attention, but really nothing like *Uncle Tom's Cabin*, which got 150,000 in sales. I have read that *Moby-Dick* sold only 1,500 copies in Melville's lifetime. I read other figures, too, so I don't really know what the exact figure would be.

Writing in a different era, I could be much more frank about homosexuality than Melville could. Moby-Dick is praised for being inclusive with people from every race and every religion. He barely mentioned women, but that was the standard line about him. I wanted to be inclusive, too; I wanted to include slavery, which Melville had left out. And I wanted to take advantage of the opportunity, because as we all know, homosexuality has existed forever, and I wanted to include it.

Interviewer: One of the really memorable, but a little bit ambiguous, parts of *Ahab's Wife* for me was the part regarding the homosexuality between Giles and Kit. It's something that seems to have caused a rift between the two for a while, and Kit seems to view it as a violation. In a later section, homosexuality is portrayed very lovingly between Robin and the judge. Can you talk a little bit about what that act signifies between Giles and Kit?

Naslund: Well, I think your reading of it is accurate, and if you are going to have a balanced book, there are some people who are tormented by the unconventional sexual orientation. Many young people commit suicide, as Giles probably did; that is also ambiguous, but I think he probably did. He bothered to get an earring from Una, which is a mark of identity. I read that sailors wore an earring in case their bodies washed ashore and they were unrecognizable. The gold would survive the salt sea, so it was a way of preserving the identity. The people in the early part of the book are young and inexperienced about any kind of sexuality. Una is confused about it, about which one of those two guys she prefers. She is quite ambivalent about it. I think many young women are confused about those things. I just tried to get the canvass full of human possibilities and just embrace it all.

Interviewer: You mentioned the guilt or torment regarding homosexuality that was plaguing Giles and Kit. Also, the suicide, or possible suicide, comes after the cannibalism. Are the two linked as some unspeakable act?

Naslund: Well, I don't think that they're linked in any way except to say that both go beyond the conventional strictures. I think cannibalism was a torment for Giles, especially since he was something of a leader in that [he loved his friends enough to do something quite morally suspect]. The book certainly doesn't condemn any of them, for cannibalism or homosexuality. There is an element of painful confusion that haunts Giles and Kit. Una suffers when she is unable to differentiate between them. To whom does she really belong, where does her nature fit? It fits partly with one and partly with the other. That's a quest, too, for sexual identity and patterns of behavior that are consistent with the inner person.

Interviewer: One thing I noticed as a pattern in the novel was quite a bit of contrasting white and black imagery. Una's mother, when she died, was in the white snow, but her skin had turned black. Giles said he'd gone to an African American church and said, "My skin was white, but my heart was black." And of course the two whales, the black one that sinks Una's ship and the white one that sinks Ahab's. Can you comment on the significance of this color symbolism?

Naslund: Well, I was trying to play a little bit on Melville's playing board. He has the famous chapter "The Whiteness of the Whale." So I was just trying not to neglect the symbolic concerns but to play it again. I didn't feel that it was as essential to my thinking as some of the other issues. I mean to me the business about "My skin is white, but my heart is black" was funny. It's presented as a virtue, whereas in Christian mythology, to have a black heart is to have a heart full of sin. I was just having fun with something Melville had started in that case.

Interviewer: And with the two whales, was there any symbolic significance with the white and the black?

Naslund: Well, I did see them as counterparts, but Una is going to survive her experience with the black whale, whereas the white whale is a more deadly creature psychologically. In a way, I'm trying to let those things, the whiteness and blackness, cancel each other out and just say in the long run that it's all the same. I hadn't thought about that particular question for a long time, and there might be some things in there that I have forgotten.

Interviewer: Well, I think that your point about canceling each other out is very interesting. Are you suggesting then more about the people involved and less about the symbolic associations?

Naslund: Yes.

Interviewer: I hadn't really made the connection between Susan and Una in bed and Queequeg and Ishmael, but now that you point it out, it makes perfect sense. What I thought about

Naslund: while I was reading that part was Susan emerging from between the mattresses.

Naslund: Birth.

Interviewer: Yes, and there is imagery that suggests that Susan is the symbolic child of Una. There is also the part where she nurses, or at least to ease the pressure in Una's breast; in what sense is Susan Una's symbolic child?

Naslund: Well, at one point, Una calls her a number of names, mother and sister as well as angel, so with the black and white images and having that list of things, I'm trying to avoid the black/white dichotomy. I think in a true friendship, especially between women, that we automatically play the mother or daughter role for each other. We don't even think about it; we just switch according to the needs of the other person. I think that was true with Una and Susan, that sometimes one took care of the other. They do switch roles about. To freeze us in a fixed position of mother or daughter is to falsify friendship. The best friendships have that suppleness to them, and it doesn't lock anybody into a specific role. There is a freedom in the diversity within.

Interviewer: That makes sense. There's the connectedness also that you were suggesting, that we are connected. It's not as simple as black and white, as you said. The two of them are part of each other.

Naslund: Right, right.

Interviewer: Some of my questions have to do with the metafictional quality of your novel. There are several different places where you make reference to people creating meaning out of things. For example, when Una's mother says that "we create our own truth about God" early on in the book, and when Kit says something like, "We make each other up, people make one another up." Ahab warns Una that words can mean different things to different people. Can you comment at all about the point you might have been making about interpretation or understanding?

Naslund: Well, I think that it's a similar point to saying that our roles are flexible roles, and we are indefinable. In a way this is Virginia Woolf's view of character, in the way that she rebelled from earlier writers who would rigidly design a character and keep the character within those parameters. Her characters are always dissolving into the landscape and into each other and constantly changing. There is a "Woolfian" influence in my sense of character and meaning. I love words, and I rely on words, but I'm also suspicious of them because of the literalness with which they are often taken. These instances

	which you have mentioned are all rather against literalism. The novel I just finished writing, *Adam & Eve*, is obviously a reference to the book of Genesis, which is taken quite literally by a large part of the American population. This [*Adam & Eve*] is a book that stirs around in the thoughts and asks for an imagination. Also, it asks one to embrace the imagination, not as something false, a poor substitute for reality, but, on the contrary, as the best we could do; we should glory in it. That's my own view of course. All these books overlap somewhat thematically, and you can see in one the beginning of others. I can, at least—after the fact, but I can.
Interviewer:	You mean in your own novels, one overlaps another?
Naslund:	Well, I'll tell you an odd occurrence in my short-story collection *The Disobedience of Water*. The first story is called "I Am Born," which of course is a reference to the first chapter of Dickens in *David Copperfield*, but there is a little girl sitting on her steps in Birmingham [Alabama], and she is drawing with a piece of gravel, and what she draws is a whale, a star, and a ship. This was ten years before I thought of writing *Ahab's Wife*. When I created the character who was going to represent myself, those are the central images that I put in her mind.
Interviewer:	That is sort of eerie.
Naslund:	It is a bit eerie. That story is about a birth scene, and here we are just talking about the birth scene of *Ahab's Wife*.
Interviewer:	Is *Adam & Eve* out yet?
Naslund:	No, I'm still revising it. I finished the first drafts, and my friends who are readers have sent me things back. I just need a little more feedback, and I'll start revising it. I revised *Ahab's Wife* four times, each time thinking it was the final revision. It is very thoroughly revised from beginning to end. Of course, the earlier parts were revised more than fifty times. I know that, because for a period of time, more than two months, I worked on it every day, and every day I started at the beginning and revised it again. Every day I thought I had gotten it, fifty times, forty-nine times I was wrong.
Interviewer:	That must have made it a very slow writing process.
Naslund:	It didn't matter to me. I wasn't thinking about that. I just wanted to write the best book I could, and it was thrilling that I got to keep on trying. It was summer, and I didn't have to teach. You know how hard it is.
Interviewer:	It's hard to get a lot of work done during the semesters.
Naslund:	It really is.
Interviewer:	There was another section where Una is referring to language and she says, "Words are but a mask. . . . A mask such as the

	ancient Greek actors wore, a mask that expresses rather than conceals the inner drama." Were you making a similar point about writing as you were earlier?
Naslund:	Yes, what I get around to saying is (a) I love language, (b) I'm suspicious of words, and (c) nonetheless, it [language] can go a long way. The masks were very large so that audiences could see them in the back of the amphitheater. So they were masks that revealed, which is a paradoxical idea that tickles me.
Interviewer:	Right, masks that help reveal emotions and clarify things but at the same time are hiding things.
Naslund:	Yes. It's really both always. It is an infinite regress. We can never get behind the final mask, let alone strike through it.
Interviewer:	Near the end, Una says about writing that "adherence to fact is slavery." Can you elaborate about her philosophy on writing, and is it the same as yours?
Naslund:	I can't exactly remember what she is doing when she says that. Where is that in the book?
Interviewer:	It's near the end, after it has already become clear to the reader that she is writing her own novel and after her sister sends her out to write on the beach.
Naslund:	Oh yes, I remember now. Well, for me as a writer, a hard stage to get over was the imperative to tell the truth in the ordinary sense. I call it the tyranny of fact. What it does is it makes an aesthetic shape difficult or even impossible if one is simply going to try or attempt to literally represent things the way they were. I would say memory and imagination are very close together. There are various psychological tests that prove this. Like the famous witnesses that all see the same thing but all think they see something quite different. Because Una's a beginning writer in a self-conscious sense at that time I guess I just wanted to acknowledge a step that I had also had to take to learn how to handle using things from my own life but having aesthetic control over them. That would have been an important thing to me, so I gave it to her.
Interviewer:	So, it's sort of liberation to imagine and create without having to enslave oneself to facts.
Naslund:	Right. Being a good reporter is a worthy thing to do, but it's a different thing from being a creative artist. I wanted to try to be a creative artist.
Interviewer:	There were just a couple more questions that I had. These have more to do with characterizations or plot elements. Una meets Henry James, Margaret Fuller, Frederick Douglass, Hawthorne, and Maria Mitchell. And Maria Mitchell lived in Nantucket; I read an interview that you gave where

	you talked about having gone to Maria Mitchell's house. Why did you decide to introduce the other historical figures into the novel?
Naslund:	Well, the two most important historical figures, for me, were Margaret Fuller and Maria Mitchell: one a great woman of letters and one a great woman of science. They were both abolitionists and feminists, and I wanted them in the book, because I knew some critics would want to say that there were not real people like Una, that I had imposed modern standards on the time. So, I protected myself by bringing these historical examples that anybody would agree had the values that I had given Una. I actually envisioned them as Wonder Woman's bracelets to reflect the spheres of science and literature. The other historical characters just came in, because they gave the intellectual flavor of the time and I was interested in what were the big issues: Unitarianism versus Trinitarianism was one of the big issues and the whole transcendentalist group. I read and reread the intellectual movements of the time, because I wanted it to be accurate in that way. Of course Frederick Douglass, how could I resist? He did give the speech in Nantucket. Nobody knows exactly what he said, so I didn't say exactly what he said. But William Lloyd Garrison's question to the audience, "Should this man be a slave after he has given a wonderful speech?" is historically accurate. It was part of the slavery motif to include him. Hawthorne, I had a grudge against him, and I put him in there in order to stick some pins in his back.
Interviewer:	Why did you decide to pair Una with Ishmael at the end?
Naslund:	I didn't know that that was going to happen until I was near the end of the book, and it occurred to me that that was the inevitable ending. I said, "I got it, I got it, I know who she is going to marry. The critics will howl." And my husband ran in and said, "Wait a minute. Are you sure this is the kind of reaction you want?" And I said, "Yes!" It just came to me out of nowhere. I was looking for it all the time. At first I thought she might just marry some Unitarian minister, but she was resistant to that. Characters sometimes do things that surprise you. Most writers testify to that happening from time to time. I certainly could. But it just came to me, like "Captain Ahab was neither my first husband nor my last" came to me. Partly because I could see Una wanted to become a writer, and Ishmael was a writer. It seemed like a fun thing to do, too. After I've been writing for a long time, I look for some fun if it's been serious and heavy.
Interviewer:	Fun for you and the reader?

Naslund: Mostly fun for me though.

Interviewer: Well, those were all the questions that I had written down. Were there other things that you wanted to add?

Naslund: I thought of a question that people often ask me about Susan that we hadn't talked about. People say, "Why did you have her turn around and go back when she escaped?" First of all, it was something of a surprise to me when she did. It was another one of those things that just happen. It is also connected to my reading of Toni Morrison's *Beloved*, which is based on a real case of a woman in Ohio that killed her child rather than be returned to slavery. When I read *Beloved*, I saw that Morrison was withholding that scene; it comes late in the book. A good bit of suspense is generated about that. You want to see that payoff scene; in a way, that's what this book is about. I admire *Beloved* a great deal, but not for that scene. I don't think that scene comes off emotionally.

Interviewer: When she kills the child?

Naslund: I thought that even though it was a historical event, she had not made it seem true that this mother would do this in the novel. The fact that it corresponds to reality is no vindication for the coherence of the fictive world. I think that as liberal persons, we have consoling hierarchies of value, and people like to think that being free is more important than being alive. I question that, and I thought that being with people she loved might be more important to Susan than being free. She has on the back burner the idea that she would lead them to freedom; of course, she finds out her mother's been maimed and is not going to be able to run. She doesn't know that at the point when she makes the decision to return, and she decides then to stay on there with her mother. It was another way of challenging conventional values and the sentimental hierarchy that a good person, a worthy, noble person, would choose to murder a child rather than to return to slavery. I just wanted to be at cross purposes with assumed values. I wanted to subvert them. I wanted to say, "You can be just as much a human being and make a different choice." And none of these are absolute decisions dictated by the grand morality of the universe. We have to do what is true to our own natures. So, that was more or less why I sent her back. But there is a sequel to her story in the next novel I wrote, *Poor Spirits*, where a descendent of Susan is a character in the Civil Rights movement, and you find out what happened to Susan. It's just a small part. But I liked leaving some questions open in the end. What happened to [Kit and] Charlotte is open, and whether Susan and Una ever reunite is open. I do

	think that it's true to life to leave loose ends. I don't want a Dickensian ending where everything is tied up.
Interviewer:	Is there any sequel between Kit and Charlotte?
Naslund:	Nope, not so far.
Interviewer:	Susan's return to slavery reminded me of a Charles Chesnutt short story, "The Passing of Grandison." In that story, a plantation master's son is trying to get the slave Grandison to run off in order to impress his antislavery girlfriend. But Grandison refuses to leave. He takes him to Canada, and Grandison refuses to run off even when the master's back is turned, and so the young master finally just abandons him there and goes home and tells everyone the slave ran off. Grandison comes home, and you find out the reason he came home is his family is still there. He has a wife and children, and he doesn't want to leave without them. But in this story, he does eventually escape with his wife and children.
Naslund:	I didn't know that story. I've heard it referred to, but I didn't know that was the essence of that story. I feel vindicated.
Interviewer:	Well, thank you so much for talking with me. I enjoyed your book very much, and I really admire you for it. You kind of conquered a whale yourself by writing the novel.
Naslund:	Well, thank you very much. I hope your book goes well for you.
Interviewer:	I do, too.

Notes

NOTES TO CHAPTER 1

1. Poe also had a brief and conflicted connection with the Young America movement, a mid-nineteenth-century group of literary nationalists. I briefly discuss Nathaniel Hawthorne's and Herman Melville's long-standing affiliation with this group in the next two chapters. For a detailed account of Poe's relationship with Young America, see Meredith L. McGill's essay "Poe, Literary Nationalism, and Authorial Identity."
2. Other critics have noted other examples of intertextual borrowing in Poe's works. Silverman, for example, notes that Poe based his short story "William Wilson" on a "brief article" by Washington Irving (149–150). Galvan points out that Charles Dickens's "A Confession Found in a Prison in the Time of Charles II" (1840) might have inspired "The Tell-Tale Heart" and "The Black Cat" (1843), and that Dickens's "A Madman's Manuscript" might also have influenced "The Tell-Tale Heart" (13–14).
3. See also Peeples ("Love and Theft" 39–40) and Whalen (217) for a discussion of puns and misinterpretation within the story. On the other hand, Joseph Dewey says that Poe's story "glorifies the sheer capacity of the intellect to make its way to solution" (58).
4. See the introduction for a more detailed explanation of these connections.
5. "The Purloined Letter," for example, has often been read as a paradigm for reading, for discovering clues in a text and interpreting them (Kempton 1; Harris 19).
6. For an introduction to this evolutionary understanding of narrative, see the introduction and see Boyd and Sugiyama.
7. On the same topic, Powers comments in an interview with Stephen J. Burn, "There is no place *except* the map, and yet we make the map together, by reading ourselves into one another, through conventions and codes, all of them provisional."
8. In an essay titled "Secret Writing," Poe repeats this statement more forcefully: "Yet it may be roundly asserted that human ingenuity cannot concoct a cipher that human ingenuity cannot resolve" (Rosenheim 10).
9. J.T. Thomas convincingly argues, "[T]hese four lines function as an acknowledgments page," the letters being the initials of those Powers wishes to acknowledge (9).
10. See the introduction for a fuller explanation of the reading function in intertextual writing.
11. In addition Bayard quotes from two of Poe's poems, "Ode to Science" and "To Helen."

12. Stereotomy is a method of paving, and it reminds the narrator, according to Dupin, of atomies [atoms], and then to Epicurus, who believes everything to be composed of atoms (Poe, MRM 246).
13. As we have already seen, Poe also wrote "The Gold-Bug," a tale about the rewards of deciphering codes, as a way to make money. Bayard states that the reconfiguration of the works of past writers can itself be a marketing strategy, because it allows the writer to insert a marker with which the reader is familiar within a newer text, creating a type of literary code that the skilled reader can take pleasure in deciphering.
14. Interestingly Poe receives his first clue in what he believes to be his channeled writing of an acrostic poem bearing the message "MATTIE DIED" through the initial letters of each line.

NOTES TO CHAPTER 2

1. Before publishing *The Scarlet Letter*, Hawthorne had lost his post at the Custom-House due to a change in the political administration. This loss may account for his ambivalent attitude toward the building and the government it represents.
2. Also see Updike, "Special Message" 858.
3. See the introduction for a more in-depth discussion of these ideas.
4. See the introduction, pages 9 and 10.
5. According to Leland S. Person, "There is no evidence that the scarlet letter or these papers ever existed outside Hawthorne's imagination" (Hawthorne 27, n. 9).
6. See, for example, Moraru 162.
7. "Part of a hypertext that identifies the hypotext for the reader" (Genette 306).
8. According to Judie Newman, "Between the 1780s and 1830s, Salem was a major international port for the East Indies and China trade—silk, tea, chinaware, textiles, and above all the pepper trade, of which Salem had a virtual monopoly" (72).
9. In another example, Mukherjee begins each section of the book with an epigraph from Keats's "Ode on a Grecian Urn." Rastogi sees in these epigraphs further evidence of artwork connecting disparate cultures: "In 'Ode on a Grecian Urn,' Keats acknowledges the presence of ancient Greece, both in his own creative fashioning and in that of the English literary tradition in general. By using couplets from this poem to open the four parts of her novel, Mukherjee makes an analogy that acknowledges the debt owed by American literature to the Indian presence" (278).
10. See Tomc.

NOTES TO CHAPTER 3

1. See, for example, Steven B. Hermann, who says that Ishmael and Queequeg are "the first portrait of same-sex marriage in American literature" (65). Leland S. Person notes the homoerotic language of Melville's "Hawthorne and His Mosses," in which Melville writes that "Hawthorne drop[s] 'germinous seeds' into Melville's soul and then shoot[s] his 'strong New-England roots' into the 'hot soil' of Melville's 'Southern soul'" (239). Person also notes, "Edwin Miller argued that an 'advance' from Melville that Hawthorne experienced as an 'assault' caused the two writers to become estranged in 1851" (239).

NOTES TO CHAPTER 4

1. Cynthia Ozick wrote in 1982, "I read *Little Women* a thousand times. Ten thousand" (Alberghene and Clark xv); Ursula K. LeGuin wrote in 1988, "Jo March must have had a real influence upon me when I was a young scribbler" (xvi); Ann Petry wrote in 1994, "I felt as though I was part of Jo and she was part of me" (xvi); and Anna Quindlen wrote in 1994, "*Little Women* changed my life" (xvii).
2. According to Lundin, "Louisa's famous father, Bronson Alcott, spoke of [Bunyan's] text in fervent praise: 'This book is one of the few that gave me to myself. . . .' Like father, like daughter: presented with her own copy of the book at the age of eight, Louisa 'thought and spoke through it' too."
3. In addition to her homage to a beloved childhood story, perhaps Kingsolver's desire to reconfigure *Little Women* is at least in part a savvy marketing strategy, just as Alcott wrote her own book to make money. A successful film version of Alcott's novel debuted in 1994, and the next several years saw an increase in Alcott-inspired merchandise, articles, and fiction (Alberghene and Clark xviii–xix). Published just four years later, *The Poisonwood Bible* can be viewed as an attempt to capitalize on the renewed interest in *Little Women* created by the film's success.
4. The brief mentions of African Americans occur when Amy proclaims that she does not mind helping at the Chester's charitable fair, because it benefits the freedmen (275), and when readers learn that one of the misfit boys at Jo's Plumfield school is "a merry little quadroon, who could not be taken in elsewhere, but who was welcome the 'Bhaer-garten,' though some people predicted that his admission would run the school" (444).
5. A recent *New York Times* editorial about the history of the phrase "one nation under God" provides evidence of the association of Christianity and capitalism in U.S. history. According to Kevin M. Kruse, in an effort to bolster public opinion of big businesses in response to Franklin D. Roosevelt's New Deal, American business leaders solicited the help of clergymen. One of these men, "[t]he Rev. James W. Fifield, pastor of the elite First Congregational Church of Los Angeles, led the way in championing a new union of faith and free enterprise. 'The blessings of capitalism come from God,' he wrote. 'A system that provides so much for the common good and happiness must flourish under the favor of the Almighty.'"
6. The dedication reads "For Darleen and Cassie—by no means little women," and the epigraph is a quotation from *Little Women,* in which Jo thinks sadly "of father far away, where the fighting was."
7. For example, according to Catherine Lavender in "The Cult of Domesticity and True Womanhood," nineteenth-century society saw the world at large as "rough" and "full of temptations, violence, and trouble. A woman who ventured out into such a world could easily fall prey to it, for women were weak and delicate creatures." The ideal home was a refuge from the "evils of the outer world" (Lavender), which explains why men would be reluctant to violate this space and the women it contained with tales of violence and abuse.

NOTES TO CHAPTER 5

1. For example, the Internet Movie Database lists nine big-screen and made-for-TV versions of the novel produced between 1920 and 1993.

2. Janet Smiley's 1998 *The All-True Travels and Adventures of Lidie Newton* also reconfigures *The Adventures of Huckleberry Finn*. See O'Loughlin for a discussion of the ways Smiley critiques Twain and American society.
3. Van Wyck Brooks makes this observation in *The Ordeal of Mark Twain*, published by E.P. Dutton & Company, 1920.
4. DeVoto makes this comment in *Mark Twain at Work*, published by Harvard University Press, 1942.
5. When asked in 1995 by a student at the University of South Carolina if he would ever write a sequel to *Deliverance*, Dickey emphatically said no, but added, "You'd have to do that. When you do it, or if you do it, show it to me first" (Thesing and Wright 39). Here, Dickey suggests a possible future reconfiguration of his own novel.
6. Fiedler's *Love and Death in the American Novel*, which contains this essay, was part of Dickey's library and was donated with Dickey's other books to the University of South Carolina.
7. In nineteenth-century canonical pairs like Huck and Jim, Ishmael and Queequeg, Natty Bumpo and Chingachgook, Fiedler sees

    an essential aspect of American sentimental life: . . . a kind of passionless passion, at once gross and delicate, homoerotic in the boy's sense, possessing an innocence above suspicion. To doubt for a moment this innocence, which can survive only as *assumed,* would destroy our stubborn belief in a relationship simple, utterly satisfying, yet immune to lust; physical as the handshake is physical, this side of copulation. . . .
    It is this self-congratulatory buddy-buddiness, its astonishing naivete that breeds at once endless opportunities for inversion and the terrible reluctance to admit its existence, to surrender the last believed-in stronghold of love without passion. (4–5, emphasis in original)

    Despite Fiedler's use of such archaic and homophobic terms as "inversion," he suggests that the oft-declared belief in the "innocence" of such unions, in their immunity to lust, is a naive form of denial on the part of the authors.
8. As the author says when discussing literary interpretations of his work, "I can't say that these things that they [critics] see in my work aren't there. I didn't intend some of them . . . I didn't consciously intend a lot of them. But sometimes I did. . . . But when a thing is gone, when it's on paper and goes out into the public domain, then it's gone" (Davis 20–21). In the same interview, Dickey adds, "When somebody says that he loves somebody else, a man loves a woman, say . . . for somebody to cut in on that and tell me why I do, and analyze my motives for doing it, what I hope to gain by it, and what I hope to compensate for, overcompensate for, what degrees of guilt there are in connection with it and so on—I get very uneasy and also a little bit angry" (22). Dickey would no doubt disapprove of the following reading of *Deliverance*, but the uneasiness and anger he admits resemble some of the unconscious regulatory devices discussed herein. In his 2000 biography of James Dickey, Henry Hart notes the author's interest in homosexuality, expressed through claims of past homosexual encounters and through unaccepted overtures toward male friends.
9. Of course, Freud's essay "Mourning and Melancholia" serves as the foundation for Butler's concept of gender melancholia. Freud theorizes the role of mourning a lost attachment in identity formation, and Butler applies his theories specifically to gender formation. Butler's comparison of the psyche to an archaeological dig alludes to Freud's *Civilization and Its Discontents* (16–18), wherein he compares the psyche to the layers of the city of Rome.
10. See Fiedler, "Come Back to the Raft Ag'in."

11. According to the informational site "Alton and the Civil War," "The Alton prison opened in 1833 as the first Illinois State Penitentiary and was closed in 1860, when the last prisoners were moved to a new facility at Joliet." It was reopened as a Civil War military prison from 1862 to 1965 (Huber).

NOTES TO CHAPTER 6

1. Later in this chapter, I discuss how my reading of Tyler's ending differs from that of Jones.
2. In "'A Language Which Nobody Understood': Emancipatory Strategies in *The Awakening*," Patricia Yaeger makes a similar point, suggesting that the parrot that opens the novel speaking "a language which nobody understood," (1), a language that annoys Monsieur Pontellier, is a representation of Edna's need for a new type of language to voice her desires.
3. Some of Edith Wharton's short stories might have served as good models for Delia, especially "The Other Two," which describes the two divorces and three marriages of the main female character, and "Autre Temps," which portrays a mature divorced woman's return to American society to stand beside her grown daughter, who also divorces and then quickly remarries.
4. See the introduction for a more in-depth overview of scripts.
5. Bender notes that Chopin begins *The Awakening* "where she knew that life itself had begun according to *On the Origin of the Species* . . . [with] Edna 'advancing at a snail's pace from the beach' with Robert" (466).

NOTES TO CHAPTER 7

1. See, for example, Hogan, Kodat, Novak, and Ramos.
2. Although the ghosts in *Absalom, Absalom!* are figurative, albeit garrulous and outraged (4), Ramos points out that in a narrative sense, the Quentin who narrates *Absalom* can be viewed as a ghost, because this character committed suicide in *The Sound and the Fury* (1929), a novel written earlier but set chronologically after the events described in *Absalom* (59–60).
3. Bradley's symbolic use of snow also resembles Leonard Jeffries's Afrocentrist labeling of whites as cold, unfeeling "ice people" and African Americans as warm, caring "sun people." Jeffries, a City College of New York professor, based this label on the theories of Senegalese Afrocentrist scholar Dr. Cheikh Diop. Jeffries's lectures, beginning in the 1970s, roughly the temporal present of the novel, were associated with black nationalism and reverse racism (Jeffries 14 of 17; Goldblatt 1 of 2), and his views seem similar to those of Old Jack and, at some points in the novel, to those of John; for example, despite the fact that he lives with a white girlfriend, John sees both whites and women as threats to black men.
4. As I have argued in "Passing as Miscegenation: Whiteness and Homoeroticism in Faulkner's *Absalom, Absalom!*" Quentin and Shreve's verbal and nonverbal communication suggests that one of the desires Quentin fails to acknowledge openly, yet which causes his blood to surge warmly, is the homoerotic.
5. As Frederick Douglass declared to a white audience in 1852, "The Fourth of July is *yours* not *mine*" (1824). Many black Americans in the twentieth century felt that they had still not fully collected on America's promise of freedom.
6. John's dream shows him becoming a literal "ice person," the figurative label that Leonard Jeffries had given to the white race.

7. This concept of death fits into the West African concept of Great Time, which African American writer John Edgar Wideman describes as "the ancestral time. It's non-linear. It is, if anything, like a river, like the sea—and we kind of swim through it" (267). That John's experiences are part of Great Time is illustrated by the fact that, as Jane Campbell puts it, "John's quest takes place over three days that span centuries" (137).
8. Of course, this reading necessitates viewing *The Sound and the Fury* (1929) as a "prequel" to *Absalom, Absalom!* (1936) and the Quentin Compson that appears in each novel as the same character.
9. See, for example, Beston, Egan, Ensslen, and Kubitschek. Cathy Brigham, Albert Stone, and Ashraf Rushdy (*Remembering*) acknowledge the possibility of John's suicide.

NOTES TO THE CONCLUSION

1. The reconfiguration of a classic text to align better with the contemporary cultural context is a process noted and celebrated among American folk musicians. In the 1930s and 1960s, such musicians as Woody Guthrie and Pete Seeger updated traditional songs to reflect their current sociopolitical concerns. In the 1990s with "The Ghost of Tom Joad," Bruce Springsteen updated Guthrie's "Tom Joad" (1940), based on John Steinbeck's *The Grapes of Wrath* (1939), to reflect his economic and social concerns about his American society. See Simon and Deverell, Bayles, and Skinner.
2. See, for example, Harold Scudder's "Melville's Benito Cereno and Captain Delano's Voyages," Richard McLamore's "Narrative Self-Justification: Melville and Amasa Delano," and Debra Ripley's "Herman Melville's Exploitation of Cognitive Features: Amasa Delano as Paradigm of Failure."
3. See, for example, Sue Parill's *Jane Austen on Film and Television* and Lynda E. Boose and Richard Burt's *Shakespeare, the Movie: Popularizing the Plays on Film, TV, and Video*.
4. *Adaptation* usually refers to a relatively faithful transformation of a novel into a movie, where setting, characters, and plot remain, for the most part, true to the original.

Bibliography

Abraham, Nicolas, and Maria Torok. *The Shell and the Kernel: Renewals of Psychoanalysis*. Trans. Nicholas T. Rand. Chicago: U of Chicago P, 1994. Print.
"Ahab's Wife." *Kirkus Reviews Magazine* 1 Oct. 1999. Web. 15 June 2011.
Alberghene, Janice M., and Beverly Lyon Clark. Introduction. *Little Women and the Feminist Imagination: Criticism, Controversy, Personal Essays*. Ed. Janice M. Alberghene and Beverly Lyon Clark. New York: Garland, 1999: xv-liii. Print.
Alcott, Louisa May. *Little Women*. 1869. New York: Signet, 2004. Print.
Allen, Brooke. "Anne Tyler in Mid-Course." *New Criterion* 13.9 (1995): 27–34. EBSCOHost. Web.
Armstrong, Nancy. *Desire and Domestic Fiction: A Political History of the Novel*. New York: Oxford UP, 1987. Print.
American Association of Physical Anthropologists. "AAPA Statement on Biological Aspects of Race." *American Journal of Physical Anthropology* 101 (1996): 569–570. Web. 27 June 2006.
Anderson, Benedict. *Imagined Communities: Reflections on the Origin and Spread of Nationalism*. 1983. New York: Verso, 2006. Print.
———. "Narrating the Nation." *Times Literary Supplement* 13 June 1986: 659. Print.
Arac, Jonathan. "Why Does No One Care about the Aesthetic Value of *Huckleberry Finn*?" *New Literary History* 30.4 (1999): 769–784. Print.
Athenot, Eric. "'Nostalgia for the Whole and the One' in *The Gold Bug Variations*." *Revue Francaise d'Etudes Americaines* 4.94 (2002): 70–77. Cairn. Web. January 19, 2009.
Avery, Gillian. "Home and Family: English and American Ideals." *Stories and Society: Children's Literature in the Social Context*. Ed. Dennis Butts. London: Macmillan, 1992. 37–49. Print.
Barbour, James. "'All My Books Are Botches': Melville's Struggle with The Whale." *Writing the American Classics*. Ed. James Barbour and Tom Quirk. Chapel Hill: U of North Carolina P, 1990. 25–52. Print.
Barnett, Pamela. "Rape and Repudiation, Masochism and Masculinity in *Deliverance*." *James Dickey Newsletter* 20.1 (2003): 1–19. Print.
Bayard, Louis. *The Pale Blue Eye*. New York: Harper, 2006. Print.
Bayles, Martha. "The Strange Career of Folk Music." *Michigan Quarterly Review* 44.2 (2005): 304–317. Print.
Baym, Nina. "Revisiting Hawthorne's Feminism." *Hawthorne and the Real: Bicentennial Essays*. Ed. Millicent Bell. Columbus: Ohio State UP, 2005. 107–124. Print.

BBC Online Services. "Mughal Empire (1500s, 1600s)." *BBC: Religions*. BBC Online Services, July 2009. Web. 3 June 2011.
Bedell, Madelon. *The Alcotts: Biography of a Family*. New York: Potter, 1980. Print.
Beer, Gillian. *Arguing with the Past: Essays in Narrative from Woolf to Sidney*. New York: Routledge, 1989. Print.
Bender, Bert. "The Teeth of Desire: *The Awakening* and *The Descent of Man*." *American Literature* 63.3 (1991): 460–473. Print.
Berninghausen, Thomas F. "Writing on the Body: The Figure of Authority in *Moby-Dick*." *New Orleans Review* 14.3 (1987): 5–12. Print.
Bernstein, Adam. "Judith Rossner, 70; *Mr. Goodbar* Author." *Washington Post* 11 Aug. 2005: B05. Web. 6 May 2009.
Benston, Kimberly W. "I Yam What I Am: The Topos of (Un)Naming in Afro-American Literature." *Black Literature and Literary Theory*. Ed. Henry Louis Gates, Jr. New York: 1984: 151–173. Print.
Blades, John. *John Keats: The Poems*. New York: Palgrave, 2002. 115–126. Print.
Blake, Susan L., and James A. Miller. "The Business of Writing: An Interview with David Bradley." *Callaloo* 21 (1984): 19–39. Print.
Bleikasten, André. "Fathers in Faulkner." *The Fictional Father: Lacanian Readings of the Text*. Ed. Robert Con Davis. Amherst: U of Massachusetts P, 1981. 114–146. Print.
———. *The Western Canon: The Books and School of the Ages*. New York: Harcourt, 1994. Print.
Bone, Martyn. "'All the Confederate Dead ... All of Faulkner the Great': Faulkner, Hannah, Neo-Confederate Narrative and Postsouthern Parody." *Mississippi Quarterly* 54.2 (2001): 197–211. Print.
Boose, Lynda E., and Richard Burt, eds. *Shakespeare, the Movie: Popularizing the Plays on Film, TV, and Video*. New York: Routledge, 1997. Print.
Boudreau, Gordon V. "In the Beginning Was the Word ... 'Whale' ... the Letter H...." *Melville Society Extracts* 122 (2002): 1–6. Print.
Bowie, Malcolm. *Lacan*. Boston: Harvard UP, 1993. Print.
Boyd, Brian. "Evolutionary Theories of Art." *The Literary Animal*. Ed. Jonathan Gottschall and David Sloan Wilson. Evanston, IL: Northwestern UP, 2005. 146–176. Print.
———. "Getting It All Wrong." *American Scholar* 1 Sept. 2006. Web. 27 March 2009.
Bradley, David. *The Chaneysville Incident*. New York: Harper, 1981. Print.
Brennan, Timothy. "The National Longing for Form." *Nation and Narration*. Ed. Homi K. Bhabha. New York: Routledge, 1990. 44–70. Print.
Brickhouse, Anna C. "'I Do Abhor an Indian Story': Hawthorne and the Allegorization of Racial 'Commixture.'" *ESQ: A Journal of the American Renaissance* 42.4 (1996): 233–253. Print.
Brightwell, Gerri. "Charting the Nebula: Gender, Language and Power in Kate Chopin's *The Awakening*." *Women and Language* 13.2 (1995): ProQuest. Web. 15 June 2011.
Brister, J.G. "*Absalom, Absalom!* and the Semiotic Other." *Faulkner Journal* 22.1-2 (2006–2007): 39–53. Print.
Brooks, Geraldine. *March*. New York: Penguin, 2005. Print.
Brown, Gillian. "Hawthorne's American History." *The Cambridge Companion to Nathaniel Hawthorne*. Ed. Richard H. Millington. New York: Cambridge UP, 2004. 121–142. Print.
Bruner, Jerome. "Life as Narrative." *Social Research* 54.1 (1987): 11–32. Print.

Bryant, John. "Moby Dick as Revolution." *Cambridge Companion to Herman Melville*. Ed. Robert S. Levine. New York: Cambridge U Press, 1998. 65–90. Print.

———. "Rewriting *Moby-Dick*: Politics, Textual Identity, and the Revision Narrative." *Journal of the Modern Language Association of America* 125.4 (2010): 1043–1059. Print.

Buell, Lawrence. "Hawthorne and the Problem of 'American' Fiction: The Example of *The Scarlet Letter*." *Hawthorne and the Real: Bicentennial Essays*. Ed. Millicent Bell. Columbus: Ohio State UP, 2005. 70–87. Print.

Burns, Stephen J. "An Interview with Richard Powers." *Contemporary Literature* 49.2 (2008): 163–179. Print.

Butler, Judith. *Bodies That Matter: On the Discursive Limits of Sex*. New York: Routledge, 1993. Print.

———. *Gender Trouble: Feminism and the Subversion of Identity*. New York: Routledge, 1990. Print.

———. *The Psychic Life of Power: Theories in Subjection*. Stanford: Stanford UP, 1997. Print.

Calinescu, Matei. "Secrecy in Fiction: Textual and Intertextual Secrets in Hawthorne and Updike." *Poetics Today* 15.3 (1994): 443–465. Print.

Campbell, Jane. *Mythic Black Fiction: The Transformation of History*. Knoxville: U of Tennessee P, 1986. Print.

Carroll, Virginia Schaefer. "Wrestling with Change: Discourse Strategies in Anne Tyler." *Frontiers* 19.1 (1998): 86–109. Print.

Carruthers, Peter. *Language, Thought, and Consciousness: An Essay in Philosophical Psychology*. New York: Cambridge UP, 1996. Print.

Castiglia, Christopher. "Alienated Affections: Hawthorne and Melville's Trans-Intimate Relationship." *Hawthorne and Melville: Writing a Relationship*. Ed. Jana L. Argersinger and Leland S. Person. Athens: U of Georgia P, 2008. 321–344. Print.

Changnon, Greg. "'Ahab's Wife' a Big, Bold Whale of a Tale; Books: Reviews and Commentary." *Atlanta Journal-Constitution* 31 Oct. 1999: 14L. Print.

Chen, Tina, and S.X. Goudie. "Holders of the World: An Interview with Bharati Mukherjee." *Jouvert: A Journal of Postcolonial Studies* 1.1 (1997). Web. 28 July 2010.

Chopin, Kate. *The Awakening*. 1899. New York: Norton, 1976. Print.

Clabough, Casey. "Space, Landscape and the Practice of Merging in James Dickey's *Deliverance*." *Southern Studies* 9.4 (1998): 1–26. Print.

Clayton, Jay, and Rothstein, Eric. "Figures in the Corpus: Theories of Influence and Intertextuality." *Influence and Intertextuality in Literary History*. Ed. Jay Clayton and Eric Rothstein.Madison: U of Wisconsin P, 1991: 3–36. Print.

Clinch, Jon. "Dangerous Words, Dangerous Ideas: A Prescription for Literature That Lasts." *RH Magazine: Censorship and Banned Books* 4: 64–65. Print.

———. *Finn*. New York: Random House, 2007. Print.

———. "Reading and Book Talk." Public library, Oxford, PA. Web. 15 May 2008.

Cook, Guy. *Discourse and Literature: The Interplay of Form and Mind*. Oxford: Oxford UP, 1994. Print.

Cowart, David. *Literary Symbiosis: The Reconfigured Text in Twentieth-Century Writing*. Athens: U of Georgia P, 1993. Print.

Cuddy, Lois A., and Claire M. Roche. Introduction. *Evolution and Eugenics in American Literature and Culture, 1880–1940*. Ed. Lois A. Cuddy and Claire M. Roche. Lewisburg: Bucknell UP, 2003. 9–53. Print.

Culley, Margaret, ed. Contemporary Reviews. *The Awakening*. 1899. New York: Norton, 1976. 145–159. Print.

Currie, Mark. *Postmodern Narrative Theory*. New York: Palgrave, 1998. Print.
Davis, Will. "James Dickey: An Interview." *James Dickey: Splintered Sunlight*. Ed. Patricia De La Fuente. Edinburg, TX: Pan American U, 1979. Print. 6–23.
De La Torre, Miguel A. "Confessions De Un Macho Cubana" (Originally "Beyond Machismo"). *Annual of the Society of Christian Ethics* 19 (1999): 213–233. Web. 18 Sept. 2003.
Demory, Pamela H. "Into the Heart of Light: Barbara Kingsolver Rereads *Heart of Darkness*." *Conradiana* 34.3 (2002). Bloomsburg University. Harvey Andruss Library. Proquest. Web. 7 Aug. 2006.
D'Erasmo, Stacey. "Call Me Una." *New York Times* 3 Oct. 1999, late ed.: Sec 7. Print.
Derrida, Jacques. *Archive Fever: A Freudian Impression*. Chicago: U of Chicago P, 1998. Print.
DeVoto, Bernard. *Mark Twain's America*. Lincoln, NE: Bison, 1997. Print.
Dewey, Joseph. "Hooking the Nose of the Leviathan: Information, Knowledge, and the Mysteries of Bonding in *The Gold Bug Variations*." *Review of Contemporary Fiction* 18.3 (1998): 51–66. Print.
Dickey, James. *Deliverance*. New York: Dell, 1970. Print.
———. Introduction: Boys of the River-God. *The Adventures of Tom Sawyer and The Adventures of Huckleberry Finn*. By Mark Twain. New York: Signet, 1979. Print.
Dickson, Rebecca. "Kate Chopin, Mrs. Pontellier, and Narrative Control." *Southern Quarterly* 37.3–4 (1999): 38–44. Print.
Doherty, Martin J. *Theory of Mind: How Children Understand Others' Thoughts and Feelings*. New York: Psychology, 2009. Print.
Douglass, Frederick. *Narrative of the Life of Frederick Douglass, An American Slave, Written by Himself*. Ed. David W. Blight. New York: Bedford/St. Martin's, 2003. Print.
———. "What to a Slave Is the Fourth of July." *Heath Anthology of American Literature*. Vol. 1, 3rd Ed. Ed. Paul Lauter. New York: Houghton, 1998. 1818–1837. Print.
Doyle, Laura. "'A' for Atlantic: The Colonizing Force of Hawthorne's *The Scarlet Letter*." *American Literature* 79.2 (2007): 243–273. Print.
Drabelle, Dennis. "Fooling around DC: Dennis Drabelle Interviews Comic Novelist Louis Bayard." *Lambda Book Report* May 1999: 6–8. Print.
Eakin, Paul John. *How Our Lives Become Stories: Making Selves*. Ithaca: Cornell UP, 1999. Print.
———. *Living Autobiographically: How We Create Identity in Narrative*. Ithaca: Cornell UP, 2008. Print.
Egan, Philip J. "Unraveling Misogyny and Forging the New Self: Mother, Lover, and Storyteller in *The Chaneysville Incident*." *Papers on Language and Literature* 33.3 (1997): 265–288. Print.
Elbert, Monika M. "'A' as Hester's Autonomy in Nathaniel Hawthorne's *The Scarlet Letter*." *Women in Literature: Reading through the Lens of Gender*. Ed. Jerilyn Fisher and Ellen S. Silber. Westport, CT: Greenwood, 2003. 256–259. Print.
Eliot, T.S. "Tradition and the Individual Talent." 1922. . *Bartleby.com*. Web. 1 Sept. 2009.
Ellis, R.J. "'No Authority at All': Harriet Prescott Spofford's 'Down the River' and Mark Twain's *Huckleberry Finn*." *Mark Twain Annual* 4.1 (2006): 33–53. Print.
Englund, Sheryl A. "Reading the Author in *Little Women*: A Biography of a Book." *American Transcendental Quarterly* 12.3 (1998): 198–219. Print.
Ensslen, Klaus. "Fictionalizing History: David Bradley's *The Chaneysville Incident*." *Callaloo* 35 (1988): 280–296. Print.

Entzminger, Betina. "Passing as Miscegenation: Whiteness and Homoeroticism in Faulkner's *Absalom, Absalom!*" *Faulkner Journal* 22.1–2 (2006): 90–105. Print.
Faulkner, William. *Absalom, Absalom!* 1936. New York: Vintage, 1990. Print.
———. *The Sound and the Fury*. 1929. New York: Vintage, 1990. Print.
Fiedler, Leslie. "Come Back to the Raft Ag'in, Huck Honey." *A New Fiedler Reader*. New York: Prometheus, 1999. 3–12. Print.
Fishkin, Shelley Fisher. *Was Huck Black? Mark Twain and African American Voices*. New York: Oxford UP, 1993. Print.
Fokkema, Aleid. "The Author: Postmodernism's Stock Character." *The Author as Character: Representing Historical Writers in Western Literature*. Ed. Paul Franssen and Ton Hoenselaars. New Jersey: Associated UP, Inc., 1999. 39–51. Print.
Foucault, Michel. *The Archaelogy of Knowledge and The Discourse on Language*. Trans. A.M. Sheridan Smith. New York: Random House, 1972. Print.
———. *The Foucault Reader*. Ed. Paul Rabinow. New York: Pantheon, 1984. Print.
Frank, Lawrence. "'The Murders in the Rue Morgue': Edgar Allan Poe's Evolutionary Reverie." *Nineteenth-Century Literature* 50.2 (1995): 168–188. Print.
Freud, Sigmund. *Beyond the Pleasure Principle*. New York: Liveright, 1961. Print.
———. *Civilization and Its Discontents*. Trans. James Strachey. New York: Norton, 1962. Print.
———. "Mourning and Melancholia." *The Standard Edition of the Complete Psychological Works of Sigmund Freud*. Trans. James Strachey. Vol. XIV. 1957. London: Hogarth, 1962. Print.
Galvan, Fernando. "Plagiarism in Poe: Revisiting the Poe-Dickens Relationship." *Edgar Allan Poe Review* 10.2 (2009): 11–24. Print.
Gannon, Susan R. "Getting Cozy with a Classic: Visualizing *Little Women* (1868–1995)." *Little Women and the Feminist Imagination: Criticism, Controversy, Personal Essays*. Ed. Janice M. Alberghene and Beverly Lyon Clark. New York: Garland, 1999: 103–138. Print.
Gates, Henry Louis. *The Signifying Monkey: A Theory of African-American Literary Criticism*. New York: Oxford UP, 1988. Print.
Genette, Gerard. *Palimpsests: Literature in the Second Degree*. 1982. Trans. Channa Newman and Claude Doubinsky. Lincoln: U of Nebraska P, 1997. Print.
Glendening, John. "Evolution, Narcissism, and Maladaptation in Kate Chopin's *The Awakening*." *American Literary Realism* 43.1 (2010): 41–73. Print.
Goldblatt, Mark. "Jeffries Redux." *National Review Online* 18 Dec. 2001. Web. 8 Aug. 2004.
Goldstein, Jane. "A Daughter's Place: The Intertextuality of Gene Stratton-Porter's *Laddie* and Louisa May Alcott's *Little Women*." *Canadian Children's Literature* 111–112 (2003): 50–59. Print.
Goldstein, Philip. "Black Feminism and the Canon: Faulkner's *Absalom, Absalom!* and Morrison's *Beloved* as Gothic Romances." *Faulkner Journal* (2004–2005): 133–147. Print.
Gonzalez, Laura Peco. "Rewriting Tradition in the Old and New World: *The Holder of the World* and *The Tree Bride*." *New Literatures of Old: Dialogues of Tradition and Innovation in Anglophone Literature*. Ed. Jose Ramon Prado-Perez and Didac Llorens Cubedo. Newcastle Upon Tyne, UK: Cambridge Scholars, 2008. 136–143. Print.
Greiner, Donald J. "Updike on Hawthorne." *Nathaniel Hawthorne Review* 13.1 (1987): 1–4. Print.
Grodal, Torben. "Evolution of Narrative Forms." *Routledge Encyclopedia of Narrative Theory*. Ed. David Herman, Manfred Jahn, and Marie-Laure Ryan. New York: Routledge, 2005. 152–154. Print.

Grossman, Jay. "'A' Is for Abolition? Race, Authorship, *The Scarlet Letter.*" *Textual Practice* 7.1 (1993): 13–30. Print.
Guillory, John. *Cultural Capital: The Problem of Literary Canon Formation*. Chicago: U of Chicago P, 1993. Print.
Gura, Philip F. "Language and Meaning: An American Tradition." *American Literature* 53.1 (1981): 1–21. Print.
Hart, Elizabeth F. "The Epistemology of Cognitive Literary Study." *Philosophy and Literature* 25 (2001): 314–334. Print.
Hart, Henry. *James Dickey: The World as a Lie*. New York: Picador, 2000. Print.
Harvey, Bruce A. "Science and the Earth." *A Companion to Herman Melville*. Ed. Wynn Kelley. Malden, MA: Blackwell, 2006. 71–82. Print.
Hawthorne, Nathaniel. *The Scarlet Letter and Other Writings*. Ed. Leland S. Person. New York: Norton, 2005. Print.
Haynsworth, Leslie. "Sena Jeter Naslund: An Epic of Her Own." *Publishers Weekly* 9 Sept. 1999: 65. Print.
Herendeen, Wyman H. *From Landscape to Literature: The River and the Myth of Geography*. Pittsburg: Duquesne UP, 1986. Print.
Herman, David. *Story Logic: Problems and Possibilities of Narrative*. Lincoln: U of Nebraska P, 2002. Print.
Herman, David, Manfred Jahn, and Marie-Laure Ryan. *Routledge Encyclopedia of Narrative Theory*. New York: Routledge, 2005. Print.
Herrmann, Steven B. "Melville's Portrait of Same-Sex Marriage in *Moby-Dick*." *Jung Journal: Culture and Psyche* 4.3 (2010): 65–82. Print.
Higginson, Thomas Whitworth, ed. *Emily Dickinson's Letters*. Early Women Masters. Web. 25 Feb. 2010.
Hogan, Michael. "Built on the Ashes: The Fall of the House of Sutpen and the Rise of the House of Sethe." *Unflinching Gaze: Morrison and Faulkner Re-Envisioned*. Ed. Carol A. Kolmerten, Stephen M. Ross, and Judith Bryant Wittenberg. Jackson: UP of Mississippi, 1997. 167–180. Print.
Hogan, Patrick Colm. *Cognitive Science, Literature and the Arts: A Guide for Humanists*. New York: Routledge, 2003. Print.
Huber, Don J. "Alton Prison: Alton in the Civil War." *Altonweb*. Alton Historical Society. Web. 1 Sept. 2009.
Hull, Richard. "Puns in "The Gold Bug': You Gotta Be Kidding." *Arizona Quarterly* 58.2 (2002): 3–18. Print.
Hunt, George W. *John Updike and the Three Great Secret Things: Sex, Religion, and Art*. Grand Rapids: Eerdmans, 1980. Print.
Huntington, Samuel P. *Who Are We? The Challenges to America's National Identity*. New York: Simon, 2004. Print.
Hurt, James. "Narrative Powers: Richard Powers as Storyteller." *Review of Contemporary Fiction* 28.3 (1998): 24–41. Print.
Hutcheon, Linda. "Historiographic Metafiction." *Intertextuality and Contemporary American Fiction*. Ed. Patrick O'Donnell and Robert Con Davis. Baltimore: Johns Hopkins UP, 1989: 3–32. Print.
———. *A Poetics of Postmodernism: History, Theory, Fiction*. New York: Routledge, 1988. Print.
Irwin, John T. *The Mystery to a Solution: Poe, Borges, and the Analytic Detective Story*. Baltimore: Johns Hopkins UP, 1994. Print.
Jacobson, Kristin J. "The Neodomestic American Novel: The Politics of Home in Barbara Kingsolver's *The Poisonwood Bible*." *Tulsa Studies in Women's Literature* 24.1 (2005): 105–127. Print.
Jarrett, Gene. "This Expression Shall Not Be Changed: Irrelevant Episodes, Jim's Humanity Revisited, and Retracing Mark Twain's Evasion in *Adventures of Huckleberry Finn*." *American Literary Realism* 35.1 (2002): 1–28. Print.

Jay, Elisabeth. "'Who Are you Gentle Reader?': John Updike—*A Month of Sundays* (1975)." *Literature and Theology* 19.4 (2005): 346–354. Print.
Jehlen, Myra. "Reading Gender in *The Adventures of Huckleberry Finn*." *The Adventures of Huckleberry Finn: A Case Study of Critical Controversy*. Ed. Gerald Graff and James Phelan. New York: Bedford, 1995. 505–518. Print.
Jeffries, Leonard. "Our Sacred Mission" Speech at the Empire State Black Arts and Cultural Festival, July 20, 1991. *Feast of Hate and Fear*. Web. 12 April 2007.
Johnson, Sarah Anne. "Nancy Rawles: I Try to Write Rhythmically." *The Very Telling: Conversations with American Writers*. Lebanon, NH: U of New England P, 2006: 169–180. Print.
Jones, Paul Christian. "A Re-Awakening: Anne Tyler." *Critique: Studies in Contemporary Fiction* 44.3 (2003): 271–283. EBSCOHost. Web. 1 March 2007.
Kanner, Ellen. "Barbara Kingsolver Turns to Her Past to Understand the Present." *BookPage*. 1998. Web. 27 April 2009.
Kaplan, Amy. "Manifest Domesticity." *American Literature* 70.3 (1998): 581–606. Print.
Kaye, Frances W. "Race and Reading: The Burden of *Huckleberry Finn*." *Canadian Review of American Studies* 29.1 (1999): 13–48. Print.
Keats, John. "Ode on a Grecian Urn." *John Keats: The Poems*. Ed. John Blades. New York: Palgrave, 2002. 115–126. Print.
Kelman, Edna. "Song, Snow, and Feasting: Dialogue and Carnival in 'The Dead.'" *Orbis Litterarum* 54 (1999): 60–78. Print.
Kempton, Daniel. "The Gold/Goole/Ghoul Bug." *Journal of the American Renaissance* 33.1 (1987): 1–19. Print.
Kennedy, Janice. "'Captain Ahab Was Neither My First Husband Nor My Last': Sena Jeter Naslund Reinterprets a Classic from a Female Perspective." *Ottawa Citizen* 6 Nov. 1999, final: B6. Print.
"Kentucky and the Underground Railroad." *Kentucky's Underground Railroad*. Kentucky Educational Television. 9 May 2006. Web. 1 Sept. 2009.
Kerber, Linda K. "Can a Woman Be an Individual? The Limits of Puritan Tradition in the Early Republic." *Texas Studies in Literature and Language* 25.1 (1983): 165–178. Print.
Kerby, Anthony Paul. *Narrative and the Self*. Bloomington: Indiana UP, 1991. Print.
Keyser, Catherine. "Jane Eyre, Bondswoman: Hannah Craft's Rethinking of Charlotte Bronte." *In Search of Hanna Crafts: Critical Essays on* The Bondswoman's Narrative. Ed. Henry Louis Gates, Jr., and Hollis Robbins. New York: Perseus, 2004: 87–105. Print.
King, Jeannette. "The Resisting Writer: Revisiting the Canon, Rewriting History in Sena Jeter Naslund's *Ahab's Wife, or The Star Gazer*." *Metafiction and Metahistory in Contemporary Women's Writing*. Ed. Ann Heilmann and Mark Llewellyn. New York: Palgrave, 2007. 182–194. Print.
Kingsolver, Barbara. "F.A.Q." *Barbara Kingsolver*. 2007. Web. 27 April 2009.
———. *The Poisonwood Bible*. New York: Harper, 1998. Print.
Knoper, Randall. "Mark Twain and Nation." *Companion to Mark Twain*. Ed. Peter Messent and Louis Budd. Malden, MA: Blackwell, 2005. 3–20. Print.
Kodat, Catherine Gunther. "A Postmodern *Absalom, Absalom!*, a Modern *Beloved*: The Dialectic of Form." *Unflinching Gaze: Morrison and Faulkner Re-envisioned*. Ed. Carol A. Kolmerten, Stephen M. Ross, and Judith Bryant Wittenberg. Jackson: UP of Mississippi, 1997. 181–198. Print.
Kopacz, Paula, and Bonnie Plummer. "Taking on the Icons: Naslund's 'Takes' on Sherlock and Ahab." *Kentucky Philological Review* 17.1–2 (2002): 23–28. Print.

Kopley, Richard. *The Threads of* The Scarlet Letter: *A Study of Hawthorne's Transformative Art*. Newark: U of Delaware P, 2003. Print.

Koza, Kimberly A. "The Africa of Two Western Women Writers: Barbara Kingsolver and Margaret Laurence." *Critique* 44.3 (2003): 284–294. Print.

Kreyling, Michael. "The Divine Mr. F." *American Literary History* 3.1 (1991): 153–161. Print.

Kroeber, Karl. *Retelling/Rereading: The Fate of Storytelling in Modern Times*. New Brunswick, NJ: Rutgers UP, 1992. Print.

Kruse, Kevin M. "For God So Loved the 1 Percent. . . ." *New York Times Online* 17 Jan. 2012. Web. 19 Jan. 2012.

Kubitschek, Missy Dehn. "'So You Want a History, Do You?' Epistemologies and *The Chaneysville Incident*." *Mississippi Quarterly* 49.4 (1996): 755–795. Print.

LaCapra, Dominick. *History in Transit: Experience, Identity, Critical Theory*. Ithaca: Cornell UP, 2004. Print.

Ladd, Barbara. "'The Direction of the Howling': Nationalism and the Color Line in *Absalom, Absalom!*." *American Literature* 66.3 (1994): 525–551. Print.

———. *Nationalism and the Color Line in George W. Cable, Mark Twain, and William Faulkner*. Baton Rouge: Louisiana State UP, 1996. Print.

Lal, Vinay. "Aurangzeb: Religious Policies." *Manas: India and Its Neighbors*. Vinay Lal. Aug. 2009. Web. 3 June 2011.

Lavender, Catherine. "The Cult of Domesticity and True Womanhood." Web. 6 June 2011.

LeClair, Tom. "As the *Pequod* Sailed. . . ." *The Nation* 13 Dec. 1999: 44–46. Print.

LeMenager, Stephanie. "Floating Capital: The Trouble with Whiteness on Twain's Mississippi." *ELH: English Literary History*. 71.2 (2004): 405–431. Print.

Lethem, Jonathan. "The Ecstasy of Influence: A Plagiarism." *Harper's Magazine* Feb. 2007. Web. 6 June 2008.

Levine. Robert S. "Genealogical Fictions." *Hawthorne and Melville: Writing a Relationship*. Ed. Jana L. Argersinger and Leland S. Person. Athens: U of Georgia P, 2008. 227–247. Print.

Lewis, R.W.B. *The American Adam: Innocence, Tragedy, and Tradition in the Nineteenth Century* (1971). Chicago: U of Chicago P, 1995. Print.

Linde, Charlotte. "The Acquisition of a Speaker by a Story: How History Becomes Memory and Identity." *Ethos* 28.4 (2001): 608–632. Web.

Lippincott, Gail. "Thirty-Nine Weeks: Pregnancy and Birth Imagery in Kate Chopin's *The Awakening*." *This Giving Birth: Pregnancy and Childbirth in American Women's Writing*. Ed. Julie Tharp and Susan MacCallum-Whitcomb. Bowling Green, Ohio: Bowling Green State U Popular P, 2000: 55–66. Print.

Lock, Helen. "The Paradox of Slave Mutiny in Herman Melville, Charles Johnson, and Frederick Douglass." *College Literature* 30.4 (2003): 54–70. Print.

Lott, Eric. "Mr. Clemens and Jim Crow: Twain, Race, and Blackface." *The Cambridge Companion to Mark Twain*. New York: Cambridge UP, 1995. 129–152. Print.

Lundin, Anne. "Little Pilgrims' Progress: Literary Horizons for Children's Literature." *Libraries and Culture* 41.1 (2006): 133–152. Wilson. Web. 16 Jan. 2012.

Luo, Shao-Pin. "Rewriting Travel: Ahdaf Soueif's *The Map of Love* and Bharati Mukherjee's *The Holder of the World*." *Journal of Commonwealth Literature* 38.2 (2003): 77–104. Sage, Bloomsburg U. Web. 28 July 2010.

Lynch, Paul. "Not Trying to Talk Alike and Succeeding: The Authoritative Word and Internally-Persuasive Word in *Tom Sawyer* and *Huckleberry Finn*." *Studies in the Novel* 38.2 (2006): 172–186. Print.

Lyotard, Jean-Francois. *The Postmodern Condition: A Report on Knowledge.* Trans. Geoff Bennington and Brian Massumi. Minneapolis: U of Minnesota P, 1984. Print.
Macpherson, Heidi Slettedahl. "Comic Constructions: Fictions of Mothering in Anne Tyler's *Ladder of Years.*" *Southern Quarterly* 39.3 (2001): 130–140. Print.
Maddox, Lucy. *Removals: Nineteenth-Century American Literature and the Politics of Indian Affairs.* New York: Oxford UP, 1991. Print.
Maibor, Carolyn. *Labor Pains: Emerson, Hawthorne, and Alcott on Work and the Woman Question.* New York: Routledge, 2004. Print.
Marx, Leo. *Machine in the Garden: Technology and the Pastoral Ideal in America.* New York: Oxford UP, 1964. Print.
———. "Mr. Eliot, Mr. Trilling, and *Huckleberry Finn.*" *The Critical Response to Mark Twain's* Huckleberry Finn. Ed. Laurie Champion. New York: Greenwood, 1991: 50–59. Print.
Matchie, Tom. "*Ahab's Wife, or The Star Gazer*: A Wider/Deeper View of Melville's Tragic Hero and His Times." *Journal of American and Comparative Cultures* 24.1–2 (2001): 85–91. Print.
Matthews, John T. "The Word as Scandal: Updike's *A Month of Sundays.*" *Arizona Quarterly* 39.4 (1983): 351–380. Print.
Mazur, Zygmunt. "The Purpose of Art: Sena Jeter Naslund's Ahab's Wife." *Homo Narrans: Texts and Essays in Honor of Jerome Kinkowitz.* Ed. Zygmunt Mazur and Richard Utz. Krakow, Poland: Jagiellonian UP, 2004. 147–155. Print.
McGill, Meredith L. "Poe, Literary Nationalism, and Authorial Identity." *The American Face of Edgar Allan Poe.* Ed. Shawn Rosenheim and Stephen Rachman. Baltimore: Johns Hopkins UP, 1995: 271–304. Print.
McIntire-Strasburg, Janice. "Mark Twain, Huck Finn, and the Geographical 'Memory' of a Nation." *Mark Twain's Geographical Imagination.* Ed. Joseph A. Alvarez. New Castle Upon Tyne: Cambridge Scholars, 2009. 83–99. Print.
McKay, Nellie. "An Interview with Toni Morrison." *Conversations with Toni Morrison.* Ed. Danille Taylor-Guthrie. Jackson: UP of Mississippi, 1994. 138–155. Print.
McLamore, Richard. "Narrative Self-Justification: Melville and Amasa Delano." *Studies in American Fiction* 23.1 (1995): 35–53. Print.
McLarin, Kim. "Loose the Shackles: When Fiction Writers Brave the Harsh Realities of Slavery." *The Free Library.* Web. 5 Sept. 2009
McWilliams, John P., Jr. *Hawthorne, Melville, and the American Character: A Looking-Glass Business.* New York: Cambridge UP, 1984. Print.
Melville, Herman. "Hawthorne and His Mosses." *The Confidence Man: His Masquerade. A Hypertext.* Ed. Scott Atkins. April 1996. Web. June 15, 2010.
—-. *Moby-Dick; Or, The Whale.* 1851. New York: Norton, 2002. Print.
Menke, Pamela Glenn. "Chopin's Sensual Sea and Cable's Ravished Land: Sexts, Signs and Gender Narrative." *Crossroads* 3.1 (1994–1995): 78–102. Print.
Milburn, Colin Nazhone. "Monsters in Eden: Darwin and Derrida." *MLN: Modern Language Notes.* 118 (2003): 603–621. Print.
Milder, Robert. "Herman Melville, 1819–1891: A Brief Biography." *A Historical Guide to Herman Melville.* Ed. Giles Gunn. New York: Oxford UP, 2005. 17–58. Print.
Miller, J. Hillis. *Ariadne's Thread: Story Lines.* New Haven: Yale UP, 1992. Print.
Mink, Louis O. "Narrative Form as a Cognitive Instrument." *The Writing of History: Literary Form and Historical Understanding.* Ed. Robert H. Canary and Henry Kozicki. Madison: U of Wisconsin P, 1987. Print.
Mitrano, Mena. "Judith Butler and the Images of Theory." *Butler Matters: Judith Butler's Impact on Feminist and Queer Studies.* Ed. Margaret Sonser Breen and Warren J. Blumenfeld. Burlington, VT: Ashgate, 2005: 57–79. Print.

Moraru, Christian. *Memorious Discourse: Reprise and Representation in Postmodernism*. Madison: Fairleigh Dickenson UP, 2005. Print.
Morrison, Toni. *Beloved*. 1987. New York: Penguin, 1988. Print.
———. "Faulkner and Women." *Faulkner and Women: Faulkner and Yoknapatawpha, 1985*. Ed. Doreen Fowler and Ann J. Abadie. Jackson: UP of Mississippi, 1986. 295–302. Print.
———. "Interview with Melvyn Bragg." *The South Bank Show*. Dir. Alan Benson. BBC, 1987. Video recording.
———. *Playing in the Dark: Whiteness and the Literary Imagination*. 1992. New York: Vintage, 1993. Print.
Moss-Coane, Marty. "Radio Times Interview with Jon Clinch." WHYY Radio. *The Horsehair Couch: The Blog of Jon Clinch*. 3 April 2007. Web. 1 Sept. 2009.
———. *Rewriting: Postmodern Narrative and Cultural Critique in the Age of Cloning*. Albany: State U of New York P, 2001. Print.
Mukherjee, Bharati. "A Four-Hundred-Year-Old Woman." *Critical Fictions: The Politics of Imaginative Writing*. Ed. Philomena Mariani. Seattle: Bay, 1991: 24–28. Print.
———. *The Holder of the World*. New York: Fawcett, 1993. Print.
Naslund, Sena Jeter. *Ahab's Wife; Or, The Star-Gazer*. New York: Harper, 1999. Print.
Newman, Judie. "Spaces In-Between—Hester Prynne as the Salem Bibi in Bharati Mukherjee's *The Holder of the World*." *Borderlands: Negotiating Boundaries in Post-Colonial Writing*. Ed. Monika Reif-Hüsler. Atlanta: Rodopi, 1991. 69–87. Print.
Nielson, Jim. "An Interview with Richard Powers." *Review of Contemporary Fiction* 18.3 (Fall 1998): 13–23. Print.
Nolan, Elizabeth. "The Awakening as Literary Innovation; Chopin, Maupassant and the Evolution of Genre." *Cambridge Companion to Kate Chopin* (2008). 118–131. Print.
Norling, Lisa. *Captain Ahab Had a Wife: New England Women and the Whalefishery, 1720–1870*. Chapel Hill: U of NC P, 2000. Print.
Novak, Phillip. "Signifying Silences: Morrison's Soundings in the Faulknerian Void." *Unflinching Gaze: Morrison and Faulkner Re-envisioned*. Ed. Carol A. Kolmerten, Stephen M. Ross, and Judith Bryant Wittenberg. Jackson: UP of Mississippi, 1997. 199–216. Print.
Nunning, Ansgar. "Historiographic Metafiction." *Routledge Encyclopedia of Narrative Theory*. Ed. David Herman, Manfred Jahn, and Marie-Laure Ryan. New York: Routledge, 2005: 216. Print.
Oates, Joyce Carol. "Time to Say Goodbye." *Times Literary Supplement* 4805 (1995): 22. Web.
Ochs, Elinor, and Lisa Capps. *Living Narrative: Creating Lives in Everyday Storytelling*. Cambridge, MA: Harvard UP, 2001. Print.
Olick, Jeffrey C. *States of Memory: Continuities, Conflicts and Transformations in National Retrospection*. Durham: Duke UP, 2003. Print.
O'Loughlin, Jim. "Off the Raft: *Adventures of Huckleberry Finn* and Jane Smiley's *The All-True Travels and Adventures of Lidie Newton*." *Papers on Language and Literature: A Journal for Scholars and Critics of Language and Literature* 43.2 (2007): 205–223. Print.
Packer, Randall. "Virtual Reality—Cultural Implications." *Science Encyclopedia*. Web. 18 Aug. 2011.
Parill, Sue. *Jane Austin on Film and Television: A Critical Study of the Adaptations*. Jefferson, NC: McFarland, 2002. Print.
Parker, Herschel. "Melville's Reading and *Moby-Dick*: An Overview and Bibliography." *Moby-Dick*. Ed. Herschel Parker and Harrison Hayford. New York: Norton, 2002. 431–437. Print.

Pearl, Nancy. "Book Lust with Nancy Pearl." *Seattle Channel's Art Zone*. 7 Jan. 2007. Web. 5 Sept. 2009.
Peeples, Scott. "Love and Theft in the Carolina Lowcountry." *Arizona Quarterly* 60.2 (2004): 33–52. Print.
———. "Poe's 'constructiveness' and 'The Fall of the House of Usher'" *Cambridge Companion to Edgar Allen Poe* ed. Kevin J. Hayes. New York: Cambridge UP, 2002: 178–90. Print.
Pennebaker, James W., and Janet D. Seagal. "Forming a Story: The Health Benefits of Narrative." *Journal of Clinical Psychology* 55.10 (1999): 1243–1254. Print.
Person, Leland S. "Gender and Sexuality." *A Companion to Herman Melville*. Ed. Wynn Kelley. Malden, MA: Blackwell, 2006. 231–246. Print.
Petit, Arthur G. *Mark Twain and the South*. Louisville: UP of Kentucky, 1974. Print.
Plate, Liedeke. *Transforming Memories in Contemporary Women's Writing*. New York: Palgrave, 2011. Print.
Plath, James. "Giving the Devil His Due: Leeching and Edification of Spirit in *The Scarlet Letter* and *The Witches of Eastwick*." *John Updike and Religion: The Sense of the Sacred and the Motions of Grace*. Ed. James Yerkes. Grand Rapids: Eerdmans, 1999. 208–227. Print.
———. "Updike, Hawthorne, and American Literary History." *The Cambridge Companion to John Updike*. Ed. Stacey Olster. Cambridge: Cambridge UP, 2006. 122–133. Print.
Poe, Edgar Allan. "The Gold-Bug." *The Selected Writings of Edgar Allan Poe*. Ed. G.R. Thompson. New York: Norton, 2004. 321–348. Print.
———. *The Letters of Edgar Allan Poe*, Ed. John Ward Ostrom. New York: Gordion Press, 1966. Print.
———. "Magazine Writing." *The Edgar Allan Poe Society of Baltimore*. 9 June 2010. Web. 9 Sept. 2011.
———. "The Murders in the Rue Morgue." *The Selected Writings of Edgar Allan Poe*. Ed. G.R. Thompson. New York: Norton, 2004. 239–266. Print.
Post, Sheila. "Melville and the Marketplace." *A Historical Guide to Herman Melville*. Ed. Giles Gunn. New York: Oxford UP, 2005. 105–132. Print.
Powers, Richard. *The Gold Bug Variations*. New York: Harper, 1991. Print.
Rajan, Tilottoma. "Intertextuality and the Subject of Reading/Writing." *Influence and Intertextuality in Literary History*. Ed. Jay Clayton and Eric Rothstein. Madison: U of Wisconsin P, 1991. 61–74. Print.
Ramos, Peter. "Beyond Silence and Realism: Trauma and the Function of Ghosts in *Absalom, Absalom!* and *Beloved*." *Faulkner Journal* 23.2 (2008): 47–66. Print.
Rastogi, Pallavi. "Telling Twice-Told Tales All Over Again: Literary and Historical Subversion in Bharati Mukherjee's *The Holder of the World*." *Form and Transformation in Asian American Literature*. Ed. Zhou Xiaojing and Samina Najmi. Seattle: U of Washington P, 2005. 268–284. Print.
Rawles, Nancy. *My Jim*. New York: Three Rivers, 2005. Print.
Reed, Ishmael. *Flight to Canada*. 1976. New York: Scribner, 1998. Print.
Renza, Louis. "Never More in Poe's Tell-Tale American Tale." *Edgar Allan Poe Review* 4.2 (2003): 22–40. Print.
"Results from the 1860 U.S. Census." *The Civil War Home Page*. 2009. Web. 3 June 2009.
Reynolds, David S. "Hawthorne's Cultural Demons: History, Popular Culture, and *The Scarlet Letter*." *Novel History: Historians and Novelists Confront America's Past (and Each Other)*. Ed. Mark C. Carnes. New York: Simon, 2001. 229–234. Print.
Ripley, Debra. "Herman Melville's Exploitation of Cognitive Features: Amasa Delano as Paradigm of Failure." *Consciousness, Literature, and the Arts* 10.2 (2009). Web. 9 March 2012.

Ritivoi, Andreea Deciu. "Identity and Narrative." *Routledge Encyclopedia of Narrative Theory*. Ed. David Herman, Manfred Jahn, and Marie-Laure Ryan. New York: Routledge, 2008: 231–235. Print.

Rodriguez, Maria Soledad. "A Little Miss in the Land of Little Women: Louisa May Alcott and Jamaica Kincaid." *Jamaica Kincaid and Caribbean Double Crossings*. Ed. Linda Lang-Peralta. Newark: U of Delaware P, 2006. 16–32. Print.

Rosenheim, Shawn James. *The Cryptographic Imagination: Secret Writing from Edgar Poe to the Internet*. Baltimore: Johns Hopkins UP, 1997. Print.

Rossner, Judith. *His Little Women*. New York: Simon, 1990. Print.

Royal, Derek Parker. "An Absent Presence: The Rewriting of Hawthorne's Narratology in John Updike's *S*." *Critique: Studies in Contemporary Fiction* 44.1 (2002): 73–85. Print.

Rushdy, Ashraf H.A. "Daughters Signifyin(g) History: The Example of Toni Morrison's *Beloved*." *American Literature* 64.3 (1992): 567–597. Print.

———. *Neo Slave Narratives: Studies in the Social Logic of a Literary Form*. New York: Oxford UP, 1999. Print.

———. *Remembering Generations: Race and Family in Contemporary African American Fiction*. Chapel Hill: U of North Carolina P, 2001. Print.

Sacks, Oliver. "Making up the Mind." *New York Review of Books* 8 April 1993: 42–49. Web. 12 Dec. 2009.

Satchell, Michael. "The Reigning Icon of Womanly Evil." *US News and World Report Special Issue* 27 Dec. 2005. LexisNexis Academic. Web. 3 March 2011.

Schank, Roger C., and Robert P. Abelson. "Knowledge and Memory: The Real Story." *Knowledge and Memory: The Real Story*. Ed. Robert S. Wyer, Jr. Hillsdale, NJ: Erlbaum, 1995. 1–85. Print.

Schiff, James A. *Updike's Version: Rewriting* The Scarlet Letter. Columbia: U of Missouri P, 1992. Print.

Schreiber, Paul. "Orphaned Orpheus; The Exiled Writer in *Moby-Dick*." *Writing of Exile* (2001): 13–26. Print.

Schwartz, Lawrence H. *Creating Faulkner's Reputation: The Politics of Modern Literary Criticism*. Knoxville: U of Tennessee P, 1988. Print.

Scudder, Harold. "Melville's Benito Cereno and Captain Delano's Voyages." *PMLA: Publications of the Modern Language Association* 43.2 (1928): 502–532. Print.

Sedgwick, Eve. *Epistemology of the Closet*. Berkeley: U of California P, 1990. Print.

Seelye, John. *The True Adventures of Huckleberry Finn*. Evanston: Northwestern UP, 1970. Print.

Sen, Krishna. "America as Diaphor: Cultural Translation in Bharati Mukherjee's *The Holder of the World*." *American Fiction of the 1990s: Reflections of History and Culture*. Ed. Jay Prossner. New York: Routledge, 2008. Print.

Shapiro, Stephen. "'Stock in Dead Folk': The Value of Black Mortality in Mark Twain's *The Adventures of Huckleberry Finn*." *Representations of Death in Nineteenth-Century US Writing and Culture*. Ed. Lucy E. Frank. London: Ashgate, 2007. 61–70. Print.

Showalter, Elaine. "Tradition and the Female Talent: *The Awakening* as a Solitary Book." *The American Novel: New Essays on* The Awakening. Ed. Wendy Martin. Cambridge, UK: P Syndicate of the U of Cambridge, 1988: 33–57. Print.

Silverman, Kenneth. *Edgar A. Poe: Mournful and Never-Ending Remembrance*. New York: Harper, 1991. Print.

Simon, Brant, and William Deverell. "Come Back Tom Joad: Thoughts on a California Dreamer." *California History* 79.4 (2000–2001): 180–191. Print.

Simon, Bruce. "Hybridity in the Americas: Reading Conde, Mukherjee and Hawthorne." *Post-Colonial Theory and the United States: Race, Ethnicity and Literature*. Ed. Peter Schmidt. UP of Mississippi, 2000. 412–443. Print.
Simon, Herbert. "Literary Criticism: A Cognitive Approach." *SEHR: Stanford Electronic Humanities Review*. 4.1 (1995). Web. 11 July 2011.
Skinner, Katherine. "'Must Be Born Again': Resurrecting the *Anthology of American Folk Music*." *Popular Music* 25.1 (2006): 57–75. Print.
Slattery, Dennis Patrick. "Watery World/Watery Words: Ishmael's Write of Passage in *Moby-Dick*." *New Orleans Review* 11.2 (1984): 62–66. Print.
Smiley, Jane. *The All True Travels and Adventures of Lidie Newton*. New York: Random, 1998. Print.
Smith, Gayle L. "The World and the Thing: *Moby Dick* and the Limits of Language." *Emerson Society Quarterly* 31.4 (1985): 260–271. Print.
Smith, Stewart, and Ruth Sullivan. "Narrative Stance in Kate Chopin's *The Awakening*." *Critical Essays on Kate Chopin*. Ed. Alice Hall Petry. New York: Hall, 1996. Print.
Solmsen, Friedrich. "Epicurus and the Growth and Decline of the Cosmos." *American Journal of Philology* 74.1 (1953): 34–51. Print.
Sommer, Doris. *Proceed with Caution*. Cambridge: Harvard UP, 1991. Print.
Spickard, Paul R. *Mixed Blood: Intermarriage and Ethnic Identity in Twentieth-Century America*. Madison: U of Wisconsin P, 1989. Print.
Spillers, Hortense. *Black, White, and in Color: Essays on American Literature and Culture*. Chicago: U of Chicago P, 2003. Print.
Spolsky, Ellen. "Darwin and Derrida: Cognitive Literary Theory as a Species of Post-Structuralism." *Poetics Today* 23.1 (2002): 43–62. Print.
Stauffer, John. "Melville, Slavery and the American Dilemma." *A Companion to Herman Melville*. Ed. Wynn Kelley. Malden, MA: Blackwell, 2006. 214–230. Print.
Steinbrink, Jeffrey. "Who Shot Tom Sawyer?" *American Literary Realism* 35 (2002): 29–38. Print.
Strehle, Susan. "Chosen People: American Exceptionalism in Kingsolver's *The Poisonwood Bible*." *Critique* 49.4 (2008): 413–428. Print.
Sugimori, Masami. "Racial Mixture, Racial Passing and White Subjectivity in *Absalom, Absalom!*" *Faulkner Journal* 23.2 (2008): 3–21. Print.
Sugiyama, Michelle Scalise. "Reverse-Engineering Narrative." *The Literary Animal*. Ed. Jonathan Gottschall and David Sloan Wilson. Evanston, IL: Northwestern UP, 2005: 177–195. Print.
Sullivan, Jane. "A Whale of a Time; BOOKS." *The Age* 17 June 2000, late ed., Saturday extra: 11. Print.
Sullivan, Ruth and Stewart Smith. "Narrative Stance in Kate Chopin's *The Awakening*." *Critical Essays on Kate Chopin*. Ed. Alice Hall Petry. New York: G. K. Hall, 1996: 147–158. Print.
Sundquist, Eric. *Faulkner: The House Divided*. Baltimore: Johns Hopkins UP, 1983. Print.
Tanner, Tony. "The Literary Children of James and Clemens." *Nineteenth-Century Fiction* 16.3 (1961): 205–218. Print.
Thesing, William B., and David A. Wright. "Dealing with 'Immortal Works': James Dickey's Last Public Discussion of *Deliverance*." *James Dickey Newsletter* 24.2 (2008): 36–42. Print.
Thomas, J.D. "Science and the Sacred: Intertextuality in Richard Powers's *The Gold Bug Variations*." *Critique: Studies in Contemporary Fiction* 51.1 (2010): 18–31. Print.
Thomas, J.T. "Deciphering the Code in Richard Powers's *The Gold Bug Variations*." *Notes on Contemporary Literature* 36.5 (2006): 9–10. Print.

Todorov, Tzvetan. *The Poetics of Prose*. Trans. Richard Howard. Ithaca: Cornell UP, 1977. Print.
Tomc, Sandra. "A Change of Art: Hester, Hawthorne, and the Service of Love." *Nineteenth-Century Literature* 56.4 (2002): 466–494. Print.
Traber, Daniel S. *Whiteness, Otherness, and the Individualism Paradox from Huck to Punk*. New York: Palgrave, 2007. Print.
Trilling, Lionel. "Huckleberry Finn: 1948." *American Educator*. Fall 2002. Web. 10 June 2009.
———. Introduction. *The Adventures of Huckleberry Finn*. New York: Holt, 1948: v-xvii. Print.
Trites, Roberta Seelinger. *Twain, Alcott, and the Birth of the Adolescent Reform Novel*. Iowa City: U of Iowa P, 2007. Print.
Turner, Mark David. *The Literary Mind*. New York: Oxford UP, 1996. Print.
Twain, Mark. *The Adventures of Huckleberry Finn*. 1885. Toronto: Dover, 1994. Print.
Tyler, Anne. *Ladder of Years*. New York: Random, 1995. Print.
United Nations Development Programme. *Human Development Report 1995*. New York: Oxford UP, 1995. Web.
Updike, John. *A Month of Sundays*. New York: Fawcett, 1974. Print.
———. *Roger's Version*. New York: Fawcett, 1986. Print.
———. *S*. New York: Fawcett, 1988. Print.
———. "A 'Special Message' for the Franklin Library First Edition of *Roger's Version*." *Odd Jobs: Essays and Criticism*. New York: Knopf, 1991. 856–858. Print.
———. "Unsolicited Thoughts on S." *Odd Jobs: Essays and Criticism*: 858–859. Print.
Vernon, Alex. "The Origin of Story and the Survival of Character in Faulkner's *Absalom, Absalom!*" *Evolution and Eugenics in American Literature and Culture, 1880–1940*. Ed. Lois M. Cuddy and Claire M. Roche. London: Bucknell UP, 2003. 116–130. Print.
Vogler, Thomas A. "The Economy of Writing and Melville's Gold Doubloon." *New Orleans Review* 24.2 (1998): 45–61. Print.
Watkins, Mel. "Thirteen Runaway Slaves and David Bradley." *New York Times Book Review* 19 April 1981. Web.
Weissberg, Liliane. "Black, White, and Gold." *Romancing the Shadow: Poe and Race*. Ed. J. Gerald Kennedy and Liliane Weissberg. New York: Oxford UP, 2001. 127–156. Print.
Weldon, Roberta. *Hawthorne, Gender, and Death: Christianity and Its Discontents*. New York: Palgrave, 2008. Print.
Whalen, Terence. *Edgar Allan Poe and the Masses: The Political Economy of Literature in Antebellum America*. Princeton, NJ: Princeton UP, 1999. Print.
Whitman, T. Stephen. *The Price of Freedom: Slavery and Manumission in Baltimore and Early National Maryland*. Louisville: UP of Kentucky, 1997. Print.
Widdowson, Peter. "'Writing Back': Contemporary Revisionary Fiction." *Textual Practice* 20.3 (2006): 491–507. Print.
Wideman, John Edgar. "Storytelling and Democracy (in the Radical Sense): A Conversation with John Edgar Wideman." *African American Review* 34.2 (2000): 263–272. Print.
Williams, Michael. "'The Language of the Cipher': Interpretation in 'The Gold-Bug.'" *American Literature* 53.4 (1982): 646–660. Print.
Wilson, David Sloan. "Evolutionary Social Constructivism." *Literary Animal: Evolution and the Nature of Narrative*. Ed. Jonathan Gottschal, et al. Evanston, IL: Northwestern UP, 2005. Print.

Wilson, Eric. "Melville, Darwin and the Great Chain of Being." *Studies in American Fiction*. 28.2 (2000): 131–150. Print.
Wilson, Matthew. "The African American Historian: David Bradley's *The Chaneysville Incident*." *African American Review* 29.1 (1995): 97–108. Print.
Wilson, Raymond J., III. "Roger's Version: Updike's Negative-Solid Model of *The Scarlet Letter*." *Modern Fiction Studies* 35.2 (1989): 241–250. Print.
Wood, James. *The Broken Estate: Essays on Literature and Belief*. New York: Random House, 1999. Print.
Wynter, Sylvia. "1492: A New World View." *Race, Discourse, and the Origins of the Americas*. Ed. Vera Lawrence Hyatt and Rex Nettleford. Washington, DC: Smithsonian Institution Press, 1995: 5–57. Print.
Yaeger, Patricia. "'A Language Which Nobody Understood': Emancipatory Strategies in *The Awakening*." *Novel: A Forum for Fiction* 20.3 (1987): 197–219. Print.
Young, Kay, and Jeffrey L. Saver. "The Neurology of Narrative." *SubStance* 30.1–2 (2001): 72–84. Print.
Zackodnik, Teresa. "Fixing the Color Line: The Mulatto, Southern Courts, and Racial Identity." *American Quarterly* 53.3 (2001): 420–451. Print.
Zunshine, Lisa. "Theory of Mind and Experimental Representations of Fictional Consciousness." *Introduction to Cognitive Cultural Studies*. Ed. Lisa Zunshine. Baltimore: Johns Hopkins UP, 2010: 193–213. Print.

Index

A

abolitionist, 74, 100, 167, 207, 211
Adam and Eve, 11, 12, 49, 60, 102, 151–2,
aesthetic reasons for reconfiguration, 3, 4–5
Africa, 19, 90–97, 128, 159, 161, 162, 163, 164, 165, 220
Alchemy, 55
Alcott, Bronson, 85, 98, 217
Alcott, Louisa May, 70; *Little Women*, 1, 3, 16, 19–20, 83–103, 104, 170, 217
American culture, 1, 3, 44, 54, 84, 104, 106, 134, 171
American Dream, 84
Anderson, Benedict, 10–11, 170
angel of the house, 87, 96
archive fever, 12
autobiography, 10, 11, 81, 84, 86, 123, 126, 141

B

Bach, Johann Sebastian, 28, 30, 31
Barth, John, 1, 16–17
Bayard, Louis, 5; *Fool's Errand*, 37; *Mr. Timothy* 175–176, 177, 178, 179; *The Pale Blue Eye*, 1, 19, 21, 23, 33–42
bible, 4, 11, 58, 102, 103, 204; in *The Gold-Bug Variations*, 31–32; in *The Scarlet Letter*, 45, 50; in *Moby Dick*, 68, 73; in *Little Women*, 85; in *The Poisonwood Bible* 91, 96; in *Adventures of Huckleberry Finn*, 106
biological determinism, 29
biracial, 130, 131, 132
blackface minstrelsy, 105, 127, 180
Boyd, Brian, 18, 29, 87, 215
Bradley, David: *The Chaneysville Incident*, 17, 21, 154–165, 166, 169, 219
Brooks, Geraldine: *March*, 17, 19, 83, 85, 86, 97–102, 103
Bunyan, John: *Pilgrim's Progress*, 45, 77, 84, 85, 217
burlesque, 2
Bushnell, Horace, 77–78
Butler, Judith, 114, 117, 118, 120, 218

C

California Gold Rush, 24, 110
capitalism, 10, 25–26, 91, 93, 94, 97, 170, 217
cannibalism, 72, 199, 200, 206–07
canonical literature, 2–3, 4–6, 8, 10, 13–18, 19, 70, 133, 143, 146, 169, 170–171, 173, 196; and Poe, 22–23, 178; and Hawthorne, 43–44, 54–55; and Melville, 68–69, 70, 218; and Alcott, 84, 86; and Twain, 104, 126, 128, 130–31, 218; and Chopin 135, 149; and Faulkner, 150, 152, 167
Civil War, 20, 21, 83, 94, 97–101, 105, 127, 151–2, 204, 219
Chopin, Kate, 70; *The Awakening*, 3, 20, 71, 135–9, 141–5, 147–9, 170, 203, 219
Christianity. 45, 58, 75–76, 91, 92–3, 95–7, 98, 122, 129, 207, 217
clergy, 20, 45, 46, 77, 90, 92, 97, 98, 102, 122, 158, 185, 205, 211, 217
Clinch, John: *Finn*, 1, 3, 6, 20, 106, 128–34, 171

238 Index

cognitive psychology, 3–4, 6–11, 15, 16, 18, 102, 173; and Poe, 27, 38; and Hawthorne, 45; and Mukherjee, 54, 58, 63; and Naslund, 69, 71; and Rawles, 126; and Faulkner, 152, 166; and Melville, 220
Cold War, 25, 90, 150, 151
collective consciousness, 11, 12, 18; and Poe, 26, 27, 31–32, 35; and Hawthorne, 46, 48; and Melville, 69–70; and Alcott 103; and Faulkner 152, and Bradley, 162
Columbus, Christopher, 10, 11, 56, 60
commercialism, 5, 26, 55, 128, 185, 192
commodification , 94, 96
construction of narrative, 1–2, 4, 6–8, 16, 18, 38, 103, 173; and Poe, 22; and Powers 28, 29; and Updike, 46, 51–52; and Hawthorne, 50; and Mukherjee, 58–59; and Melville, 79; and Naslund 81–82; and Rawles, 126-7, and Clinch, 133; and Faulkner, 152-3; and Bradley and Morrison 154
contextual anchoring, 53
cryptography, 23, 24, 27–28, 30, 39–41, 216
cultural narrative, 4, 10–11, 13–16, 18, 19, 20, 69–70, 81, 102–03, 154, 170-3; and Bayard, 35, 42; and Hawthorne, 44, 46, 48; and Naslund, 66, 73, 82; and Melville, 69, 73, 82; and Rawles, 128; and Chopin, 135, 146; and Tyler, 136, 139, 143, 146; and Faulkner, 151-2, 168; and Morrison, 169

D

Darwin, Charles, 12, 15, 49, 75, 137–38, 141, 145; *Origin of Species*, 37, 152
death instinct, 102
Declaration of Independence, 166
DeFoe, Daniel: *Robinson Crusoe*, 26–27, 28
Derrida, Jacques, 12, 77
De Saussure, Ferdinand, 78, 141
detective story, 19, 33–34, 37, 38, 75, 176, 178, 186, 190

DeVoto, Bernard, 104, 106, 107, 108, 218
Dickens, Charles, 176, 178, 195, 196, 209, 213, 215
Dickey, James: *Deliverance*, 20, 106, 110–20, 127, 128, 132, 134, 218
Dickinson, Emily, 4
domesticity, 83, 85, 96, 147, 170, 186, 217
Douglass, Frederick, 74, 121, 122, 123, 172, 210, 211, 219
Duyckinck, Evert, 43

E

Eakin, John Paul, 6, 8, 16, 173
Eden, Garden of, 12–13, 28, 32, 49, 60, 61, 103, 128, 170
Eliot, T.S., 14–15, 70, 104, 179
Epigraph, 5, 41, 47, 64, 81, 84, 89, 97, 128, 216, 217
epiphany, 4, 27, 28, 129
Emerson, Ralph Waldo, 67, 80, 84, 100
ethos, 84, 151
Evans, Augusta Jane, 70
evolutionary literary criticism , 6, 15, 18, 27, 29, 31, 37, 49, 87, 114, 135, 146, 149, 172–3, 215

F

family, 8, 11, 19, 62, 68, 128, 130, 132, 156, 160, 162, 213; and Alcott, 83–86; and Rossner, 86–88; and Kingsolver, 88–97; and Brooks, 97–99, 101; and Rawles, 120–4; and Tyler, 136–40, 142, 144–9; and Faulkner, 150–3, 163
Faulkner, William, 3, 150–1; *Absalom, Absalom!*, 20–21, 151–5, 159, 161–7, 169, 170, 171, 219; *The Sound and the Fury*, 153, 163, 219, 220
Feminism: and Naslund, 19, 70, 72–73, 211; and Tyler, 20, 136, 145, 147; and Mukherjee, 53, 54, 59–60; and Alcott, 84, 86, 95; and Brooks, 99; and Rawles, 141; and Chopin, 41, 145, 149
Fiedler, Leslie, 70, 73, 107, 111, 112–3, 116, 186, 218
film/movie adaptations, 84, 172, 217, 220
forefather(s), 34, 150

foreshadow, 73, 117
Foucault, Michel, 13, 15–16, 49, 69
fourth of July, 158, 219
fourth wall, 2
Freud, Sigmund, 47, 102–3, 116, 193, 218
Fuller, Margaret, 72, 210–11

G
Gates, Henry Louis, 2, 3
gender oppression, 33, 59, 86, 88–9, 96, 98, 100, 110, 114–5, 116, 120, 123, 125, 155, 158, 218
Genette, Gerard, 16, 53, 70, 216
ghosts, 101, 154–5, 162, 168, 188, 219, 220

H
Hawthorne, Nathaniel, 43, 83, 84, 150, 199, 205, 210, 211, 215; Hester Prynne, 11, 19, 44–47, 50, 53, 55, 59–61, 71, 143, 203; *The Scarlet Letter*; 3, 19, 43–62, 64–65, 66, 67, 68, 75, 102, 170, 203, 216
Herman, David, 8, 53–4, 63, 71, 202
heterosexuality, 117, 120
hillbillies, 113, 116–9
Hinduism, 52, 57, 61, 62
historiographic metaficition , 2, 17, 82
Holmes, Sherlock, 193–4, 195, 199–200
homoeroticism, 36–7, 73, 111, 113, 116–7, 119, 185–6, 205, 216, 218, 219
homosocial, 113, 186
Hutcheon, Linda, 2, 13, 17, 82
hypercanonization, 105
hypocrisy, 48, 61, 122
hypotext, 3, 16, 70, 216

I
ideology, 8, 15, 23, 82, 85
identity: necessity of narrative for, 6–7, 9–11, 16, 18, 20, 38, 82, 92, 123, 128, 136, 140–2, 173; social construction of 18, 29, 118, 120, 133, 218; American cultural identity, 20, 22–3, 38, 44–5, 69–70, 81, 82, 85–6, 91, 95, 103, 104, 111, 131, 133–4, 146, 150–51, 171, 215; personal identity, 40, 52, 63, 105, 110, 125, 133, 136, 137–8, 140, 144–5, 160, 188, 206; gender and sexuality identity, 73, 91, 97, 114, 118, 207
imagined communities, 5, 10, 170
imperialism, 15, 56, 96, 98
India, 19, 52–8, 60–4, 216
interconnectivity, 31, 156
internationalism, 54, 94, 216
intertextuality, 1–2, 8, 14, 16–17, 27, 34, 215
internal narrative, 7, 71
Islam, 52, 61, 62

J
Jacobs, Harriet, 121, 123, 124, 166
James, Henry, 179, 180, 210; *Daisy Miller*, 143
Johnson, A.B., 78

K
Keats, John, 28, 64–5, 216
Kingsolver, Barbara: *The Poisonwood Bible*, 1, 6, 16, 19, 83, 86, 89–97, 98, 99, 101, 102, 103, 217
Ku Klux Klan, 158

L
Lacan, Jacques, 12, 28, 49
linear narrative, 80, 92, 119, 127, 133, 220
Lumumba, Patrice, 90, 91
Lyotard, Jean-Francois, 15

M
manumission, 23, 108, 109, 121, 122
market-driven reconfiguration, 3, 5–6, 26, 128, 216, 217
Marvell, Andrew: "The Unfortunate Lover," 45
materialism , 42, 51, 87
master narratives, 16, 32, 36, 93, 96, 155, 157, 164
McCullers, Carson, 143
Melville, Herman, 43, 66–7, 150, 198–9, 215, 216; *Moby Dick*, 1, 3, 12, 17, 18, 19, 66–70, 73–82, 83, 84, 102, 111, 170–3, 180, 186, 194–207; *The Confidence Man*, 67; *Benito Cereno*, 172, 220
memory talk, 8
memory-nation nexus, 10
metacognition, 102
metafiction , 2, 16, 17, 82, 205, 208
metanarratives, 15, 23, 29, 38

metaphor, 12, 24, 49, 63, 75–8, 111, 113, 137, 139
metatextual, 17, 52, 78–9, 81, 82, 171
Milton, John: *Paradise Lost*, 45, 77
miscegenation, 56, 64, 153, 155, 219
misogyny, 33, 59, 73
Mitchell, Maria, 72, 199, 210–11
Moraru, Christian, 1, 2, 18, 53, 54, 216
Morrison, Toni, 131, 153; *Beloved*, 21, 154–5, 165–9, 212
Mukherjee, Bharati: *The Holder of the World*, 19, 44, 48, 52–65, 70, 125, 216
myth of origin, 3, 4, 9, 11–13, 19, 44, 46, 48–9, 52, 56, 60, 65, 103, 110, 151

N

Naslund, Sena Jeter, *Adam & Eve*, 80, 209: *Ahab's Wife*, 1, 6, 17–8, 19, 21, 66, 68–77, 79–82, 125, 171, 193–213
nationalism, 10, 23, 43, 44, 83, 151, 215, 219
Native American/Indian, 45, 55, 56, 57–8, 60, 62, 64
Native Son, 156
New Critics, 151

O

Oedipal phase, 103
ontology, 38, 42, 75

P

parody, 2, 17, 24, 82, 122, 183–4
pastiche, 3
patriarchy, 85, 89, 91, 93, 96, 97, 141, 166
perception, 6, 7, 9, 14, 17, 20, 102, 134, 153, 171; and Powers, 29–30; and Bayard, 35, 38; and Hawthorne, 45, 48; and Mukherjee, 63–5; and Naslund, 66, 69, 79; and Rossner, 89, 103; Kingsolver and Brooks, 103; and Twain, 104, 106; and Seelye, 108; and Dickey, 116; and Clinch, 133; and Tyler, 139, 146–7, 149; and Faulkner, 151–2, 153
phallic symbol, 71, 117, 118, 119
Poe, Edgar Allan, 1, 3, 22–3, 42, 66, 75, 83, 84, 102, 150, 175–6, 178–9; Auguste Dupin, 33, 34, 36, 37, 38, 41, 186, 190, 216;
Tales of the Grotesque and Arabesque, 2; "The Black Cat," 215; "The Fall of the House of Usher," 19, 34, 35, 181, 182, 184, 188, 189; "The Gold Bug," 6, 19, 22–8, 30–33, 34, 35, 38, 40, 170, 180–1, 216; "The Murders of the Rue Morgue," 19, 33, 34, 36, 37, 181, 186, 190; "The Philosophy of Composition," 33, 34–5, 181; "The Purloined Letter" 19, 34, 181, 190, 215; "The Raven," 24, 33, 173; "The Tell-Tale Heart," 19, 34, 39, 45, 181, 182, 215
Plate, Liedeke, 5, 53, 70, 86, 171
postmodernism, 1, 2, 3, 5–7, 13, 15, 29, 38, 68, 81, 134; and Poe 23; and Powers 27, 32, 42; and Melville, 77, 78; and Naslund, 80; and Dickey, 110; and Clinch, 129, 134; and Tyler 146; and Bradley and Morrison, 154
post-structuralist, 12, 18, 29, 49
Powers, Richard: *The Gold Bug Variations*, 6, 19, 23, 25–6, 28–34, 37, 38, 41, 42, 110, 215
pre-conscious, 12, 48
prelapsarian, 31, 32, 152
pre-linguistic, 12, 48
presentist bias, 35–6, 60, 125
Promethean Fire, 5, 192
Puritan, 44–8, 52, 56, 58, 60, 61–2, 64, 84–5, 95, 96, 170

Q

quest: for metaphysical origins, 13, 23, 25, 26, 49, 50, 75, 77, 102, 110, 145, 151, 156, 166–7, 170, 172, 201–02, 220; for meaning, 19, 30, 77, 156; for unity, 26, 32, 76, 102, 123; for treasure, 33; for literary origins, 34, 41, 170; for adventure, 68, 71–2, 195, 197, 201; for revenge, 79; for liberation, 123, 136, 207

R

race, 1, 15; in Bayard, 35–6, 180–01; in Hawthorne, 55; in Mukherjee, 62–3; in Melville, 73–4; in Naslund, 74, 204, 206–08; in Alcott and Kingsolver, 91, 94–8, 101; in Twain, 105, 108–10; in Dickey, 113–4,

116–7, 119; in Rawles, 121, 124, 125; in Clinch, 129–33; in Faulkner, 151, 154–6; in Bradley, 157–165, 166, 219;
Rawles, Nancy: *My Jim*, 20, 106, 121–8, 132, 134, 172
reading function (in literary texts), 4, 16, 17, 20, 86, 215; in Powers, 25, 31; in Poe, 28; in Bayard, 34, 40; in Updike, 51; in Mukherjee, 53; in Naslund, 71, 80; in Clinch, 133; in Tyler, 139, 142–5; in Faulkner, 159
realism, 7, 30, 107–10, 123, 137, 142
reconstruction, 105, 125, 132
Reed, Ishmael: *Flight to Canada*, 1, 2
rememory, 166
repression: and Puritanism, 47, 53, 61, 95; repressed memory/past, 56, 70, 155, 157–8, 161, 167; of emotion, 100, 103, 143, 164; of sexuality, 113, 117–120, 132,
retelling, 1, 3, 5, 16, 19, 20, 46, 152, 159, 166, 171–3, 192, 193
Rosner, Judith: *His Little Women*, 19, 83, 86–9, 98, 101, 102, 103

S

schemata/schema, 8–9, 14, 16, 114, 115, 171
Scopes Monkey Trial, 152
script, 8, 58, 71, 110, 114, 115, 142, 144–5, 147, 148, 149, 219
Seelye, John: *The True Adventures of Huckleberry Finn*, 20, 106–10, 127, 131, 134
self-narration, 6, 8, 14, 69, 114, 123, 144–5, 153
self-referentiality, 30, 78–9, 205
sex, 1; in Poe, 33, 37, 180, 182, 185–6; in Bayard, 34, 37, 187, 188, 189; in Hawthorne, 45; in Updike, 46–51; in Mukherjee, 60; in Naslund, 73–4, 82, 205, 206–07; in Rossner, 87; in Kingsolver, 94; in Brooks, 98; in Seelye, 108; in Dickey, 110, 113–4,; 117–120, 218; in Rawles, 123, 124, 125; in Clinch, 130; in Tyler, 136, 143, 148; in Chopin, 138, 141, 148; in Morrison, 166; in Melville, 216
Shakespeare, William, 4, 66, 68, 71, 76, 77, 106, 172, 197, 198, 199, 200, 203, 220

sign/signifier/signified, 12–13, 24, 28, 42, 47, 49, 78–9, 101, 115, 134, 152
signification, 3, 12–13, 27, 38, 49, 151, 164
sinusoidal structure, 137
social-constructivist theory, 1, 29; and national identity, 10, 22, 58, 106; and personal identity, 13, 18, 22, 28, 29, 50, 114–7, 120, 123; and social order, 93, 103, 119, 120
Southworth, E.D.E.N., 70
Spofford, Harriet Prescott, 105
Stowe, Harriet Beecher: *Uncle Tom's Cabin*, 2, 70, 74, 96, 121, 122, 123, 206

T

The Great Gatsby, 143
The Norton Anthology of Literature of Women, 135
The Sun Also Rises, 143
theory of mind, 7, 102–03
Thoreau, Henry David, 78, 84
Tower of Babel, 31
Truth, 4, 13, 16, 18, 44, 69; in Melville, 19, 77; in Naslund, 19, 79, 80, 82, 208, 210; in Poe, 29; in Powers, 29; in Bayard, 40; in Updike, 44; in Mukherjee, 44, 59, 63–5; in Hawthorne, 50, 59; in Rossner, 86–8; in Kingsolver, 92, 93; in Brooks, 99, 101; in Seelye, 107–08; in Twain, 113; in Dickey, 113; and Rawles, 125–7; in Clinch, 128, 132; in Faulkner, 155, 161; in Bradley, 156–8
Turner, Mark David, 6, 58
Twain, Mark: *Adventures of Huckleberry Finn*, 1, 3, 12, 20, 66, 68, 104–11, 116, 119–25, 127, 128–34, 170, 171, 186, 218; *A Connecticut Yankee in King Arthur's Court*, 172
Tyler, Anne: *Ladder of Years*, 3, 20, 135–49; 219

U

underground railroad, 109
unity, 13, 15, 26, 28, 32, 35, 40, 48–9, 52, 56, 102, 103, 123
unreliable narrator, 17, 39–40, 42, 50–52, 154, 177

Updike, John, 65, 216; *A Month of Sundays*, 6, 19, 44, 46, 48–51; *Roger's Version*, 6, 19, 44, 46–8, 50–1; *S.*, 6, 19, 44, 46, 47–8, 51–2
utopia, 61, 85

W
West Point Academy, 33, 34, 36, 40, 181, 183, 185, 186–7
white privilege, 91, 94–5, 96–7

writing function (in literary texts), 4, 17, 20, 46, 49–51, 79–80, 86, 99, 133, 159

Y
yonic symbol, 80
Young America, 43, 44, 66, 67, 171, 215

Z
zeitgeist, 129

For Product Safety Concerns and Information please contact our EU representative GPSR@taylorandfrancis.com
Taylor & Francis Verlag GmbH, Kaufingerstraße 24, 80331 München, Germany

www.ingramcontent.com/pod-product-compliance
Lightning Source LLC
Chambersburg PA
CBHW050011010526
44115CB00026B/1942